THE
FEDERAL
GOVERNMENT
&
URBAN
HOUSING

SUNY SERIES IN URBAN PUBLIC POLICY

C. Theodore Koebel, editor

THE
FEDERAL
GOVERNMENT
&
URBAN
HOUSING

THIRD EDITION

R. ALLEN HAYS

SUNY
PRESS

Published by State University of New York Press, Albany

For information, contact State University of New York Press, Albany, NY
www.sunypress.edu

Production by Ryan Morris
Marketing by Anne M. Valentine

Library of Congress Cataloging-in-Publication Data

Hays, R. Allen, 1945-
    The federal government and urban housing / R. Allen Hays. — 3rd ed.
        p.   cm. — (SUNY series in urban public policy)
    Includes bibliographical references and index.
    ISBN 978-1-4384-4166-5 (pbk. : alk. paper) — ISBN 978-1-4384-4167-2 (hardcover : alk. paper)
    1. Housing policy—United States—History. 2. Housing—United States—History. I. Title.
    HD7293.H394 2012
    363.5'80973—dc23
                                                                                2011018384

10 9 8 7 6 5 4 3 2 1

CONTENTS

List of Illustrations   vi

Introduction to the Third Edition   vii

CHAPTER 1
Power, Ideology, and Public Policy   1

CHAPTER 2
The Ideological Framework for Housing Policy   15

CHAPTER 3
Housing and Human Needs   59

CHAPTER 4
Federal Housing Assistance from the Depression   87
to the Moratorium: 1934–1973

CHAPTER 5
New Directions in Housing Assistance: 1973–1980   139

CHAPTER 6
The Federal Role in Community Development   165

CHAPTER 7
Retrenchment and Recovery: Reagan and George H. W. Bush   223

CHAPTER 8
Stagnation and Progress: The Clinton Era   253

CHAPTER 9
Housing in the Twenty-first Century   283

References   307

Index   333

ILLUSTRATIONS

Figures

1-1	Ideology and Public Policy	13
3-1	Housing Cost Burdens by Type of Household	66
3-2	Consumer Price Indeces for Basic Necessities: 2000–2008	81
4-1	Assisted Housing Production: 1969–1973	115
4-2	Section 235 Performance	121
4-3	Section 236 Production and Foreclosures	128
5-1	Assisted Housing Production: 1969–1984	152
6-1	Budget Outlays for Community Development	197
6-2	Community Development as a Percent of all Outlays	198
8-1	HUD Approproations: FY 1994–2008	268
9-1	Selected HUD Housing Expenditures: 1997–2006	285

Tables

3.1	Basic Housing Services by Type of Household: 1997–2007	64
3.2	Breakdowns or Interruptions of Service: 1997–2007	65
3.3	Cost Burdens	67
3.4	Selected Neighborhood Conditions: 1997–2007	71
4.1	Section 236 Cumulative Assignment and Foreclosure Rates: 1977	129
5.1	Characteristics of Section 8 and Section 236 Projects	155
6.1	CDBG Dollar Shares by Type of Recipient	200
6.2	Regional Distribution of CDBG Funds	201
6.3	Uses of CDBG Funds	206
8.1	The Pros and Cons of the Hope VI "Mixed Income" Strategy	273

INTRODUCTION
TO THE THIRD EDITION

When the first edition of this book was published in 1985, housing and community development policy in the United States had just passed through a period of turmoil and change. The decade of the 1970s began with a commitment to greatly increase the federal government's role in ensuring that all citizens had access to affordable housing, utilizing both public sector production and subsidized private sector production. The Fair Housing Act of 1968 was a big step toward guaranteeing that full and fair access to housing wouldn't be denied on the basis of race. It also began with major reforms in the community development process designed to increase the benefits and reduce the costs of redevelopment to the lower income citizens who had so often been callously displaced by urban renewal efforts.

Unfortunately, over the course of the next two decades, a great deal of the momentum toward addressing the housing needs of low and moderate income households was lost. Public housing came in for severe criticism and for serious cutbacks in production. Private subsidy programs also lost support. In both cases, the decline in support was due to a combination of disillusionment with the way these programs were being executed and a shift toward the right in the political climate, which encouraged the scaling back of virtually all Great Society efforts. Meanwhile, federal community development efforts were scaled back so that, even though they had a less destructive impact on poor neighborhoods, they had less capacity to transform declining central cities. In addition, HUD lacked both the political will and the enforcement tools to overcome the tremendous inertia and resistance that perpetuated housing segregation based on race. From the perspective of the early 1980s, it seemed that the nation might virtually abandon any serious national efforts to address housing inequality and deprivation.

Now, looking back from the perspective of twenty-five years later, it is apparent that neither total recommitment to nor total abandonment of federal housing and community development efforts has occurred. In terms of the number of low to moderate income units produced or subsidized by the federal government, the level of effort displayed in the 1970s was never restored. The chief mechanism of assistance shifted from direct subsidies for housing production to vouchers that subsidized the consumer's purchase of housing services, but even these new subsidy mechanisms were funded at much lower levels than the older ones. Moreover, a significant portion of the new vouchers issued had to be used to maintain assistance to families who were losing support under the older system. Production of new, affordable housing units was shifted almost entirely to state and local governments and to nonprofit providers, who received indirect federal subsidies through the tax system. Even though this retrenchment began under two Republican presidents, Richard Nixon and Ronald Reagan, Democratic presidents have shown little enthusiasm for reversing it when they have come into office.

Redevelopment of central business districts and central city neighborhoods was also turned over almost exclusively to state and local actors. Block grant funding and tax free industrial development bonds often provide critical gap financing for central city projects, but the bulk of the funds now come from private investors and state/local sources. Residential neighborhoods near the central city have followed one of two paths; either they have undergone gentrification as upper-middle-class families reoccupied parts of the central city or they have been left to experience further disinvestment and abandonment. Neither of these outcomes is favorable to their former low income residents.

However, in spite of the persistently weak commitment of the national government to addressing housing needs, one can take heart from the fact that many of the assisted units that were available in the early 1970s have either been maintained or converted to vouchers, with the result that net losses in this original assisted housing stock have been much more limited than was feared in the 1980s. A number of extreme proposals to abolish the federal effort came to naught in Congress, even when Republicans were in the majority. One can also take heart from the fact that hundreds of thousands of units of low to moderate income housing have been produced in communities throughout the nation, by packaging state and local assistance with the limited federal assistance that has been available. In all parts of the country, there are numerous community leaders who recognize that substandard housing can blight the entire community and that families who are forced to spend large percentages of their incomes on housing may encounter other problems as a result. A broad spectrum of political leaders has been unwilling to totally abandon low income families to the tender mercies of the private market as they seek adequate shelter.

This book was initially written with two purposes in mind. The first was to provide a comprehensive history of housing policy since the Great Depression, something that was lacking when it was first published. The second was to place housing policy in the context of the overall political process in the United States; that is, to show how struggles for power among those with different visions of how a democratic capitalist society should be run have affected the specific outcomes of housing policies and programs. These remain the two central purposes of the Third Edition.

The first two chapters set the stage by presenting a model of the public policy process in which competing ideologies play a central role in framing and resolving issues. The liberal and the conservative outlooks are really two variations on the central ideology of democratic capitalism, but they still diverge greatly in their visions of the proper working of the system. These outlooks have continued to evolve during the entire eighty year period covered by this book, but the basic polarity that they represent remains the same. Liberals believe that the state needs to play a more active role in regulating the economy and ameliorating social inequality, in order for the system to provide maximum benefits to all. Conservatives believe that the state's role should be less active, with minimal regulation of the private sector and minimal public redistribution of goods and services. This fundamental split remains, even though important cultural/religious elements have been added to both ends of the spectrum. In writing the first edition, I believed it was necessary to defend the central place of ideological conflict in my analysis, since so much public policy seemed to emerge in the realm of centrist consensus. However, ideological polarization within the American political system has increased so much during the last twenty years that its influence on public policy is glaringly obvious in the current era.

Chapter 3 is new in this edition. Its purpose is to provide additional theoretical grounding for the examination of housing policy by exploring how housing relates to fundamental human needs. Abraham Maslow's hierarchy of needs provides a general framework for this exploration. This chapter also presents data on the extent to which the nation's current housing stock meets, or fails to meet, these basic needs.

The remaining chapters of the book provide the basic historical narrative of the evolution of housing policy from 1933 until 2010. As was done in the Second Edition (1995) the earlier sections of the narrative have been condensed somewhat, in order to focus on those issues most salient to later housing policy developments. However, in the process, an attempt was made to retain the richness of the descriptions of particular periods of policy development. In chapters 8 and 9, developments since 1995 have been described in detail.

The old saying that "History repeats itself" is, of course, not literally true. Each era of political struggle and policy development has its own unique set of circumstances and dilemmas. However, this historical narrative does reveal recurring themes and patterns. In every era, housing has been recognized as an important human need, and yet the low income groups who need it most are repeatedly stigmatized and isolated by more privileged members of society. This stigmatization makes it difficult to provide them with adequate housing. Provision of housing in clearly identified, publicly owned structures has often intensified the stigmatization of their inhabitants, and yet programs that induce the private sector to create housing for low income people in less clearly identifiable concentrations have also encountered serious difficulties. Meanwhile, housing assistance to the prosperous through tax deductions remains a political sacred cow, as liberals and conservatives continue to struggle over how much housing assistance to provide to the poor and what level of housing services the recipients really "need." And, of course, the specter of racial privilege and racial segregation casts a long shadow over the entire process.

Nevertheless, in spite of these recurring struggles, there has been a learning curve with regard to many aspects of housing provision. Strategies for housing assistance have become more sophisticated and flexible. The toolbox of strategies is there to be opened, whenever political leaders can summon the political will to use it. During the last twenty years, there has been political support for maintaining earlier commitments but not for bold expansions of these initiatives, even when liberal Democrats have been in control of the White House and/or Congress. During the last three years, the meltdown of housing credit for all classes of people has added serious economic barriers to the political barriers preventing the provision of decent, affordable housing to those who need it most. However, a historical review of the struggles over housing policy such as the one provided in this book can still provide useful insights to those who continue to seek opportunities to meet the essential housing needs of their fellow human beings, even in the currently bleak political and economic landscape.

CHAPTER 1

Power, Ideology, and Public Policy

The study of policy and the study of power are closely related. Power is usually operationally defined in terms of policy outcomes—that is, as the ability of a political actor to influence the behavior of others in such a way as to gain a preferred outcome. Students of power and of policymaking generally assume that power is not distributed haphazardly among the population but, rather, that any society develops stable influence patterns in and around governmental and nongovernmental institutions. In short, power is exercised within some kind of power structure, no matter how changeable and ambiguous that structure may be.

During the two decades following World War II, the prevailing paradigm among political scientists was the pluralist model. In this model, power is not controlled by a single ruling elite (as in the minority view expressed by Mills [1959], Kolko,[1962], and others) but by fragmented elite groups which are divided both geographically and functionally. Though ordinary citizens do not participate actively, this system was viewed as providing a reasonable approximation of democratic representation in at least three ways. First, the leadership of organized interest groups represents the concerns of many citizens not directly involved in the political process. Second, the democratic rules of the game help ensure the openness of the system to new groups activated by some compelling need for government action; and this openness is further encouraged by the fact that no single elite controls all areas of policy. Third, elected officials act as brokers who balance competing interests through compromise, thus building consensus on the direction of public policy (Dahl 1971).

During the 1960s and 1970s, the pluralist view was challenged by McConnell (1966), Lowi (1979), and others. Their critique was reinforced by studies of "subgovernments" in the public administration and policy literature (Maas 1951; Freeman 1965). In addition, leading pluralists such as Charles Lindblom (1977) later published substantial modifications of their views. These critics agreed that power is highly fragmented, with different collections of interests dominating policy areas of immediate concern to them, but they differed as to the openness of the system to new groups. Existing groups often succeed in excluding from the decision-making process new groups with differing views or interests. A common strategy for such control is to develop close alliances with key members of Congress and with administrative agencies responsible for existing policies. These subgovernments strongly resist intervention not only by competing groups but by top-level political leaders representing broader constituencies, such as the president and congressional party leaders. As Baumgartner and Jones (1993) argue, these arrangements are not totally immune to challenge and may, in fact, dissolve during periods of rapid policy change, but they can be stable for long periods of time.

Lowi further argues that the operation of the power structure may vary according to the issues involved. With regard to issues raising fundamental questions about the existing distribution of wealth among large groups within the population, a greater degree of top-level control exists than in other policy areas. That is, policy change is highly dependent on initiatives made at the highest levels of the Executive Branch, and the formulation of these initiatives will be done by small groups of presidential advisors, assisted by specialists in the area. Thus, the power structure, though basically fragmented along policy lines, is capable of accommodating high level coordination when fundamental redistributive issues are at stake (Lowi 1964; Ripley and Franklin 1991). Of course, interest groups supporting social welfare policies are continuously active in their attempts to influence policy (Hays 2001), and opponents can also mobilize powerful allies to fight presidential initiatives with all the resources at their command, as has been illustrated by the battles over health care reform, of which President Barack Obama's struggle is only the most recent.

These revisions of pluralism bring it closer to the reality of U.S. politics. However, while those writing about specialized structures of power suggest widely shared U.S. political values, which legitimize the system of interest group power, they do not give full weight to the effects on the political process of fundamental similarities across fragmented power centers. Thus, an examination of another element of political reality, that is, ideology, is critical to the development of a more complete understanding of the policy process.

The relevance of strongly shared beliefs to the study of power was argued by Bachrach and Baratz in their classic article, "The Two Faces of Power" (1962). They argue that strong limits are placed on the range of decisions possible in the system by the shared values and assumptions of its participants. Certain problems, or certain alternative means of solving them, are never discussed or debated by decision makers due to their shared assumption that these problems or solutions are not legitimate topics for political debate. The authors refer to these tacit acts of exclusion as "non-decisions."

While stressing the need to look at shared beliefs, Bachrach and Baratz's discussion of non-decisions does not take us very far in understanding *how* participants' beliefs shape the decision-making process. They suggest that non-decisions operate to the advantage of established groups and to the disadvantage of "outsiders" such as the poor. However, ideologies clearly do more than provide criteria for those whose concerns are *in* and whose concerns are *out*. To better understand the impact of ideology on political decisions, it is first necessary to explore the general structural features of ideologies and to see how abstract belief systems take on an operational form that influences day to day policy decisions.

Operational Ideologies

An ideology is a set of interrelated assertions about the social and political world which guides the behavior of individuals and groups. To many, the term *ideology* conveys the notion of a complex, logically structured set of beliefs that has been refined to a fairly high level of intellectual sophistication. Certainly, many political actors have worked out fairly consistent sets of beliefs, which guide their decisions. However, in order to influence political behavior, an actor's ideology need not be fully and thoroughly reasoned out. Rather, influential ideologies may also consist of imperfectly articulated assumptions. These assumptions shape the worldviews with which actors relate to political events and issues.

Political ideologies contain three types of statements. First, they contain assertions about reality—that is, statements that purport to be empirically valid generalizations about the nature of the world or of human beings. Second, they contain ethical prescriptions for human behavior derived from the assertions they make about reality. These ethical assertions are often, but not always, based on religious beliefs. Third, they contain, as a special case of their ethical precepts, prescriptions for the arrangement of social institutions in ways consistent with their central values. No ideology is a totally consistent package that explains all aspects of reality. Most have major internal contradictions which emerge as they are applied and elaborated. Furthermore, the institutions these ideologies purport to justify do not exist in a vacuum. Complex societies contain familial, economic, political, and religious institutions, each legitimized by slightly different ideological principles. In a stable society, these institutions and ideologies tend to reinforce each other, but there is also competition for influence between institutions. Major inconsistencies often exist between beliefs supporting different institutions of the same society. The complex agreements and contradictions existing between democracy and capitalism will be discussed in chapter 2.

As a result, ideologies enjoying wide acceptance in a society usually develop a set of *operational* assumptions and values that may deviate significantly from the *pure* ideals contained in formal statements of the ideology. The ideals set forth clearly and consistently what is to be valued most by believers. However, these moral absolutes rarely enter directly into the political process except as vague symbols, brought out on ceremonial occasions to legitimize the system as a whole. The operational form of the ideology, in contrast, stresses the concepts and behavior patterns most crucial to the long-term survival of the institutions which the ideology justifies, and it incorporates the compromises those institutions have made to survive. As such, the operational ideology is much more likely to directly influence political behavior, and it is only when we look for ideologies in their operational form that we can fully gauge their impact. It should also be emphasized that an operational ideology, as defined here, is more than a haphazard bundle of exceptions to the ideal. Rather, it is a transformation of the ideal into another, fairly consistent set of concepts which correspond more closely to current political experience.

Because ideologies are so closely related to institutions and because individuals and organizations tend to interpret common ideologies in ways that match their unique situations, there has been a tendency among Western political analysts to see ideology as a dependent variable which is shaped by a much more potent source of human motivation: interests. An *interest* may be thought of as consisting of two elements: (1) a need or desire experienced by an individual or a group; and (2) an external object or state of affairs that is seen as fulfilling that need or desire. Interests are immediate and concrete, and they are believed to be the main driving force behind political behavior. Material interests are usually seen as the most important type, but desires such as power, security, prestige, or growth also serve to inspire political involvement. In this view, individuals and groups use ideology primarily to convince themselves of the justice of their demands and to legitimize them to others.

A more thorough examination of the relationship between ideologies and interests shows, however, that it is much more complex than this view suggests (Stone 1997). At the heart of this complexity is the fact that interests are not the concrete, self-evident motivators that interest-based notions of politics make them out to be. Of the two elements constituting an interest—a need plus an object or state of affairs that is seen as satisfying that need—the need element would appear the least ambiguous. Although there is disagreement among students of motivation as to what are the most basic human needs, one can generally identify some widely shared human need behind most political actions. The other element of an interest—the object that can satisfy that need—is much more variable and ambiguous. Any human need can be satisfied in a variety of ways, and, in most situations, it is not clear in advance which of several alternative future states will best satisfy a need.

Thus, in order to pursue his or her interests, the individual must first identify which object or state of affairs will best satisfy his or her needs. Then, means must be chosen to achieve the desired future state. These often involve intermediate goals and objectives, which also appear on the political scene as interests. Moreover, these choices are often made with limited information as to the full costs and benefits of any alternative and in the face of unpredictable responses from others with a stake in the decision. As Schlozman and Tierney (1986) point out:

> Clearly, then, our definitions of what is best for us are rarely free, self-conscious choices, made in the way we assess the merits of the limited number of items on a restaurant menu—that is, made in the knowledge of all the relevant alternatives. Rather, our preferences are influenced by a multitude of socially structured factors in our background and experience. (Scholzman and Tierney 1986, 20)

If interests are more accurately viewed as points in a complex decision-making process, rather than fixed, self-evident motivators, then one must ask, "What are the common methods by which actors determine their interests in a given situation?" Many studies of political decision making emphasize the large amount of policy-relevant information from a variety of competing sources which the typical decision maker is asked to interpret (see, for example, Nakamura and Smallwood 1980; Kingdon 1984). He or she must also attempt to predict the actions and reactions of multiple sets of competing actors. The typical actor lacks the time, resources, and expertise to fully and rationally analyze the costs and benefits of each alternative. As a result, actors try to maintain established patterns of behavior which they regard as successful and tend to evaluate new data in terms of simplified decision rules which they feel have worked in the past. (See, for example, Aaron Wildavsky's analysis of the decision rules used by the House Appropriations Committee [1979].)

Given that actors try to organize and simplify reality in this way, it is likely that widely shared ideologies serve as potent and readily available sources of the expectations and of the preconceived decision rules brought into any situation by political actors. As noted above, ideologies contain both descriptive and prescriptive elements. Thus, they create expectations as to the behavior of others in concrete situations. To the extent that these expectations become operative as predictors of the future, ideology becomes deeply intertwined in the process of interest formulation. Actors use ideology not only to justify behavior but also to interpret data from their own experience and to predict the costs and benefits of future actions. To be sure, they may deliberately manipulate shared ideological precepts to cloak self-seeking behavior. But the worldview upon which they draw for this "symbol manipulation" (Edelman 1964; Stone 1997) has also shaped their own perceptions of the situation and through these the very interests they pursue.

To suggest that ideological categories are used as a source of decision rules is not, however, to suggest that a uniform set of values guides the thinking of all or most political actors. Widely shared ideologies are broad enough in their structure to permit wide variations in interpretation. There are, of course, idiosyncratic variations between individual interpretations of shared values. However, an equally common pattern is the development of two or more distinct sets of interpretive frameworks, each held by a certain group within the society's active decision makers, which involve different notions of how common ideologies should be applied to concrete social problems. Each of these interpretive frameworks supplies a different set of decision rules to be used in specific situations, and the differences in these approaches generate much of the ongoing political conflict over policy alternatives. The choice of one framework or another is usually influenced by the concrete interests of the actor. However, similar viewpoints are likely to be shared by a broad spectrum of actors from a variety of institutional roles. A succinct label for these competing interpretive frameworks is *coalition ideologies,* because they link together actors whose specific interests may vary.

The competing coalition ideologies that will be discussed in this work are subsumed under the terms *liberal* and *conservative.* While I will argue later that the principles widely attributed to these two viewpoints are sometimes inaccurate reflections of their actual operational values, it is clear that these two terms symbolize distinct interpretations of a common ideology, democratic capitalism, which dictate different solutions to common problems. Both have been influenced by other belief systems besides capitalism. Some liberals have incorporated socialist ideas while many conservatives adhere to notions of government enforcement of private morality which predate and may contradict both the capitalist market and democratic individualism. Nevertheless, in their actual usage, these two outlooks are firmly rooted in a common capitalist worldview. They both support the central economic institutional arrangements of capitalism, but they differ as to how these institutions, and the social order which supports them, can best be stabilized and perpetuated.

Shared ideologies may also be elaborated into specific sets of preconceptions about particular areas of public policy. While widely shared ideologies encourage consistency in the way decision makers respond to a variety of problems, each substantive policy area has its own unique history, which tends to create shared assumptions among those involved about what can be and what should be done to solve problems in that area. Both Heclo (1978) and Kingdon (1984) suggest that policies are framed within distinct policy communities, composed of interest groups and governmental specialists concerned with a particular set of issues. Participation in these communities may be somewhat fluid, but common ideas and assumptions develop that lend support to current policy arrangements (Baumgartner and Jones 1993). These assumptions are linked to the immediate interests of the actors involved, but their roots can also be traced to the ideological frameworks within which the policy developed. In part, they represent the application of general ideological assumptions to that policy area.

The description of ideological preconceptions just presented applies most directly to political elites who are directly involved in the decision-making process. In addition to these activists, there exists a somewhat larger attentive public, who are concerned enough about an issue to articulate a consistent set of beliefs about it (Cobb and Elder 1981). However, the degree to which ideology influences the attitudes of ordinary citizens is not as clear. Research on public opinion shows that most voters are poorly informed about issues and that their views don't fit neatly along the liberal-conservative continuum that applies to the politically active. They may have *schemata* organized around specific political events, but many of them lack a clear ideological framework within which policy preferences are organized (Conover and Feldman 1984b; Hamill, Lodge, and Blake 1985).

At the same time, members of the mass public often possess strong personal identities, constructed out of the social and political values associated with groups that they consider themselves to be a part of. These identities can enter strongly into politics, even though the persons involved may lack a sophisticated knowledge of public policy issues. Moreover, these identities contain elements of prevailing ideologies which have been strongly internalized. For example, Thomas Frank (2004) has discussed how identity politics based on fundamentalist Christian values can override what others might perceive as the direct economic interests of many people in guiding their political participation. He argues that the political Right has become very sophisticated in appealing to identity issues, by portraying itself as the defender of "basic American values" and of the hardworking, independent people who share those values. The more recent "Tea Party" movement also appears to be based on the capitalist values of individualism and self-reliance, which its members see as having been compromised by the actions of the Obama administration. In sum, one cannot dismiss the influence of ideological precepts on mass behavior, even if they are often inchoate in their articulation.

If, in fact, ideologies and values penetrate the decision-making process as pervasively as has just been suggested, then they may be expected to exert a profound influence on public policy outcomes. As suggested above, this influence will be in the direction of an underlying continuity in assumptions and approaches across many policy areas, even when each area is dominated by different functional groups. There are at least two ways in which shared ideologies act to generate such continuities. First, they act as intellectual and emotional filters through which policy initiatives must pass before they are considered acceptable and responsible proposals. Again, this *filtering* is often seen as a matter of interest protection—that is, proposals will not be considered that seriously threaten the power, wealth, or status of groups or individuals currently active. However, this is only part of the picture, for these preconceptions strongly influence judgments as to *whether* an alternative threatens the interests of those in power. A proposed expansion of governmental activity will, in part, be evaluated by affected groups on the basis of short-term concrete benefits, but they will also look at its long-term effects. If they have strong ideological biases against any government involvement in their affairs, this assumption will create the expectation of long-term harm which may override their desire for short-term gains.

Closely related to the ideological filtering of policy initiatives is the ideological filtering of participants in the political process. On the surface, it would appear that the U.S. system allows for the expression of a wide variety of concrete interests. Industry groups compete vigorously for government favors and protection, while labor unions, farmers, and groups of public-spirited citizens also enter the fray, often with direct challenges to the pursuit of profit by particular firms. Yet, underlying this seeming plurality of interests are shared assumptions, often unstated, as to which groups and which types of individuals can be trusted to follow the rules of the game (i.e., to confine their pursuit of interests to methods that will not disrupt or threaten the system as a whole).

The most obvious set of criteria for the inclusion or exclusion of participants consists of the manifest beliefs of the individual or group in question. Those who espouse ideologies that are opposed to prevailing beliefs will find it difficult to move into positions of permanent stable influence, due to the profound distrust they engender in other participants. In addition, biases concerning social class and education act as selection criteria (Scholzman 1984). Businessmen and professionals find access to the political process much easier than the poor or working class, and where the latter are represented it is by leaders who have been co-opted into the prevailing value structure. Finally, institutional position itself is a criterion for inclusion in the larger decision-making arena. A person who has risen to a position of authority in a large public or private organization is not only recognized as a spokesperson for that organization, but is also presumed to have demonstrated the skill, reasonableness, and social conformity necessary to be a responsible participant in the larger political process.

Having noted the general types of filters that apply to virtually all aspects of decision making, I will now look at some of the more specific institutional expressions of broad ideological perspectives in the political process. The revised pluralist model described earlier calls attention to the narrowness of the concerns and interests that motivate most political actors. Yet, to view government as exclusively composed of a series of discrete, isolated decision-making arenas is a distortion. One must also take into account the institutions that permit and encourage the formation of broader ideological coalitions.

The most prominent of these institutions is the presidency. Writers on the presidency such as Neustadt (1980) have justifiably emphasized the limits on the power of the president—the need for him to bargain with and persuade not only Congress but segments of the bureaucracy which he nominally heads. Yet there is also tremendous power inherent in the administrative and the agenda-setting role of this office. Interest groups and agencies, entrenched in their policy subsystems, may be able to defeat the president on specific issues, and they may be able to rewrite the detailed language of legislation so as to maximize its benefits or minimize its costs to them, but the president has a powerful influence on the overall political atmosphere. He is the source of most major policy initiatives, and so interest groups often find themselves in a reactive position vis-à-vis issues he has forced them to address (Kingdon 1984).

It is also clear that each administration has a distinct ideological flavor. Each president chooses a team of advisors and cabinet officers who reflect his own ideological perspective. Usually his views correspond with one of the broad liberal or conservative ideologies prevalent at that time. Voters may not be clear on the values or issue positions of the candidate they choose, but party elites and other active, informed groups understand them more clearly, and they are ready to see their worldview put into action when a sympathetic president is elected. More than any other single political leader, the president is expected to respond to issues with a coherent philosophy, rather than with adjustments to interest group pressures.

Ideological motivations are also prominent in Congress. It is certainly true that most members of Congress are policy specialists with strong commitments to interest groups and programs in their district and in their specialized areas of expertise. Voting patterns on these issues of immediate concern may, therefore, follow subgovernment loyalties, which are not always ideologically consistent. Yet, on the vast majority of issues, each member has little intimate knowledge and no overwhelming commitments. On these issues, ideology becomes an important predictor of voting behavior (Savitch 1979; Caraley 1976). In addition, the election of an individual by a certain constituency often reflects that constituency's ideological flavor, and the recruitment of a particular member to a specialized policy subsystem is influenced by that individual's value preferences.

Numerous observers have noted an increase in ideological polarization within Congress during the last thirty years.(Cohen, Fleischer, and Kantor 2001) The rhetoric on both sides has, in many cases, become so completely mutually contradictory as to call into question whether they are talking about the same reality. As will be discussed in more detail below, changing economic and social conditions, plus geographical shifts in the "center of gravity" of the major political parties have made both conservative Democrats and liberal Republicans increasingly rare. Initially, many observers of voting behavior asserted that the mass of voters were still in the middle of the road, despite this polarization of elites. However, more recent analyses have suggested that substantial segments of voters have followed their leaders into polarized camps (Patterson 2003).

One other important dimension of the influence of ideology on the policymaking process must be dealt with before these general comments can be applied to the creation of an analytical model appropriate to the examination of housing policies. This is the dimension of change in ideological perspectives. It is common to look at the process of change in beliefs as shaped by events in the external environment. In this view, the actor may start out with preconceptions about the world. These beliefs are then crushed, altered, or expanded by the sheer impact of reality—by glaring inconsistencies between the actual behavior of others and the behavior predicted by one's initial beliefs.

However, as suggested above, the separation between events and beliefs is somewhat artificial for several reasons. First, the expectations with which actors enter a situation strongly affect their behavior and, therefore, shape the reality of that situation. Second, unless the impact of a policy is direct and powerful, there is always room for interpretation as to whether the policy has actually failed or succeeded. Political leaders are bombarded with feedback about program outcomes from many sources, and they can choose to listen to and believe those that confirm their predispositions (Hays 1986). Finally, even when unanticipated and/or harmful consequences are too obvious to ignore, the actor will often try to explain failure in terms that maintain the overall structure of his or her worldview intact. There is no doubt that genuine changes in attitudes occur, but they are likely to be incremental and actors will often deny that any real change has occurred. And, the resiliency of beliefs in the face of changed circumstances leaves open the possibility that the same mistakes or problems will occur repeatedly.

Looking at the larger political arena, another possible response to changing circumstances becomes apparent. Since shared ideologies are broad enough to be subject to conflicting interpretations which crystallize into coalition ideologies, it becomes likely that in the face of failure of the environment to respond as predicted by the overall ideological system, political leadership will shift back and forth between differing ideological coalitions. Rather than question their fundamental assumptions, elites may struggle for the power necessary to try out their conflicting applications of these assumptions to the current situation. Out of this struggle, gradual change may emerge, as one coalition or the other incorporates new ideas. Yet, the struggle may also produce drifting or incoherent policies, as none of the solutions acceptable in terms of current beliefs prove to be relevant or effective.

An awareness of the struggle between competing ideological perspectives also draws our attention to the centrality of compromise. Compromises occur on hundreds of technical and substantive points during the policy process. However, beyond these specific concessions, it appears that policies that have long-term success exist in a political equilibrium between opposing groups. Proponents of a program must usually push it through in the face of considerable opposition. In the process, they must modify it to attract marginal supporters and to satisfy key interest groups. The final product, if it is to survive over the long term, must be acceptable not only to a short-term coalition of supporters but to a more stable majority, because opponents will continue their efforts to weaken or eliminate it. If support for the program grows, these opponents will reduce their efforts at drastic change and concentrate on containment of its impact. At this point, even if opponents succeed in preventing the program from attaining the degree of impact desired by its most ardent supporters, it will have gained a secure niche in the system until conditions generate broader support for new directions. Programs attaining equilibrium usually contain provisions that make them palatable to a rather broad range of ideological perspectives.

This notion that policy is shaped by an equilibrium between opposing ideologies might, at first glance, appear incompatible with some recent research on public policymaking. Kingdon (1984) and others stress the fluid, almost haphazard way in which problems and proposed solutions emerge, and they emphasize the changing cast of actors moving in and out of various policy arenas. However, this incompatibility is more apparent than real, since it is not being suggested here that ideological orientations rigidly dictate specific policy options. Within shared ideological perspectives, various options are put forth by a wide variety of actors. Nevertheless, Kingdon stresses that the source of an idea is not as important to its adoption as the existence of an overall political climate in which the idea is taken seriously. He also suggests that the ideological predispositions of decision makers are an important part of that climate (Kingdon 1984, 75–82).

Summary and Conclusions

Figure 1.1 schematically summarizes the broad analytical framework suggested in the last few pages. As is readily apparent, the decision-making subsystems surrounding each distinct policy area form a central element in this framework. These subsystems will, in some policy areas, be organized along the lines of the subgovernment alliances suggested by Freeman. In others, participation may be more fluid and open, as suggested by Heclo and Kingdon. In either case, these subsystems play a central role in shaping the problems that reach the public agenda and the alternatives considered. Moreover, each subsystem has its own history, in which certain approaches have been accepted as technically or politically viable. This creates resistance to change within each area which, as the incrementalist decision model suggests, tends to make new proposals differ as little as possible from the status quo. Because of the importance of these subsystems, the

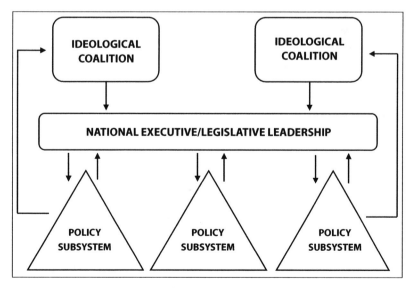

Figure 1-1 Ideology and Public Policy

use of broad ideological orientations and coalitions as a major variable in explaining policy decisions should not be seen as an attempt to substitute an idealized, bipolar issue conflict for the convoluted processes by which ideas and decisions emerge. Rather, ideological conflicts must be seen as a central element in the broader political environment in which specialized policy subsystems operate. This framework also outlines the processes by which ideological orientations influence policy subsystems. Broad ideological coalitions within the political/economic elite compete for control of legislative and executive institutions. The coalition currently in a dominant position will, based on its ideological orientation, generate strong messages to policy subsystems concerning the kinds of general policy directions considered acceptable or unacceptable. These messages will then be interpreted by the participants and applied to the problems with which they are concerned. The nature of the national leadership will also affect the ideological makeup of participants in various subsystems, either directly through key appointments, or indirectly through the types of ideas viewed as current or acceptable.

Finally, the framework presented in Figure 1.1 also suggests that the outputs created by each policy subsystem generate feedback, which is utilized in the broader ideological debates over the direction of public policy. Conclusions about the positive or negative effects of programs are publicized in the media, and programs are evaluated by various governmental and nongovernmental institutions. These conclusions are usually interpreted differently by those with different ideological perspectives and, thus, become ammunition in the ideological struggle (Hays 1986).

Scholarly treatments of public policy generally take one of two routes to an understanding of an area. One is to examine the broad historical sweep of policy change and to account for it in terms of shifting conditions and attitudes. The other route is to narrow the focus to specific decisions and look in detail at participants and processes. The present study generally follows the first route, and it is from this perspective that ideology emerges as an important influence on the course of public policy. However, this study also gives sufficient details about crucial policy choices to illuminate the impact of longer-term changes on specific outcomes. Therefore, on the theoretical level, I have tried to suggest patterns by which changes in ideological climate and national leadership influence more narrow decision-making processes. The model presented here will guide the treatment of housing policy decisions in subsequent chapters.

CHAPTER 2

The Ideological Framework for Housing Policy

Part I—the General Ideological Context

In order to establish an overarching ideological framework for the examination of housing policy, this chapter will proceed from the more general ideological context to the more specific frameworks affecting housing policy. Since this is a work concerning public policy, rather than political philosophy, the ideas will not be thoroughly explicated but will be presented in the general form that they assume as they actually guide the policy process. It is a basic premise of this work that ideas matter because social reality is, to a significant extent, constructed by the beliefs that people hold (Berger and Luckman 1966). Prevailing assumptions about social reality are translated into action and thus become part of that reality.

Democratic Capitalism

The dominant political ideology in the United States is democratic capitalism. In its ideal form, the democratic element in this ideology includes the following beliefs:

- A belief in the fundamental political equality of all citizens, rooted in a moral belief in the inherent worth and dignity of all persons.
- A belief in the freedom of all citizens to participate in the political process through open expression of their political views and through freely joining with other citizens to pursue their political aims.
- A belief that the selection of political leaders and the making of policy decisions should occur through majority rule.
- A belief that minority rights require protection against abuse by the majority, including limitations on majority rule where necessary.

The capitalist element in this dominant ideology includes the following beliefs, as described by Dolbeare (1971):

- A belief that the basic driving force behind human productive activity is the individual's desire to enhance his or her material well-being and to compete with others for recognition and advancement. The chief corollary is that society must encourage and reward acquisitiveness and competition if it is to achieve the highest overall level of prosperity.
- A belief that the market is the most efficient and least coercive allocator of goods and services for the society as a whole, since its operation enables each individual's desires to maximize wealth and to make personal consumption choices to be harmonized with society's collective development.
- A belief that government should play a secondary and supplementary role to the private market in regulating human interactions, leaving individuals to make their own consumption choices and private firms to produce whatever goods they wish. (Friedman, M. 1962)

Elements of these two basic belief systems that comprise democratic capitalism are profoundly contradictory in important respects but also profoundly reinforcing in other important respects. Capitalism celebrates inequality, whereas democracy is based on equality. The extremes of wealth and poverty that are generated by capitalism make it very difficult for democracy to function in the open and egalitarian way that it is supposed to, while capitalists are constantly on the defensive against the leveling tendencies (i.e., the extension of political equality to include economic equality) inherent in popular government. However, both capitalism and democracy depend on an open society in which ideas can be freely exchanged. They also depend on the rule of law to temper both political and economic competition. Finally, they both celebrate the right and the capacity of individuals to advance themselves without the restraint of hereditary or traditional relationships and obligations. The complex and contradictory nature of this relationship is one major reason why there is room for broad disagreements over how a democratic capitalist system should be governed.

The operational form of the democratic capitalist ideology contains important modifications to its ideal form. These modifications have evolved out of the historical experience of the United States, and they shape the attitudes that guide daily activities within the system. One set of modifications relates to the role of shared values and morality in the operation of the system. Since colonial times, the culture of the United States has been dominated by the Judeo-Christian religious tradition. Although interpretations of this tradition have varied over time, a common thread is the notion that even an open, individualistic society such as that fostered by both democracy and capitalism must be governed by a strong set of shared moral beliefs that restrain individual choices and individual self-interest. These moral beliefs call for both negative restraints on some kinds of behavior and for a positive obligation to engage in other behaviors, with some religiously motivated actors emphasizing one while others emphasize the other.

On the restraint side, Judeo-Christian morality has been defined in terms of refraining from certain behaviors that are seen as destructive to ordered social relationships, such as, for example, drinking, gambling, and sexual activity outside marriage. The state has repeatedly been called upon to legally enforce these moral prohibitions, up to and including the 1919 ratification of a constitutional amendment (the Eighteenth) prohibiting the sale and consumption of alcoholic beverages. These calls for legal prohibition of immoral acts exist in constant tension with the belief in the freedom of individual choice that is inherent in the role of democratic citizen and free market consumer. The modern "culture wars" are, to a significant degree, a replay of earlier struggles over morality within American society, even though they deal with a uniquely contemporary set of issues.

On the positive behavioral side, Judeo-Christian morality has repeatedly emphasized a sacred obligation to behave compassionately toward those who are economically deprived or who are otherwise rendered in need of assistance by life's circumstances. Jesus placed the Christian obligation to the poor in a central ethical and theological position, but he was echoing earlier, similar sentiments in the Jewish scriptures on the importance of compassion. This religious message has often been muted so as to require only token compassion on the part of the rich for the poor, and poor people are sometimes condemned for their alleged failures to conform to traditional morality. However, throughout American history, the religious obligation to help the poor has frequently operated as a strong counter-weight to the capitalist belief that people are only entitled to what they can earn through the competitive market system.

A second set of important modifications of the democratic capitalist ideology consists of beliefs supporting the differential allocation of status and opportunity based on racial/ethnic identity. Early colonial capitalists found it useful and vital to their economic ambitions to isolate African

Americans as a low cost, enslaved workforce. In seventeenth-century colonial America both white and black laborers started out as indentured servants, but black laborers were gradually pushed into slavery, while white laborers were able to move toward freedom (Allen 1994). In order to support this economic arrangement, an ideology of the racial inferiority of people of African descent was promulgated, so that the high-minded phrases about liberty made by America's founders could be seen as not applicable to them. A similar racist ideology was applied to American Indians, in order to justify the expropriation of their lands and their near extermination (Brown 1971).

Economic development in the early United States benefited tremendously from trade in the commodities produced by slave labor, but, at the same time, there was a fundamental underlying tension between slavery and the free labor system that was developing in the North. Northerners began to see the South as a backward region that was holding back the full capitalist development of the nation. This tension helped fan the sectional divisions that led to the Civil War (Goodwin 2005). However, the abolition of slavery did not result in the full integration of African Americans into the free labor system, in large part because the underlying racism that supported it remained strong. Rather, African Americans remained in the South as agricultural workers or in other low-paying occupations. Even after economic expansion drew millions of African Americans to northern cities during and after World War II, they still suffered discrimination and exclusion from the full benefits of this expansion. The ideology of capitalism clearly supports advancement through individual efforts and merit, but the actual operation of the system incorporates numerous mechanisms that preserve white privilege (Lipsitz 2006).

A third set of modifications relates to the role that the government can play in economic growth. A corollary to the core principles of the capitalist ideology is the belief that economic growth is an important and worthy goal in and of itself. The market itself is viewed as the best overall mechanism for promoting economic growth, and individual entrepreneurs within the system benefit greatly from the expanding markets that are created by economic growth. However, there has never been a time in the history of capitalism when strategic investments by governments were not also a critical element in economic growth. First, government investment has been directed at manifestly "public goods," such as infrastructure, where it is impossible or impractical to deny access to additional users once the good has been created (Stiglitz 1986). Secondly, public subsidies, loans, and loan guarantees have been directed at reducing initial risks and costs for private firms so that new markets will develop more quickly than they might without intervention. Thirdly, while government regulation has often been bitterly resisted by private firms, it has also at times been embraced as a way to limit "excessive" competition and make their environments more predictable.

As a result, those embracing the prevailing capitalist ideology have almost universally accepted the idea that government intervention is acceptable when it promotes overall economic growth, or, as in the case of the 2008–09 bailouts of banks and automobile companies, when it is seen as necessary to prevent a massive economic disaster. Savitch (1979) refers to these types of interventions as "reinforcing" in that they almost always provide the most direct benefits to firms and individuals who are already "market winners" with benefits to other members of society assumed to trickle down from these investments at the top. Even when a firm is seeking tax breaks or other subsidies that benefit only itself or its particular industry, it can often be successful if it ties these benefits to the overall goal of economic growth. Where liberals and conservatives disagree, argues Savitch, is over whether government interventions aimed at redistributing wealth or services to the less advantaged members of society (he calls these "ameliorative" interventions) are also necessary to strengthen and stabilize the democratic capitalist system in the long term.

A fourth modification of the democratic capitalist ideal type has occurred in the nature of political participation. The large disparities in wealth generated by the economic system inevitably lead to large inequalities in influence within the political process, thus undercutting the basic idea of the equal political role of all citizens. However, many citizens share the belief expressed in recent Supreme Court decisions (*Buckley v. Valleo*), that political donations (no matter how large) are a form of free speech that should not be regulated by the government. In addition, the capitalist system encourages individuals to make work and consumption the central activities of their lives, and these activities often leave little room for an active, responsible citizen role (Putnam 2000). As noted in chapter 1, this situation led pluralists to argue that having most citizens represented by proxy through organized groups was the best approximation of democracy that could be achieved in a modern industrial society. Even though levels of political participation have ebbed and flowed over the history of the United States, high levels of citizen apathy and disengagement have been a constant.

Liberal and Conservative Ideologies

OVERVIEW

To begin the discussion of conservative and liberal ideologies, it is useful to outline the basic features of each perspective. Any such outline, of course, greatly oversimplifies reality. People who call themselves liberals or conservatives may disagree with any one of these elements, or they may embrace them hypocritically while practicing the opposite. Also, these core beliefs are constantly evolving. This list would have been different if prepared in the 1950s, and it will probably change again as the twenty-first century progresses. However, this list accurately summarizes where these competing belief systems have stood for at least the past forty years.

The modern liberal variant of the democratic capitalist ideology has the following main elements:

- A belief in the active use of the state to redistribute resources in order to ameliorate the living conditions of those who are seriously disadvantaged by the labor market and in order to enhance economic opportunity for these individuals.
- A belief in the active use of the state to regulate markets in order to, among other things, prevent financial instability, protect consumers, and control negative externalities such as environmental degradation.
- A belief in the active use of the state to protect the rights of racial and ethnic minorities, women, those with alternative sexual orientations, and persons with disabilities—all groups with long histories of discrimination and exclusion in American society.
- An emphasis on international cooperation and negotiation in addressing the international interests of the United States, coupled with a willingness to utilize military power aggressively to protect core U.S. interests.
- Cultural support for nontraditional families, nontraditional lifestyles, and nontraditional religious and cultural beliefs.

Even though liberals believe in the active use of the state, they still support capitalism as the optimal mode of organizing the means of production. Their redistributive efforts rarely challenge the basic structure of the private economy. In addition to their activism to ameliorate inequality, many liberal leaders have, as noted above, also supported state subsidies for economic development by capitalist firms, on the grounds that economic growth benefits all elements of society.

The modern conservative variant of the democratic capitalist ideology has the following main elements:

- A belief that the state should not intervene to ameliorate economic inequality except in the most extreme circumstances. This belief is based, in turn, on two pillars:
  - That the state is an ineffective problem solver that worsens, rather than improves economic and social conditions through its interventions.
  - That amelioration of inequality harms the initiative and independence of those receiving the aid, while it unjustly and inefficiently redistributes wealth from society's "winners."
- A belief that unregulated markets produce the optimal distribution of goods and services in the society and maximize the total wealth of the society. Regulating negative externalities, such as pollution, reduces efficiency and productivity.
- An emphasis on the aggressive and often unilateral projection of American military and economic power in the international arena, supported by a strong belief in the superiority of American values and intentions.
- A belief that, while individual acts of discrimination are wrong, disadvantaged minorities should not claim "group rights" for special consideration or compensation.
- Cultural support for traditional, heterosexual, patriarchal family relationships and for the privileged position of the Christian religion within American society. (Note: This last element is generally not shared by those who consider themselves to be libertarian conservatives.)

Even though conservatives are generally hostile to state intervention in the economy, they too have supported state intervention on behalf of economic development, through subsidies to capitalist firms. Many conservatives have also embraced state intervention to proscribe behavior that violates their core cultural norms.

THE DEVELOPMENT OF CONTEMPORARY LIBERAL BELIEFS

During the nineteenth century, as the capitalist system continued to evolve from its eighteenth-century roots, the pressure to ameliorate the extremes of inequality that it generated also grew. In the developed capitalist economies of Western Europe, a strong labor movement initially embraced the Marxist call for total transformation of the capitalist system, but it gradually evolved into a social democratic movement which utilized political and economic pressure to modify, rather than overthrow, capitalism (Bernstein 1961). This shift was enabled, in large part, by the growing productivity of the capitalist system. Contrary to Marx's prediction of the progressive impoverishment of the working class, the economic surplus generated by capitalism enabled increases in both wages and social benefits without a radical redistribution of wealth away from the capitalist class.

In the United States, a mass, working-class social democratic movement never developed. In her thorough analysis of the origins of the American welfare state, Theda Skocpol (1995) attributes this, in part, to the fact that democratic modes of participation were organized along regional and local lines, decades before the industrial working class emerged in the United States. Urban and rural political machines mobilized working-class voters but resisted class-based appeals. In addition, the existence of slavery created a racial chasm dividing the labor force that proved difficult for workers to overcome, even after slavery was abolished. After the Civil War, the South continued to be dominated by a reactionary white elite that strongly resisted challenges to inequality of any sort, whether based on race or on class. In addition to the racial divide, the ethnic diversity of the largely immigrant working class proved a major obstacle to working-class solidarity.

The absence of a social democratic movement did not, however, mean that class issues were totally organized out of American politics. Throughout the late nineteenth and early twentieth centuries, labor unions struggled to establish themselves against strong, and often violent, capitalist resistance. By the 1920s, they had an unrealized agenda of union recognition and expansion of social benefits that the Great Depression would give them the opportunity to achieve. Their vehicle was, of course, the Democratic Party. However, this party was, from the Depression on, hampered by the contradiction of needing to retain its reactionary Southern base while at the same time trying to build a progressive coalition in the rest of the country. As Skocpol demonstrates, this contradiction severely limited President Franklin D. Roosevelt's ability to pass progressive social programs, as each new program had to be modified so as not to challenge racial apartheid in the South (Skocpol 1995). This contradiction ultimately contributed to the fracturing of the "New Deal Coalition" in the late 1960s.

It was President Roosevelt who popularized the use of the term *liberal* to refer to the belief in an activist national government that the New Deal embodied. In using this term, he was attempting to link his movement to the notion of progress and also to the notion of "liberality," that is, generosity and tolerance toward those less fortunate. This new usage contradicted the nineteenth-century meaning of the term, in which being a liberal meant that one supported the unfettered development of the capitalist market system over against older, aristocratic social institutions. This older usage is still reflected in the philosophical use of the term *liberalism* to describe the individualistic beliefs supporting the creation of a modern, democratic capitalist society. It is also reflected in the recent use of the term *neo-liberal* to describe the market oriented reforms that have been enacted in developed capitalist countries and have also been imposed on developing countries by the World Bank and the International Monetary Fund (Stiglitz 2002).

New Deal liberals were focused on issues of economic recovery, economic justice, and on issues of regulating the economy to prevent future disasters like the Great Depression. Many Southern Democrats supported these initiatives because of the exceptionally bleak economic conditions that the Depression had created in their region, but, as the price for their support, they insisted that the New Deal not challenge racial inequality. However, in the post–World War II era, conflicting streams concerning racial equality began to pull the elements of the New Deal Coalition in different directions on race. On the one hand, the important role that African Americans played in World War II, plus the contradiction of fighting racism in Europe with a racially segregated army, generated some public and elite support for challenging American apartheid. In addition, thousands of African Americans were moving from the South to the urban North, where their presence made them natural additions to the multiethnic coalition upon which Democratic support in the cities rested.

On the other hand, the Southern wing of the party continued to strongly resist any initiatives toward black equality, and many segments of the white working class in the North were equally resistant to progress toward racial equality. For example, as shall be discussed in chapter 4, the Depression-era FHA housing program came into its own after the war, as it assisted millions of white households to purchase new homes in the suburbs. However, African Americans were almost totally excluded from the benefits of this program, due to the closeness of the FHA to real estate interests, both north and south, who wanted to perpetuate segregation. In addition, in the 1940s, Southern Democrats joined Republicans in resisting the expansion of New Deal social programs to include more public housing and a national health care system.

The burgeoning civil rights movement of the late 1950s and early 1960s thus presented the liberal leaders of the Democratic Party with a difficult dilemma. On the one hand, both their values and their political interests outside the South dictated support for the African American struggle. In addition, there was broad popular support for the civil rights movement, as long as it was focused on elements of Southern apartheid, such as segregated public facilities, that were less prevalent in the rest of the country. On the other hand, they recognized that by embracing the goals of the civil rights movement, they would potentially lose the solid Democratic loyalties of the South which had enabled them to control Congress and the presidency. An number of historians have chronicled how President Lyndon Johnson, a Southerner, made the choice to embrace black equality with his eyes open as to the negative political consequences for his party (Milkis 2005, 20–21).

The embrace of African American civil rights by the Democratic Party profoundly shaped the nature of the new social legislation that emerged in the 1960s and of the new liberalism that accompanied it. First, while the two civil rights acts passed in 1964 and 1965 were directed at Southern problems, much of the legislation included in the Great Society initiative was directed at the complex social and economic problems of Northern central cities, where African Americans were being concentrated into impoverished ghettos. The goal of the War on Poverty was to build up these neighborhoods and improve economic opportunity for their residents. Such social transformation proved to be a much more difficult task than simply redistributing income, and the failure of these programs to live up to their ambitious goals would later be used by conservatives to discredit liberalism (Haveman 1977).

Secondly, the new liberal initiatives of the 1960s were couched in what has since been referred to as "rights language." That is, instead of focusing on the economic goal of simply preventing deprivation, as earlier New Deal programs tended to do, they were focused on guaranteeing the dignity and opportunity of individuals in all aspects of life, particularly those groups who had been arbitrarily excluded in the past. Thus, the guarantee of individual rights by the state became a central part of the liberal belief system. Moreover, once this "rights language" was introduced into the liberal vocabulary, it was embraced by additional groups who believed that their members had been excluded by discrimination from the full benefits of American society. The feminist movement of the early 1970s was the first to use the language generated by the black civil rights movement. Later on, in the 1980s and 1990s, persons with disabilities and GLBT (Gay, Lesbian, Bisexual, and Transgendered) persons would utilize the same language to demand fair treatment.

Meanwhile, other social and economic transformations were occurring that would profoundly shape the nature of American liberalism. The first was the gradual decline in the political and economic influence of the labor movement from the 1970s on. Although this decline had multiple causes, the main driving force behind it was the globalization of manufacturing (Goldfield 1987). As communications and transportation technology improved, corporations found it increasingly possible to move large segments of their manufacturing operations to developing countries with vastly lower wage scales than the United States. This increasingly international and decentralized system of production undermined the bargaining power that unions had gained in the more centralized, Fordist system of industrial production that had concentrated jobs in developed countries such as the United States earlier in the twentieth century. In addition, American industries where jobs could not be exported found it increasingly easy to import cheap labor through both legal and illegal immigration. Although the labor movement has retained considerable influence within the Democratic Party, its declining power has led to the increasing marginalization of some of its key issues, such as restrictions on free trade. Also, the declining power of unions to mobilize the working class along economic lines left them susceptible to mobilization on noneconomic issues such as racial and cultural resentments.

Secondly, the cultural values of the middle and upper middle class underwent rapid transformation from the early 1960s onward. The affluence generated by the postwar economic boom led them to focus less on stable, economically responsible family units and more on individual freedom and personal exploration. In addition, the percentage of women completing college increased greatly, and college-educated women were less likely to be contented with the limited role of suburban housewife that had been staked out for them after World War II (Friedan 1983). This educational shift thus contributed greatly to the emergence of a second wave of feminism in the 1970s (the first wave being the struggle for the vote in the early twentieth century), which swept away many of the remaining gender-based restrictions on employment and political participation (Baxandall 2005). Women were also partially liberated from the constant risk of pregnancy by the birth control pill and were thus able to more fully explore other options besides those dictated by motherhood. Finally, the capitalist system found it necessary to encourage the development of an individualistic, consumer culture in order to continue to expand markets after more basic consumer needs had been satisfied. This consumer culture provided additional support for the centrality of individual fulfillment as a societal value.

A small but significant number of white middle-class persons became actively involved in the civil rights movement, and their consciousness of the remaining injustices in American society was thereby greatly increased. However, it was the issues arising from the involvement of the United States in the cold war against Russia and China that created the most radical generational split within the middle and upper middle classes. A small middle-class peace movement emerged around the issue of nuclear war in the early 1960s (the so-called Ban the Bomb movement), but it was the war in Vietnam that created a truly mass-based peace effort. Since the emergence of the cold war in the late 1940s, the United States had been fighting proxy wars in developing countries to prevent the expansion of Russian and Chinese influence, but the proxy war in Vietnam escalated to include a direct American combat role that required the conscription of significant numbers of young Americans. Young people on college campuses were threatened by the draft, and they had access to information that challenged the official version of what was happening in Vietnam. As a result, opposition to the war morphed with other cultural changes to produce an antiwar movement dominated by a "counterculture" that also embraced increase sexual and cultural freedom (Roszak 1995).

Members of the white and black working class lacked the educational draft deferments of the middle class and above, and so they disproportionately became those who actually fought and died in Vietnam. This fact, plus their innate patriotism, led many white working-class citizens to bitterly resent collegiate protesters, whom they viewed as privileged, middle-class draft dodgers. In addition, a significant segment of the middle class failed to embrace the values and lifestyle of the counterculture. Many of these working and middle-class persons came to view themselves as the defenders of traditional American values against what they saw as the permissiveness and self-indulgence of the counterculture. These folks were ripe for recruitment into the resurgent conservative movement that will be described below.

Divisions over the Vietnam War, and the attendant cultural divisions, presented another difficult dilemma for the Democratic Party. Progressive intellectuals had, along with working-class voters, always been a key element in the Democrats' liberal coalition, and yet these intellectuals were now participating in demonstrations against the very president, Lyndon Johnson, who had represented the apex of liberal influence earlier in the 1960s. In the late 1960s, opinion within liberal Democrats began to shift against the war and against Johnson, leading many to support the insurgent candidacies of Senators Eugene McCarthy and Robert Kennedy in the presidential election of 1968 and to support Senator George McGovern in 1972. The Democratic Party felt a strong pull toward supporting both the foreign policy positions and the cultural stances of this key element in their coalition. However, at the same time, by embracing these new middle-class voters, they risked further alienating the white working-class voters who had traditionally supported their party. The racial divisions of the 1960s and the cultural divisions of the 1960s and 1970s would continue to weaken the party in the ensuing decades, thus creating the opportunity for conservatives to regain influence.

With the election of Ronald Reagan in 1980, the liberal coalition became a minority coalition, which had to fight a rearguard action to protect some of the gains of the 1930s and the 1960s. This minority coalition was quite different from the coalitions that had brought the New Deal and the Great Society into being. The loss of the South to the coalition became permanent and almost total, as large majorities of white Southern voters switched to the Republican Party. The loss of the white working class was less clear-cut. In the election of 1980, the media focused attention on the so-called Reagan Democrats, formerly solid, blue-collar Democratic voters who had voted for Reagan. This attention obscured the fact that working-class voters continued to vote Democratic in larger proportions than voters of higher socioeconomic status (Pomper 1981). What was perhaps more damaging to Democrats was the fact that many working-class voters simply dropped out of the political process. Declines in voter participation were steady from 1980 through 2000, and this lack of participation was most notable among younger people who lacked a college education (Patterson 2003). In addition, increasing numbers of working-class persons were not citizens and, thus, could not participate at all.

The withdrawal of working-class voters left an increasingly affluent electorate, who were divided along cultural and ideological lines that were not always clear-cut. People in education and the "helping" professions tended to be more liberal, whereas people employed in business tended to be more conservative, although not always. People who worshipped in the so called "mainline" Protestant denominations such as Presbyterian, Episcopal, and Methodist tended to be more liberal, whereas people in evangelical churches tended toward conservatism. Among the middle-class liberals who supported the Democrats, issues of personal freedom, the environment, and foreign policy tended to be more important than traditional economic issues. The only element of the broad-based, cross-class coalition that remained reliably within the liberal coalition consisted of African Americans, who voted Democratic by a margin of eight or nine to one. Hetherington and Larson (2010) present data showing that the new liberal coalition is separated from conservatives on the basis of personal values and identity more clearly than on the basis of the economic issues that were dominant in the New Deal Coalition. Liberals strongly embrace tolerance for groups and lifestyles, such as GLBT persons, that are equally strongly rejected by conservatives.

Since 1980, the liberal coalition has clearly lost the power that it once had to shape the national agenda. However, one is not necessarily justified in seeing it as a permanent minority coalition during the period from 1980 to 2008. Determining how liberal or conservative the electorate actually is has become a tricky proposition. Polls often show majorities agreeing with basic liberal positions, such as reforming health care or protecting the environment. However, many of these same citizens will actually vote for conservatives, based on national security or cultural issues. Some political analysts have argued for a "de-alignment," in which voters no longer reliably support either party or ideology but, rather, respond to short-term issues and personalities. Other analysts have challenged this, citing data that show a significant segment of the electorate which is deeply polarized along liberal-conservative lines (Hetherington and Larson 2010). These conclusions may not be totally contradictory but rather time bound to the particular years in which the data were collected. Despite all this ambiguity, one is still justified in labeling the period from 1980 to 2008 as a conservative era, in that conservatives came to frame the terms of the national debate in the way that liberals had done in the 1930s and 1960s. Therefore, I will now turn to a discussion of the formation of the conservative ideology, as it has developed in the late twentieth and early twenty-first centuries.

The Conservative Ideology

During the nineteenth century, as the political struggle in Western Europe shifted from advancing capitalism within an aristocratic milieu to modifying capitalism to meet workers' demands, the label "conservative" came to be applied to those who defended a relatively unfettered market economy, rather than to those defending the older order. The notion of "laissez-faire" capitalism was always more of a political myth than a description of reality, because, as noted above, there was never a time in the development of capitalism when the state did not play an active role in supporting and regulating the development of market economies. However, there was still considerable room for disagreement as to the exact nature and extent of state intervention, and conservatives believed that such intervention should be kept to a minimum, especially with regard to ameliorating inequality. In addition, conservatism retained some of the features of the earlier aristocratic version, in that its spokespeople argued for respect for established institutions and asserted the need for change to be slow and incremental.

In the United States, the Progressive Era of the early twentieth century saw the emergence of rhetoric that labeled wealthy capitalists as "plutocrats" who were resisting needed modification and modernization of the market system. During the New Deal, President Franklin Roosevelt adopted and amplified this rhetoric, denouncing business opponents of his programs as "moneyed interests" who were resisting the public interest. In the presidential election of 1936, support for and opposition to Roosevelt were clearly sorted out along class lines, with many affluent voters solidifying their rejection of the New Deal while less affluent voters overwhelmingly supported Roosevelt. This new alignment reinforced the association of conservatism with resistance to the expanded role of the state, particularly at the national level. It also reinforced the association of conservatism with the Republican Party.

Voting studies conducted during the 1950s and 1960s showed that the conservative, Republican position was a minority position among the voters, even though Republicans were occasionally able to win the presidency based on short-term issues (Campbell et. al. 1964). When Dwight D. Eisenhower became the first Republican president since the New Deal, he did not try to overturn basic New Deal programs such as Social Security, and some analysts were moved to declare the "end of ideology" in which there was consensus on the basic direction of policy and only technical issues remained to be resolved (Bell 1965). However, this analysis ignored the deep philosophical divisions over the nature and role of the state which lay beneath the surface of this apparent consensus.

When John F. Kennedy was elected president in 1960, his electoral and congressional margins of support were too narrow to allow any bold expansions of the social welfare role of the federal government. However, his more modestly funded proposals, such as the War on Poverty, were clearly moving in the direction of a more activist government. In addition, Kennedy increasingly came to embrace the goals of the African American civil rights movement, albeit with great caution and ambivalence. In response to these changes in policy, a new, more rigidly conservative faction began to emerge within the Republican Party. Its popular base was concentrated in the South and West, where both the business and popular ideology had always been more conservative than in the North and Midwest.

Some of its energy came from those who continued to embrace the militant anticommunism that had emerged at the beginning of the Cold War, particularly during the McCarthy era. Resistance to the spread of communism abroad was linked, in this view, to resistance to progressive groups and policies at home, which they labeled as subversive. They believed that the United States should attempt to aggressively roll back communism abroad, and they wanted to purge the government of anyone who counseled restraint and accommodation. From the beginning, they viewed liberals as "soft on communism" and as weak in their patriotism, but this issue did not develop mainstream purchase in the late 1950s and early 1960s, when there was a broad elite consensus supporting a strong anticommunist foreign policy. However, when the Vietnam War led students from the New Left to begin an across the board critique of American motives and intentions in international affairs, this reinforced conservatives' conviction that liberals were disloyal to American values.

After America's defeat in Vietnam in 1975, conservatives would create and popularize the narrative that this defeat was due to internal dissent and irresolute leaders in the United States, not to the military and political effectiveness of the communist insurgents. In addition, a group of conservatives, later labeled "neo-conservatives," developed a strong critique of the Nixon administration's détente with the Soviet Union and, with the help of funding from the defense industry, created organizations such as the Committee on the Clear and Present Danger that supported virtually unlimited expansion of the American nuclear arsenal and opposed any arms limitation treaties (Mann 2004). Under the influence of this group, the Republican Party successfully positioned itself as the leader of a resurgence of American pride and patriotism in the 1980s and cemented its popular image as "stronger in defending American interests" than the Democrats. They were assisted in this effort by liberals' seeming inability to craft a coherent, progressive vision of foreign policy that could be effectively sold to the American public.

Another source of conservative energy came from resistance to the civil rights movement for African Americans. These new conservatives eschewed the traditional Southern white rhetoric of racial superiority and instead couched their arguments against civil rights legislation in terms of individualism and property rights. Conservatives such as Senator Barry Goldwater strongly opposed the civil rights legislation of the 1960s, but, once it was passed, conservatives used its existence to argue that further attempts to correct past inequalities, such as affirmative action, were unnecessary. They argued that African Americans, women, and other disadvantaged groups were asserting "group rights" over against the individual's right and obligation to better himself or herself through his or her own efforts. This argument completely ignored the operation of the "group rights" of whites in the perpetuation of white privilege (Lipsitz 2006). By embracing this philosophy, the Republican Party positioned itself to take advantage of the white backlash against African American gains that grew in the late 1960s all across the country and also to claim the loyalties of white Southerners who were abandoning their traditional Democratic loyalties.

In the late 1960s, resistance to the black struggle for equality was linked to resistance to student protests against the Vietnam War under the "law and order" theme. The race riots that erupted in most American cities in the mid-1960s helped undercut support for the civil rights movement among many whites, and student protests were also seen as creating disorder and lawlessness. Conservatives have always shown a preference for preserving and respecting the prevailing social order, and this preference was again brought to the fore by the intense social conflicts of the 1960s. There was a strong overtone of racism in the law and order rhetoric, because those who were trying to change their disadvantaged status were viewed primarily as a source of social disruption, rather than as groups with legitimate grievances.

In addition, liberals who sought to respond to urban disorder through new social programs were characterized as too permissive toward those who had violated the law, and this critique of permissiveness was extended to their treatment of ordinary criminals, as well as rioters. Their perceived permissiveness toward lawbreakers was, in turn, linked to their permissiveness in accepting new social and sexual norms, as described above. Conservatives thus positioned themselves as defenders of conventional middle- and working-class families who were working hard and playing by the rules. This positioning helped them to undermine the loyalties of many voters to the Democratic Party, a loyalty that had been based on economic issues rather than these social issues.

It is at this point in the evolution of modern conservatism that evangelical Christianity began to become important. Evangelical Protestantism has always been a strong element in American culture, undergoing periodic revivals in response to social and economic change. In the late twentieth century, many people turned again to these beliefs as a way to justify and support their resistance to the social changes that were sweeping the country. The Bible clearly offers a great deal of support for a very traditional, patriarchal view of the family, and it has also been interpreted to support capitalist values of self-reliance and self-improvement (Weber 1992). In addition, the evangelical worldview provides reassurance that proper belief and behavior will lead to eternal rewards from God, a reassurance that is very attractive in times of social turmoil and disruption.

In the 1970s, it was the women's movement that presented the greatest challenge to these traditional beliefs. Women were increasingly leaving the exclusive roles of childbearer and homemaker and seeking individual fulfillment through education and careers. Their increasing ability to earn income in the workplace made them, in turn, less economically dependent on men and, thus, better able to leave marriages that they found destructive or unfulfilling. They were also claiming increasing control over their own sexuality and reproduction. All of these changes disrupted the patriarchal family relationships that were supported in the Old and New Testaments.

However, many women came to view liberated attitudes as a threat to their traditional value in the home, not as an opportunity to increase their value as human beings. More educated and affluent women were entering the labor force for independence and fulfillment, but those from less educated backgrounds were often entering the labor force out of economic necessity, as declining real wages made it ever more difficult for families to support themselves with a single breadwinner. Even though the dual roles of breadwinner and homemaker put incredible stress on women, many still clung to their role in the home as the primary nurturers of children as the central source of their identities. Encouraged by male religious leaders, these women came to see such issues as abortion as an attack on their values rather than as an enhancement of their choices.

The economic and foreign policy conservatives who dominated the Republican Party at first approached evangelical Christians with ambivalence. The cultural issues that were of central concern to this group were not the main concerns of those for whom economics defined their political positions. However, the hostility of evangelicals toward liberal Democrats, coupled with their demonstration of effectiveness in mobilizing voters on their issues proved irresistible to Republican leaders. Thus, Christian conservatives were gradually incorporated as one of the core constituencies of the party. Of course, not all of those who embrace evangelical Christianity are politically conservative. Surveys show greater diversity in their political views than popular media coverage would lead one to expect. Nevertheless, the voices of conservative evangelicals were the loudest and best organized and thus came to be viewed as speaking for the entire group.

Finally, the contemporary version of conservatism was fueled by the conviction among conservative businessmen and other white middle-class citizens that the role of the national government in American society was growing too large. Far from accepting the New Deal as *fait accompli*, the early conservative standard bearer, Senator Barry Goldwater, of Arizona, argued that it had gone "too far" and needed to be curtailed. He viewed his opposition as not only consisting of Democrats but of moderate Republicans who, in the view of Goldwater and his followers, were too accommodating to the liberal ideology and programs of the Democrats (Schoenwald 2001). Goldwater's overwhelming defeat by Lyndon Johnson in the presidential election of 1964 tended to obscure the significance of his movement in introducing a new, militantly conservative element to political activism within the Republican Party. This element would connect with prominent conservative intellectuals and form an audience for their strong critiques of the New Deal and the Great Society. Although conservatives' support of Richard Nixon's successful bid for president in 1968 represented a compromise with a moderate, pragmatic candidate, they continued to generate energy and ideas that would form the base for a growing conservative influence within the party.

Pierson and Skocpol (2007) provide convincing evidence that the period from 1960 to 1990 was an era of the steady, overall expansion of the role of the national state in American life, despite conservative successes in rolling back certain programs. More areas of life were regulated, and more distinct groups of Americans were assisted by federal programs than had ever been in the past. This steady expansion of government fueled the intensity of conservative resistance, and their positions hardened to preclude almost any constructive role for the federal government in addressing social problems. They developed a network of conservative think tanks that produced research supporting their categorical antigovernment stance. They also learned that they could disseminate stories and statements purporting to demonstrate the total incompetence of government, first through talk radio and later through the Internet. The empirical basis of many of these stories was weak to nonexistent, but they were widely accepted as gospel by those whose beliefs they reinforced.

It is not surprising that American business leaders would resist the expansion of regulatory programs that constrained their business decisions and of redistributive programs that increased their tax burdens. However, as noted earlier, the development of hard-line conservative positions and their movement into the mainstream of the Republican Party was also influenced by important changes in the nature of capitalism. The globalization of markets favored more conservative capitalists who were willing to ruthlessly cut costs by resisting union demands, by fighting regulations, or by moving jobs elsewhere. In addition, the shift in the American economy from traditional manufacturing to services and high tech industries favored the South and West, in part due to the concentration of massive defense spending (which spawned technology) in those areas (Mollenkopf 1983). As the political and economic power of these regions increased, it was to be expected that their more conservative attitudes would move to the fore in national politics.

As many authors have pointed out, it is quite possible to be economically conservative and socially liberal. The libertarian strain in conservatism, in which government interference both in the economy and in the private lives of citizens is opposed, has provided a strong and vigorous minority voice. Nevertheless, many conservatives find a deep connection between social and economic conservatism. Both support an established social order in which those who work hard are rewarded, and those who don't must suffer the consequences. The fact that many conservatives work in innovative, rapidly changing industries does not alter their opposition to change at the social level. As Thomas Frank (2004) has suggested, a religiously sanctioned economic and social conservatism provides a clear identity for ordinary people. It is an identity that stands in clear opposition to the identity that is typical of liberals (Hetherington and Larson 2010). Liberal efforts to woo voters away from this identity through purely economic arguments have often proved unsuccessful.

Summary

The liberal and conservative polarities just described have strongly shaped the political debate and the policymaking process since the 1930s. However, as a result of the social and economic changes just described, the late twentieth and early twenty-first centuries found both ordinary citizens and political elites more strongly polarized into competing ideological camps than in previous decades. Liberals and conservatives now disagree not only on values but on their basic narratives as to how the system works and should work. Each of these camps tends to be dominated by more privileged middle- and upper-middle-class voters, since poor and working-class voters are no longer as effectively mobilized as they were in the nineteenth and early twentieth centuries. Those in the working class who are mobilized are often pulled in the conservative direction by their cultural values, while they are also pulled in the liberal direction by their economic concerns, so that neither the Democrats nor the Republicans can assert an exclusive claim to be a truly working-class party. Conservative opposition to any government programs that seek to ameliorate inequality has become more rigid and absolute, while liberals have become more ambivalent in their support for such programs. This polarized atmosphere does not encourage broad new initiatives to help the poor, including those relating to housing.

Part II—Housing Policy and Ideology: Multiple Frames of Reference

As suggested in chapter 1, the application of the liberal and conservative orientations just described to a particular policy area is shaped by the unique traditions, values, and interests associated with that policy area. On the one hand, one can predict that the responses of liberals or conservatives to housing policy will be similar to their responses in other policy areas. On the other hand, housing policy has its own history, which influences any given decision. Programs are proposed, debated, implemented, evaluated, and either maintained or rejected. Each stage of the process is influenced greatly by what has gone before, that is, by the success or failure attributed by various actors to various programs.

Yet, delineating the values that influence a policy area is never a simple process. The notion of *policy areas* suggests that the activities of government can be meaningfully divided according to the substantive problems at which these activities are directed, such as, for example, transportation, defense, health, housing, etc. However, the numerous problems faced by individuals and communities are interdependent, and a program usually cannot define and address a particular problem without also affecting many related problems. Such multiple impacts are often the result of deliberate attempts by decision makers to please diverse groups with a single program, or they may be unanticipated consequences of the complexity of problems. In either case, both the way in which a policy subsystem evolves and the way in which national leadership of varying ideological persuasions may view specific programs are greatly influenced by the sets of problems or issues seen as forming the *context* of a particular program. If the primary goal of a program is seen as X, that program may be linked, in the eyes of decision makers, to a whole set of values and assumptions about programs of X-type. If a program is viewed as primarily directed at Y, another set of assumptions related to Y-type programs may influence them. Policy subsystems often contain different sets of actors who view the same programs as X or Y, a fact which can either weaken or broaden program support, depending on the circumstances.

Therefore, if the impact of broader ideologies on policy outcomes is to be fully understood, one must look at the various contexts or frames of reference within which a given policy or program has been viewed. The intended and unintended consequences of programs often cause them to be linked with more than one set of problems simultaneously, and broadly shared ideological assumptions may be applied to programs in different ways, depending on the primary frame of reference in which the program is being viewed at any given time. In the case of housing policy, there are three frames of reference within which housing programs have been viewed. First, housing has been viewed as one of a set of programs subsumed under the label *social welfare policy.* Second, housing has been viewed as a *community development policy.* Finally, housing policy has been viewed in the larger context of *macroeconomic policy* which has influenced a wide range of government programs. In the next few pages, these frames of reference will be described in general terms, as a preface to the more detailed analysis in later chapters.

The Social Welfare Context

A social welfare program may be broadly defined as any program that utilizes public resources, in the form of direct financial aid, in-kind assistance, or publicly funded expertise to alleviate problems confronted by individuals and families which are considered beyond their capacity to deal with on their own. Since housing has traditionally been viewed as one of the basic elements of a minimum standard of living (along with food, clothing, medical care, and education), decisions concerning housing programs have been heavily influenced by the overall history of social welfare efforts.

Though social welfare programs serve other groups in the population, the poor are their most frequent targets. Therefore, U.S. cultural and political orientations toward poverty play a major role in shaping the scope, design, and implementation of such programs. The central problem of poverty may be briefly stated in the following way. The natural workings of the labor market—that is, the way it allocates resources to individuals in the absence of intervention by government or other authoritative institutions—provides vastly unequal material reward for various roles in the process of production and virtually no reward for nonparticipation. People at the lower end of this reward structure cannot afford the level of consumption of basic goods and services that society defines as adequate. Therefore, a group of people exists who, in their own eyes and in the eyes of others, are impoverished. Material deprivation is accompanied by social and psychological stress, contributing to above average incidence of psychological disorders and social conflict among this group.

The size and composition of the group labeled *the poor* has changed substantially over time. While the overall distribution of wealth in the United States has stayed relatively constant since 1900, rapid increases in productivity have brought about a general increase in the standard of living. Yet, a substantial group remains at a level of existence far below that of the majority—the "other America" that Michael Harrington brought so forcefully to the nation's attention (Harrington 1971). Housing falling below widely accepted minimum standards has always been a significant and visible feature of poverty.

The central beliefs of the capitalist ideology have as a major corollary a justification of the social inequality created by the market economy. Two arguments are central to this justification. One stresses the *necessity* of poverty as an element in the stable functioning of the economic system. In this view, the threat of poverty serves as an incentive for individuals to contribute their labor to the economic system and to advance within its hierarchies. Without such a threat, the productivity of the system declines, resulting in a smaller "pie" for the whole society to divide. Also, the price of labor (particularly unskilled labor) is kept low by the threat of even worse deprivation as a result of unemployment. This, in turn, reduces the cost of goods and services to the rest of society.

Another central argument relates to the *justice* of poverty as a fate befalling individuals. This defense rests on the premise that impoverishment is a result of the individual's lack of character and discipline—an unwillingness to make the effort necessary to advance or a cynical attempt to take a free ride at the expense of society. Such a justification is, of course, closely related to a more sweeping defense of the whole system of inequality. Not only do the poor deserve to be where they are, but those at higher rungs of the economic ladder are there because they have exhibited hard work and strength of character. Therefore, they deserve to enjoy the fruits of their labors undisturbed by governmental redistribution or by guilty consciences. In addition, those at the highest levels may justly exercise a disproportionate share of economic, political, or social power due to the wisdom and virtue which their position purportedly reflects (Lewis 1978).

For many Americans, hostility toward the poor extends beyond an intellectual defense of inequality to include a visceral dislike of the poor as a group. Many undesirable traits are attributed to them, including laziness, slovenliness, dishonesty, an inability to plan for the future, and a propensity to drug addiction and violence. These perceptions are used not only to justify resistance to social welfare, but also to justify the geographic and social isolation of the poor. In addition, the process of defining one's own status in the U.S. system of stratification is often linked to the ability to limit the social interactions of self and family to persons of equal or greater socioeconomic status. As a result, if social programs such as housing subsidies locate the poor in physical proximity to higher status groups, or enable them to enjoy a comparable quality of life, they are seen as a threat to the status of these groups.

Though there is no logically necessary association between hostility toward the poor and racism, the two are often closely linked in a circular, self-reinforcing thought process. Discrimination in employment leads to disproportionate concentrations of African Americans and Latinos among the poor, which leads, in turn, to an association between the characteristic black or Latino and the negative characteristics attributed to the poor. This association leads to further discrimination since it reinforces the belief that such groups lack the character or intelligence for higher status occupations. It also intensifies demands for geographic and social isolation of poor persons who are members of racial or ethnic minorities, and the notion of providing services to the poor in general becomes associated with racial integration of those services (Ladd and Ladd 1991).

The attitudes just described are widespread in American society and affect political actors at both ends of the political spectrum. However, clear differences have emerged between liberals and conservatives as to how these cultural values have been interpreted and applied. In particular, the issue of the proper *governmental* response to the problem of poverty divides, perhaps more clearly than any other single issue, the liberal and conservative ideologies described in Part I. Therefore, a brief examination of these two competing attitude sets is necessary in order to understand clearly their impact on housing policy.

Conservatives are generally characterized by stricter adherence to the two central justifications for poverty just mentioned, in contrast to liberals who have qualified their support for market-generated inequalities in important ways. However, what most clearly distinguishes the conservative position is the linkage of these justifications of inequality to a rather complex set of attitudes toward the role of government in solving social problems. The strict laissez-faire position stresses the potential economic inefficiency of any government role in the allocation of goods and services. However, as previously noted, this outlook is not the operational ideology of most conservative political actors. Instead, they tend to support government interventions that protect or enhance the opportunities of market winners, while, in contrast, interventions that force market participants to reallocate resources in uncongenial ways receive the full force of the laissez-faire critique. Clearly, programs directed at alleviating poverty fall into the latter category.

The type of social welfare program that most arouses conservative resistance is one in which the government takes over a segment of the productive apparatus and becomes a direct provider of goods and services, thereby competing with the private sector. Nationalization of key industries or transportation facilities, the direct employment of surplus labor by the government, and publicly owned housing or health facilities have all been bitterly opposed on the grounds that they confer too much power on the public sector and are inefficient uses of resources.

Somewhat more acceptable have been programs in which the government subsidizes private firms in order to make the provision of low-cost goods and services profitable. As shall be discussed in chapter 4, this form of housing subsidy program became very popular in the 1960s. Although arrangements vary from program to program, the basic design is as follows: the provider charges what is determined to be a fair market price for the item; the impoverished consumer pays whatever price governmental guidelines say he or she can afford; and the government pays the difference. Such programs are defended on the grounds that private entities can produce the desired goods with less overhead than public sector agencies. They are also defended on the grounds that they create less government bureaucracy, which is to say they confer less overall power on the public sector than would be the case under direct government control of production. Finally, such subsidies are said to provide additional economic benefits by stimulating production in key private industries. Subsidies to the poor become subsidies to market winners as well, thus bringing them closer to the type of governmental intervention acceptable to most conservatives.

Another major strand in conservative opposition to social welfare programs relates to the total resources devoted to such programs. Often the debate over programs to alleviate poverty hinges on the scale of such efforts rather than yes or no choices as to government involvement. If proposals appear too costly at the onset or are perceived as rising too rapidly in cost, they will be opposed vigorously. The criterion for what constitutes excessive costs is generally an incremental one, that is, costs must not surpass those of previous levels of effort by too much, too quickly. If so, the program is denounced as a drain on the treasury which the country cannot afford, often without regard for the relationship between the current level of expenditures and objective measures of the need for the program. Underlying such objections to increases in the scale of such programs is, of course, a desire to contain the power of the public sector and to limit the resources allocated by nonmarket mechanisms.

This emphasis on controlling the scale of government intervention introduces a paradox into the conservative stance on programs for the poor. Their basic belief that the individual's status is determined by hard work and self-discipline would seem more compatible with programs that extend modest amounts of aid to individuals somewhat higher on the socioeconomic scale than the very poor. A blue-collar worker who puts in forty hours of hard work each week but whose wages do not provide the surplus necessary to cope with such problems as old age, illness, or layoffs would seem a more deserving recipient of aid than an unskilled, chronically unemployed member of the "underclass." As a matter of historical fact, it was just such programs (Social Security, unemployment insurance, etc.) that became the largest and most permanent features of the U.S. welfare state, but this occurred over the bitter opposition of many conservatives. Any attempts to broaden the base of benefits included in these original New Deal measures are resisted on the grounds that funds should be reserved only for those most in need. Also, recent concerns with the financial soundness of Social Security have been utilized by conservatives to construct an argument for the radical restructuring of this program along private investment lines, even though it is not clear that privatization would solve (and it might even exacerbate) the system's financial woes.

The reason for this contradiction lies in the large amount of resources involved in offering even modest levels of benefits to the relatively better off members of the working and middle classes. Although these persons might be deserving, the broadening of aid to include them would involve the government in large-scale reallocations of national wealth. These enhance the power of the public sector and reverse market decisions in ways that are too extensive from the conservative point of view. Therefore, they have consistently argued for restricting federal programs in housing and other areas to those at the very bottom of the income scale, as a way to control their costs and to limit political support for such programs.

As the conservative movement gained momentum and intensity from the 1980s on, some conservatives began to question the value of *any* government assistance to the poor, no matter how limited in scope. Charles Murray (1984) wrote a best-selling book in which he argued that welfare payments perpetuate poverty by encouraging women without other economic means of support to have children. This argument relied on an oversimplified image of welfare recipients as consisting mostly of long-term dependents, when in fact a majority of recipients were on welfare for relatively short periods of thme (Danziger and Haveman 2001). Nevertheless, this and similar arguments contributed to political support for the lifetime limits on welfare payments that were enacted in the welfare reform measure passed in 1996.

Although the prevailing cultural image of the poor has been negative, a number of strands in the U.S. cultural weave support the alleviation of poverty on moral or ethical grounds, and the contemporary liberal position has arisen, in part, from these strands. First, the Judeo-Christian belief in the ultimate dignity and worth of each human being, regardless of social rank, has led to efforts by church leaders to encourage the privileged to extend aid to the poor. Second, the American belief in democratic equality, while generally applied only to the political realm, has been extended by many to include notions of government-protected equality of opportunity and of a publicly guaranteed floor under market-generated inequality. Finally, though socialism has never enjoyed widespread support in the American working class, the notion of a fair share of society's wealth for those who help produce it has influenced the thinking of many of its leaders and their professional allies.

However, arguments of *moral obligation* by themselves rarely provide a sufficient basis for winning political coalitions in favor of social welfare programs. One reason is that beliefs supporting inequality have such a direct and powerful link to the immediate interest of the business, financial, and professional elites who dominate policy formulation in the United States. Moral suasion alone has been insufficient to dislodge this link, especially when guilt about the poverty of others can easily be assuaged by piecemeal, paternalistic, private charity.

Another reason is that working- and middle-class citizens who have supported various egalitarian reforms tend to have ambivalent attitudes toward those below them on the economic scale. They often resent the taxes necessary to support social welfare programs, even when they agree with the ends of such programs in the abstract (Wilensky 1975; Free and Cantril 1967). In addition, they share with elites a strong belief in the work ethic, and they relate gains they have made to the self-discipline required by their own very real struggles.

To overcome these sources of resistance and gain broader support, advocates of social programs have, therefore, moved beyond moral suasion to strategies appealing more directly to the interests and concerns of economic and political elites and of the mass of working- and middle-class citizens. They have created an alternative set of beliefs by which these groups can link their interests to those of the poor. The result has been the development of what Lawrence Friedman (1968) calls "social cost" justifications. These arguments have in common an emphasis on the costs the suffering of the poor imposes on the rest of society. Thus, they represent a fundamental shift away from the older notion that poverty is beneficial to society.

Three distinct types of social cost justification can be identified. The first stresses the long-term threat to the stability of the economic and political system posed by the sufferings of the poor. According to this view, the frustrations of the poor incline them toward violent, socially disruptive behavior and make them receptive to the revolutionary appeals of radical counter-elites. Thus, those benefiting from the system must be willing to limit its most flagrant deprivation, even if it springs naturally from its underlying structure. Such an argument is especially appealing in times of system crisis, such as the Great Depression, when calls for radical alternatives gain momentum.

The second social cost argument emphasizes the immediate impact of the deprivations of the poor on other members of society. In the nineteenth century, when infectious diseases such as cholera were still common, this argument stressed the direct link between pestilence bred in the slums and the health of the community as a whole. Later, as these threats receded, other themes were emphasized, such as reductions in crime and in the costs of institutionalizing the victims of poverty. With regard to housing, an essentially aesthetic argument was often used. Slums were described as physically ugly, blighted areas of the community which were an offense to the sensibilities and pride of the whole. Getting rid of slums was seen as a way of cleaning up the community which was presumed to benefit slum dwellers as well, though in most cases they were simply displaced into other blighted areas.

The third social cost justification views the individual in poverty as a potential human resource. The individual's contribution to the productivity and well-being of society is, in this view, wasted by poverty. Moreover, this wastage results not from individual character flaws but from material deprivation, a negative social environment (family, school, neighborhood, etc.), and psychological stress. The negative effects of all these factors should be counteracted by proper public intervention in order to maximize each individual's contribution to their own and to the collective well-being (Waxman 1983).

Radical critics of these social cost justifications, such as Piven and Cloward (1966; 1971; 1982), point out that programs implemented with social costs as their rationale often contain strong elements of control and suppression of the poor behind a humanitarian facade. They ignore the structural causes of poverty within the overall system of labor utilization and treat individual characteristics of the poor as the primary causes of their status. Such a control element fits well with the basic appeal to the self-interest of groups other than the poor which is at the heart of social cost justifications. These approaches emphasize poverty as a problem of maintaining the larger social order, not the absolute value of the poor as human beings. Such a view also reinforces the status of those middle-class professions that have arisen to take care of such problems.

The social cost critiques of poverty just described form the core of the liberal justification of social welfare. As Savitch (1979) notes, mainstream liberalism in the United States has stopped short of advocating fundamental changes in the market system. This tendency toward moderate reform can be traced, in large part, to the fact that the needs of the poor are usually expressed not by the poor themselves but by more privileged members of society on their behalf (Hays 2001). Liberal members of the politically active stratum have a stake in expanding services to the poor, but they also have a stake in the existing system of inequality, and they have close ties to those at the top of the system who provide the funds for research and service endeavors.

However, the historical record also shows that liberals have often been quite willing to expand social welfare and other forms of social engineering much farther than is reflected in existing policies. Therefore, one must look at the political balance of forces between liberal and conservative coalitions to understand the limited nature of U.S. social welfare efforts, not just at the characteristics of liberals themselves.

The necessity of compromise puts both factions in the position of defending policy outcomes they regard as less than optimal. This, after all, is the nature of politics. However, compromise is, perhaps, more politically costly for liberals since it is they who are defending government action. Liberal politicians usually have to fight hard to get any sort of program put into place, no matter how limited in scope or design. Yet, the very limits they must accept make the program vulnerable to valid criticisms from other liberal scholars, journalists, and policy advocates concerning its design, administrative procedures, comprehensiveness, or equity. The ultimate purpose of such critiques may be improvement or expansion of the program in question, and, to the extent that the analysis encourages effective political demands for change on the part of clients and/or stimulates legislators and administrators to initiate improvements, it may have the desired effect. At the same time, in a political atmosphere of elite dissensus as to just what the overall role of the public sector should be, such critiques may actually undermine political support for existing programs, rather than generate pressures for expansion.

This occurs in at least two ways. First, conservatives use such critiques to argue for the overall unworkability of the program and the consequent need to scrap it. Or, they may cite the problems of several programs in support of the even more global claim that government social welfare programs don't work (Schwarz 1988). Second, while constant critical analysis by liberals of programs whose overall intent they support is an important and necessary part of experimentation and improvement, it also serves to create division and uncertainty within their ranks, making programs more vulnerable to curtailment or elimination. In the face of a dual onslaught from the left and from the right, defenders of existing programs are left on rather barren intellectual and emotional ground. Statements such as "It may not be perfect but it's the best we could get" or "We know there are problems but look at the program's successes" may be empirically accurate, but they hardly serve as clarion calls to political action on the program's behalf (Mollenkopf [1983] applies this argument in a thorough and sophisticated way in his treatment of urban liberalism).

The above should not be construed as a suggestion that liberals stop making intellectually valid critiques of social welfare programs. To do so would not only be unethical but would surely invite even worse political disasters. Rather, it is to point out the precarious and ambivalent position in which liberals find themselves in their efforts toward greater government involvement in social welfare problems. As will be made abundantly clear in the following discussion of housing policy, our nation's seeming inability to arrive at coherent government policies is not solely a result, as has often been suggested, of insufficient planning or information, but of the simultaneous existence of two intellectual and political struggles—one over *whether* government should get involved and the other over *how* public involvement should be organized and executed.

The Community Development Context

The second frame of reference within which housing policy has been viewed is that of community development policy. Community development, in its broadest sense, is the total process by which a geographic or political entity improves the quality of its physical structures, its economic life, and its social relationships. However, the major issues in this arena tend to revolve around *physical* improvements and their interaction with other factors.

Housing policy decisions are influenced by this environment because housing is not just an item of immediate consumption or a service to particular families but also a physical resource. Since it occupies a large portion of the available space in the community, it shapes the qualitative and quantitative allocation of that space. Each dwelling unit is also linked to a package of neighborhood and community services and amenities that, in addition to the physical condition of the unit itself, help determine the quality of life for several generations of families. Thus, housing programs have become embroiled in a larger debate over the shape and direction of community growth.

Community development policy has been dominated by two distinct, but interrelated sets of issues. One consists of issues pertaining to the role of local government vis-à-vis the private sector in the control of economic growth and physical development. The other set of issues relates to the changing distribution of power between federal, state, and local governments as they have assumed differing roles in the local community development process. The latter is, of course, but one subset of a whole range of policy problems in intergovernmental relations, but community development issues have raised intergovernmental conflicts more clearly and forcefully than many other issues.

Ideological divisions among elites are not as clear with regard to community development issues as with social welfare issues. As shall be shown, community development policies tend to be pursued by different groups for different reasons. However, a clear division has emerged with regard to the proper direction community development should take. Most liberals and most conservatives have, since the New Deal, supported some federal role in community development activities, but they have differed as to the nature of that role. These liberal/conservative differences are an important part of the environment in which housing policy has been formed.

The community development process in the United States has been primarily in private hands from the earliest days of settlement. The rate at which cities have grown, the allocation of the physical space they occupy, and the distribution of the benefits of development among the population have largely been determined by private economic decisions based on market considerations (Chudacoff and Smith 2000; Savitch 1979). Nevertheless, public services and amenities have always been seen as a necessary element in this growth.

In the mid-nineteenth century, many U.S. cities began to grow rapidly. The massive influx of immigrants and the rapid pace of economic development required new investments in public services such as transportation, utilities, and police, even though the services expected of government were much more limited than today. In response to the stresses of growth, political machines formed in many cities, with leaders who "coordinated" the development of public services through bribery and kickbacks, enriching themselves greatly in the process. This form of extralegal centralization enjoyed the support of business interests for a considerable period. However, as business began to change from the entrepreneurial to the professional managerial style, a new breed of managers and professionals became increasingly frustrated with the corrupt, personalistic style of machine rule. Tired of paying the financial price and eager to apply to government the same principles of scientific management to which they aspired in private endeavors, they supported the municipal reform movement which greatly reshaped local politics early in the twentieth century (Judd and Swanstrom 2010).

Business and professional leaders pushing for reform often received the support of middle-class social reformers who wanted to improve living conditions and opportunities for the poor. These reformers saw the bosses as exploitative, in spite of their ostentatious charitable endeavors. Yet, the leadership of reformed cities often proved even more insensitive to the needs of the poor and working classes than the bosses. Defenders of reform institutions spoke of a unified public interest for the whole community, but, in fact, the new institutions were dominated by upper-middle- and upper-class groups who closely identified the public interest with their own interest in economic growth. The concepts of minimum government and sound financial management they advocated often meant an absence of services to the poor.

Lawrence Friedman (1968) has documented the attempt early housing reformers made to utilize this notion of a community interest in the shape of development. According to Friedman, Jacob Riis and other early advocates of housing for the poor borrowed a term from biology—*blight*—to describe slum conditions. This term implied that slums were a disease that threatened the whole community, just as blight on one branch of a tree could soon spread to the whole tree. Yet, in the hands of business-oriented elites, the concept soon came to focus on the physical existence of the slums, not the problems of the people inhabiting them. The goal of removing blight was used to justify physical destruction of the slums with little regard for the fate of their inhabitants.

These conflicting uses of the term *blight* highlighted the conflicting values which physical planning and other deliberate public efforts at community development would come to serve. In one sense, such efforts contradicted the laissez-faire notion of city growth. The forerunners of the modern planning profession, people such as Frederic Law Olmstead and Daniel Burnham, dreamed of transforming the crowded hodge-podge of the market-generated city into planned, orderly, convenient, aesthetically pleasing communities. For example, in carving Central Park out of Manhattan's crowded street grid, Olmstead clearly went against the land use that market forces would have dictated, in order to create open space and greenery for city dwellers. And, other early planners optimistically predicted that physical improvements would alleviate the social problems of the poor. Thus, professionals involved in physical planning seemed to share a common goal with those involved in expanding social welfare programs, namely, the need for conscious public modification of market outcomes in order to benefit society as a whole (Mohl and Richardson 1973).

In another sense, the kind of professionalization involved was quite different from the commitments to social reform that gradually evolved among other groups. Although both contravened strictly market-driven growth (which allocates space to the highest bidder and rewards each citizen according to the market value of his or her labor) physical planning is an intervention that clearly reinforces the interests of most economic elites.

First, it fits their notion of civic pride, in that planning can easily justify the creation of showy public facilities and open spaces which improve the community's image and attractiveness to new investment. Attractive public spaces and facilities are utilized to sell potential investors on the desirability of living and doing business in the community. Also, certain planned public developments, such as sports stadiums housing professional teams, are designed to signal that the community has "arrived" as a major hub of commerce.

Second, physical planning can be used to meet the need for some rational ordering of public services, facilities, and land use to support private economic development. Thus, zoning was transformed from a tool for orderly growth to a tool for excluding "undesirables" from certain neighborhoods, and for the strategic enhancement of property values. Even transportation and utilities planning became the design of streets and sewers to serve areas already developed by private enterprise (Chudacoff 2000). Social welfare programs, in contrast, present a more direct challenge to ideological justifications of inequality, and their long-term contribution to the stability of any given community is often not so readily apparent.

Thus, a liberal/conservative split emerged over the scope and direction of community development. Strict, laissez-faire conservatives have been reluctant to support any active government role, even in physical planning and redevelopment (Anderson 1964; Welfeld 1974). However, many otherwise conservative actors, who oppose social welfare measures, support such a governmental role as a justifiable subsidy to private investors. These supporters believe that public community development programs should have economic growth as their main objective, even when that imposes costs on lower-income persons.

Liberals, too, have supported the use of public funds for physical planning and economic development, and in administering the nation's first major community development program, urban renewal, some politically liberal local leaders proved very insensitive to the needs of the disadvantaged. Nevertheless, the overall thrust of liberal action with regard to community development has been to urge that it directly address the needs of the poor, in addition to serving general economic development needs. As shall be shown in chapter 6, this liberal/conservative struggle became very important in the later years of the urban renewal program, and it shaped the debate over the uses of Community Development Block Grant funds.

Debates over the role of local government in community development can be traced to the nineteenth century, but, prior to the Great Depression, most participants in these debates saw no legitimate role for the federal government in the process. During this crisis, in contrast, many cities were gripped by social, physical, and financial problems far exceeding the capacity of local governments to respond. The federal government was the only entity with sufficient resources to deal with long lines of the unemployed or to provide needed public works when most city treasuries were nearly empty. Nevertheless, this increased federal role went against a long tradition of decentralization in U.S. politics. The defenders of this tradition, while unable to block federal involvement, influenced it profoundly.

The notion that state and local governments are closer to the people than the federal government has been a staple of U.S. political rhetoric throughout most of the country's history. However, it was James Madison who, in making his case for a strong federal government, first warned that smaller units of government might be more easily dominated by a single faction which could then guide governmental decisions exclusively in its own interest (Cooke 1961). Grant McConnell (1966) expanded this line of thought, arguing that privileged groups have an easier time controlling political decisions in smaller, decentralized units of government. The elite in each unit is more homogeneous, facilitating communication and the formulation of common interests. Also, the unit is more likely to be dominated by one or two major economic activities, which control most of the resources for public action. Conversely, people whose resources are small are weakened by their inability to join with large numbers of others in a common cause.

Another reason why political decentralization tends to benefit economic elites, emphasized by Peterson (1981) and Mollenkopf (1983), is the increased bargaining power which large economic entities have vis-à-vis government. As the U.S. economy has developed, the private sector has become more and more international and interdependent in scope. While even a large firm incurs substantial costs in moving its operations, the fact remains that economic units are mobile in relation to units of government. This forces states and localities to compete for economic development. In order to stimulate local growth, governments must strike a bargain with private entities favorable enough to attract and keep them. Of course, important parts of the bargain are not controllable by local government, such as climate and proximity to markets; but this makes them even more eager to manipulate those they can control, such as taxes, subsidies, and regulations. This weak bargaining position makes it very difficult for any locality to impose costs or regulations on the private sector, no matter how well such measures might serve the needs of local citizens. Only the federal government is in a position to impose strong, uniform regulations or obligations which firms cannot avoid by moving out of town or out of state (although even federal leverage is increasingly reduced by their ability to move out of the country altogether).

It is, therefore, no accident that the lines of political division over the

issue of centralization versus decentralization closely parallel the liberal/
conservative split over the role of the government in altering market decisions. Even though the economic crisis of the 1930s shifted the American
elite consensus to support some federal involvement, the liberal/conser-
vative split soon reemerged in a slightly different form around issues
concerning the extent and direction of such involvement. Conservatives
continued to oppose programs that aided the poor, such as public housing,
but many became more willing to accept physical development aid that
reinforced existing market tendencies, provided that such aid was administered locally, and so did not interfere with local elite prerogatives or
alter program benefits in favor of the disadvantaged. Liberals, in contrast,
supported both physical redevelopment and social welfare efforts. They
were willing to accept greater federal planning, guidance, and financing
of local efforts as a means to ensure more equitable treatment for those
disadvantaged by the market.

On the other side of the coin, states and localities are sometimes inclined
to take a more pragmatic and less ideological approach to social and
community problems than are national political leaders. At the local level,
it is often possible for people of different political persuasions to agree on
concrete solutions to concrete local problems. For example, a conservative
business owner may be philosophically opposed to government assistance
to the poor, but he or she can agree to support a housing project that is
publicly subsidized because it "cleans up" a low income neighborhood,
thereby enhancing the community's overall image. As shall be shown, this
pragmatism allowed states and localities to assume a greater leadership
role in housing for the poor when the federal government greatly reduced
its support.

The Macroeconomic Context

The third frame of reference which has influenced housing policy, along
with virtually every area of governmental activity, is that of macroeconomic
policy. Since the Depression, and even more since World War II, the federal
government has assumed the responsibility of deliberate macroeconomic
intervention, in order to minimize the peaks and valleys of prosperity and
recession to which the market economy is subject. This larger environment
interacts with housing policy in three ways:

- First, since virtually every actor in the system feels a strong stake in
  the outcomes of economic policy, the struggle between liberals and

conservatives over the proper macroeconomic interventions frame their struggles in more narrow policy areas.

- Second, the behavior of the economy as a whole, whether in response to its internal dynamics or in response to government intervention, has a direct impact on the housing sector of the private market. Long-term economic trends, such as inflation, greatly affect the availability and cost of housing. Moreover, as these trends interact with broad social and demographic trends in urban communities, they create different problems for different segments of the population. These problems, in turn, have an influence on the kinds of federal housing policies that appeal to decision makers.
- Third, as the economic crisis of 2008–2011 has illustrated, investments in housing and in housing credit instruments constitute a large sector of the economy, so that downturns or restructuring in this sector can have a negative effect on the entire economy.

FISCAL AND MONETARY POLICY

As a result of the Great Depression, the ideas of British economist John Maynard Keynes became widely accepted as a basis for policy in the United States and elsewhere. Keynes argued that public expenditures and taxation could be used to dampen the swings of the market economy from periods of rapid growth and inflation back to periods of recession and job loss. He believed that it was acceptable for a government to run a modest deficit, if that was necessary in order to provide such countercyclical interventions. In addition to wide acceptance of the Keynesian notion of fiscal policy, the idea that government could and should manipulate the money supply in order to address the twin evils of inflation and stagnation also came to be widely accepted. In the 1950s and 1960s, fiscal and monetary policies were seen as two powerful and valuable tools for preventing future depressions of the scale that occurred in the 1930s.

The conservative ideology includes a visceral dislike of most of the activities and expenditures of government, with the exception of defense spending. To most conservatives, taxes are always "too high" and government programs are always "wasteful." Therefore, the notion of utilizing public expenditures in a countercyclical fashion has always been at odds with conservatives' basic inclinations. In the post–World War II era, Keynesian fiscal policy displayed a degree of success, and a bipartisan consensus appeared to have formed behind its use. However, economists such as Milton Friedman began laying the groundwork for a conservative counterattack, in which it was argued that governmental intervention should be minimal and should be centered on monetary, rather than fiscal policy (Immergluck 2004).

During the 1970s, the economy presented a new and less tractable set of problems. Up until this decade, fiscal policy had been guided, in part, by the Philips Curve, which described a trade-off between inflation and unemployment. When unemployment rose to unacceptable levels, government would stimulate the economy with additional spending, until the point at which economic growth would begin to produce inflation. At that point, fiscal policy makers would rein in public spending in order to slow the economy down. During the 1970s, this trade-off ceased to work as predicted. High levels of inflation began to coexist with high unemployment in a pattern known as "stagflation."

Stagflation had multiple causes. The most important was the slowing of economic growth as the postwar economic boom enjoyed by the United States came to an end. The economies of Western Europe and Asia had recovered and were competing with American firms for both domestic and international markets. This slowing of growth meant that incomes were not rising as fast, so that taxes were seen as an increasing burden by the middle class and above. In addition, productivity growth also slowed. This meant that raises given to employees did not always match their increases in productivity, and, therefore, that wage increases tended to have a more inflationary impact. In addition, the politically motivated embargo by oil producers in the Middle East raised the cost of an essential input into the productive process, energy, at a time when prices were already being pushed upward by other forces.

The resulting loss of confidence in standard fiscal tools reignited the debate over what the government's economic role should be. The stagflation debate coincided with the rapid expansion of both social benefit programs and the regulatory activities of government. Rather than attack these new programs on their individual merits, conservatives constructed an argument that the overall level of public taxation, spending, and regulation were to blame for the economic troubles of the era. In this view, taxes and regulations depress productivity, while public spending stimulates inflation. As inflation and interest rates soared in the late 1970s, this argument began to find a receptive public audience. The Republican candidate for president in 1980, Ronald Reagan, argued that most of the nation's economic problems could be laid at the feet of "big government."

In the 1980s, fiscal policy took a different turn, one that was not the preferred outcome for either liberals or conservatives. President Reagan pushed through substantial tax cuts, but the political popularity of many domestic programs (plus Democratic control of the House of Representatives) forced him to accept much smaller spending cuts than he wanted. Meanwhile, he was substantially expanding defense expenditures. This combination of decreasing revenues and increasing overall expenditures led to rapid increases in the federal deficit. Unlike the temporary deficits linked to short-term fiscal stimulus that were envisioned by Keynes, these were structural deficits, reflecting a long-term gap between revenues and expenditures for the federal government. These deficits were not created as the desired outcome of deliberate fiscal policy choices but rather were the result of the political stalemate between liberals and conservatives.

However, conservatives learned an important lesson from the 1980s. It was that capping revenues to the point of creating deficits was a much more effective way of restraining liberal spending initiatives than tackling programs one at a time (Greider 1981). In previous decades, conservatives had denounced deficits as the product of liberal profligacy and fiscal irresponsibility. Once they discovered that the ongoing large deficits gave them leverage to oppose liberal programs, they began to lose enthusiasm for serious efforts to reduce the deficit, especially if it meant tax increases. They continued to ritually denounce deficit spending and to call for draconian budget cuts to eliminate it, but in fact they saw deficits as an effective way to derail new programs. Any liberal who proposed new spending for anything faced the hurdle that the government was already swimming in red ink.

The ability of conservatives to pursue this tactic was enhanced by the fact that deficit spending did not have some of the dramatic negative effects on the overall economy in the 1980s that many economists had predicted. This was due to two other factors. First, the Federal Reserve acted to counter the inflationary effects of the deficit by tightening the money supply. In 1982, the Fed forced a recession through restricting the money supply but, in so doing, it effectively ended the threat of double digit inflation that had arisen in the late 1970s. Inflation has stayed at manageable levels since that time. Second, the crowding-out effect, in which federal borrowing makes less credit available to private borrowers, was muted by large purchases of U.S. debt instruments by other countries, such as China. During the 1980s, the United States was transformed from a creditor nation to a debtor nation, but this did not produce any immediate, visible harm to the economy.

This lesson was carried forward into the administration of George W. Bush, from 2001 until 2009. Bush and the Republican majority in Congress enacted large tax cuts and then proceeded to incur even larger structural deficits than had occurred during the Reagan administration. They attempted to conceal the full extent of the deficit by taking expenditures for the wars in Iraq and Afghanistan "off budget" when computing it, but they were, in fact, tolerating a huge structural gap. When the economy was on the verge of collapse in 2008, these structural deficits made it more difficult to enact the kind of stimulus measures that were called for in the Keynesian model.

During the 1980s and 1990s, liberals continued to defend programs piecemeal, and, as Pierson and Skocpol (2007) document, they were successful in preventing conservatives from shrinking government to the extent that they desired. However, liberals were unsuccessful in projecting a convincing overall model of managing the economy that could counter the conservative message that "the government is the problem." In fact, many centrist Democrats embraced the notion that the government's role had to be reduced, and put forward a milder version of the conservative agenda. Polls showed that distrust of government was widespread, so that even though a majority of voters might agree with the liberal goal of helping those who are in need, expanding the government's role proved a hard sell. President Bill Clinton's spectacular failure to enact health care reform in 1994 is an excellent example of the operation of these cross-currents (Skocpol 1996).

Housing is affected by fiscal policy in several ways. First, because the demand for housing is highly dependent on the availability of credit, changes in interest rates can have an immediate, drastic effect on the housing market. For example, interest rates fell in the late 1990s and stayed low by historical standards through much of the next decade. This was helpful to the overall economy, but in the housing sector, it helped fuel rising demand and rising prices. People were encouraged to make highly leveraged purchases by both the low rates and the anticipation that the value of their property would increase. The resulting housing boom helped keep the overall economy healthy, but it set the stage for a precipitous collapse when favorable lending conditions changed.

Secondly, home purchases are subsidized by the federal government through the federal tax deductibility of mortgage interest and property taxes. The National Low Income Housing Coalition estimates, based on data from the Office of Management and Budget that the 2011 value of these tax breaks is $210 billion (National Low Income Housing Coalition 2011, 38). During the 1980s, there was considerable discussion of the fiscal impact of "tax expenditures," that is, tax deductions targeted at specific groups or specific activities, which many economists view as equivalent to the government granting money for these purposes. However, this issue has not entered actively into the fiscal policy debate since that time. These kinds of subsidies are politically popular, especially with conservatives, because they do not show up in the budget as expenditures, and they do not involve the creation of new public agencies to administer them. However, once they are established, tax deductions become entitlements, which are difficult to rescind, even when their costs rise rapidly. The mortgage interest deduction is one of the most costly of these tax expenditures, and it disproportionately subsidizes those at higher incomes. It also reduces the effective interest rate paid by purchasers, thus further stimulating demand for housing, especially at the high end of the price range. For example, a taxpayer in the 26 percent bracket who is paying a 5 percent nominal interest rate experiences an actual interest rate of 3.7 percent. Nevertheless, any attempt to restrict it would encounter stiff political resistance from both taxpayers and housing producer lobbies.

REGULATORY POLICY

Beginning in the Progressive Era of the early 1900s and continuing through the Great Depression of the 1930s, there was a great expansion of federal government involvement in regulating the financial sector of the economy, in order to ensure the availability of credit for housing and economic development and to restrict speculative practices that can cause the entire economy to collapse. According to Dan Immergluck (2004) there were, by the end of the New Deal period, a wide range of regulations in place, including:

- Federal Reserve requirements that banks maintain minimum reserves;
- Federal Deposit Insurance Corporation protection for the accounts of individuals;
- A "firewall" between depository institutions and investment firms, created by the Glass-Steagall Act of 1933.

In addition, a number of regulations and subsidies had been enacted that were specifically targeted at housing finance:

- Federal subsidy and regulation of savings and loan associations, whose sole purpose was to finance housing;
- Creation of the Federal Housing Administration (FHA) program of

mortgage insurance that fundamentally changed the way housing loans were made, from short-term mortgages to long-term, fully amortized loans;

- Creation of the Federal National Mortgage Association (FNMA, or "Fannie Mae") to foster the development of a secondary mortgage market that would increase the liquidity of housing capital. (Immergluck 2004, 19–51)

However, as memories of the Great Depression faded over the next three decades, so, too, support for the Depression-era regulatory structure began to erode. The first big casualty was the savings and loan system, during the late 1980s. As inflation took off in the late 1970s, and as interest rates rose with it, the federally restricted interest rates offered by savings and loans became much less attractive to depositors. These institutions requested a lifting of these restrictions and, as a result, they were able to offer higher interest money market accounts and certificates of deposit. They also lobbied for, and received, authorization to invest in commercial real estate, as well as housing. However, the lifting of these regulations was not sufficient to counteract the loss of deposits, and many institutions suffered massive losses from risky investments in commercial real estate. The federal government stepped in with a $124 billion bailout that saved many investors, but over the next few years, the savings and loan system was largely absorbed by banks and other types of housing lenders.

During the 1970s and 1980s, the deregulation philosophy came to be enthusiastically endorsed by conservatives and many "middle of the road" liberals. A number of industries, such as airlines, were deregulated, and it was inevitable that pressure to deregulate financial markets would follow. Among the most important deregulatory measures were:

- The federal override of state usury laws that limited the interest rates that could be charged to consumers;
- A federal law permitting interstate banking that led to massive mergers within the banking industry
- The repeal of the Glass-Steagall Act's firewall between banking and other investment activities.

The effect of these measures, acting in combination with the growth of the secondary mortgage market, was to create a national, standardized market for mortgages. Historically, mortgage markets had been localized, and they depended on the intimate knowledge of the community and of borrowers that was held by local banks and savings and loans. From the 1980s on, credit criteria and ratings became standardized, so that investors in a part of the country distant from where a loan was originated could feel confident as to its soundness. Standardization also encouraged a rapid increase in the popularity of mortgage-backed securities, which are bonds backed by revenues from bundled groups of mortgages. Securitization involved a partial transfer of risk from the initial lender to new investors. This factor, coupled with the elimination of usury laws, caused a large number of higher interest, higher risk, sub-prime loans to be introduced into the mortgage mix during the first decade of the twenty-first century.

Viewed from the perspective of the hindsight generated by the 2008–2010 collapse of the mortgage market, the flaws and potential risks of such a system are readily apparent. However, the embrace of the neoclassical, free market ideology by key decision makers blinded them to the risks. Friedman's notion that financial markets, when left alone, naturally achieve equilibrium and efficiency was accepted as gospel, despite much historical evidence that such markets are unstable and require careful regulation. Even after the crisis, many conservative commentators tried to blame it on government action, rather than the increasingly risky behavior of private investors.

Post-Crisis Politics

President Barack Obama owed his election in 2008 to the economic crisis. Analyses of polling and voting data suggest that, in the absence of this overwhelming economic disaster, many voters' reservations about Obama's race and about his image as a very liberal candidate could have given Republican candidate John McCain the election (Campbell 2008). However, managing the economic crisis has proved extremely challenging for President Obama during his first years in office. As noted earlier, the structural deficits left over from the Bush administration have meant that Obama's stimulus spending, which would otherwise be a fairly modest Keynesian intervention, has produced deficits that are an unprecedented share of GDP and that raise the concerns of some liberal economists, as well as conservatives. In addition, the economy did not respond quickly to the stimulus but remained in a sluggish growth pattern with ongoing high unemployment rates. This, in turn, threatened the credibility and political capital that Obama needed to push through his progressive legislative agenda.

During this crisis, the primary focus of concern in housing policy has been rescuing home owners that were experiencing foreclosure and stabilizing the mortgage lending process through new regulations. As shall be discussed in chapter 9 the impact of this crisis on housing for low income people has not received equal attention. Housing for the poor had not been a central feature of Obama's progressive agenda, but it is likely that voters' judgment as to his economic stewardship will affect his ability to address this issue, along with many others. Macroeconomic management issues are obscure to most citizens, but voters do judge presidents on their overall record of economic management. Therefore, the liberal/conservative struggle over a variety of issues will be profoundly affected by Obama's perceived success or failure in this arena.

CHAPTER 3

Housing and Human Needs

Introduction

In chapters 1 and 2, the political and ideological frameworks within which housing policy is created have been described. This chapter addresses the fundamental question of why housing is important to human existence. Public policy is not always directed toward meeting fundamental human needs; it may address symbolic outputs designed to provide citizens with a psychological sense of the legitimacy of the state or of recognition of their place in society. However, policy makers do put a great deal of effort into meeting what they perceive to be fundamental needs, and certainly housing policy has been guided by a sense that housing represents one of the essential elements in human existence. Therefore, in order to understand housing policy decisions, one must understand clearly what human needs housing is expected to satisfy. This chapter will show that housing addresses a full range of complex human desires and needs. Each of these needs has come into play at various times as housing policies have been formulated and debated.

The previous discussion of ideology has shown that there are profound philosophical differences within American society as to how fundamental needs are to be satisfied. Should society be designed to maximize each individual's pursuit of her or his own needs, with the market mechanism assuring an overall efficient distribution of goods and services, or does society have a collective obligation to provide certain essential needs for people who lose out as a result of market outcomes? The answer to this question depends, in turn, on whether or not one views the satisfaction of the needs of individuals as fundamentally interdependent in ways that the market mechanism cannot fully capture. Therefore, the final section of this chapter discusses the relationship between housing as a set of fundamental needs and housing as a market commodity.

Part I—Housing and the Hierarchy of Needs

What is a human need? Obviously, a full answer would take us into complex realms of psychology and philosophy that are far beyond the scope of this work. For current purposes, a serviceable, commonsense definition is adequate. At its heart, the concept of a human need is related to some element of human existence that people require in order to thrive and to fully develop their potential. If they are deprived of this essential element, they may still figure out ways to live productively, but their struggle to do so is much less likely to meet with success than when this need has been met.

Why is housing included in virtually any list of basic needs? The immediate and obvious need that human beings have for "a roof over their heads" might make the answer seem obvious or simple. However, the relationship between housing and human needs is far from simple, because housing simultaneously addresses (or fails to address) a variety of needs. As one examines housing policy, one continually encounters multiple needs that housing is intended to address. Therefore, an understanding of housing policy should be grounded in a theoretical understanding of this complex panoply of needs. This theoretical framework provides a point of reference as one navigates the complex currents of housing demands and policy responses.

In defining human needs in the way just described, one must acknowledge the implicit normative content in this definition. Those who care about human needs generally do so out of a normative belief that it is "good" for the human needs of others to be fulfilled. One could take an alternative perspective (as many people do) that views life as a "zero sum" struggle in which one's own need satisfaction is primary, even if it must be achieved at the expense of others. However, almost all world religious and philosophical traditions reject this purely self-centered view. Coming from a wide variety of perspectives, these traditions arrive at the similar conclusion that reciprocity and mutual care among human beings achieve much more positive outcomes for all individuals, in the long run. To look at it in terms of individual well-being, whatever sacrifice of one's immediate desires is required to respect the needs of others "pays off" in terms of one's own long-term happiness and fulfillment. While a lot of empirical evidence to support this conclusion could be presented, it is in the end an ethical conclusion, based in part on a leap of faith that life will turn out better for all human beings if mutual concern prevails.

Having acknowledged this ethical underpinning, one may then proceed to explore how basic human needs can be identified and defined. Immediately, one encounters the problem that statements of "need" are socially constructed. What individuals believe they need in order to survive and thrive is shaped by the culture into which they are born. For example, in the individualistic culture of the United States, most people would argue that children "need" the privacy of having their own bedrooms, especially as they get older, while in other, more communal cultures this level of personal privacy would neither be expected or desired. This social construction of needs is the root of the confusion that often arises over the boundary between needs and wants. If one defines a "want" as an expectation of some desirable future state, then clearly not all wants are needs. However, as cultures change and differentiate, the boundary between needs and wants constantly shifts. What was at most a vague aspiration or luxury at one point in history (for example, indoor plumbing) comes to be regarded a "basic necessity of life" at another time.

The fuzzy and culturally dependent nature of these boundaries should not, however, cause one to abandon the search for a definition of basic human needs. Intuitively, one can conclude that certain basic elements of life are more important than others in enabling human beings to live a full, meaningful life. What these elements are, and how a "meaningful life" is defined will vary from one culture to another, and how society is organized will also affect the ways in which needs are experienced. However, experience within a multicultural world suggests that some human needs are so fundamental as to transcend any particular cultural milieu. In addition, in looking at human needs within a particular culture, such as will be the case in this study of U.S. housing policy, it is perfectly valid to rely upon the values of that culture as a basis for framing needs, since it is those values that will shape the expectations of those who create and are affected by public policy.

Maslow's Hierarchy of Needs

In the 1940s, psychologist Abraham Maslow developed his well-known "hierarchy of needs," and his formulation quickly escaped the halls of academia to become a part of popular culture. In creating a *hierarchy* of needs, Maslow intended to show that the satisfaction of different types of needs is interdependent and that the satisfaction of certain needs, such as basic physiological needs, is primary (or, in Maslow's terminology, *prepotent*) in that the individual cannot satisfy "higher" needs within the hierarchy unless the more basic needs have been satisfied. He *did not* argue that the progression was absolute. Humans can pursue different levels of needs at once and gain at least partial satisfaction of a higher type even when a more basic need remains unfulfilled. However, he did argue that the individual could not *fully* satisfy the higher needs without underlying, more basic needs having been addressed, because the individual's energy and attention will still be primarily engaged in satisfying the more basic needs. For some, the notion of a hierarchy might suggest that those needs at the top are in some sense "better" than the needs at the bottom. For Maslow, those at the bottom are more fundamental to human existence than those at the top, but humans only realize their full potential when they are achieving satisfaction at all levels (Maslow 1970; Madsen 1974).

Maslow's five categories provide a useful classification of the range of drives and desires which shape human existence, and this classification also highlights the interdependence of various types of needs. These categories have wide popular appeal precisely because most human beings can see that most of what they believe they need and want can fit into one of these five basic categories. In addition, one may observe that persons who are chronically unable to fulfill one of these sets of needs are often in despair and may experience multiple conflicts with other human beings. Therefore, Maslow's categories form a useful basis for understanding where housing fits into the overall pattern of human existence. The provision of housing touches all five of Maslow's categories of need, and its role in serving all five of these needs has been reflected in many of the public policies designed to enhance the provision of housing.

What follows is a brief discussion of the ways in which the provision of housing impacts each of these categories. As each need is outlined, data on the current ability of the U.S. housing stock to provide that need will be presented. The end result will be a comprehensive look at the adequacy of the provision of the basic human needs addressed by housing in the United States.

Housing and Physiological Needs

Human beings share with many other living things the basic need to protect themselves from the extremes of the elements with some form of shelter. This need for shelter becomes particularly acute when the vulnerable young are being nurtured. Our compassion is particularly touched, then, by people who must live out of doors without shelter or by people who seek shelter in places not designed for human habitation. However, as human housing has become more densely packed into limited spaces, and as housing provision has become more technologically sophisticated, the physiological elements of housing needs have become more complex than simply keeping out the elements (Goldstein, Novick, and Schaffer 1990). Consider the following elements of modern shelter and their relationship to physical well-being:

- Human health is related to adequate light and ventilation in a dwelling, a condition that is compromised by cramming dwellings together into small areas or by shoddy construction.
- Density exacerbates the problem of disposing of human waste and garbage in such a way that they do not spread disease. Basic sanitation thus becomes a crucial physiological element in housing. Proper waste disposal also links individual units to a complex, community-wide infrastructure that must be financially supported by those receiving the services, including the management of the waste stream so as to prevent broader negative impacts on the environment and on public health.
- As housing has acquired more sophisticated heating and electrical systems, these systems can become a threat to human health (and even life) if not properly designed and maintained. A health threat can be specific to a particular unit—for example, carbon monoxide poisoning due to a faulty furnace—or it can be community-wide pollution created by power generation.
- The increasing use of synthetic construction materials has raised the threat of unhealthy chemical residues in housing units. Consider, for example, the long and costly struggle to remove lead-based paint, which can cause serious health problems for children, from houses built before 1978.
- The location of housing units in flood plains, in areas of poor drainage, or in areas contaminated by dangerous chemicals (for example, Love Canal near Buffalo, New York) also poses a threat to the health of their inhabitants.

During the first half of the twentieth century, the U.S. Census designation of a dwelling as "lacking some or all plumbing" was useful as a proxy variable for identifying seriously inadequate housing. This classification reflected both the fact that indoor plumbing had become a basic component of adequate housing and that many units still lacked that component. However, from the 1960s on, the number of units in that category began to shrink drastically, to the point where this designation was no longer a useful indicator of housing quality. Therefore, the Census Bureau included a range of other quality criteria in the American Housing Survey that it began to conduct in 1973. Among other things, it recognized that just because plumbing, electricity, and heating systems are present in a unit does not mean that they are in proper working order or that they pose no danger its inhabitants.

Out of the current list of conditions of dwellings utilized by the American Housing Survey, one may identify the following that are potential threats to the basic physiological needs of the occupants of a unit:

- Lack of complete kitchen facilities or lack of basic plumbing;
- Water that is not considered safe, or recent water stoppages;
- Recent (last three months) breakdowns in toilets or sewage disposal;
- Malfunctions of heating systems leading to an uncomfortable degree of cold;
- Repeated tripping of circuit breakers or blowing of fuses, indicating a dangerous or inadequate electrical system.

The data from American Housing Surveys covering the past ten years presented in Tables 3.1 and 3.2 suggest that of all occupied dwellings in the United States, only small percentages experience serious problems in these

Table 3.1 Basic Housing Services by Type of Household: 1997–2007

		1997	1999	2001	2003	2005	2007
All occupied units	Lacking complete kitchen	2.3	1.7	1.5	1.5	1.6	1.6
	Lacking some or all plumbing	1.2	1.4	1.3	1.3	1.2	1.1
	Water not safe	11.0	9.7	8.8	9.1	9.0	8.0
Black Householder	Lacking complete kitchen	3.5	3.0	2.5	2.6	2.7	2.5
	Lacking some or all plumbing	2.0	1.9	1.9	2.0	1.8	1.9
	Water not safe	14.4	12.1	11.4	11.3	11.2	9.9
Hispanic Householder	Lacking complete kitchen	2.0	1.6	1.8	1.6	1.9	2.4
	Lacking some or all plumbing	1.2	1.4	1.2	1.3	1.3	1.5
	Water not safe	14.3	14.8	15.9	18.3	17.9	18.5
Poverty Household	Lacking complete kitchen	8.6	5.6	4.8	3.4	4.2	4.0
	Lacking some or all plumbing	4.7	4.3	3.8	3.1	3.2	2.6
	Water not safe	25.3	18.8	16.4	15.6	15.7	12.7

Source: American Housing Survey

Table 3.2   Breakdowns or Interruptions of Service: 1997–2007

		1997	1999	2001	2003	2005	2007
All Households	Water stoppage	4.3	4.4	3.8	3.4	3.2	3.4
	Without working toilet	—	4.5	2.8	2.1	2.0	1.9
	Sewage disposal breakdown	1.3	1.8	1.4	1.5	1.0	1.3
	Heating failure	7.7	6.1	6.7	6.9	6.7	8.2
	Electrical breakdown	5.2	5.6	5.0	4.2	4.1	4.1
Black Householder	Water stoppage	3.9	3.6	3.7	3.3	2.4	2.9
	Without working toilet	—	4.7	4.9	3.5	3.3	3.8
	Sewage disposal breakdown	1.4	2.5	2.7	1.9	1.3	1.7
	Heating failure	10.9	9.6	10.2	9.5	9.2	10.0
	Electrical breakdown	11.2	11.3	10.5	8.4	7.8	8.5
Hispanic Householder	Water stoppage	2.2	2.9	3.1	3.1	2.9	2.7
	Without working toilet	-	2.6	3.2	2.9	2.3	2.2
	Sewage disposal breakdown	0.7	1.4	1.5	1.5	1.2	1.2
	Heating failure	4.9	5.6	6.3	6.4	6.2	6.7
	Electrical breakdown	4.6	5.3	6.2	5.8	5.6	5.3
Poverty Household	Water stoppage	8.5	8.1	6.6	5.0	4.8	4.2
	Without working toilet	-	7.3	7.5	5.1	4.4	4.6
	Sewage disposal breakdown	2.0	2.9	2.8	2.4	1.5	1.6
	Heating failure	17.3	14.6	14.2	12.0	11.8	13.3
	Electrical breakdown	15.9	15.3	12.4	11.0	10.5	8.5

Source: American Housing Survey

areas, and that most of these problems have declined in frequency since 1997. However, African American and Latino householders experience these problems in considerably higher proportions than the white population, and much higher percentages of these problems are found among households with incomes below the poverty line. In 2007, 1.8 million households reported severe physical problems and 5.2 million households reported moderate physical problems with their dwellings (U.S. Census, 2007).

Housing Costs and Basic Needs

Because of the generally good condition of American dwellings, as reported in these surveys, many authors have described housing deprivation in the United States as primarily a cost problem, rather than a physical problem. That is, most families are able to obtain housing that is in reasonably good condition, but lower income families are forced to pay large percentages of their income to obtain any housing at all. However, one may view this cost problem as posing a threat to basic physiological needs that are potentially just as serious as bad plumbing. This is due to the crowding out effect that such high housing costs have on expenditures for other basic necessities, such as food and health care. A family in poverty that is spending 60 percent of its meager monthly income on rent in order to keep a roof over their heads may place its children at risk by feeding them an inadequate diet or by neglecting preventive health care.

Figure 3.1 shows the average percentage of income that is expended for housing by American households, as reported in the American Housing Survey. For all households, the median percentage of income devoted to housing has remained in the modest 20 percent range over the last six American Housing Surveys. However, both African Americans and Latinos are paying higher percentages of their incomes for housing than the population as a whole. In addition, persons with incomes below the poverty line were paying 45–46 percent of their income at the time of the two most recent surveys. This indicates a substantial cost burden for households with limited incomes.

Since the early 1980s, the federal criterion for housing affordability has been that a household should pay no more than 30 percent of its income

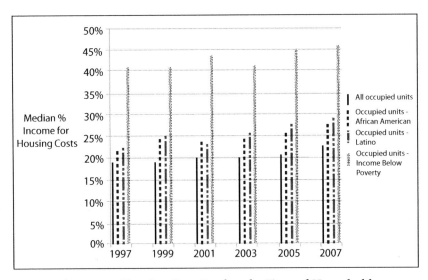

Figure 3-1 Housing Cost Burdens by Type of Household

Source: U.S. Bureau of the Census and Department of Housing and Urban Development, American Housing Survey: 1997–2007.

for all housing costs combined. Table 3.3 shows the percentages of various population groups that are paying more than this proportion of their incomes. Several trends and relationships are clearly revealed by the data presented in this table:

- The total proportion of households whose housing costs exceed this threshold increased substantially between 1997 and 2007, from 26.2 percent to 33.2 percent. There was a substantial dip in this percentage in the 2001 survey, conducted at a time when the economy was booming and incomes were higher, but the overall trend has been upward.
- Renter households bear a significantly heavier cost burden than owner households. This is primarily due to their substantially lower incomes.
- African American and Latino households have cost burdens that are substantially higher than are typical for all households.
- In 1997, only about 30 percent of poverty households lived in housing that was affordable according to the 30 percent of income criterion, and

Table 3.3 Cost Burdens: Percent of Households paying > 30 of Income for Housing[1]

	1997	1999	2001	2003	2005	2007
All occupied units	26.2	25.1	20.3	28.1	30.8	33.2
Owner Occupied	19.0	18.1	15.0	21.1	24.3	26.3
Renter occupied	42.0	41.2	33.3	45.5	47.6	50.7
Occupied units— African American	35.6	35.0	27.8	36.9	40.1	43.8
Occupied units— Latino	41.2	37.6	31.1	42.7	45.7	54.4
Occupied units— Income Below Poverty	70.3	69.6	63.5	71.6	74.3	75.1

[1]These percentages exclude households paying 100% or more of income for rent, households with zero or negative income, and households paying no cash rent. In these cases, the actual cost burden is indeterminate. These exclusions affect a substantial portion of the households below the poverty line, thus making the proportion for this group somewhat uncertain. However, the exclusion of households over 100% and households with zero rent balance each other out to some extent, thus permitting the conclusion that the proportions reported here are generally accurate.

Source: American Housing Surveys 1997–2007

this had declined to approximately 25 percent in 2007. This remains the case in spite of the existence of several million federally and locally assisted housing units for low and moderate income families.

The notion of using a fixed percentage of income as the criterion for excessive costs has come under criticism by some scholars as too simplistic. In his excellent analysis of the relationship between shelter costs and expenditures for other basic necessities, Michael Stone (2006) shows that different shelter costs have different impacts on families, depending on their composition and the amount that they must spend to obtain other essential items, such as an adequate diet and health care. For small families, the 30 percent criterion may overstate their cost burden, since their other expenses are lower, but for large families it may greatly understate the strain that providing housing makes on their resources, since such families must find larger units (often a difficult and expensive effort) and must also pay more for other necessities. However, he argues that the relative inflexibility of housing costs frequently leads lower income families to sacrifice other necessities first, in order to avoid homelessness. His larger point is that families experience "shelter poverty" any time that housing costs threaten their ability to obtain other essential elements of survival.

Physiological Needs and the Environment of the Dwelling

Yet another type of threat to physiological well-being can come from a dwelling's immediate physical environment, as well as from the dwelling itself. The environmental justice movement has called attention to the fact that low income communities in general, and communities of color in particular, are disproportionately affected by hazardous waste dumps and other environmental dangers. When decisions are being made about the location of such sites, government and corporate decision makers look for areas where political power and resistance will tend to be less, and lower income areas fall into this category (Bullard 2008).

Recent major natural disasters, such as Hurricane Katrina (2005) and serious floods in the South and Midwest (2007 and 2008), have highlighted the importance of reasonable protection from severe weather as an important element in the protection of life and health that is derived from the physical surroundings of one's dwelling. No dwelling can provide absolute protection from catastrophic natural events, but in many communities throughout the United States, thousands of housing units are located in flood plains and other areas that present much higher than average risks to one's life, health, and possessions. Not surprisingly, many (though by no means all) of these dwelling units are occupied by low to moderate income households, because the higher risk and overall lower desirability of such areas makes housing that is located there cheaper. Thus, when floods occur (whether induced by hurricanes or heavy rainfall) the lives and health of already vulnerable people are jeopardized. In the case of Hurricane Katrina, these negative effects were exacerbated by the appalling lack of priority given by governmental authorities to warning and then evacuating people in the lower income, predominately black neighborhoods of New Orleans (Bates and Swan 2007).

When the floods recede, questions are raised as to whether rebuilding should be allowed in these flood-prone areas. The answer given by federal, state, and local governments has increasingly been "No." In one sense, this is beneficial, because people are moved out of harm's way from future flooding, and because ongoing federal investment in flood reconstruction is reduced. However, such displacement often reduces the already limited supply of modestly priced housing, and in some cases it obliterates entire low income neighborhoods. Individuals may receive sufficient compensation to find adequate replacement housing, but the overall supply of affordable housing may be negatively affected. In light of the recent increase in severe weather events that has been linked to climate change, this type of housing problem may get worse in the future.

Housing and Safety Needs

Safety consists of the basic need to feel secure from violations of one's person and possessions by others. This category obviously overlaps with physiological needs, in that, as noted above, the safety of one's person is a fundamental biological imperative. Thus, fire or flood safety in housing involves both the physiological need to stay alive and the emotional need not to be exposed to the danger of catastrophic loss. However, the element of safety in housing also involves other considerations than immediate physical well-being:

- The ability to control one's interactions with others. Different cultures have different expectations concerning privacy, but the underlying issue is whether an individual can exercise effective choice concerning how and when to limit interactions with others (Dovey 1985). An important element of housing quality is the degree of control of internal and external interactions that it provides. Internal interactions occur with those that share the housing unit, and these are affected by the amount of space and the demarcation of space within a dwelling. External interactions are those between inhabitants of the unit and those outside it. Housing can provide either an effective or an ineffective physical barrier between its inhabitants and the outside world. External interactions are also affected by how the unit is situated in relation to common areas that are shared with residents of adjacent units. As Newman (1972, 1995) demonstrated, some common areas are "defensible space" that is under the effective control of surrounding residents, while others do not allow them to monitor or control the presence of outsiders who may mean them harm.

- The ability to keep one's material possessions secure. Possessions require scarce resources to acquire, so that loss of key possessions can greatly affect one's overall quality of life. In addition, possessions are psychological extensions of the self, so that protecting them is also protecting a piece of one's identity. This is reflected in the fact that people whose homes have been robbed often report a sense of personal violation that goes beyond the financial losses involved in the robbery (Brown and Harris 1989).

Clearly, the satisfaction of safety needs by a dwelling is greatly affected by its neighborhood surroundings, as well as the physical characteristics of the dwelling itself. Even if one's own unit is secure, this provides little comfort if one must be fearful every time one leaves it. The poignant, widely reported story of some elderly residents of Chicago who died during a heat wave because their fear of crime prevented them from opening their windows is an extreme example of neighborhood safety impinging on personal safety. When one inhabits a dwelling, one also inhabits its immediate surroundings, and these surroundings often have a profound effect on all levels of need in Maslow's hierarchy.

The American Housing Survey contains a number of indicators of the overall quality and safety of neighborhoods in the United States. Data on these indicators are presented in Table 3.4. They include such items as:

- The perceived level of crime in the neighborhood and whether this level of crime is "bothersome" to the households reporting. (Note: in 2007 this measure was changed to ask respondents just to report "serious crime" in their neighborhoods. Since these data are not comparable to previous years, they are not presented in Table 3.4.)
- Other "bothersome" neighborhood conditions including:

- The presence of boarded up buildings or buildings with bars on the windows in close proximity to the respondents' dwelling units;
- The presence of trash and litter in the neighborhood as an indicator of the overall level of maintenance of public areas.

Table 3.4 Selected Neighborhood Conditions: 1997–2007

		1997	1999	2001	2003	2005	2007
All Occupied Units	Crime bothersome	10.4	8.2	8.7	8.5	8.7	N/A
	Other bothersome conditions	15.2	15.0	14.1	13.5	14.1	15.7
	Unsatisfactory shopping	16.7	16.4	16.1	16.0	16.3	0.0
	Nearby buildings with bars on windows	9.2	8.7	7.5	7.2	7.0	9.5
	Nearby buildings vandalized	5.0	4.9	4.7	4.6	4.7	5.1
	Trash/Litter/Junk	9.5	8.8	9.2	8.8	8.6	8.8
Black Householder	Crime bothersome	17.4	13.9	16.4	15.5	14.3	N/A
	Other bothersome conditions	17.0	16.9	16.4	16.4	16.1	19.1
	Unsatisfactory shopping	19.5	18.3	18.0	16.9	17.3	N/A
	Nearby buildings with bars on windows	22.3	20.8	17.6	17.5	15.7	21.1
	Nearby buildings vandalized	13.2	12.0	12.5	12.0	11.5	12.1
	Trash/Litter/Junk	17.2	15.6	16.5	15.8	14.9	14.5
Hispanic Householder	Crime bothersome	8.2	7.7	7.6	9.7	9.6	N/A
	Other bothersome conditions	8.5	9.8	11.0	12.0	11.4	14.4
	Unsatisfactory shopping	6.8	6.9	8.5	8.7	9.2	N/A
	Nearby buildings with bars on windows	13.1	14.2	12.1	14.1	13.3	21.0
	Nearby buildings vandalized	4.3	4.7	4.3	4.9	4.6	5.7
	Trash/Litter/Junk	9.0	8.9	9.8	11.4	9.8	10.9
Poverty Household	Crime bothersome	25.2	17.9	17.5	15.0	16.0	N/A
	Other bothersome conditions	25.2	23.2	20.2	16.3	18.0	19.5
	Unsatisfactory shopping	37.1	29.7	29.0	24.2	24.3	N/A
	Nearby buildings with bars on windows	26.3	21.2	15.7	13.5	13.2	17.7
	Nearby buildings vandalized	16.6	14.2	12.0	11.3	11.3	10.6
	Trash/Litter/Junk	28.4	23.9	21.2	19.3	18.1	15.9

Source: American Housing Survey

The data in Table 3.4 show that all households experience a variety of neighborhood problems at higher rates than they do problems with their own dwellings. Crime, litter, vandalism, and security measures on windows present bothersome levels of disorder in a range of neighborhoods. However, minority neighborhoods and poverty neighborhoods experience significantly higher rates of all of these problems in comparison with the rates for all households. This coincides with higher rates of problems with individual dwellings to create much more serious problems with the neighborhood environment for these groups than for other segments of the population.

Crime rates are often viewed as a fundamental measure of the personal safety of the residents of a neighborhood, and urban crime rates have fluctuated considerably during the past four decades. However, the rate of reported crime reflects not only residents' responses to immediate threats to their personal safety but also law enforcement priorities. For example, many cities experienced a dramatic spike in murders and other serious crimes during the 1980s, much of it related to struggles over control of the emerging market for crack cocaine, as well as more traditional drug markets. In response, federal, state, and local authorities intensified their "War on Drugs." This war targeted not only perpetrators of drug-related violence but many nonviolent drug offenders as well. More arrests, plus the imposition of mandatory long sentences, dramatically swelled the prison population in most states, and these arrests and convictions were disproportionately targeted at people of color. Thus, while authorities claimed they were making neighborhoods safer with their war, they were drastically harming the life chances of thousands of young male residents of these neighborhoods by funneling them into the criminal justice system (Agid 2007; Bertram, Blachman, Sharpe, and Andreas 1996).

The net result of such law enforcement practices was a dual threat to the safety of those dwelling in low income neighborhoods, especially those of color. On the one hand, these residents were the primary victims of the violent crime that did occur, and police efforts at protecting them from this violence were often either ineffective or overly draconian and oppressive. On the other hand, families in these areas were subject to the additional threat of the loss of (largely) male family members due to imprisonment for nonviolent drug offenses, a practice that frequently does more harm than good to both the incarcerated individual and the surrounding community (Mauer 2009; Alexander 2010; Weitzer and Tuch 2006).

Another item reported in Table 3.4 is the presence of convenient neighborhood shopping. At first glance this might appear to be purely an amenity, but it can substantially contribute to or detract from the quality of life in the neighborhood. When this shopping affects access to the basic necessities of life, then it can be harmful to the physiological needs mentioned above. For example, many large supermarket chains have effectively abandoned low income urban neighborhoods, and those that stay often sell their poorest quality produce at their inner city sites. If there are no convenient grocery stores, residents are forced to pay higher prices for lower quality food at neighborhood convenience stores. This can have very negative effects on the long-term health of families. In some cities, there have been serious efforts to encourage vegetable gardening or locate farmers' markets where they are accessible to lower income residents.

Housing and "Belonging" Needs

Maslow chose the term *belonging* to describe the basic human need for satisfying emotional attachments to other human beings. These can involve attachments between parents and children, attachments between siblings, attachments to an extended family, friendships, romantic /marital attachments, and attachments to a larger network of community relationships. Among the impacts of housing on the satisfaction of the need for belonging are the following:

- A housing unit can either promote or interfere with the development of positive family relationships. If the unit violates prevailing cultural standards for crowding, then the sense of being crammed into too small a space can exacerbate tensions between family members, and it can interfere with the emotional and cognitive development of children. Jonathan Kozol (2006) provides a powerful and poignant discussion of the impact on a family of being forced to live together in a single room in one of New York City's "welfare hotels." The conclusions of his case study are supported by a broad range of psychological studies (Gifford 1997).
- A sense of belonging is also related to the control issue mentioned above. Hostile interactions with neighbors can affect relationships within families, as well as one's overall sense of community, especially if one lacks effective ways to limit or avoid these interactions.
- The neighborhood in which a dwelling is located can provide either positive or destructive interactions with neighbors. This can particularly affect children or youth, who may be exposed to positive or negative

role models, but adults are also affected.

- Neighbors may possess resources that are helpful to other families and individuals, and a sense of community among neighbors facilitates access to these resources, while, at the same time, the sharing of resources also reinforces a sense of community.
- Positive networks of associations with neighbors can form the basis for more effective participation in the larger political community (Saegert, Thompson, and Warren 2001).
- The attachment to "home" as a physical space bears a close association in the minds of many people with their sense of attachment to their nuclear and extended family, as well as powerful memories of the process of growing up. Environmental psychologists have documented that the surroundings in which one is raised imprint expectations on the child as to what a physical dwelling "should" look like, expectations that continue to operate in adult housing choices, albeit at an unconscious level (Marcus 1992). Growing up in dilapidated housing could potentially create a strong desire to acquire better surroundings as an adult, but it could also lower the child's expectations as to what kind of housing he or she "deserves."

A weakening of ties of belonging within families may occur for a variety of reasons besides housing quality, ranging from interpersonal conflict to severe economic distress. Lack of male commitment to marriage and parenting has been strongly linked to lack of economic opportunity for males (Mare and Winship 1991). When males abandon the family, then a household headed by a single female results, and these households have the highest rate of poverty of any category of household, due to having only one breadwinner and due to the lower earning power of women relative to men. The children may suffer from the economic and psychological distress of the single parent, and the boys in particular may be harmed by the lack of a strong, male role model in their lives. They grow up without the expectation that they will ever be stable providers, and so the cycle perpetuates itself.

However, the type of dwellings that such families occupy may figure importantly in their overall instability and distress. Poor-quality dwellings expose them to stress and danger and they confer a stigma on them that is frequently internalized. There may also be considerable instability in the housing situation of these low income households. Temporary loss of income can lead to eviction, and the family must then find another dwelling that they can afford or join the ranks of the homeless. Children may be constantly moved from school to school, which can exercise a powerful downward drag on their educational commitment and performance.

Neighborhood attachments have been frequently studied, but are notoriously hard to pin down. People rely on their neighborhoods for a wide range of interactions and assistance, ranging from casual small talk to child care and help with home maintenance. This is particularly true for modest income neighborhoods, where adults lack the community-wide ties and relationships that more affluent citizens gain through their jobs and civic involvement. If a neighborhood suffers from a high rate of violent crime, then fear may limit these neighborly interactions, yet some research has shown that strong networks of interdependence can be formed in even the most depressed and violent areas (Stack 1974). Many modest income neighborhoods are also able to create formal neighborhood associations which take collective action against the neighborhood's problems.

Considerable scholarly and practitioner attention has been directed at the relationship between housing characteristics and residents' degree of neighborhood attachment. Home ownership is widely believed to increase a household's neighborhood commitment and engagement, by creating a sense of permanence and by adding an element of economic self-interest to the preservation of the neighborhood. On the other hand, the residents of many upper income owner-occupied neighborhoods are quite content to exist with no formal neighborhood ties, because of their extensive networks outside the neighborhood. Many aspects of housing design have been examined for their impact on neighborhood attachment, including discussions of designs that create or fail to create "defensible space" (Newman 1995) and designs that encourage or fail to encourage regular neighborly interactions (Congress for the New Urbanism 2000). Observers disagree as to whether housing acts as an independent variable that affects these commitments or whether it simply reflects or signals other social characteristics that have positive or negative effects on interaction.

Housing and Self-Esteem

According to Maslow, individuals seek to reinforce their sense of self by seeking status and recognition in ways that are appropriate to their culture. A person whose basic sense of self-worth is undermined by negative parental messages or by social stigmatization often lacks the self-confidence to succeed in personal relationships, in education, or in the work environment. However, even those persons who have a solid, underlying sense of self-worth often seek additional reinforcement through various forms of social acknowledgment of their worth. This can take the form of recognition for individual accomplishments, or it can take the form of being identified as a member of a socially desirable or prestigious group. In the latter case, self-esteem and belonging needs can become closely intertwined.

In examining the relationship between housing and needs for self-esteem one must recognize a truth that has been skillfully articulated by Liechty and Clegg (2007) in their study of religious sectarianism. It is that a variety of genuine and legitimate human needs can be sought in ways that are harmful to other groups within a society. Some groups of people may seek to satisfy both the need for belonging and the need for esteem in ways that exclude and /or stigmatize other groups within a society. This is certainly a powerful element in the way that housing has been allocated spatially within communities. Consider the following:

- In American society, the type and location of one's housing is a powerful symbol of one's social prestige and acceptance. A spacious, elegant house in a "good" neighborhood signals that a family has "arrived" at a higher place on the social and economic scale. This prestige element is directly translated into the market value of the dwelling, so that the household's economic interest in their investment powerfully reinforces their desire for social prestige.
- The prestige of the neighborhood is affected not just by the type of housing but by who lives there. Even where most of the dwellings in an area are of high social and economic value, their residents will strongly resist the proximity of even a small number of residents of lower socioeconomic status. They will also resist any kind of alternative housing or land use (such as, for example, group homes) which they believe will reduce the status and value of their investments.
- As a result of the exclusion of households of lower socioeconomic status from "better" neighborhoods, these households are compelled to live in areas that bear a negative stigma. This stigma harms residents both economically, in terms of reduced opportunities and wealth, and psychologically, in terms of their loss of a sense that they are valued and capable members of the larger community. In addition, the lower prestige of the area combines with the low purchasing power of the residents to create disinvestment in the housing stock by private owners and investors. The neighborhood's physical deterioration then further reinforces the perceptions of higher income persons that the people living in such neighborhoods are undesirable as neighbors.

- For people of color, socioeconomic stigmatization is magnified by racial stigmatization. Considerable research has shown, for example, that lower income African Americans are much more geographically isolated than white families with similarly low incomes (Massey and Denton 1993). In addition, repeated testing experiments sponsored by the Department of Housing and Urban Development and by private organizations have shown that even middle-class members of racial minorities frequently find themselves steered and pushed into neighborhoods where housing values are lower than for comparable housing in predominately white areas (Smith and Cloud 2010).

In sum, the human need for esteem, while a normal and healthy part of human development, has been channeled into incredibly destructive patterns of social exclusion, and these patterns are nowhere more clearly and dramatically illustrated than in housing development.

Housing and Self-Actualization

By self-actualization, Maslow means the need to fully and creatively express one's talents and capacities as a human being. He argues that once the more basic needs have been satisfied, human beings are free to pursue activities that lead to a broader sense of satisfaction and growth. The activities through which self-actualization is sought will vary greatly among individuals; some may seek it through artistic endeavors, others through economic success, others through intellectual endeavors, and still others through seeking to serve the larger community. This aspect of Maslow's theory has been one of its most controversial elements. Some critics see in it an implicit justification for the self-absorption of privileged middle-class Americans while others see the concept as simply too vague to create a separate, meaningful category of motivation (Daniels 1988; Geller 1982). Toward the end of his life, Maslow himself sought to expand and clarify the concept, by adding another level of fulfillment that includes the dedication of the self to deeper spiritual awareness and to serving the common good (Kolto-Rivera 2006).

However, as with his other categories, it is clear that Maslow is onto something with his specification of the desire for self-expression and the desire to fully realize one's potential as elements of human motivation that are distinct from other types of needs. Certainly, as one looks at the role of housing in people's lives, one can see this need clearly expressed, in the following ways:

- Individuals treat their physical environments as expressions of their personalities, and they seek to shape them in ways that reflect their tastes and inclinations. According to Dovey (1985), housing forms are a mix of cultural norms and individual expression. She views the transformation of personal space as part of "the dialectic between personal change and environmental change, in which we change our environment and we are in turn changed by environmental experience" (48). From the college student who puts up posters in his/her dorm room to the homeowners who pore over home decorating catalogs, people with sufficient disposable time and income frequently devote a considerable amount of both to decorating and redecorating their living spaces. Differences in tastes and styles of utilizing their space among people sharing the same living space can lead to serious conflicts.
- When differences in housing preferences are displayed in an overt fashion, they may lead to conflicts between the right to self-expression inherent in the notion of "property rights" and the needs and values of neighbors. If I decide to express my environmental values by turning my front yard into a "natural prairie" my neighbors with neatly trimmed lawns may object that what they view as my "weed patch" is detracting from the aesthetics and value of their homes. If their verbal protests don't work, they may seek the assistance of their attorneys. These concerns are reflected in the property maintenance covenants that residents of some high prestige neighborhoods are compelled to sign.

While it may be tempting to dismiss these matters of taste as mere surface manifestations of housing, one must consider that those whose incomes and/or tenure status prevent effective self-expression through altering their living environment may come to view their drab surroundings as one more form of stigmatization, and they may, in turn, contribute to the physical decline of neighborhoods by ceasing to invest any energy in maintaining their dwelling units. The lack of control over the physical appearance of their dwellings becomes one more way that they are rendered powerless and denied an important means of self-expression.

In addition, self-actualization through education and the pursuit of a rewarding and successful work life is also seriously hampered by the physical and social isolation that low income neighborhoods impose on their residents. Of course, the physical isolation of one's dwelling is only one of several factors blocking such achievements, and others such as lack of educational attainment and racial discrimination may have more powerful effects. However, the neighborhood in which a household lives may help to foster and to concentrate all these other facets of disadvantage. In the eyes of many of its residents, as well as more affluent people looking at it from the outside, the low income neighborhood symbolizes despair and hopelessness, and its residents are viewed as trapped in a cycle in which their full potential will never be realized. The relative few who are able to break out and to find success and fulfillment may be viewed as "exceptions that prove the rule."

Housing Needs and Physical Determinism

The intimate connection between housing and the full range of human needs and values has created a strong tendency among social analysts and planners toward what has been termed "physical determinism" (Smith 2006; Hays 2002), This is the tendency to view the nature of the physical space occupied by human beings as determinative of the quality of their social existence. According to this view, people who live in positive surroundings experience more positive social relations, while those in negative surroundings experience more negative relationships. The history of cities in both North America and Europe is replete with efforts at social engineering through housing and neighborhood design (Bauman, Biles, and Szylvian 2000).

On one level, physical determinism is easy to discredit. A simplistic version of this idea was used to justify the removal of entire neighborhoods of poor people, on the grounds that these areas exerted a "blighting influence" (note the disease metaphor) both on their occupants and on the surrounding community. Economic elites who coveted slum land for other purposes created the fiction that they were "solving" the problems of poor neighborhoods by obliterating them. Of course, numerous sociological studies, beginning with Marc Fried's pioneering work (1966), demonstrated the heavy social and psychological costs of such displacement, despite the fact that the poor neighborhoods being destroyed truly were undesirable environments in many ways.

On another level, however, physical determinism is difficult to dismiss out of hand. Extensive research by environmental psychologists has shown that social relationships and the physical spaces in which they occur exist in a dynamic interaction with each other. While the best-designed physical space cannot eliminate social isolation or social conflict, the design, distribution, and control of physical space sends powerful messages about what kinds of human activities can occur there. For example, in the 1950s and

1960s public shopping streets were privatized into shopping malls, in which merchants, supported by various court rulings, came to exert virtually complete control over what activities could occur there. This control was used to forbid any kind of political solicitation or organizing activities, thus eliminating one of the formerly important uses of public space. Similarly, the design and control of housing spaces exerts a strong influence on what kinds of activities tend to occur within and among housing units.

In making an argument for the vital role of housing in meeting human needs, one is not necessarily taking a position in favor of physical determinism. Like all forms of human expression or endeavor, housing simultaneously shapes and is shaped by the desires and intentions of those utilizing housing. While it is certainly true that "good" housing doesn't automatically produce "good" people, it is also true that the environment created by housing can either enhance or detract from the positive potential of both individual and collective human activities. In advocating for improved housing for the poor, progressives have at times fallen prey to simplistic determinism, but this should not detract from advocates' vital point that decent housing is an important component in human well-being on many levels of need and motivation.

Part II—Housing as a Commodity

In our contemporary mixed private/public economic system, most housing units are provided through transactions in the private market. Figure 3-2 shows that while increases in medical costs have soared, increases in housing costs have tracked closely the overall rate of increase in the Consumer Price Index for Urban Consumers. These data support the conclusion that the rising proportions of income paid for housing by American households is as much an incomes problem as a housing problem. The Economic Policy Institute reports flat or declining real incomes for households in the bottom two quintiles of the income distribution during most of the last decade, even during years when the economy was expanding (Mishel, Bernstein, and Allegretto 2009). More recent data from the U.S. Census show that the median income for all households, while increasing during the prosperous years of the late 1990s, has stayed flat since then, with exception of modest decreases during the recession that began in 2007 (U.S. Census 2010). The result of this lack of income growth is that housing costs have risen in relation to household incomes even as the overall inflation rate for housing costs has not exceeded that for other commodities. Of course,

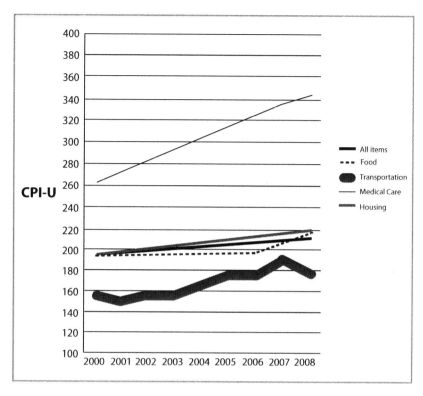

CPI-U

**Figure 3-2 Consumer Price Indeces for Basic Necessities: 2000–2008
(1982–1984 = 100)**

Source: CPI Detailed Report, Historical Tables, 2008

there is great variation in housing costs among American communities, and those communities with rapidly rising costs have seen prices for decent quality housing slip out of reach of an even larger proportion of their residents.

When viewed as a commodity to be purchased by consumers, housing has certain characteristics that render housing markets quite different from markets for other basic commodities. First, when compared to other consumer goods, housing is relatively expensive to produce and, therefore, highly dependent on credit in order to be constructed and consumed. Thus, housing availability can be drastically affected by the availability of credit. Moreover, because a large portion of the credit market in the United States is committed to housing finance, a crisis in the housing market can easily generate a crisis in the economy as a whole, as has been forcefully demonstrated by the events of 2007–2011.

In addition, because the construction of a dwelling requires the assembly of a diverse set of components, the fate of the industries that produce these components becomes dependent on the performance of the housing market. Loss of jobs in these industries further exacerbates the economic consequences of a housing downturn.

Secondly, housing is distinct from other commodities such as food and clothing in that it is consumed over a relatively long period of time, and the same housing unit is usually occupied by multiple households during its extended lifespan. This means that, in order to remain an asset to the community and to individual households, it must be constructed soundly enough to meet the needs of multiple consumers, not just its immediate occupant. Throughout its lifespan, each housing unit stands as a major feature of the built environment within a community. Therefore, its physical condition, along with the behavior of its various inhabitants, creates either positive or negative externalities for the surrounding dwellings and for the community as a whole. It is this extended lifespan, plus the fact that it occupies land with the potential for many uses, that lends housing its dual properties of an investment and a service that is consumed. Each unit has both "use value" and "exchange value." Its use value consists of the vital services that it provides to those who inhabit it. Its exchange value consists of its market value as a commodity, which includes the value of the land upon which it stands as well as of the dwelling itself.

In the ideal competitive market, there should be no gap between use value and exchange value. According to this model, households allocate their resources to different commodities in order to maximize their utility. Different households will choose to allocate their resources differently, with some choosing to spend more on housing and some choosing to spend less. These choices represent their preferences as to how much housing they want to consume. The equilibrium prices for various types of housing would be determined by many such exchanges (Levy 1995).

In reality, there is often a large gap between the use value and the exchange value of housing. First, there is the issue of the resources available to households in relation to the cost of housing. The competitive market model takes the existing distribution of resources as a given in calculating the efficient allocation of goods and services. If the underlying distribution of incomes is highly unequal, then, as documented above, many households will lack sufficient resources to obtain adequate housing at the prices it is available without sacrificing other basic necessities such as food and health care. Of course, this income distribution is also the result of a market, the market for labor, so that changes in modes of production cause changes in the value of various kinds of labor, leading some groups to benefit and others to lose out in the distribution of resources.

Some free market advocates have argued that the housing affordability problem is largely the result of the artificial floor under the price of housing that is created by government regulations such as zoning and building codes. Without these regulations, entrepreneurs could provide housing at an affordable price for any household, albeit at a very low level of quality for the poorest households (Seidel 1978). This is essentially what happens in developing countries where poor people are allowed to construct housing out of whatever materials are available and then gradually upgrade it as funds become available. However, few Americans would accept the presence of the resulting shanty towns around their cities, with the attendant threats to the health and safety of their inhabitants and to the rest of the community. In the United States and other developed countries, the operating assumption is that housing needs are not fully met without the establishment of minimum standards for a dwelling unit. If these minimum standards increase the cost of producing housing to more than people of low incomes can afford, then the answer is to subsidize either their incomes or production costs or both.

A second effect of the gap between use value and exchange value is that a dwelling that provides vital shelter needs to a lower income household may have a very low exchange value on the market. This low exchange value encourages disinvestment in maintaining the quality of the dwelling on the part of the owner, whether it is that household or their landlord. Alternatively, the exchange value of the dwelling or the land it occupies may be driven upward through speculation to the point where its inhabitants can no longer afford to purchase the bundle of services it provides. Even at the middle range of the price scale, the sales or rental prices of adequate housing typically exceed what families of low or even moderate incomes can afford.

A third effect of the gap between use value and exchange value is the concentration of housing investment at the high end of the housing market. Households with higher incomes can demand larger houses with more amenities, and, because the costs of inputs of materials and labor do not rise in exact proportion to the size and quality of the dwelling, more expensive dwellings can be produced at a higher profit than less expensive dwellings. (To put it in simpler terms, the materials and labor required to produce a 4,000 square foot house cost less than twice as much as those required for a 2,000 square foot house, but the latter will command more than twice the price.)

The result is that new housing is almost never produced for low and moderate income households without some form of government subsidy, which increases the developer's return on investment. In the market economy, absent government subsidy, the main mechanism for the provision of housing for people of modest incomes is the filtering of used housing units down to them from higher income households (Grigsby 1965). If the housing is sturdy and well maintained, then this may not create a problem, but in many cases housing units are made available to lower income households only after considerable disinvestment in maintaining their physical condition has taken place, and the lower incomes of their new inhabitants virtually guarantee that such disinvestment will continue. The one exception to the lack of investment in new housing for lower income people is manufactured housing, but it is often of mixed quality, is concentrated in stigmatized areas such as "trailer parks," and lacks the investment value of "stick built" housing. (Most manufactured homes depreciate in value like an automobile, rather than providing stable or increasing equity for their owners.)

A fourth effect of the difference between use value and exchange value is a tendency of middle and higher income households to overinvest in housing, because they are basing their decision on the investment value of the home rather than strictly on its capacity to meet their families' needs. In times when house prices are rising, households may strain their budgets to the limit to purchase a house that they really cannot afford, in anticipation of the house rising rapidly in value so that they can recoup their investment along with a substantial capital gain when it is sold. They may also fear that prices will rise totally out of their reach if they wait. (Federal tax breaks to homeowners also encourage this tendency.) Traditionally, the risk aversion of banks and other mortgage financers, reflected in underwriting practices, acted as a restraint on households' tendency to acquire more than they could afford. However, over the last twenty years, as was discussed in chapter 2, these lenders moved toward more flexible and creative ways to finance housing purchases, and they became less and less risk averse. Both buyers' and lenders' eagerness to cash in on the rising exchange value of housing led them to ignore the inevitable end of the period of rising prices, with disastrous consequences for both.

The discussion of the relationship between housing and basic needs presented in this chapter makes a strong case for housing to be considered what economists call a "merit" good, that is, one that is so essential to human survival that the market cannot be allowed to be the sole determinant of its allocation and consumption (Stiglitz 1986). In a competitive market, the value of a good is simply the intersection between what the buyer is willing to pay for the marginal unit of a good with the marginal cost of that unit to the producer. There is no moral judgment as to the value of the good to the individual or to society, because different consumers may value a given product differently (Levy 1995). However, in terms of social reality, we do have to make moral judgments that place a value on goods in terms of whether or not consumption of these goods is essential to the long term well-being of both the individual and society. The range of fundamental human needs that housing serves suggests that it is important for individuals and households to obtain adequate use value out of their housing at a price that does not compel them to sacrifice other basic necessities. The price at which dwellings can be produced on the private market while providing a competitive return to producers is often far more than many families can afford without such sacrifices. Therefore, public and nonprofit sector involvement in the provision of housing becomes imperative if these families are to benefit from an adequate dwelling.

CHAPTER 4

Federal Housing Assistance from the Depression to the Moratorium: 1934–1973

Part I—The Emergence of Federal Housing Assistance; 1934–1968

In this and the following chapter, the development of housing policies in the social welfare policy context will be examined. This history must be explored at three levels of generality. First, housing policy must be placed in the context of the broad shifts in political climate that have occurred since the 1930s. It was suggested in chapters 1 and 2 that ideology is a major element in this general climate, shaping decisions in many policy arenas. In the following pages, shifts in the balance of forces between liberals and conservatives at the national level will be shown to correspond to major changes in the scope and direction of housing efforts. In particular, the impact on housing programs of liberal and conservative attitudes toward social welfare policy will be shown.

Yet, simply establishing a correspondence between such ideological shifts and changes in housing policy does not fully reveal the impact of liberal and conservative values on the housing programs that have emerged. One must also identify issues and concerns central to the housing policy arena itself, and a relationship must be shown between these issues and the overall political climate. The analysis of issues unique to housing will constitute the second level of generality at which this policy will be explored.

Four issues have been central to virtually every housing policy decision: the quantity of housing produced; the quality of the housing; the cost of the programs; and equity (i.e., the fairness of the programs in serving various income groups). Liberals and conservatives have taken conflicting positions on all of these issues, and the outcomes have been shaped by compromises based on the relative power of liberal and conservative coalitions.

Finally, the history of housing policy is the history of specific programs. Congress does not enact philosophies or approaches, but rather programs embodying these broader ideas. As noted in chapter 1, problems encountered by specific programs become feedback which is variously interpreted by liberals and conservatives and incorporated as ammunition in their political struggles. Moreover, new programs evolve in response to the shortcomings of the programs preceding them, as well as in response to broader attitudinal shifts. Thus, the third level of generality at which housing policy must be explored consists of the unique problems encountered by each major housing program; FHA, public housing, Section 235 and 236, and Section 8.

While this book focuses mainly on changes in housing policy during recent decades, a longer historical perspective is vital to understanding recent events. The present chapter begins by examining housing policy from the Depression to 1968. Friedman (1968) traces the debate even farther back, to the mid-nineteenth century, when reformers began to pressure local governments to do something about the vile tenements spawned by rapid urbanization. He notes the continuity between the social cost arguments then raised by Jacob Riis and other reformers and the arguments used in contemporary battles. Nevertheless, the debate over the federal government's role in housing for the poor began in earnest during the Great Depression of the 1930s, for it was only then that liberals had enough national political power to initiate serious federal involvement. Furthermore, the history of two major housing initiatives stimulated by the Depression—the Federal Housing Administration's mortgage insurance program and the public housing program—played a major role in shaping later political struggles.

The Changing Role of the FHA

As discussed in chapter 2, the Great Depression of the 1930s was a time of ascendancy for the liberal point of view, although conservative forces displayed their strength on certain issues. A broad consensus that government action was needed to respond to the country's multifaceted crisis enabled the federal government to expand into areas where its intervention would previously have met overwhelming resistance. Both the Federal Housing Administration (FHA) and the public housing program represented just such novel interventions and, while neither was without opposition, both were enacted by large congressional majorities.

The major rationale for the establishment of the FHA by the National

Housing Act of 1934 was clearly to aid families in need. Widespread loss of jobs and income in the Depression led to astronomical foreclosure and eviction rates, as both borrowers and creditors succumbed to the crisis. This, in turn, led to a rapid drop in housing construction, accelerating unemployment in the building trades. In 1933, Congress created the Home Owners Loan Corporation (HOLC), providing emergency loans to homeowners in imminent danger of foreclosure. However, the 1934 Act introduced federal regulation and support of the housing credit system through FHA mortgage insurance. Thus, it went beyond correction of immediate problems and fundamentally restructured the way people borrowed money for home purchases. By introducing the long-term, low-down-payment, fully amortized, level-payment mortgage, in place of the short-term, high-down-payment, balloon notes of earlier years, the FHA greatly broadened the segment of the U.S. population who could afford a home (Immergluck 2009). The working- or middle-class family with modest but steady income now found mortgage payments within reach. It was these persons, whom Friedman called the "submerged middle class," that the FHA program helped rescue.

The FHA program did not, however, address the problems of those too poor to purchase a home, and during its subsequent history, this shift toward service to the white middle class was accentuated. After World War II, the program was expanded (and supplemented by the parallel Veterans Administration program) to aid the housing industry in meeting the vast new demand generated by returning veterans and by rising incomes across the board. But those aided were largely white middle- or working-class families with enough income to purchase the new suburban tract housing springing up around American cities. African Americans were first officially and later unofficially excluded from eligibility for loans by the FHA, and the spiral of decline affecting central city neighborhoods was accelerated by the FHA's refusal to underwrite mortgages in such areas. Thus, the FHA was an important provider of housing to people of modest means, but a large segment of the population was bypassed (Semer 1976; Bradford 1979).

The FHA program was vast in scope, a factor that might have been expected to engender opposition from conservatives, in spite of the respectability of the middle income groups being served. However, the FHA began during one housing crisis and substantially broadened its clientele during another period of housing shortages. The large degree of popular support it developed made it politically difficult to attack. Therefore, while other housing proposals were subjected to intense scrutiny by the more conservative post–World War II Congresses, the FHA remained relatively unscathed, and the inclusion of funding for this program in any broader housing legislation smoothed the way for its passage.

Also of great importance to the political acceptance of FHA was the fact that it was part of a package of programs developed to bail out a group that in normal times would be major beneficiaries of market allocations—bankers and other investors. The near-collapse of the banking system during the Depression led to substantial government intervention in banking and investment problems. In housing credit, the Federal Home Loan Bank Act, championed and signed into law by President Herbert Hoover, created the Federal Home Loan Bank Board. This act virtually created a new form of intermediary by molding a fragmented, locally based group of building and loan associations into a nationwide, government regulated system of savings and loans (Immergluck 2004, 36). In order to encourage the flow of capital into mortgage loans, the regional Home Loan Banks set up by this act provided credit for savings and loan associations that wanted to lend beyond their own capital. However, savings and loans were strictly regulated. They were not allowed to make investments beyond mortgages, and they were restricted in the interest they could pay out on deposits. As shall be shown, this closely regulated system, which functioned well as a source of credit for households for forty-plus years, began to unravel in the late 1970s.

In 1938, relatively late in the Depression era, the federal government took a further step to encourage the free flow of capital for housing loans, through the establishment of the Federal National Mortgage Association (FNMA, or "Fannie Mae"). Fannie Mae purchased FHA insured mortgages from banks and other lenders, thus freeing up their capital for additional loans. Then, Fannie Mae sold "mortgage backed securities" to investors, which provided a return based on the interest payments on the underlying mortgages held by Fannie Mae. This indirect form of investment generated even more capital, because investors were no longer tied to the long payout periods of the underlying mortgages. As long as the lending practices that supported Fannie Mae's investments were fiscally sound, it could play a vital and constructive role as an intermediary whose activities ultimately benefited families who wanted to purchase homes. As Immergluck describes it, Fannie Mae became a second major "circuit" for mortgage capital that supplemented the circuit provided by the Federal Home Loan Bank system (Immergluck 2009, 33). However, when mortgage lending practices began to veer toward ever more risky lending during the first decade of the twenty-first century, Fannie Mae became a major participant in the mortgage finance meltdown of that decade.

Federal mortgage insurance was crucial to the success of both of these new systems, since it provided sufficient security to permit the national flow of housing capital (Semer 1976; Immergluck 2009). Thus, the FHA was, in a very critical sense, a conservative program as this term has here been defined. Since it facilitated profitable business transactions among a key group of private market participants, it was guaranteed political support by a very powerful interest group that at other times had opposed governmental activism.

In a manner typical of programs that aid market winners, the FHA gradually became closely identified with the industry it served. Responsibility for processing FHA mortgages was assumed by private savings and loans and by mortgage bankers, with the result that the concepts of sound underwriting prevalent in the banking industry became those which governed FHA lending (Bradford 1979). FHA policies of discrimination against African Americans and central city neighborhoods were, to some degree, merely reflections of widespread business practices, rather than any unique malevolence of the FHA. However, the codification of racial discrimination by the federal government provided powerful reinforcement for a dual housing market. White families could take advantage of the new federal programs to improve both their housing quality and their wealth accumulation. African American families were largely denied this crucial opportunity for upward mobility and for improvement in their living conditions (Freund 2007).

It should also be noted that the new long-term FHA mortgages enhanced the value of tax benefits which had been available to homeowners since the inception of the income tax in 1913; the deductibility of mortgage interest and local property taxes from federal taxable income. Such deductions gradually grew to become a major *tax expenditure* on behalf of home ownership, one that was of greater benefit to higher income persons because of their higher tax rates (Aaron 1972). Again, this large loss of federal revenue was not seriously questioned by either conservatives or liberals, because of its benefits to market winners.

Throughout the Eisenhower years, the presidency was in the control of moderate conservatives. Though their ability to shape policy was limited by the countervailing power of liberals in Congress, the Eisenhower administration succeeded in slowing the growth of federal social welfare programs. In this atmosphere, the FHA's role as an aid to private bankers serving the middle class was not seriously questioned. However, the election of

John F. Kennedy in 1960 signaled the return of liberals to executive power and a gradual increase in pressure toward more governmental aid to the disadvantaged. The FHA became the target of some of this pressure.

The liberalism of the 1960s was initially different in spirit from that of the New Deal. As noted in chapter 2, the social welfare programs of the New Deal were undertaken to deal with a massive economic crisis, whereas the Kennedy-Johnson proposals were initially seen as modifications of an essentially prosperous and productive economic and social order, which would bring the disadvantaged into the mainstream. Nevertheless, the events of that decade led to a growing sense that such programs were needed as a response to a new crisis. According to Piven and Cloward (1971), Democratic leaders saw African Americans, particularly the growing urban black population, as a pivotal element in the party's winning coalition and, therefore, responded to the demands of the civil rights movement. When the largely nonviolent protest of the early 1960s was augmented by the urban riots of 1965 to 1968, the Democrats' sense of urgency increased, and their focus shifted from the abolition of legal segregation in the South to the economic concerns of the Northern urban ghettos. As a result, the Johnson administration sought to create new programs and modify existing ones to better aid the urban poor. The FHA, which had generally ignored the needs of the inner city, became a logical target for their efforts.

One way the agency became involved was through use of its mortgage insurance to back subsidized rental housing programs such as, in 1961, the Section 221(d)(3) program and, in 1968, the Section 236 program (to be discussed later in this chapter). A second avenue of FHA involvement was the modification of its single family home ownership program in an attempt to meet the needs of central city and minority neighborhoods. This initiative bears some discussion at this point.

It began in the mid-1960s with FHA administrative rule changes aimed at altering insurance underwriting criteria to accommodate central city areas. One HUD directive stated that in dealing with these new "high risk" areas, FHA approved lenders should refrain from lending in "only those instances where a property has so deteriorated or is subject to such hazards . . . that the physical improvements are endangered or the livability of the property or the health or safety of its occupants are seriously affected" (quoted from HUD internal documents in Bradford 1979, 326). The Housing Act of 1968 added Section 223(e) to the Housing Act of 1934, which "gave legislative sanction to waiving or relaxing FHA property standards to permit mortgage insurance for housing in blighted areas of central cities" (Semer 1976, 23).

The 1968 Act further enhanced the FHA's role in insuring housing for the disadvantaged by creating the Government National Mortgage Association (Ginnie Mae) to supplement the work of the Federal National Mortgage Association (Fannie Mae). The purpose of Ginnie Mae was to buy mortgages on higher risk low income housing projects at a higher price and to resell them at market rates, absorbing the loss as a government subsidy. It was split from Fannie Mae to avoid any threat to the marketability of the latter's mortgage-backed securities, and it soon became the major purchaser of mortgages for low income projects.

Finally, the 1968 Act added Section 235, which provided a federal subsidy of mortgage payments to persons of modest income wishing to purchase their own homes. This subsidy covered the difference between the mortgage payment at the regular FHA interest rate and the same payment at 1 percent interest (or 20 percent of the purchaser's income, whichever was greater) (Semer 1976, 124). Two attitudes, or perceptions, contributed to the choice of home ownership programs as a vehicle to aid urban areas.

One was a growing awareness that credit problems were both a symptom and an important cause of housing and neighborhood decline. *Redlining* is now a standard term of opprobrium in the vocabulary of urban affairs, but the fact that property owners in certain areas could not easily obtain credit for purchase or property improvement because lending institutions had written off the area as high risk, was just rising into public consciousness in the mid-1960s. Though the returning white gentry of the 1970s were to find that redlining was more than a racial problem, in the 1960s it was viewed primarily in those terms as one more form of discrimination contributing to the despair and frustration of African Americans.

A second attitude was a widely held belief in the beneficial social effects of home ownership. The purchase of a single family home has always been a central part of the American Dream. However, proponents of home ownership for the poor went one step farther than recognizing it as a legitimate aspiration. They argued, in addition, that home ownership would instill a sense of personal pride which would counteract the culture of poverty, thereby improving not only the care that individuals devoted to their dwellings but their overall outlook on life. In the words of Wright Patman (D, Texas), chair of the House Banking and Currency Committee, "Pride of ownership is a subtle but powerful force. Past experience has shown us that families offered decent homes at prices they can afford have demonstrated a new dignity, a new attitude toward their jobs. . . . By extending the opportunity for home ownership to low- and moderate-income families, we will give them a concrete incentive for striving to improve their own lives" (*CQ Almanac* 1968, 329).

Furthermore, it was felt that home ownership would create a greater sense of commitment to the neighborhood and the community, which would lead to more responsible forms of participation. As Senator Charles Percy (R, Illinois) bluntly stated, "People won't burn down houses that they own" (U.S. Congress, Senate 1967). Interestingly enough, though this argument was essentially a liberal social cost justification, it was very appealing to many conservatives, and all thirty-nine Senate Republicans co-sponsored Senator Percy's proposal for a home ownership provision in the 1968 Housing Act (McClaughry 1975).

One other source of political support for the expansion of FHA activities into central city and minority areas should be mentioned here, although it will also be discussed in connection with subsidized rental housing. This was the growing tendency in the 1960s for key segments of the private housing industry to support government intervention on behalf of the housing needs of the poor, especially where the private sector was the provider. Government subsidy for privately produced housing services was not a new idea. It had been proposed in the 1930s as an alternative to public housing and explored thoroughly by a commission on housing appointed by Eisenhower in the early 1950s. Nevertheless, since the New Deal, home builders, realtors, and bankers had been more or less united in their opposition to any expansion of the government role in housing beyond the regulations and insurance programs already in place, particularly where that expansion involved assistance for the poor. They viewed the long-term threat of government competition and regulation as outweighing any short-term gains from federal subsidies. They concentrated on limiting the incursion already made by public housing, rather than risk a nominally private sector program that might ultimately increase the government's role (Freedman 1969).

In the 1960s, the National Association of Real Estate Boards (NAREB), whose concerns tended to focus on sale and rental of existing dwellings, and who thus saw government-stimulated supply increases or subsidies as a threat to their market, continued to resist new subsidy programs. In contrast, the National Association of Home Builders gradually became a strong supporter of such programs. They became, in fact, part of a policy subsystem alliance which also included the Housing and Home Finance Agency (HHFA, later to become HUD) and the pro-housing members of the House and Senate Banking and Currency Committees. The Kennedy and Johnson administrations actively courted such support by emphasizing the need for a public-private partnership in solving housing problems, and they were supported in this instance by a number of moderate Republicans. The new FHA home ownership programs were seen as prime examples of such a partnership.

As a result of these interests and attitudes, the FHA entered the 1970s at the helm of programs that had previously been foreign to its basic values. Such an uneasy marriage contained great potential for problems, and the emergence of these problems in the first two years of the decade created an image of program failure which was to shape the policy debate which followed. Before addressing these problems, however, the other major element in the historical picture, public housing, must be examined.

Public Housing

The public housing program was enacted by Congress in 1937, relatively late in the New Deal period. Though there was organized opposition led by NAREB, they were unable to block it, due to wide congressional support engendered by the dual crisis in housing and in construction trades employment (Semer 1976). However, the program was unable to capitalize on its initial support because it had barely begun to produce units when World War II began. War needs diverted materials from housing construction, and public housing was mainly utilized for war industry workers rather than the poor. In addition, NAREB and its allies succeeded in imposing budget cuts in the late 1930s, which curtailed production (Gelfand 1975).

Because of this hiatus, major political conflicts over the program did not emerge until after the war, when the liberal New Deal coalition had lost strength. In 1946, Truman proposed major new funding for the program as part of his comprehensive housing proposal, but the public housing provisions proved to be the most unpopular sections of the bill and barely escaped deletion from the final legislative product, the Housing Act of 1949. Even this commitment was later to be seriously undermined, as shall be shown.

The complex history of public housing can best be understood in terms of four basic issues which were the focus of debate and struggle between its opponents and proponents. These are:

- Site selection
- The target population
- Cost and financing problems
- Problems of administration and project design.

In each of these areas, the political balance of forces created contradictory pressures which made it difficult for the program to meet its objectives. Moreover, some of these contradictions continued to affect later alternatives to public housing.

SITE SELECTION

The issue of site selection arose early. The precursor to the public housing program, the Housing Division of the Public Works Administration, ran a centralized program, in which the federal government itself bought and developed project sites. Because of the political appeal of decentralization and because of legal challenges to the federal government's right to use eminent domain for such a purpose, proponents of a permanent public housing program opted for local control (Mandelker 1981). Local housing authorities would be created by special legislation in each state to develop and administer the federally financed projects. In addition, local governments would be given a role in site selection through a *cooperation agreement* between the public housing authority and the local government regarding payments in lieu of taxes for fire, police, and other public services. Battles over public housing site selection had both a class and a racial dimension.

Unfortunately, but not surprisingly given the negative attitudes toward the poor described earlier, middle-class neighborhoods greeted public housing with the same enthusiasm as they might have greeted the introduction of bubonic plague. And citizens' groups could generate more heat than local politicians were willing to endure. Local opposition was further fanned by a vigorous national propaganda campaign carried out by NAREB. Legislation in many states required that local participation in the program be subject to direct voter approval by referendum. These referenda gave opponents the opportunity to excite public fears. In Seattle, for example, opponents published a map purporting to show intended sites for public housing in middle-class areas, even though the local housing authority had made no such decisions (Freedman 1969). Even where referenda were not required, pressure was exerted through aldermen representing various areas, as in the Chicago case documented by Meyerson and Banfield (1955).

In spite of such resistance, many of the public housing developments built immediately before and after World War II became popular and attractive places to live for white working-class families. The rent was low and the public landlord easier to deal with than private landlords (Vale

2000). However, increasing postwar affluence, plus the FHA and VA home ownership programs, enabled many white working-class public housing residents to become homeowners in the suburbs. Their places were often filled by impoverished African American migrants from the South who were moving into large cities in great numbers. Since African Americans were prevented by segregation from pursuing other housing opportunities, many public housing projects became black ghettoes from which escape was difficult.

In addition, many cities used public housing as a deliberate tool of racial segregation. Residents of white neighborhoods were very threatened by the postwar influx of African Americans into Northern cities. Blockbusting and racial tipping led to the rapid transformation of many areas from white to black, and whites in other neighborhoods were willing to do anything, including resorting to violence, to prevent this from happening. One way for city officials to respond to these fears was to build large, high rise public housing developments in neighborhoods that were already African American and then channel the postwar influx of black residents into what came to be called "vertical ghettos."

The city that best exemplified this process was Chicago. Chicago's South Side became home to huge, high rise projects such as the Robert Taylor Homes, which housed thousands of black families in one concentrated area. Some public housing was also built in white areas, but a few feeble attempts to integrate it were rebuffed by white violence and harassment against African American tenants (Venkatesh 2000).

Most localities managed to build some public housing, but the political pressure to locate new units in areas already occupied by the poor was overwhelming. Any large concentration of disadvantaged persons in a single development would have borne a certain stigma. However, the stigma was intensified by the construction of new projects in the midst of vast expanses of dilapidated housing already bearing the label of slums (Meehan 1979). This stigma was self-fulfilling, insofar as it influenced the behavior of the poor themselves. Many families with dreams of upward mobility avoided what they called "the projects," even when the low rent would have helped financially. This left a greater concentration of the most desperate, down and out poor with no other place to go. In addition, those who responded to the pressures of poverty with sociopathic behavior found the huge projects to be fertile ground on which to practice criminal activity. Critics could then point to the deterioration of the quality of life in public housing as evidence that it should never have been built.

POPULATION SERVED

The population to be served was a second major problem for public housing. In other industrialized countries, publicly owned or subsidized housing has served a broad segment of the population (McGuire 1981). In the United States, in contrast, it was assumed from the beginning that only the very lowest income persons, those so desperately poor as to have no chance of obtaining housing on the private market, should be served.

The 1937 Act limited income in two ways. First, tenant income could not exceed five times the rent, with the exception of large families. Second, it authorized the federal public housing agency to set dollar limits on income, to reflect the legislative intent that only low income people should be served. The limits set during the first twenty years of the program were, according to Freedman, so low as to ensure that occupants were among the poorest persons in the United States (Freedman 1969, 107). In 1959, these restrictions were removed, and limits were left to local discretion (Mandelker 1973). However, a 1971 study of seventy-four cities indicated that throughout the 1960s, local authorities' limits remained well below the median incomes in their communities (U.S. Congress, House 1971).

Such a policy satisfied vertical equity, in that those with the greatest need had the highest priority for help. This principle has been defended vigorously by liberals as the only fair way to distribute the typically slender resources allocated to social welfare programs. Nevertheless, the application of this principle presents severe problems for the programs involved, as was amply illustrated by public housing.

One problem was that for twenty-five years, the nation's major housing assistance program did not serve a large segment of the population with genuine housing needs. It appeared grossly unfair to families who worked hard to earn slightly better incomes than public housing tenants, but who ended up occupying worse housing or paying a much larger percentage of income to secure decent quarters. A second, and related, problem was that strict income limits penalized upward mobility by public housing tenants. During the 1940s and 1950s, most authorities evicted tenants whose incomes rose above the prescribed ceiling. Any laxity in this policy exposed the agencies to public criticism for letting allegedly "well off" people live in subsidized housing (Freedman 1969, 107). However, the sudden eviction of such a family often put them in worse financial shape, since comparable private housing cost more. The projects were hurt, too, in that these upwardly mobile persons could have provided stability and community leadership.

A third problem with strict income ceilings was that they reinforced the public's negative image of public housing tenants. This problem was not as severe during the early years of the program, when the typical tenant was a temporarily poor but otherwise respectable family who needed aid as a result of the difficulties of war or the Depression. Many housing authorities tried to maintain respectability by designing other admissions standards to screen out all but these families. However, during the 1950s the composition of the American poor as a whole gradually shifted from the temporarily disadvantaged to a more permanently distressed, disproportionately black underclass, and a positive image became more difficult to maintain (Wolman 1971, 31). For example, AFDC families, initially excluded in many communities, gradually came to be admitted and to comprise an increasing percentage of tenants, just as they became an increasing proportion of the low income population. This helped reinforce public perceptions of the program as one more "dole" to those already receiving aid.

The overall effect of these three problems was to undermine political support, but the restriction of the program to the very poor created another political problem as well, that of constituency. After World War II shook the nation out of its economic doldrums, the poor gradually became a minority of the population, largely without the skills, resources, or inclination to exert political pressure on behalf of programs benefiting them. As a result, the main interest group pushing for public housing consisted of its professional administrators, acting through such organizations as the National Association of Housing and Redevelopment Officials (NAHRO). The support they could muster depended not on the political clout of their clients but on an appeal to social cost arguments. These were sufficient to keep the program from extinction, but in the face of concerted attacks from the private housing industry, they were hardly a political basis upon which it could thrive (Keith 1973; Hays 2001). That the direct participation of clientele groups could have made a difference is shown by the galvanizing effect extralegal participation by the poor through the riots of 1965–68 had on this and other social welfare efforts.

FINANCIAL PROBLEMS

Eugene Meehan made the financial problems of the public housing program central to his analysis of what he considers its widespread failure. He contends that over most of its existence, the program was forced by financial starvation to provide a limited number of units and a declining quality of service (Meehan 1977, 1979), and he documents convincingly the important role played by lack of funds. Funding was used to restrict the program in several ways.

The most obvious was through the appropriation of funds for construction. Congress consistently funded far fewer units than were authorized. The largest gap occurred in the 1950s. The Housing Act of 1949 authorized approximately 135,000 units per year over the following six years. However, actual appropriations never exceeded a peak of 90,000 units in Fiscal Year (FY) 1950 and reached a low point of zero in FY 1954. More typically, appropriations fluctuated around 25,000 units. As a result, by 1960, five years after the target date for completion of 810,000 new units, less than one-quarter of these had been built (Freedman 1969, 19–32).

This outcome resulted, in large part, from political configurations within Congress. The responsibility for substantive housing legislation was lodged in the housing subcommittees of the House and Senate Banking and Currency Committees. These committees attracted senators and representatives with an intense interest in housing, who developed close ties with federal housing agencies, and with pro-housing lobbies such as NAHRO and the National Housing Conference. In contrast, the Independent Offices Subcommittee of the House Appropriations Committee, the group responsible for housing appropriations during the 1950s and 1960s, included many conservative Southern Democrats and Republicans, who were hostile to the whole concept of public housing. NAREB and other anti–public housing groups concentrated their lobbying on this more sympathetic center of power, thus preventing the achievement of the 1949 Act's ambitious goal.

Yet, continued funding limitations cannot entirely be attributed to skillful utilization of an alternative power center within Congress. Throughout the 1950s public housing remained an unpopular program, subject to periodic dismantling attempts on the floor of the House and Senate, as well as in the Appropriations Committee. In addition, the degree of presidential support had an appreciable impact. While Truman was president, he pushed for larger numbers of units (although the Korean War kept him from proposing the original goal of 135,000). Eisenhower, on the other hand, was cool to the program and, while never trying to abolish it, consistently recommended low levels of funding. Finally, local opposition affected national decisions, in that many of the units funded were subject to delay due to protracted site selection battles. Although local officials, for the most part, lobbied for more units as a means of reducing their slums, these simmering local controversies dampened congressional support.

The Kennedy administration was more enthusiastic about public housing, and immediately proposed that 100,000 units be built by 1964. When Johnson assumed the presidency, he further accelerated the program, proposing 60,000 units per year for four years in the Housing Act of 1965, and a total of 395,000 units over three years in the Housing Act of 1968. Thus, the 1960s produced a strong executive branch drive toward a larger, smoother flow of units. Congress, too, seemed more willing to appropriate funds without the vituperative rhetoric of earlier battles.

The aforementioned change in the political environment due to the civil rights movement and urban riots, coupled with liberal control of the presidency and larger liberal majorities in Congress, largely accounted for this shift. However, another rather paradoxical reason for the greater ease with which public housing expenditures made it through Congress was that the focus of debate had shifted to newer, more innovative programs such as rent supplements. Next to these, public housing seemed familiar and controllable. This point will be discussed more fully below.

Money considerations, in addition to limiting the quantity of public housing units built, greatly affected their quality. The 1937 Act funded only capital costs; that is, the principal and interest on bonds issued by local housing authorities to finance construction. Operation and maintenance were covered out of rents, and any surplus rental income had to be applied toward debt repayment (Meehan 1979). Early in the program, when units were new and the tenants were the working poor, authorities had little trouble in supporting operating and maintenance costs. However, during the 1950s and 1960s this became increasingly difficult. On the one hand, inflation increased expenses, and aging buildings required more repairs. On the other hand, tenant incomes declined. Aaron reports that between 1961 and 1970, the median family income of public housing tenants declined from 47.1 percent to 36.9 percent of the U.S. median family income (Aaron 1972, 116).

By the late 1960s, according to Mandelker, many housing authorities were in serious financial difficulty (Mandelker 1973, 82–83). Nevertheless, though Congress was funding more units, they were much less willing to confront the issue of operating subsidies. A major reason was that local authorities' problems were widely perceived as the result of inefficient or careless management, coupled with the alleged destructiveness of tenants. Even though studies by the Urban Institute and the Rand Corporation showed that price inflation, not poor management, was the main cause of the cost squeeze (Mandelker 1973, 83), most members of Congress were reluctant to provide money they felt would reduce local incentives to operate efficiently.

When the cost problem was finally addressed, it was done obliquely through congressional response to a symptom; the substantial rent increases to which many authorities resorted in order to cover costs. These increases led to tenant unrest, culminating in rent strikes in Newark and St. Louis. Congress responded in 1969 with the Brooke Amendment, which restricted public housing rents to no more than 25 percent of tenant income. Since this limitation caused a loss of revenue for many housing authorities, Congress also provided operating subsidies to cover local shortfalls (and to pay off previously accumulated operating deficits) (Mandelker 1973). Thus was created one of the housing policy controversies of the 1970s, which will be examined further later in this chapter.

MANAGEMENT AND DESIGN ISSUES

All three issues just described—site selection, target population, and cost—had an important impact on the quality and quantity of the services offered by public housing. However, the program stimulated another debate related to the quality of services it provided: a debate over the physical design of the structures and the quality of their management. Here, too, the program was caught between conflicting pressures from liberals for improvement and from conservatives for containment.

The issue of public housing design touched directly on a central question common to all such programs, namely: What level of housing quality should be enjoyed by those whom the government assists? The prevailing view among conservative critics and among many liberals as well was that the quarters provided by the government should be Spartan. Anything more than the minimum quality necessary to maintain health would, in this view, weaken the incentive of the residents to better themselves and excite the resentment of unsubsidized families. The application of this principle proved extremely destructive to public housing in the long run.

To begin with, most citizens and elected officials tended to associate cost control with control over amenities. Strict limits on the per unit cost of public housing were intended to prevent local authorities from constructing units that might be viewed as "too luxurious" for low income persons. In response, Congress placed tight limits on per unit prototype costs often setting them well below average construction costs for an area. However, such costs were at least as much related to the quality of the basic elements of construction as to extras that might make a unit luxurious. (A 1982 HUD study documented the relatively small impact amenities had on per unit costs; U.S. Department of Housing and Urban Development 1982b, 5–8.) Therefore, these limits often resulted in shoddy construction of such basic elements as doors, windows, plumbing, and heating equipment. Such short-term savings were, of course, inimical not only to the tenants' quality of life but to the taxpayers' long-term financial interest in durable units. Widespread negative perceptions of the poor obscured this problem, since the tenants themselves were blamed by the public for the poor condition of the units.

Even where basic construction was sound, cost restrictions discouraged design features that were essential to the smooth functioning of families and of the projects as communities. Units with minimal floor space, elevators that stopped on every other floor, floor plans arranged to minimize costs but maximize security problems, a total absence of site planning or recreational facilities—all of these were seen as prudent cost-cutting measures. However, the long-term costs, both to the tenants and to the public, were clearly much larger than short-term savings.

Beyond this, the absence of basic amenities was a symbol of the stigma attached to living in public housing. As Nathan Glazer has pointed out, and as discussed in chapter 3, one's concept of what level of housing services is minimal is a product of time and culture, and it is clear that the housing expectations of postwar Americans have far exceeded those of earlier generations or their contemporaries in other cultures (Glazer 1967). It is also true that individuals will generally aspire to the standard of living of those higher on the income scale and that the total equalization of housing quality with aspirations would be excessively costly. However, there is another minimum quality line which is difficult to define precisely but which, if not met, leads the individual to put less value on his dwelling and, perhaps, on himself. The failure to meet such a standard can, as a result, contribute to the deterioration of life in the project. Common public housing design items such as toilets without seats and cabinets or closets without doors would certainly fall into this category of stigmatizing deficiencies.

Yet another design controversy which negatively affected elite and mass acceptance of public housing concerned its aesthetic contribution to the community as a whole. In sharp contrast to the widespread public sentiment in favor of Spartan dwellings for the poor, a number of influential planners, architects, and social critics attacked public housing's lack of aesthetic quality as a blight on the community (Friedman, L. 1968). In the 1930s, modernist architects favored the "tower in the park" design (i.e., large high rises surrounded by open space) over what they saw as the crowding and congestion of urban slums (Bauman, Biles, and Szylvian 2000; Radford 1996). In this respect, the design of public housing mirrored larger trends in architecture that affected all types of dwellings and commercial structures.

However, the concrete or brick monoliths built in larger cities soon came to be criticized not only for their drab appearance but for their lack of *human scale*. In her classic critique of modernist planning (Jacobs 1961), Jane Jacobs argued that more traditional street layouts, far from being chaotic, fostered community through constant interpersonal interactions and informal mechanisms of social control (*eyes on the street*, to use her well-known phrase). In addition, the work of Newman on "defensible space" showed that physical design could enhance or detract from the safety of public housing neighborhoods (Newman 1972, 1995). The massive impersonal housing blocks required mothers to send their children ten floors down to play, unsupervised, in barren, rubble-strewn lots, and the hallways and stairwells of these buildings became havens for criminal activity. However, given cost constraints, the demand that public housing provide low-cost shelter for tens of thousands of people while at the same time meeting the criteria of a warm, personal, communal environment and/or making a major architectural statement, was difficult, if not impossible for public housing authorities to meet.

Closely related to the physical deficiencies of public housing were widespread perceptions of local management difficulties. In the 1950s, many agencies tried to keep their projects respectable in the eyes of the community by screening out applicants they considered undesirable and by extensive intervention into the private lives of tenants. The eviction of female tenants for becoming pregnant out of wedlock was standard policy in many localities, and tenants were often fined heavily for physical damage to the property (Steiner 1971). In the 1960s, tenants' groups challenged such regulations as paternalistic, and by the end of the decade, most authorities had loosened their parietal rules. At the same time, many other public housing managers were under fire for being too lax (i.e., for not responding vigorously to problems of physical damage, criminal behavior, or other social conflicts). Each of these criticisms was valid for some projects, and it was not impossible to find, in the same locality, strictness in some areas coupled with laxity in others. Nevertheless, the simultaneous existence of these two critiques was typical of the cross-pressures under which the program operated.

Because of numerous criticisms of public housing management during the 1960s, the decade saw the beginnings of various efforts at improvement. Existing managers received training, and tenant councils were set up to provide resident input (Peterman 1993; Monti 1993). Also, social services and recreation for tenants were expanded. These experiments had varying success, depending on the good faith with which management undertook them, the ways in which the conflicts engendered by tenant participation were handled, and the adequacy of funding. Overall, such efforts contributed to an atmosphere of uncertainty within the program, which was to affect later policy decisions.

Subsidies and Supplements

Another dimension of housing policy in the 1960s, which was to have an important impact later, was extensive experimentation with alternative ways to assist low income tenants, through the use of private sector construction and leasing. As noted in connection with Section 235, neither conservatives nor liberals were receptive to the idea of subsidies to the private sector for the provision of low income housing during the first twenty-five years of federal housing efforts. Conservatives feared expansion of the government's housing role. Liberals were concerned that the private sector would be unable to provide the service as cheaply as the public sector, thus denying benefits to lower income persons.

In addition to the ambivalence of those representing various points on the political spectrum, one also has to look at the political dynamics of the housing policy struggle in the 1940s and 1950s to explain the absence of private sector programs. Public housing became an established program, but it was under such severe attack that several moves in Congress to extinguish it nearly succeeded. Therefore, liberal housing advocates concentrated on maintaining a minimal level of activity in this existing program, and the distrust of federal involvement prevalent in the 1950s helped discourage innovation of any kind. On the other side of the battle, conservatives discovered they could not muster enough votes to kill the program, and they gradually accepted its existence on a limited scale. They found that its impact on the private market could be kept to a minimum (1) by controlling appropriations; and (2) by perpetuating local struggles over site selection, which kept the poor concentrated and isolated. By the end of the 1950s, the program, though not particularly liked by either side, was at least a known quantity.

In spite of these ideological and pragmatic factors, Kennedy came into office determined to push beyond the political equilibrium established around a 25,000 unit per year public housing program. On the one hand, his desire to improve housing conditions for the poor led him to push for expansion of public housing. On the other hand, several concerns motivated him to look at other forms of assistance.

First, qualitative criticisms of public housing from the Left were becoming more intense in the late 1950s, thus encouraging Kennedy's advisors to seek alternatives to public ownership. Second, innovations helped satisfy an urge displayed by Kennedy's advisors in many areas of policy—the urge to project an image of creativity and progress, in contrast to the stagnation they attributed to the Eisenhower years. Third, they perceived a need to aid families with incomes too high for public housing but too low to obtain standard housing on the private market. According to Milton Semer, concern among housing policy analysts that this group was not being reached by either FHA or public housing increased during the late 1950s (Semer 1976, 116). Fourth, Kennedy became president during an economic downturn which hit the housing industry particularly hard, raising unemployment in the industry to as high as 20 percent. Expanding government involvement in housing construction was a way to stimulate this key element of the private economy.

Finally, the Kennedy administration, and later the Johnson administration, placed great emphasis on the principle of public-private cooperation in solving social problems. Without the Great Depression at hand to stimulate fears of total system collapse, it seemed necessary to move beyond this kind of threat as a social cost argument and to emphasize the direct gains that the private sector could realize from helping the poor. Not only would the stability and harmony of society as a whole be enhanced, but various market winners could profitably expand their opportunities by helping the disadvantaged. Such a commonality of interests would expand the political base of social welfare programs, thereby avoiding the pariah status that direct government handouts to the poor such as public housing and AFDC had endured. Such considerations overrode the liberal concerns about vertical equity mentioned above, and led to the pursuit of public-private partnerships.

Kennedy's first housing initiative in this direction was the Section 221(d)(3) Below Market Interest Rate program, enacted in 1961. This program enabled private lenders to originate mortgages on rental housing developments at a rate below the prevailing market rates. Then, they could sell these mortgages to Fannie Mae at a price based on market rates. The loss sustained in this transaction constituted a subsidy designed to reduce rents. Participation was also encouraged by the extension of liberal borrowing terms by FHA. The Section 221(d)(3) program was directed at families with incomes too high for public housing but too low for standard private housing. The upper income ceiling was usually set at or near the median income for a particular geographical area, while the floor was the upper income limit for public housing. Another important provision was that tenants were not evicted if their income rose above a certain fixed level, but could continue residence at higher rents.

In its first four years, approximately 90,000 units were committed under the program, yet, it remained vulnerable to attack on a number of grounds and thus did not establish a stable political foothold. First, the interest subsidies did not result in as large a reduction in rents as had been hoped. In some cases, rents were only twenty dollars a month lower than conventional FHA multifamily projects, with the result that only the upper range of moderate income families could be served. This, combined with the lack of eviction due to rising income, raised the median income of 221(d)(3) tenants to five thousand dollars in 1965, a relatively high figure for that time. Media reports of allegedly well-to-do tenants living in these projects hurt the program's image.

In short, the program was caught on the opposite horn of the dilemma that ensnared public housing. Public housing served a very low income group and as a result was stigmatized as a dole for the undeserving. Section 22l(d)(3) served a slightly higher income group, and was attacked for giving aid to those who were too well-off to deserve it.

A second political difficulty arose from the nature of its impact on the federal budget. Since the entire mortgage on each project was purchased by Fannie Mae, each development required a large sum of federal money up front. Only a fraction of this amount would actually be lost to the government in the long run, since the loan was to be repaid by the developer. However, the program's large initial outlays enabled its detractors to characterize it as excessively costly and made it a target of strict funding limits.

To avoid the problem of budgetary impact, the Johnson administration sought a different type of program in 1965. Their alternative, called the *rent supplement* program, restructured the subsidy so that, instead of being applied indirectly through the government's repurchase of the mortgage at a loss, it was applied directly to the tenant's rent. FHA would insure a market rate loan to finance the project which, along with other expenses, would determine an economic rent for the project. The difference between this figure and 20 percent of the eligible tenant's income would be paid as a direct federal subsidy. While costing the same, or possibly more, this approach had the advantage of limiting the program's yearly budgetary impact.

This new proposal became the target of bitter debate in Congress. However, the focus of this debate was not the program's budgetary impact. Instead, the major bone of contention was the income group to be served. Like Section 221(d)(3), this program was aimed at families in what the Johnson administration referred to as the *20 percent gap* between public housing and private standard housing. Yet, the subsidy provided in the rent supplement proposal was somewhat deeper than that of the earlier program, and it was far more direct and visible. While the change in subsidy method minimized budgetary impact, it converted the government's effort from an indirect stimulus to *low*-cost housing construction to what opponents could characterize as a subsidy to middle income families.

This debate split supporters of federal housing programs, as well as mobilizing opponents. The National Association of Housing and Redevelopment Officials (NAHRO) opposed the program, calling it "administratively cumbersome and socially indefensible" (*CQ Almanac* 1965,361). This stance was motivated by the self-interest of local public housing authorities in keeping their program center stage, as well as an ideological objection to helping higher income groups. The proposal ultimately attracted such strong opposition that Johnson was forced to make a major modification in order to secure passage. Eligibility requirements were amended so that, instead of serving the 20 percent gap, subsidies were available only to those with incomes *at or below* public housing limits. Only by averting an expansion of federal activity into the moderate income area, thereby allaying both conservative fears of government expansion and liberal fears of abandonment of the poor, could Johnson get rent supplements through Congress.

The rent supplement debate was also fanned by increasing fears that the federal government would force socioeconomic and/or racial integration on higher income areas. Rent supplements were seen by both proponents and opponents as a more effective tool than public housing for achieving such integration. Higher income limits meant that subsidies could be extended to families who could afford to move into middle income areas, and, because it involved direct contracts between the HHFA and private builders, site selection would not require local government approval. By 1965, the federal government had become firmly identified with the cause of civil rights and with aid to the urban poor, as symbolized by the presence of African American housing advocate, Robert Weaver, as head of HHFA. Congressman Paul Fino (R, N.Y.) expressed the fears of many opponents, saying that the bill was "without safeguards to prevent the housing administrator from moving the poorest people into the best housing." This position was echoed by Senator John Tower (R, Texas) who said that the program's goal was to "get low income, middle income, and high income groups all living together." Neither of these statements explicitly mentioned racial integration, but one House member characterized race as "a major subsurface issue." (Quotes are from the *CQ Almanac* 1965,373–77,246.)

Though the rent supplement program was finally enacted, its implementation was very slow, in large part because opponents used their second line of defense, the appropriations process, to block it. Congress refused to appropriate funds in 1965, and in 1966 it cut Johnson's request in half. Also, a rider was attached to the 1966 appropriations bill which forced HHFA's successor, the new Department of Housing and Urban Development (HUD), to seek local government approval for rent supplement projects (*CQ Almanac* 1966, 245). This subjected the program to the same local site selection battles encountered by public housing. As it became clear that the program would remain small in scale, the Johnson administration sought another alternative more palatable to Congress and to the public.

The new plan was incorporated in Johnson's 1967 housing proposal and became law as the Section 236 program, a major part of the Housing Act of 1968. This program again utilized annual subsidies to private lenders rather than government loans, in order to minimize budgetary impact. But, in this program, the subsidies were not paid as direct rent supplements. Instead, the developer arranged a loan at market rates but only paid 1percent interest, the difference being made up by federal payments to the lender. Furthermore, in an effort to avoid the virulent opposition that had greeted the income provisions of the rent supplement program, the new proposal buried its income limits in the subsidy mechanism. No family paid less than a basic rent, computed on the basis of the 1 percent mortgage rate (however, 20 percent of the units in each project were set aside for additional subsidy through rent supplements). The upper income ceiling was set by a "fair market rent," calculated on the basis of rents for comparable units in the locality. No family for whom 25 percent of income was less than or equal to the fair market rent was eligible (US. General Accounting Office 1978).

However, Congress was, as Semer expresses it, "still not of a mood to turn ... [HUD] loose to work in the general vineyard of 'low- and moderate-income' housing" (Semer 1976, 126). Congress came up with a complicated formula for income ceilings, which reflected its clear desire to keep a strict income lid on the program. In the end, the new program was enacted with much less controversy than rent supplements and was funded at a much higher level than any previous subsidy program. Also, the income limits were much more liberal than those of the rent supplement program.

To complete the picture of new subsidy efforts in the 1960s, another program should be mentioned which slipped through Congress quietly in 1961—the Section 23 Leased Housing Program. Under this program, a public housing authority could locate a vacant unit, select an eligible tenant from its waiting list, and determine the rent that the tenant would pay based on its usual criteria. Then, it could sign a lease with the private landlord in which it agreed to pay the difference between the tenant's payment and the private market rent for a comparable unit. This program avoided the controversy surrounding other ventures into private sector housing because it was clearly within the control of established agencies and because it remained small scale throughout the 1960s. Its significance is that, of all the housing programs enacted during that time, it was closest to the *housing allowance* concept that was to become popular in the 1970s, and thus, it served as a model for later proposals.

Fair Housing

The Fair Housing Act of 1968 was a historic piece of legislation that was a direct response to the ongoing racial discrimination in the sale and rental of housing that had created the racially divided settlement patterns that characterized all American cities. As has been shown, the desire of privileged white citizens to maintain racial apartheid in their neighborhoods and communities affected all aspects of decision making with regard to housing. Racial considerations subverted the stated goal of the public housing program—decent affordable housing—and turned the program into a tool for perpetuating segregation. As new subsidy programs emerged, they too were shaped by the imperative of the racial divide. However, the Fair Housing Act was not directed at housing production by the government but at private acts of discrimination by landlords, realtors, and buyers/sellers of real estate. Along with the Civil Rights Act of 1964 and the Voting Rights Act of 1965, it was considered a major accomplishment of the struggle for civil rights for African Americans and other people of color.

The passage of the Fair Housing Act was accompanied by bitter debate in Congress, with opponents characterizing it as an assault on the "property rights" of white citizens. Mara Sidney (2003) documents the fact that proponents of the act, in order to develop positive language that would counter these attacks, linked it to upward mobility by African Americans. According to the narrative that they created, educated, middle-class African American families who wanted to move out of the poverty and turmoil of the ghetto could use the protections of this Act to secure housing in more stable (presumably white) neighborhoods. In this way, they turned the urban riots, a potential liability for anyone arguing for expanded civil rights in the latter half of the 1960s, into an asset by creating a set of "deserving blacks" who would be the beneficiaries of the legislation.

This framing of the issue was successful in securing passage of the Act, but it resulted in a law that was focused on individual acts of discrimination perpetuated against those who were otherwise "deserving" of being admitted to white, middle-class neighborhoods. It further put the burden on individuals by specifying that HUD could only act on the basis of individual complaints of discrimination, not on the basis of overall patterns of discrimination. Compared to the two earlier civil rights laws just mentioned, its enforcement mechanisms were incredibly weak. It took other legal actions, such as court cases and HUD regulations created in response to court cases, to directly address the issue of how housing development, whether publicly or privately sponsored, acted to perpetuate the segregation of whole neighborhoods and areas of the city.

Summary of Part I

I have attempted in Part I to set the stage for later housing policy decisions by tracing the development of three major types of subsidy programs prior to 1970: FHA single family mortgage insurance; public housing; and a collection of programs based on indirect and direct subsidies to private builders which were developed in the 1960s. By 1970, all of these programs had, by one route or another, become important parts of the federal strategy for improving low income housing.

No single piece of legislation embodied the liberal commitments of the Johnson administration more than the Housing Act of 1968. It reaffirmed the sweeping rhetorical goal of the Housing Act of 1949, "to provide a decent home and living environment for every American family," and it also set specific quantitative targets. The Act declared "that it [the goal] can be substantially achieved within the next decade by the construction or rehabilitation of 26 million housing units, six million of these for low- and moderate-income families" (HUD 1976, 143). All of the programs included in the Act were funded at levels unheard of in the previous thirty years of federal involvement. Looking at this legislation at that time, it was possible to conclude that the nation had finally made a serious commitment to the use of federal resources to improve housing conditions for lower income families.

The actual course of events was quite different. After about four years of large-scale expansion, the entire federal housing effort was brought to a halt by the Nixon Moratorium, amid charges that all the major new programs had been failures and amid calls for a totally new approach. As will be shown in Part II, the seeds of this rapid policy reversal lay in the unresolved nature of the underlying ideological and political disputes in which housing was embedded, disputes already aired in the 1950s and 1960s. In short, the ship was standing on the launching pad, with plenty of fuel and a seemingly clear flight path charted, but the captaincy changed hands and the crew was still deeply divided on the basic direction it should take. Thus, it could be expected that the mission would dissolve into midcourse wrangling, which would nearly halt the flight altogether.

Part II—From Boom to Bust in Federal Housing Assistance: 1969–1973

Dye and Ziegler (1981) argue that a presidential election cannot be treated as a mandate for particular policy directions because: (1) voters are poorly informed about the issues and candidates' positions on the issues; and (2) voters choose candidates for many reasons, of which only a small part are agreements or disagreements with specific policy stands. The election of 1968 was one in which the policy mandate was particularly murky. Voters were tired of the Vietnam War but hostile to the antiwar movement. They supported programs to aid the poor, but they wanted law and order restored in the cities, after three years of riots. The turmoil that plagued Johnson's tenure seemed at one point to be driving millions of traditionally Democratic voters away from the party, either to Nixon or the third party candidate, George Wallace. Yet, in the end, the Democratic candidate, Hubert Humphrey, gained majorities in most of the groups in the traditional New Deal Coalition, thereby rendering Nixon's victory margin razor thin (Converse et al. 1969).

Dye and Ziegler go on to say that, while the popular will as to policy options is obscure, elections do serve the function of bringing into power a new leadership group which usually has different plans for governing the country (Dye and Ziegler 1981, 210–13). In one sense, this was certainly the case in 1968. A distinctly different group assumed power when Nixon took office. Yet, in another sense, the division of power between liberals and conservatives was as complex as the voter's electoral decision, particularly with regard to social welfare policies such as housing assistance.

First, multiple perspectives were represented within the Nixon administration. Some advisors, such as Daniel Patrick Moynihan, Robert Finch, and George Romney, felt that the previous administration's commitment to solving the problems of the poor should be maintained, having been reformed and stripped of excesses by the new administration. The key to future Republican electoral success was, they felt, to move toward the center, to portray themselves as more cautions and responsible liberals than the Democrats. Others, such as John Mitchell, supported the notion of a new Republican majority, based on groups who wished to contain, if not totally reject, the demands of the poor. This majority would add to the traditional Republican core of conservatives many of the disaffected middle class who felt that their money and their values were being sacrificed to the demands of strident minorities. Nixon himself, according to several accounts, lacked a clearly articulated philosophy on domestic social programs and attached less importance to these issues than to foreign affairs (Evans and Novak 1971; Safire 1975). Therefore, the direction his administration took was greatly influenced by which group of advisors was able to gain his ear.

Second, the election of 1968 left in place forces strongly supporting Great Society programs. The election made only a slight dent in the Democratic majorities in both houses of Congress, thus leaving liberals with a strong power base. In addition, interest groups with a stake in various programs retained considerable political clout. The governments of most large cities were not Republican strongholds, but many in the party did not want to write off this political base entirely. And local officials as a group, whether Democratic or Republican, still commanded a respectful ear in Congress when speaking through such organizations as the U.S. Conference of Mayors. There were also private sector interest groups who could be counted on the side of such programs. These were not groups Nixon could afford to totally ignore.

The result of these contradictory pressures was a Nixon Administration stance on social welfare policy that gradually shifted over his five and a half years in office. Initially, following the lead of his more liberal advisors, Nixon made efforts to contain, control, and redirect, but not to reverse, major Democratic initiatives. Programs with the weakest support, such as the War on Poverty (which had alienated many in Congress with its efforts to organize the poor politically rather than simply give out benefits) were the first recommended for reorientation or reduction. Meanwhile, programs with greater support, such as housing assistance, were continued and even expanded. Yet, as Nixon's term progressed, the liberals gradually lost influence and, one by one, departed the administration. This left the more conservative group in control of domestic policy, a group inclined to use the political weaknesses displayed by various programs as opportunities to push for their curtailment. Particularly in the period between Nixon's overwhelming reelection victory in 1972 (which they interpreted as a mandate for a shift in policy in a conservative direction) and his total loss of political effectiveness in mid-1974 due to Watergate, the administration was more aggressive in pursuing reorganization measures and budget cuts.

These internal shifts in the Nixon team are stressed here because, in general, the failure of any program to perform, or its generation of undesirable side effects, are not in themselves sufficient conditions for a successful political attack on the program. As Wildavsky has pointed out, criteria for success or failure are usually ambiguous, judgments of efficacy are dependent on value perspectives, and many programs serve purposes other than their stated objectives (Wildavsky 1979). In addition, it is possible for decision makers to choose from a variety of responses to program deficiencies, ranging from minor administrative adjustments to major modifications or substitutions (Hays 1986). Therefore, in explaining instances, such as housing assistance, where concern about deficiencies led to severe curtailment or abolition of programs, one must also look for political actors with the motives and ability to utilize the programs' weaknesses to undermine support. Many Great Society programs displayed serious flaws, and the ideology of the Nixon team inclined them to favor drastic changes over adjustments.

Another aspect of Nixon's strategy bears discussion before the particular problems of housing programs are examined. This was his tendency to couch major efforts at retrenchment in the rhetoric of reform previously associated with liberal initiatives. Even though Nixon's political strength grew as his term progressed (until the Watergate scandal exploded), and although he intensified his efforts to change the direction set by the Great Society, the underlying political support for social welfare programs was sufficiently strong that he did not openly advocate a full-scale retreat from federal involvement. Instead, he cast himself in the role of a reformer, who wished to improve the fairness and effectiveness of federal efforts to help the disadvantaged. In an October 13, 1969, message to Congress, he declared that "this would be the watchword of the Administration: REFORM," and he went on to list eleven areas of reform, ranging from the draft to revenue sharing to the Office of Economic Opportunity (Nixon

1971, 11D-A). Most of these reforms would reduce the public sector's active role on behalf of the disadvantaged, and they were often accompanied by funding reductions. Such changes would, of course, be reforms from a conservative point of view, but Nixon was clearly appealing to liberals by suggesting that he sought changes in the means, not in the ends or the level of commitment. This blending of retrenchment with reformist rhetoric influenced the development of housing programs by encouraging new approaches.

Nixon's victory created great concern among housing proponents that Johnson's initiatives would quickly be abandoned (Keith 1973). However, in keeping with the cautious strategy just described, Nixon sent just the opposite signal by appointing George Romney, a pro-urban, pro-housing Republican, as Secretary of Housing and Urban Development. Romney promised greater administrative efficiency in the programs enacted in 1968 and then presided, for the next four years, over the largest boom in the construction of federally assisted housing that had ever occurred. Data on the production of units in programs run by HUD are presented in Figure 4-1. They show the extent of the boom between 1969 and 1974, and the contribution of each of the major programs begun or accelerated by the Housing Act of 1968.

If a single period can be identified during which the support for these programs began to unravel, it is probably the year 1971. As Figure 4-1 shows, this was when production reached its peak, but it was also a year in

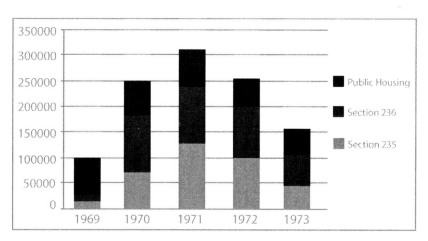

Figure 4-1 Assisted Housing Production: 1969–1973

Source: Department of Housing and Urban Development Statistical Yearbook, 1979

which investigations by Congress and the media began to uncover problems in the Section 235 and 236 programs, and in which ongoing controversies over public housing intensified. Since each program had its own path of development and decline, it is best to examine them separately.

THE SECTION 235 PROGRAM

Cities Destroyed for Cash was the lurid title of one journalist's exposé of the Section 235 program in Detroit. This book begins with figures purporting to demonstrate the program's failure on a national scale. Then, the author launches into an account of the juicier details of the Detroit scandal, including the murder of an evil realtor by a conscience-stricken man who had helped her procure houses from inner city residents at rock-bottom prices in order to sell them at huge profits (Boyer 1973).

While most descriptions of the program lacked the drama of this account, it accurately reflected the aura of scandal that enveloped it in 1971 and 1972. *The Wall Street Journal, Business Week, The National Observer*, and other influential periodicals carried stories about FHA's troubles (McClaughry 1975, 4), while several congressional investigations were begun (U.S. Congress, House Committee on Banking and Currency 1970, 1971b; Committee on Appropriations 1972; Committee on Government Operations 1971, 1972a). Meanwhile, grand juries indicted builders, realtors, and FHA officials in Detroit, New York, Philadelphia, and several other large cities. Clearly, these programs had gone awry in some communities, serving neither the interests of the general public nor their intended beneficiaries (Lilley 1972b, 1972c).

The pattern of abuse which emerged from these investigations is well summarized in this account of a home purchase under Section 235:

> In a typical case, a real estate operator would buy up a number of rundown or abandoned buildings in an inner-city slum. He would make sufficient cosmetic repairs to make the building temporarily presentable. An FHA appraiser—often a fee appraiser—would inflate the appraisal value, occasionally for an illegal kickback. The operator would find an aspiring low income family with little knowledge of the responsibilities of home ownership. The bank would make the loan, knowing, of course, that FHA would step in, in case of default. The operator would take his money and disappear. Later, the homeowner would discover that his home had many substandard conditions, conditions more expensive to correct than his limited budget permitted. Having only $200 in the deal, and facing huge expenses and protracted wrangling, the homeowner

would abandon the property and disappear. And another problem home went into the FHA inventory. (McClaughry 1975, 21)

This account identifies several key actors in the transaction; the FHA administrators, the prospective buyer, the realtor or builder, and the mortgage banker. All displayed attitudes or behavior that combined to make the outcome unfavorable. In addition, the transaction was influenced by the condition of the inner city housing market in which it was taking place. Let us briefly explore each actor's role.

The passage of the 1968 Act thrust the FHA into territory both unfamiliar and uncomfortable for its staff. After years of underwriting mortgages for middle-class, white buyers using the banker's criterion of economic soundness as a measure of risk, the FHA staff was suddenly asked to change both its criterion and its clientele. Backers of the 1968 Act were concerned that the criterion of economic soundness erected an arbitrary barrier around inner city areas, since it was based as much on the location of a house as its physical condition. Their intent was that the FHA would bring its expertise to bear on inner city problems, with a reasonable relaxation of standards to reflect inner city conditions. However, during implementation, many local FHA administrators heard a different message. In the words of a 1971 HUD Audit Report, "We were informed, both orally and in written comments [by local FHA officials] that the word was out from the Central Office to relax the inspection requirements" (U.S. Congress, House Committee on Banking and Currency 1971b, 85). This tendency to interpret a lowering of standards as a philosophy of "anything goes" was exacerbated by the push from top HUD officials for high-volume production of units, plus a lack of adequate staff in many field offices.

The result was, in some areas, a breakdown of the normal FHA review process. Properties were not inspected or given only an external, "windshield" (drive-by) inspection. In a masterpiece of bureaucratic understatement, the HUD Audit Report notes: "The conditions were so bad in some of the houses we inspected that the interior inspection by an appraiser prior to insurance is debatable" (87). In addition, the value of houses was often determined by private fee appraisers who were themselves local realtors, and their carelessly or deliberately inflated valuations were accepted without review.

With FHA willing to relax its standards, there were numerous builders and real estate agents willing to exploit the situation for quick profits. These agents could easily find willing buyers among low income persons eager to improve their housing. The agents would use FHA backing to reassure the buyer of the quality of the house. Then, they would take advantage of FHA laxity, or, in some cases, bribe officials to look the other way while the house was sold in poor condition and/or at an inflated price. They found their most fertile ground in neighborhoods that were changing racially or could be tipped toward racial change by skillful manipulation. Blockbusting was, as Bradford points out, a technique highly developed by unscrupulous inner city realtors long before the FHA program was introduced. It depended for its success on whites who were afraid of property value loss due to integration and on African Americans who, because they faced very restricted housing choices, were eager to open up new areas. However, the impact of blockbusting had, in the past, been limited by the lack of available credit, since most banks would lend to African Americans, if at all, only on the most unfavorable terms.

The new FHA initiatives opened a flood of credit to areas vulnerable to racial change. FHA mortgage insurance made lending in these areas virtually risk free for mortgage bankers and savings and loan associations. They could get FHA approval on the structure, service the loan for a nice fee, and then immediately sell the mortgage to Fannie Mae. If the mortgage defaulted, FHA covered the loss and was left with the property (Bradford 1979).

The willingness of realtors to sell inferior units to low income persons at high profits can, in one sense, be explained by sheer greed, without reference to more abstract values. Yet, in another sense, such behavior fits into a broader set of attitudes toward the poor. The fact that the middle class often stereotypes the poor as lazy, ignorant, unkempt, or destructive makes economic exploitation of them seem more ethically palatable. When challenged, entrepreneurs respond with statements such as "It's better than what they had," or, "These people don't care how it looks," or, "They'll just tear it up anyway." Where the entrepreneur is white and the client is black, such stereotyping is intensified, although black entrepreneurs may also exploit their own community. Interviews with local FHA officials conducted during HUD and congressional investigations show they often shared these types of attitudes toward the people they were serving.

To reject these stereotypes, however, is not to suggest that the attitudes and lack of knowledge of buyers had no impact. By extending home ownership to lower income persons, the FHA was reaching many who had little knowledge of the responsibilities it entailed. Typical of the problems cited by many authors is an account, given to this writer by a local government official, of a new Section 235 owner who went to the bank demanding that they fix the plumbing, as if the bank were the landlord rather than simply the mortgagee. Because of such problems, the FHA was justly criticized for a total absence of counseling of prospective home buyers or even a sense of responsibility for blatantly fraudulent representation of housing conditions by sellers to buyers. As the HUD Audit Report stated, "FHA personnel advocated . . . the *caveat emptor* concept" (84). To its credit, HUD several times requested funding for counseling, but Congress refused until 1972, after the program had been tainted by scandal.

Yet, in spite of the importance of the attitudes of low income purchasers, the tendency of many accounts to blame the problems of Section 235 on lack of buyer awareness is a subtle form of "blaming the victim" (Ryan 1976) if it is not placed within the total social and economic context of these transactions. Some accounts describe buyers who were aware of the shortcomings of houses they were buying but felt compelled to take advantage of what seemed a once-in-a-lifetime opportunity for home ownership. Contrary to the abstract economic models of many market advocates, the poor are often unable, or perceive themselves as unable, to shop freely on the open market for the best product, even when given a cash subsidy to do so. Thus, they may take what they can get, even with full knowledge of its deficiencies.

Furthermore, the problems of many purchasers seemed to stem as much from financial overextension as from inadequate cultural background. The program not only subsidized interest but reduced the down payment to as low as two hundred dollars, and even this amount was often paid by the real estate speculator. Thus, the buyer had little financial stake in the property and was more inclined to equate home buying with renting. In addition, the computation of the percentage of income to be paid for housing did not take into account maintenance expenses for which the owner would be responsible, nor did the program allow for the accumulation of a maintenance reserve to deal with large, one-time expenditures. Finally, the problems encountered by many buyers were the direct result of poor construction and thus were so costly that few homeowners could have easily paid for them. A staff report of the House Committee on Banking and Currency comments:

> The staff did find cases where homeowners failed to take care of basic maintenance responsibilities, but in such cases the result was for the most part only poor housekeeping by middle class standards. However,

no homeowner can be expected to cope with poor construction, cracked foundations, improper wiring, and a general failure of contractors to meet local building and maintenance requirements. A welfare mother with four or five children may well have a house that is in less than spotless condition, but they cannot be blamed because there is only one electrical outlet in the entire house and no . . . heating vents in any of the bedrooms on the second floor. (U.S. Congress, House Banking and Currency Committee 1971b, 106)

It is much easier to recite the well-documented catalog of Section 235 abuses than it is to establish a picture of the success or failure of the program as whole (Berger 1969). Most critiques of the program were based on case studies of a few major cities. While understandable in light of the complexity of the data involved, it is nevertheless hard to gain from a few cases an accurate picture of the program's national impact. In cities such as Detroit and Philadelphia, the program generated massive corruption and had a clearly negative impact on some of the neighborhoods involved. Other cities operated the program in a manner beneficial to the low income people affected.

Because the response of many lower income families to problem units was abandonment of the property, the rates of delinquency and foreclosure of loans are reasonably good indicators of the national incidence of the problems described above. Figure 4-2 shows the cumulative number of units in default or in foreclosure for each year from 1969 to 1979 as a percentage of the cumulative number of Section 235 loans in effect for that year. This graph shows a significantly higher proportion of loans in default or foreclosure for the Section 235 program than for FHA home mortgage programs as a whole, particularly in the period from 1971–74.

Clearly, some of the program's difficulties resulted in a much higher casualty rate than was typical in suburban and/or middle income areas. However, these default rates do not suggest total crisis or collapse. Of all the loans made, over 90 percent *did not* end up in foreclosure, an indication that the majority of the program's clients were reasonably well served. As Downs points out, Section 235 was known from the beginning to be high risk, due to the marginal neighborhoods and low income families involved. Thus, high foreclosure rates should not have been surprising. He also notes that the cost of such defaults was vastly overestimated by Romney and others on the basis of the Detroit experience. He estimates a cost of $3,000 per HUD-acquired unit for handling and resale (Downs 1973, 65).

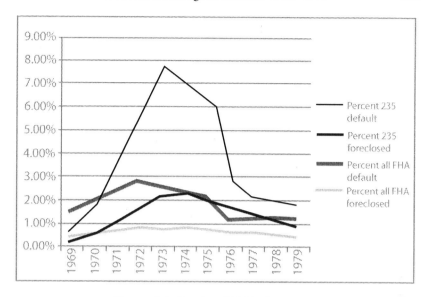

Figure 4-2 Section 235 Performance

Note: Percentages are computed based on the total number of loans in effect in any given year.

Source: Department of Housing and Urban Development Statistical Yearbook, 1979

Looking at the impact of defaults strictly in numerical terms does not, of course, take into account the social and psychological effects of abandoned dwellings and governmental callousness. Nevertheless, even if one is less sanguine about the programs' failures than Downs, a question remains as to whether the program was fundamentally flawed or could have been substantially improved through changes in design and administration. There is some evidence that such modifications could have had favorable results.

First, another look at Figure 4-2 shows an interesting pattern in the rate of foreclosures. The program began in 1969 and by 1970 showed a modest default rate of 2.0 percent and a foreclosure rate of 1.0 percent. This rate began to accelerate rapidly in 1971, and by 1973, nearly 9.0 percent of loans were in default, and about 2.0 percent were in foreclosure. However, after 1975, the rate declined rapidly, to percentages of default and foreclosure that were closer to the average for all FHA loans. To put it another way, most of the program's foreclosures occurred early in the life of the individual mortgages affected. This pattern suggests that a screening of applicants was taking place through early foreclosure that should have taken place before the sale, since most structural or financial problems that could cause default within one or two years of sale should have been apparent at the outset. Once this de facto screening of applicants occurred, the rate of foreclosure returned to a much more reasonable level. This provides more direct evidence that administrative laxity, not basic program design, was responsible for much of the abuse. Though the task of changing business-oriented FHA offices into social welfare agencies would have been difficult at best, top HUD officials made little or no effort to retrain local FHA staff. Instead, they sent down a message equivalent to "Damn the torpedoes, full speed ahead." Existing FHA appraisal and inspection procedures contained sufficient safeguards to prevent gross abuse, had the staff applied them properly (Downs 1973, 51).

Beyond this, other features likely to increase program success would not have been impractical. Extensive counseling would have minimized the role of buyer ignorance in default and abandonment, although counseling would, in many cases, have had to be backed up by financial help with maintenance costs. In addition, as McClaughry's excellent analysis suggests (McClaughry 1975), a conscious effort by the FHA to involve neighborhood groups in planning and executing the program might have curtailed blockbusting, shoddy construction, and abandonment. Such efforts would have slowed production, but they would have brought the program closer to meeting its objectives.

Evidence that such modifications could have led to success is provided by the testimony of Leonard Katz, a former FHA administrator from Milwaukee, Wisconsin. In Milwaukee, applicants were required to take three classes in home buying before being given a list of realtors to contact. For those program participants on welfare, an inspection of the home by the Welfare Department was required. If the purchaser lacked the two hundred dollars down payment, this was supplied by a grant from the St. Vincent de Paul Society. As a further safeguard, the buyer was required to personally inspect the property before purchasing, and at the closing, he or she was represented by a lawyer from the Legal Aid program. Finally, the buyer was given a class in home maintenance by the University of Wisconsin Extension Service (U.S. Congress, House Committee on Government Operations 1972a, 162–71).

This extensive interagency cooperation required an administrative effort that, in one sense, was above and beyond the call of duty for an FHA official. Yet, it yielded concrete benefits for the agency as well as for buyers, since the Wisconsin foreclosure rate, as of early 1972, was 0.09 percent, or nine

foreclosures out of 8,500 mortgages insured (McClaughry 1975, 25). Ironically, during much of this time Katz's office was being castigated by higher
HUD officials for low productivity, while the Detroit FHA Director, whose
office would later produce the worst scandal in the country, was being
praised for his "aggressive processing of inner-city homes" (McClaughry
1975, 126).

The fact that there was plenty of room for constructive change within
the existing program was frequently raised in testimony by interest groups
supporting it within the housing policy subsystem. The Mortgage Bankers
Association provided a report to the Senate Appropriations Committee
listing many individual success stories and lauding the virtues of good
counseling for prospective buyers (U.S. Congress, Senate Appropriations
Committee 1971). Other congressional supporters also emphasized the
program's positive aspects and took the Nixon administration to task
for most of its failures (see, for example, U.S. Congress, Joint Economic
Committee 1973).

This response by program supporters placed the Nixon team in a delicate
position. On the one hand, the program's failures could be used as grounds
for the disengagement to which Nixon was already inclined. Rather than
making a genuine effort at improvement, it could gradually distance itself
from the program, while claiming leadership in the search for alternatives.
On the other hand, since virtually all Section 235 production had occurred
under the Nixon administration, its spokesmen had to avoid criticizing the
program in such a way as to direct more blame on their own shortcomings.
Thus, the testimony of George Romney over the first Nixon term contains
negative appraisals of program performance, but it also attempts to play
down the extent of abuse and to emphasize the steps taken to improve it.
This ambiguous position was a further incentive for Nixon to couch later
attacks in terms of reform rather than retrenchment. He could thus cast
himself in the role of improving the tools of housing policy rather than
throwing them out after failing to use them properly.

The Section 236 Program

The Section 236 rental housing program, the 1968 Act's counterpart to the
Section 235 home ownership program, received less public attention, in
part because its concept was not as novel as home ownership for the poor.
Also, the program's failures were less massive and visible. Nevertheless, the
program's difficulties did receive attention, which contributed to the loss
of political support for housing assistance in general.

In 1972, the Surveys and Investigations Staff of the House Appropriations Committee investigated Section 236 and identified a number of
problems. These may be divided into three groups:

- Problems of site selection;
- Problems related to the motivations and qualifications of sponsors;
- Problems of excessive costs and rents.

It was noted earlier that policy makers sought to avoid lengthy local
conflicts over site selection by moving from public housing to private
sector subsidies. In Section 236, some conflict was avoided by the fact that
builders could obtain their sites through private real estate transactions.
However, the tendency to concentrate units in low income or central
city areas was not eliminated. Builders saw these areas as their natural
market and sought to locate new units accordingly. In addition, there
were delays and restrictions on construction in higher income areas
which could, under public pressure, be imposed by public bodies. Many
suburban areas had zoning laws that virtually excluded multifamily
development; and, even where this was not the case, middle-class citizens
saw Section 236 projects in the same negative light as public housing
(though tenant incomes were generally higher) and utilized all available
legal avenues to keep them out.

The concentration of Section 236 projects in central city and/or low
income areas had at least two negative consequences. First, projects sometimes inherited the negative reputation and the social problems of their
surroundings, much as public housing had done earlier. Second, some
cities experienced overbuilding of projects in relatively small geographic
areas. If this did not directly create vacancies in new units, it often was
the indirect cause of vacancies in older projects nearby, as eligible tenants
sought out the greater amenities available in newer developments.

HUD regulations mandated a careful check of marketability as part of
the processing of Section 236 proposals, but its staff often lacked detailed
knowledge of local markets. And, though the market will itself adjust
supply and demand in the long run, it does permit short-term problems of
oversupply. If such an oversupply problem pertains to fast food restaurants
on a commercial strip, then the failure of the last two built may not affect
anyone but the investors. But, in the already volatile conditions of urban
housing markets, the failure of a housing development may generate negative consequences for an entire neighborhood, as well as for the project's
owners and residents. Furthermore, when the entire program is under

close, and often hostile, scrutiny, anything that increases failure rates can cloud its future.

Section 236 sponsors could be of three types: cooperatives, nonprofit organizations, or limited dividend, profit-making corporations or partnerships. The last two types constituted the bulk of the developers. Nonprofit organizations accounted for roughly one-third of the starts. A typical pattern was that of one Midwestern city in which a consortium of churches was formed to sponsor a project. The intent of these organizations was altruistic—to improve housing opportunities for lower income persons. However, as shall be shown, these groups' lack of expertise in housing created serious problems with the units built under their sponsorship.

Limited dividend sponsors were, in contrast, investing in subsidized housing for profit. Their return on investment was formally limited to 6 percent, but there were numerous ways this return could be increased. The complex relationships that developed in this situation bear some discussion, since they affected not only Section 236 but also the Section 8 program which superseded it in 1974. The experience with the use of tax subsidies in Section 236 also influenced the design of the Low Income Housing Tax Credit, which was enacted in 1986. The following discussion is drawn from the aforementioned House staff report (U.S. Congress, House, Committee on Appropriations 1972); and from a Congressional Budget Office report on real estate tax shelters (U.S. Congress, Budget Office 1977).

As was also true for unsubsidized multifamily developments, the primary attraction of a Section 236 development to wealthy investors was not the return from rental income but the sheltering of other income from taxation. Mortgage interest and property taxes were deductible, and tax law permitted the use of accelerated depreciation on the value of the property. The investor could shelter current income by counting against it paper losses in the value of the rental units.

These losses were subject to recapture for tax purposes upon sale of the property, because the difference between the actual sales price and the depreciated value claimed in prior years was subject to capital gains tax. However, the capital gains tax rate was much lower than the income tax rate for persons in upper income brackets, and the difference between accelerated and straight line depreciation was not subject to recapture if the property was held for sixteen years or if the funds were reinvested in another subsidized housing project. In addition, the investor enjoyed the tax-free use of the sheltered income during the time the property was held. Finally, investors could, by putting up a certain percentage of the down payment, claim that portion of the total cost of the development as a basis for figuring accelerated depreciation. For example, if a development cost $1,000,000, with a down payment of $100,000, an investor could put up $20,000, or 20 percent of the down payment, and claim 20 percent of the depreciation losses for the entire $1,000,000 project.

These tax benefits led to a variety of ownership arrangements under the general rubric of *tax syndication.* The developer himself usually did not have enough income to take full advantage of the tax benefits, so he would "sell" them by setting up a limited partnership with other investors. The developer served as general partner, with responsibility for actual development process, while the liability of the others was limited to the money invested. Since subsidized housing was considered a high-risk investment, it would have been very hard to raise sufficient capital for Section 236 projects without the additional incentive of tax breaks. However, the complex ownership patterns had some disadvantages for the long-term viability of such projects.

To begin with, most of the tax benefits were realized in the first ten to fifteen years of the project's life. Therefore, investors were tempted to use the project for these benefits and then sell it, without concern for its long-term survival. (As shall be discussed in chapter 8, the loss of assisted units through such sales became a major policy concern in the 1980s.) In addition, most partners had little knowledge about management, and, since their financial risk was limited, they had little incentive to become effective watchdogs over the developer or its management agent. Finally, since income from rent was not their major source of return, investors had little incentive to pressure managers to run a tight ship in terms of maintenance or vacancy losses. Though investors had an interest in avoiding the early collapse of a project, their arm's length relationship discouraged early detection and prevention of such a collapse.

A third problem for Section 236 was that of cost and rent escalation. One source of cost escalation was the developers themselves, who had an obvious incentive to inflate construction costs in order to maximize subsidy payments. Higher profits could be inserted into development costs through land acquisition. HUD based its mortgage amount on its own appraisal, and the House Appropriations Committee staff found that the actual cost was often much lower than the appraised value. They could also inflate revenue through fees and overhead charged to the limited partnership for design, general contracting services, setting up the tax syndication, or for management.

HUD did attempt to regulate these costs, but a combination of lack of local data, general administrative laxity, and the shrewdness and determination of developers often made regulations ineffective. Paradoxically, where HUD did enforce regulations, the result was often construction delays, which themselves increased costs. The process was so complex that a group of developers arose who specialized in subsidized projects. They developed the patience and expertise to negotiate the maze of HUD approval and to turn it to their advantage. The effects of such practices were reflected in a HUD estimate that Section 236 projects cost 10–20 percent more than comparable conventional projects, not including "tax expenditures" (i.e., revenue lost due to tax breaks) (U.S. Department of Housing and Urban Development 1974a).

Problems also arose in connection with operating costs. Developers deliberately manipulated the situation by obtaining HUD agreement to low estimates of operating costs for the purpose of project approval, so that they could insert higher construction costs in the original rent levels. Once the project was in place, enforcement became more lax and increased rents to cover operating costs could be sought.

In addition to deliberate manipulation, the real costs of maintenance and utilities increased rapidly in the early 1970s. This was part of the larger trend in which the median income of tenant households increased more slowly than the costs of rental housing. This trend created serious problems for all rental housing, but its impact was especially severe on Section 236, which based its subsidy levels on costs rather than on a fixed percentage of tenant incomes. Steadily rising costs and rents reduced the potential market of eligible tenants, prevented the most needy families from benefiting from the program, and created an additional incentive for project managers to skimp on maintenance and services.

As in the case of Section 235, it is easier to recite a list of problems than to assess the total impact of these problems on the program. Again, the incidence of mortgage foreclosures is a useful indicator of the nationwide severity of program deficiencies. Figure 4-3 shows the cumulative total of units foreclosed or assigned in relation to the total number of units constructed. It reveals a low foreclosure rate in the first three years of the program, followed by a rapid increase between 1973 and 1976, when most units built under the program came into existence. In subsequent years, foreclosures moved upward only gradually, from about 56,000 in 1976 to just over 71,000 in 1979. As of that year, 16.4 percent of the units built had ended up in foreclosure.

The strong surge of early foreclosures probably reflects the initial problems of marketability and financing just discussed. These data conform to the pattern found in a 1978 General Accounting Office (GAO) report on the program, namely, that most foreclosures occurred early in the project's life, in some cases even before construction was completed. As in Section 235, this early surge of foreclosures suggests that nonviable projects were being screened out by foreclosure. This, in turn, points to the inadequacy of HUD's pre-approval screening process (U.S. GAO 1978).

In one sense, this problem is an inherent defect of such public-private programs. Evidence from many areas of public policy suggests the disadvantages in motivation and information control that regulating agencies suffer in relation to the industries they regulate, and their tendency to be co-opted by those they regulate. Also, as noted in the 1978 GAO study, the very fact that investors were protected by government insurance made them more inclined to let a troubled project default rather than working out long-term payment arrangements as was often done with private projects in financial difficulty. Yet, in another sense, this pattern of early foreclosure suggests that, even within the inherent limitations of the public oversight process, a substantial reduction might have been achieved by tightening administrative procedures. Moreover, even the foreclosures that did occur

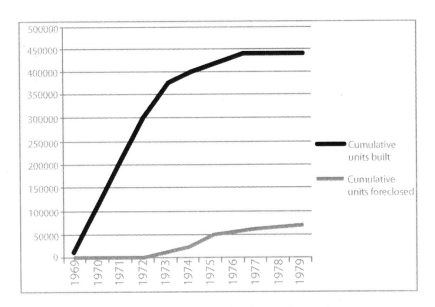

Figure 4-3 Section 236 Production and Foreclosures

Source: Department of Housing and Urban Development Statistical Yearbook, 1979

did not add up to the picture of escalating financial disaster portrayed in the media during the early years of the program.

Data on overall foreclosure rates also conceal some important differences in rates of failure between various types of Section 236 projects. Table 4.1, taken from a 1980 GAO analysis, breaks down foreclosures according to project type. It shows that projects undertaken by nonprofit sponsors had more than four times the rate of failure of those undertaken by for-profit groups. The GAO suggested this was principally due to two factors: (1) These groups' lack of experience in housing finance or management; and (2) undercapitalization of projects due to limited resources. Also notable is the fact that projects involving substantial rehabilitation had a much higher failure rate than new construction. This reflected the tenuous situation in which rehabilitation projects found themselves. Often located in declining neighborhoods, their marketability depended on improvements in the entire area, an uncertain prospect over which sponsors had little control. Also, the fact that rehabilitated units often cost nearly as much as new ones but could not command the same rents left them with a much narrower financial margin.

When these two problem categories are removed from the total, the failure rate for newly constructed Section 236 projects drops to just over 7 percent. According to the GAO, this was actually 2 percent less than the rates of the FHA Section 207 market interest rate program (for middle income rental units) for a similar period and less than the 15 percent rate experienced by the Section 221(d)(3) program. It was still substantially higher than that for privately insured multifamily developments (just over 1 percent). However, considering that the Section 236 program was designed to fund developments too risky for normal private sector investment, this higher rate should not have been surprising. In sum, had more

Table 4.1 Section 236 Cumulative Assignment and Foreclosure Rates: 1977

Type of sponsor	New Construction		Substantial Rehabilitation	
	Family	Elderly	Family	Elderly
Limited dividend (for profit)	7.1%	1.7%	31.3%	13.6%
Nonprofit	32.6%	5.9%	65.1%	12.5%

Source: U.S. General Accounting Office, Evaluation of alternatives for financing low and moderate income rental housing. PAD 80-30, 1980.

caution been taken with nonprofit sponsors and with rehabilitation, and had the tighter administrative controls mentioned above been implemented, Section 236 could have been remarkably successful in terms of the long-term financial viability of its projects.

There were, nevertheless, other questions raised about this program not directly related to its numerical rate of failure. The Section 235 program, to the extent that it was successful, conferred the substantial financial and psychological benefits of home ownership on low income persons, in addition to the benefits associated with occupying a "decent, safe and sanitary" dwelling. In this respect it had a distinct advantage over any other subsidy program.

In contrast, the Section 236 program was an alternative way to provide assisted rental housing that could be fairly compared to earlier methods of achieving the same goal. One point of comparison was vertical equity. Both liberals and conservatives criticized the program for not meeting the needs of the lowest income tenants. This criticism was later confirmed by the 1978 GAO report, which found the 1975 median income of Section 236 tenants to be $5,634, in contrast to the national median income of $11,400 and the public housing tenants' median income of $3,531. However, the group in question clearly was not affluent and had legitimate housing needs that the private market could not meet. And, given the questions raised earlier about the image and political support problems of a governmental housing effort strictly for the poorest of the poor, one may legitimately ask whether vertical equity should be so strictly followed that moderate income persons must wait in line for federal subsidies until the housing needs of *all* of the very poor have been served.

The other question raised about Section 236 was the cost of extensively subsidizing *new* construction of housing for lower income persons by the private sector. The program's attractiveness to private builders certainly contributed to its achievement, in a very short time, of a higher level of production than any other such program. Yet, in order to appeal to profit-oriented firms, it had to funnel a substantial amount of public dollars into the pockets of wealthy investors. This proved to be a major weakness of the program in the eyes of both conservatives, concerned with the size of public expenditures, and liberals concerned with utilizing funds efficiently to serve the poor. As shall be shown in chapter 5, it led to increased advocacy of programs relying on existing housing. Yet, the fact that new construction programs could add to the supply of low-cost housing and the fact that they engendered a larger constituency for subsidized housing than did publicly owned housing continued to make them appealing.

Therefore, the issue of new construction versus the use of existing units would recur throughout the 1970s and 1980s.

While the Section 235 and 236 programs were reaching new heights of production and also running into serious problems, the public housing program also enjoyed an unprecedented construction boom, as is shown in Figure 4-1. However, this boom, too, coexisted with the intensification of its earlier problems. These continuing difficulties provided a rationale for the Nixon administration's inclusion of public housing in its blanket attack on housing assistance programs. The two most significant public housing problems were those of financial management and site selection.

Since the federal subsidy to public housing covered only construction financing, the rapidly rising operating costs encountered by local public housing authorities in the 1960s had to be paid out of rents. This gave them the choice of decreasing maintenance and tenant services, increasing rents, or both. Reductions in maintenance accelerated physical deterioration. Rent increases put larger burdens on low income persons and stimulated rent strikes or other tenant protests in several cities.

Senator Edward Brooke, a liberal Republican and the first African American elected to the Senate in the twentieth century, became deeply concerned with the problems of public housing, and he spearheaded efforts to obtain federal operating subsidies. At the same time, he wished to limit the rent burden local authorities could impose. Therefore, he attached to the Housing Act of 1969 an amendment that tied increasing operating subsidies to an upper limit on rents of 25 percent of tenant income.

The passage of the Brooke Amendment was followed by a protracted struggle between HUD, Congress, and affected groups over how the new restrictions and subsidies were to be applied. According to one account, HUD officials tended to blame local administrators for their projects' financial problems, and thus were concerned that operating subsidies not encourage bad local management. Therefore, they put the most restrictive interpretation possible on congressional intent with regard to distribution of operating subsidies (Mandelker and Montgomery 1973). In the year following the Brooke Amendment, HUD spent only $33 million out of an appropriation of $75 million (Mitchell 1974, 446).

Furthermore, according to Meehan, the entire process was carried out without considering the vast accumulation of deferred maintenance problems. Congress eventually enacted a modernization program to finance correction of such problems, but it again was underfunded and did not allow localities flexibility in identifying and correcting their most serious physical deficiencies. This tendency to ignore accumulated problems, as well as a reluctance to respond to immediate problems was, according to Meehan, symptomatic of HUD's failure to answer the most fundamental question of all, namely, how much does it really cost to provide minimum adequate housing services with a reasonable degree of efficiency (Meehan 1979)?

The bottom line for most local authorities was that new funding was insufficient to cover revenue losses caused by the Brooke Amendment, especially considering inflation. The program thus began the 1970s with more new construction than ever, but with many of its older units crumbling. Symbolic of this deterioration was the demolition (beginning in 1972) of St. Louis' vast Pruitt-Igoe project, which had been rendered uninhabitable by extreme physical deterioration. Pictures of the dynamiting of those buildings (constructed a mere fifteen years earlier) made the front pages of newspapers across the country and made an indelible impression on many who knew little else about the program. The media treated Pruitt-Igoe as a symbol of the alleged total failure of the program, though thousands of other public housing units across the country continued to provide decent housing to their tenants. This new symbol added momentum to the push for new approaches to housing subsidies, which Nixon was soon to initiate.

Problems related to site selection also continued to plague public housing in the early 1970s, and the issue that increasingly dominated this controversy was the racial composition of public housing projects. In the late 1960s, the severe racial segregation of public housing became increasingly unacceptable to groups of African Americans and liberal whites striving for racial equality. As the FHA had been attacked for perpetuating segregation, so, too, public housing was criticized for creating "vertical ghettos."

As mentioned earlier, Chicago had one of the most blatant policies of public housing segregation in the country in the 1950s and early 1960s. Each city council member had de facto veto power over the location of public housing in his/her ward, with the result that virtually all units were in predominately African American areas (Lazin 1976; Meyerson and Banfield 1955). It was not surprising, therefore, that a court challenge to the Chicago program was mounted by civil rights activists in the late 1960s. This challenge, often referred to as the *Gautreaux case* (though it was actually a series of cases), resulted in a federal court order charging the Chicago Housing Authority and the city council with racially motivated site selection practices. The court also set forth several steps to be taken to reverse this pattern (Mandelker et al. 1981).

Court challenges in other cities were directed at the exclusion of public housing and other subsidized development by white, suburban communities. Such challenges were successful when, as in Lackawanna, Pennsylvania, and Black Jack, Missouri, a clear intent to discriminate through zoning and other policies could be shown. Where this could not be shown, as in the *James v. Valtierra* case, policies that had the indirect effect of excluding low income (African American) housing were upheld. In another case, *Shannon v. HUD*, the U.S. Court of Appeals ruled that HUD had to take into account the impact of a project on the racial and economic composition of the neighborhood it was to be built in and that HUD should not cause further segregation by its site selection policies (Mandelker et al. 1981, 581–90). Partly as a result of these court cases, Nixon, in 1971, ordered all federal housing agencies to actively promote equal housing opportunities, and HUD issued a series of regulations designed to make racial deconcentration an important factor in site selection.

As the long history of civil rights legislation and litigation has shown, issuing court orders and federal policy guidelines banning segregation is relatively easy, while enforcing them vigorously is much harder, and actually obtaining integration as a result of enforcement is harder still. This is shown by the events following the initial *Gautreaux* decision. Mayor Richard Daley Sr. and the Chicago City Council responded to the decision with a policy of massive resistance reminiscent of Southern segregationists. The council refused again and again to approve public housing sites in white areas which were offered by the Chicago Housing Authority and HUD in an effort to comply with the *Gautreaux* ruling. The result was a virtual halt in public housing development for several years until a further ruling was obtained which suspended the Illinois state law requiring local government approval for public housing sites and allowed the Chicago Housing Authority to proceed on its own.

As for HUD regulations, there was virtually no weapon HUD could wield over local communities strong enough to overcome determined opposition to racial or economic integration. Many were willing to forgo participation in federal programs if this was to be the price. In some instances, HUD softened the regulations so as to minimize their impact. For example, the site selection criteria established by HUD as a result of the *Shannon* decision did not forbid low income housing in minority areas but required that comparable units be available to minorities in white areas (Mandelker et al. 1981). This turned enforcement into a numbers game wherein the hypothetical possibility of an African American moving into a white apartment complex was substituted for the actual development of new units in a nonminority area. But even in cases where pressure from HUD or the courts forced the location of new housing in middle income, white areas, the current residents often voted with their feet, thereby tipping the surrounding area into majority black status (Lazin 1976).

The strength of white resistance to residential integration through federal housing programs, plus the fact that fears of racial integration seemed to increase the overall level of public and elite hostility to government housing efforts had long ago led many within the African American community and its white allies to question the use of housing integration as the major strategy for improving black housing conditions. The costs of residential segregation to African Americans are considerable (Massey and Denton 1993), yet the brick wall of white resistance led many to believe that housing improvement within African American neighborhoods was the best route to follow. These questions continued to arise throughout the 1970s. When, for example, a federal court in one of the *Gautreaux* cases approved the suspension of funds to Chicago's Model Cities program as a way to force the city council to approve new public housing sites, many African Americans protested that the integrationist strategy followed by Dorothy Gautreaux and her ACLU allies was actually hurting more than helping their community (Lazin 1976). And although the black power and black separatist movements played a key role in pushing an internal development strategy for black communities, they were not alone in the belief that segregated housing was better than no housing.

In the broader context of the development of federal housing programs, the constant struggle over the use of public housing to achieve racial integration can be seen as one more source of division among liberal supporters. Basic liberal values permit plausible arguments for housing integration as a primary or as a secondary strategy depending upon one's view of the best way to serve the long-term interests of African Americans and other minorities (Hartman and Squires 2010). Given the multiple negative impacts of segregation on the life chances of people of color, the integrationist argument is the most powerful in the long run, but in the short run, the priority of getting people of color in decent housing regardless of location may take precedence. Meanwhile, like other such divisions, it tended to strengthen conservative efforts to undermine the momentum of such programs and to keep them small and socially marginal. Though many factors set the stage for the Nixon administration's attempt at retrenchment, the continued inability of public housing to resolve its basic dilemmas was certainly an important influence.

Late in 1972, rumors began to circulate within HUD that Nixon was contemplating a moratorium on housing program activity. These rumors were taken so seriously that HUD Area Offices began to process Section 235 and 236 applications frantically, with the result that, as Nixon's new HUD secretary, James Lynn, was later to comment ruefully, "more approvals . . . [were given] in the three week period from December 15, 1972 to January 8, 1973 than in the entire fiscal year up to that time" (*CQ Almanac* 1973b, 429). These fears proved well founded. Choosing to take the battle into the camp of the "enemy," the outgoing HUD secretary, George Romney, announced the freeze in a January 8 speech to the Houston convention of the National Association of Home Builders. As outlined by Romney, the freeze included:

- A moratorium on all new commitments for subsidized housing programs, including Section 235 and Section 236;
- A hold on new commitments for water and sewer grants, open space land programs and public facilities loans until Congress establishe[d] a program of community development special revenue sharing of which these programs would become a part;
- A freeze beginning July 1 on all new commitments for urban renewal and Model Cities funding, also a part of the administration's community development revenue sharing plan;
- A freeze on new commitments for similar, smaller Farmer's Home Administration programs in the Agriculture Department. (*CQ Weekly Report* 1973a, 40)

So far, this chapter has described the major problems in existing housing programs that made them vulnerable to such a move and has outlined the general policy orientations of the Nixon administration that led them to contemplate it. However, to convey the full political context of the moratorium, it is necessary to treat several other developments which played a direct role in bringing it about.

First, the importance of Nixon's massive reelection victory must be emphasized. These were heady days, when it appeared that Nixon's approach had been endorsed by all segments of American society. True, Congress remained in Democratic hands, but in the months before the Watergate scandal began to poison all aspects of Nixon's political life, it seemed that he had gained new strength. Coupled with the conservative shift within the Nixon administration on domestic issues (symbolized, in the housing field, by George Romney's departure and his replacement by

James Lynn) this new mandate could be expected to stimulate bold new moves.

Second, the moratorium resulted from the impact on housing policy of another national policy debate—the debate over the proper role of federal, state, and local governments in administering domestic programs. Early in his first term, Nixon set forth what he called the "New Federalism." This involved two concepts. One was consolidation and simplification of the numerous federal categorical grant programs initiated during prior Democratic administrations. The other related concept was devolution of control over program administration from the national level to states and localities. As noted in chapter 2, advocacy of greater local control is a common stance among conservatives. However, the New Federalism had also struck a responsive chord among liberal local officials as well, because they saw the categorical grant-in-aid system as eroding their political and administrative control. These issues will be discussed more thoroughly in chapter 6.

Many of Nixon's New Federalism proposals were eventually enacted. In the short run, however, they encountered rough sledding in Congress, because congressional allies of many categorical programs feared loss of funds and loss of commitment to solving specific problems. The struggle between Nixon and Congress over the proposed Housing and Urban Development Act of 1972 occupied most of 1972. The proposal included both the consolidation of community development programs, such as urban renewal, into a block grant and the reorganization and consolidation of fifty existing federal housing programs. After passing the Senate in March 1972, this bill was buried by the House Rules committee in September (*CQ Weekly Report* 1972). Once the election was over, Nixon had an incentive to try dramatic action which he hoped would break the deadlock.

A third major issue affecting the moratorium was the long struggle between Nixon and Congress over executive impoundment of funds appropriated by the legislative branch. Nixon had tried impoundment on numerous occasions, succeeding in some cases, but having several others struck down by the judiciary (Mitchell 1974). The moratorium was, in effect, an impoundment of funds, but it was justified on the grounds that the programs as constituted could not be administered properly. Since these programs had serious and well-publicized problems, Nixon's advisors felt he could make this action stick both in the political arena and in court. As it turned out, they were right on both counts. In his January 8 speech, Romney laid out the elements of the administration's rationale for the moratorium. He cited an "urgent need for a broad and extensive evaluation of the entire Rube Goldberg structure of our housing and community development statues and regulations." He went on to say that:

> While the Section 235 and 236 programs appear to be working well in many parts of the country . . . they have too frequently been abused and made the vehicle of inordinate profits gained through shoddy construction, poor site location, and questionable financial arrangements. (*CQ Weekly* Report 1973d, 140)

With regard to public housing, he stated that:

> [S]ome very fundamental mistakes have been made. . . . The public housing units began to fill up with welfare families and many who exhibited antisocial behavior. . . . Gradually, criminal elements, drug addicts, and other problem elements came to dominate the environment of these units. (*CQ Weekly* Report 1973d, 140)

Two months later. Nixon reiterated these themes. He announced that a team of researchers had been assembled within HUD to conduct a thorough study of all housing programs and to produce a report by the fall of 1973, under the leadership of Michael H. Moskow, HUD Assistant Secretary for Policy Development and Research. The new HUD secretary, James Lynn, was also heavily involved in the study (Phillips 1973a, 1256–57).

Meanwhile, housing proponents in Congress reacted with dismay to the moratorium. Both pro-housing Democrats, such as Senator William Proxmire, and pro-housing Republicans, such as Senators Charles Percy and Edward Brooke, were very critical. In addition, a national coalition of forty-nine organizations, including the NAHB, the National League of Cities, the National Education Association, AFL-CIO, and the Mortgage Bankers Association, called on Congress to delay confirmation of Lynn and other Nixon appointees until the freeze was lifted.

Yet, when it came to action, Congress could not muster sufficient unity to take on the freeze directly. In May 1973, the House passed a resolution authorizing funds for housing and urban development programs. When it reached the Senate, Proxmire attached an amendment ordering the president to end the freeze. The amended resolution passed the Senate and was accepted by House conferees, but with a veto of the entire bill certain, the full House voted to recommit the conference report, thereby forcing the passage of a new resolution without the anti-moratorium provision. Other attempts to cancel the freeze during the eighteen months it was in effect also failed. Actions like the moratorium ultimately intensified resentment against Nixon for attempting to create, in the then current phrase, an "imperial presidency." This resentment helped fuel reactions to Watergate. In the short run, however, it appeared to be a decisive and highly successful attempt to alter the course of housing and community development policy in a conservative direction, and it was given judicial support by a favorable ruling in *Pennsylvania v. Lynn*. Meanwhile, he used the hiatus in housing activity he had created to promote an alternative approach to the provision of housing subsidies to lower income persons. His proposals, and their impact on housing policy, will be discussed in chapter 5.

Chapter Summary and Conclusion

From the perspective of 2012, the struggles to create effective housing programs in the 1960s and 1970s may, at first glance, appear to be primarily of historical interest. However, the issues and dilemmas that still affect current housing programs were clearly on display forty-plus years ago. The list includes: site selection, income criteria, design features, cost effectiveness, management issues, and the proper role of the private sector. Underlying all of these specific issues is the failure of the United States to clearly and effectively address the fundamental question raised in the title of a recent book on housing policy, "Where are poor people to live?" (Bennett, Smith, and Wright 2006). For many middle-class and upper-middle-class citizens, their first answer is "NIMBY!" but beyond that they have little concern for the quality of life of the poor and are very inclined to "blame the victim" for all the problems of housing assistance programs. The efforts of people who do care are bedeviled by this hostility and indifference, and yet they continue to struggle to improve the housing conditions of the poor. The next phase of this struggle occurred in the late 1970s and early 1980s, with the Housing and Community Development Act of 1974 providing the legislative framework. This will be the subject of chapter 5.

CHAPTER 5

New Directions in Housing Assistance: 1973–1980

In September 1973, HUD completed its report on housing programs and strategies. Under the title *Housing in the Seventies*, it included what had been promised, a comprehensive review of federal involvement in housing, particularly housing for the poor. Though couched in the technical language of policy analysis, it was clearly not an objective program assessment but a political document designed to achieve a certain end. One point it attempted to drive home was the alleged failure of previous housing subsidy programs, in order to legitimize Nixon's suspension of these programs. To support this point, virtually all the shortcomings mentioned in chapter 4 were emphasized. However, the report was also designed to achieve a broader goal: the justification of a new approach to addressing the housing problems of the poor. This involved much greater reliance on direct cash subsidies to housing consumers than previous programs. Therefore, in order to fully understand the direction taken by this report, it is necessary to examine the concept of housing allowances and the genesis of this idea within the Nixon administration.

The term *housing allowance* encompasses a range of possibilities. In its simplest form, a housing allowance is a cash grant to a low income household (usually based on a percentage of income deemed appropriate by policy makers for a household to spend on housing), which enables them to rent or purchase a unit of better quality than they could afford unassisted. This approach presupposes that the main reason why the poor occupy substandard units is insufficient income to obtain standard housing and that a cash grant will enable them to shop in the private market for a unit that meets their needs. Given the increase in effective demand generated by these grants, the market will respond with an adequate supply. Thus, even though "housing allowance" connotes earmarking the grant for housing purposes, the assumptions behind this approach are very similar to those underlying broader proposals of unconstrained cash grants to the poor, such as the negative income tax, that had been put forward in the late 1960s and early 1970s.

Because of a number of concerns to be discussed later, not all proponents of the housing allowance concept favored it in its pure form. Most advocated constraints or supplements to the basic cash grant. The most widely accepted constraint involved supervision of the landlord-tenant relationship by a public agency, in the form of an inspection of the unit to ensure its standard condition and varying degrees of participation in the lease agreement. The principal supplement was the linkage of the cash grant to a program of new construction to ensure that the supply of low income housing would increase along with the demand.

The housing allowance approach was proposed at various times during the first thirty-five years of federal housing efforts, but it was kept on the back burner for the reasons discussed in chapter 4. Nevertheless, this approach has always had certain features making it attractive to both liberals and conservatives. These encouraged this alternative to surface in the 1970s, after other approaches had acquired some tarnish. Housing allowances involve less active interference in the production of housing by the private market than any other type of public subsidy, because the government's role is largely one of making lower income people more effective consumers. Little or no direct government production or subsidy of production is involved. This made it particularly appealing to conservatives who wished to keep government activism on behalf of the poor at a minimum, as suggested in the discussion of Milton Friedman's position in chapter 2.

The authors of *Housing in the Seventies* transformed Friedman's argument into a seemingly more precise formulation, which they used to demonstrate the greater efficiency of cash housing grants. Utilizing survey data from public housing tenants, they attached a dollar value to the amount of housing tenants said they would consume if they were given cash, and they established a ratio between this amount and the actual cost of each of the in-kind subsidies. They referred to this ratio as "Transfer Efficiency." The cash value of the subsidy invariably amounted to less than its actual costs, thus allowing the authors to discount the overall efficiency of existing programs by ratios of less than one (U.S. Department of Housing and Urban Development 1974a, 90–91). This result is not surprising, since most consumers prefer a free to a constrained choice and since low income consumers may have low expectations as to the quality of housing they can consume. It is questionable, however, whether the precision of a hypothetical dollar figure derived from this expression of preference should have been equated to the actual dollar costs of in-kind subsidies and used as a standard of comparison. In addition, this formulation tended to play down the positive externalities generated for the neighborhood and the community by improved housing conditions.

While the appeal of housing allowances to those holding the traditional conservative belief in minimum government is obvious, one might question their compatibility with the operating ideology of many conservative political actors. Since this group has traditionally supported programs that funnel government aid to the activities of market winners, it might have been expected that the housing subsystem would have found a sympathetic audience for its emphasis on producer subsidies. To a significant degree, such subsidies were a logical extension of the government regulation and support already given to the housing industry as a whole. The extra expenditures resulting from high production costs and tax breaks could have been justified as stimulants to private investment and employment in the construction trades.

The lack of appeal of these programs to conservatives, and their subsequent attraction to housing allowances, derived, in large part, from the inability of the backers of these subsidies to disassociate them from the negative connotations attached to the ultimate beneficiaries of their programs—the poor. Other programs that subsidize private sector activities usually serve some overall goal of economic growth or national security which is widely shared by economic and political elites. The subsidy serves a particular firm or industry, but it is also compatible with an image of shared well-being in which the common interests of economic elites are identified with the public interest. In the case of housing subsidies, the funds aided certain segments of the housing industry, but the product ended up in the hands of a group viewed by most conservatives as undeserving. Therefore, to the extent that projects failed financially or deteriorated physically, the money flowing into them came to be seen as waste even though it did provide a boost to the construction industry.

In addition, housing programs based on producer subsidies violated another key conservative norm—the desire to keep low income housing programs confined to a relatively small number of people who can be labeled as truly destitute. The authors of *Housing in the Seventies* devoted much attention to the issues of horizontal and vertical equity, replaying arguments raised about moderate income housing in the early 1960s. Throughout the report they lamented that: (1) current programs served only a small segment of the eligible population; and (2) persons of moderate income were being served while some lower income people were not. Although critics of the report pointed out that it exaggerated the proportion of the low income population not served (U.S. Congress, Senate Committee on Banking and Urban Affairs 1974), these basic characterizations of the programs were correct. However, at least two responses could have been made to this lack of equity. One was to recommend expansion of both low and moderate income programs until the legitimate needs of both groups were met. Clearly, the authors of the report were not willing to accept the extensive reallocation of resources to housing from other purposes necessary to eliminate inequity in this fashion, since the report also criticized existing programs for their aggregate costs.

They recommended, instead, that existing resources be concentrated on the lowest income segment of the population and that these resources be spread out to serve as many of this group as possible. The authors clearly expected that housing allowances would do this. Since their data suggested that families wanted to spend less on housing than they were compelled to spend as a result of production subsidies, the authors concluded that housing could be provided at a smaller per unit cost if the poor were allowed to shop. Also, a larger proportion of existing housing could be used, rather than directing subsidies at relatively more expensive new construction. In sum, the report argued for the housing allowance as a means of avoiding a drastic increase in the share of the pie going to low income housing while redistributing it more broadly among those with housing needs.

The appeal of the housing allowance concept was not, of course, limited to conservatives. The typical liberal stance had been to push for expansion of the government's role in this area, but many liberals began, in the 1970s, to look more favorably on housing allowances. Both pragmatic political considerations and considerations of program effectiveness contributed to this shift. On the pragmatic side, the supplementation of public housing with federally assisted private sector projects, while it made production somewhat less subject to political blockage at various levels of government, did not succeed in improving the overall level of political support for such programs as much as had been hoped. True, it had made political allies out of a key segment of the housing industry, but, for the reasons cited above, this did not guarantee a more stable political niche. In addition, local community opposition, and the resultant concentration of projects in marginal or poor areas, was often as intense for Section 236 projects as for public housing. Regardless of private ownership and regardless of occupancy by a slightly higher income group than public housing, such projects were still seen by middle income neighborhoods as instruments of socioeconomic and/or racial integration. Finally, the argument that housing allowances would reduce per unit subsidy costs had an appeal to liberals as well as conservatives, in that it promised a larger impact from a limited amount of dollars.

Liberal views of program impact and effectiveness may be grouped around three issues: (1) the changing needs of low income households; (2) the benefits of de-concentrating the poor; and (3) the philosophical issue of empowerment. With regard to the first issue, a broad spectrum of housing policy analysts in the 1970s believed that the overall physical condition of the housing stock had improved greatly, and there was considerable evidence from the U.S. Census to support this. Therefore, they believed that the central housing problem for low income households was no longer one of residence in substandard dwellings but one of paying too large a percentage of their income for standard dwellings. A logical conclusion was that housing subsidies should shift their emphasis from production to direct support for the housing costs of the poor. Thus, the notion of housing allowances had more appeal than in the 1960s, when most studies had stressed the shortage of standard housing for the poor.

With regard to the second issue, liberal concern with the ghettoization and stigmatization of the poor through their concentration in large housing projects increased rather than decreased during the 1970s. Public housing was seen by many liberals as well as conservatives as going from bad to worse, in spite of efforts to save it financially and administratively. Nixon struck a responsive chord when he blamed this trend on the concentration of an ever-lower income segment of the population in these units. The appeal of the "culture of poverty" concept was still strong, and the multiple social problems created by the concentration of the poor in public housing were seen as manifesting this culture in its most pathological form. Moreover, some Section 236 developments spawned similar problems.

As a result, the concept of *de-concentrating* the poor through scattered-site, small-scale developments became increasingly popular among housing reformers in the early 1970s. It was seen as a way to provide the poor with decent housing while avoiding negative side effects. In the prevailing view, the poor could blend into a middle-class neighborhood in small numbers without arousing too much hostility and could learn from their middle-class neighbors the virtues of responsible community behavior. They would also enjoy the improved public services which the political clout of their middle-class neighbors could command.

The fact that the housing allowance concept went one step beyond the de-concentration of public housing by eliminating or reducing production subsidies was seen as a further enhancement of the assimilation process. Middle income neighborhoods had proved quite capable of detecting and resisting even small, scattered site developments, and such developments raised fears of infiltration similar to those voiced in connection with rent supplements a few years earlier. Also, the juxtaposition of new, government-built housing for the poor with unsubsidized working-class or middle-class dwellings often enhanced the sense of inequity felt by the units' neighbors. Such problems were eventually to occur with housing allowances as well, but at the time it was believed that the low visibility of housing allowances would substantially reduce the friction normally caused by low income housing.

With regard to the third issue, the idea of housing allowances had a certain congruence with a philosophical theme in liberal thinking that gained importance during the 1970s—the concern for *empowerment* of the poor (Beer 1978). Whereas the New Deal legacy had been one of government interventions on behalf of the poor, interventions engineered by white, middle-class professionals, the 1960s saw attacks on these interventionist institutions themselves by political organizations representing the poor (Piven and Cloward 1971). Stimulated in part by the community action rhetoric of the War on Poverty and by the direct action strategies of the civil rights movement, many leaders in disadvantaged communities began to view the bureaucracies that handed out social welfare benefits as instruments of social control designed to keep poor clients "in their place" while at the same time addressing their material needs. They demanded, and to a limited extent received, representation in institutions making and implementing social welfare policies. On the ideological level, the concepts of *empowerment* and *de-bureaucratization* began to appear in liberal writings, which had, prior to this time, tended to emphasize more paternalistic values of social engineering.

The relationship between empowerment and housing allowances is complex. When the idea was first proposed, some writers on the Left denounced it as a means of throwing the poor back onto the tender mercies of the private landlord. Chester Hartman suggested in a 1974 article that housing allowances were a "hoax." By increasing the effective demand for housing in the restricted market available to lower income persons, such allowances would, he argued, enable landlords to charge higher rents for existing units without substantially improving them and would give them more leverage in negotiating and enforcing lease provisions. Such a change would, therefore, restrict the ability of the poor to control their housing conditions. In contrast, keeping low income housing a visible public program would ultimately give the poor more leverage over its administration, especially as advisory and participatory mechanisms continued to evolve (Hartman and Keating 1974).

Nevertheless, the concept of allowing the poor to choose their own housing was very compatible with the overall liberal concern with empowerment, especially as data on increased supplies of standard housing began to reduce fears of a low income market crunch. There was also increasing distrust of the ability of public officials to make intelligent decisions for the poor. Conservatives had always questioned the competence of the public sector and now some in the liberal camp began to share that distrust.

Housing in the Seventies was not the first place where housing allowances emerged into serious consideration as a policy option. As early as 1968, the Kaiser Committee appointed by President Johnson had recommended an experimental program of housing allowances. According to Raymond Struyk's account, Harold Finger and Malcolm Peabody, members of Nixon's HUD team appointed shortly after the Kaiser report was released, picked up this recommendation and pushed it within the administration. In proposing the legislation that was to become the Housing Act of 1970, Nixon included research funds intended to cover such a study. An amendment by Senator Edward Brooke specifically mandated such an experiment, and Brooke's proposal was included in the final bill (Struyk and Bendick 1981).

This legislation marked the beginning of the Experimental Housing Allowance Program (EHAP), one of the longest, most complex, and most expensive experimental programs ever launched by the federal government. EHAP was really three different experiments, set up in different communities throughout the United States to test various aspects of the housing allowance concept. As summarized by Struyk, these were:

1. The Demand Experiment, in which the responses of low income clients to alternative payment formulas, levels of payments, and minimum housing standards were measured in terms of participation levels, mobility, and level of housing consumption;
2. The Supply Experiment, in which the response of housing markets in two communities to rapid demand increases due to large-scale participation in the program, were tested;
3. The Administrative Agency Experiment, in which the impact of various administrative structures and various levels of client services was tested in a number of locations. (Struyk and Bendick 1981, 8)

This might seem a logical point at which to summarize the findings of these complex experiments. However, in terms of the history of Nixon's policy initiatives, these findings are not immediately relevant, since EHAP was barely underway in 1973 when the moratorium was declared and *Housing in the Seventies* was written. Nixon did not wait for the results of EHAP before launching his policy initiative, and the immediate impact of the EHAP study stemmed more from the simple fact that it was being done. The existence of such a large and systematic experimental program gave housing allowances a respectability that they might not otherwise have had. Moreover, Nixon first touted the housing proposal that was to become Section 8 as a further experiment, thus linking it to EHAP.

One other element of the total environment in which Nixon's proposals were spawned—the Section 23 program—needs attention before proceeding with a full discussion of these proposals and their results. As mentioned in chapter 4, Section 23 was instituted without fanfare in 1961, as a means for local public housing authorities to gain additional units without stimulating hostile community reactions. Because of the commitment of the Kennedy, Johnson, and early Nixon administrations to production subsidies, the program remained small throughout its first twelve years. However, when housing allowances were being considered, Nixon's team looked with new interest on this program. Section 23 was not a pure housing allowance program, since the local housing authority, not the tenant, secured and leased the unit. Yet, it did involve cash payments to private landlords, and Nixon asserted in this September 1973 housing message that the program "can be administered in a way which carries out some of the principles of direct cash assistance" (*CQ Weekly Report* 1973b, 2523). Consequently, he lifted the freeze on this program and authorized HUD to process applications for an additional two hundred thousand units. He and his advisors saw it as a "tried and true" program which lent further credibility to their new proposals.

Part II—The Section 8 Programs

The Creation of Section 8

Although Nixon endorsed the housing allowance concept in September 1973, he also stated his intention to continue suspension of all programs except Section 23 while studying the problem further (*CQ Weekly Reports* 1973b). However, in late 1973 and early 1974, he came under increasing pressure to do something about housing. The president of the NAHB, George Martin, complained bitterly in Senate testimony that "[u]nder. . . .

[Nixon's] plan, all that low and moderate-income groups have to console them is the hope that 2 or 3 years in the future some type of housing allowance may be instituted on a gradual basis to help them obtain decent housing" (*CQ Weekly Report* 1973c, 2969). This complaint fell on sympathetic ears in Congress. By late 1973, Watergate revelations were eroding Nixon's strength. And, though Senator William Proxmire lamented that (presumably due to Watergate) "I just don't know how you can get the attention of the country on this," the Watergate pressure benefited housing proponents by gradually softening Nixon's stand, as he sought to earn congressional good will in any way possible.

Therefore, the Nixon administration supported an omnibus housing and community development bill, which made its way through Congress during the first half of 1974. This bill contained the major provisions of Nixon's earlier proposal, the Better Communities Act, which consolidated various community development programs into a block grant (to be discussed in chapter 7). It also proposed to rapidly phase out Sections 235 and 236, replacing them with an expanded version of the Section 23 program.

The House passed a bill on June 20, 1974, which closely resembled Nixon's proposal (*CQ Weekly Reports* 1974b). However, the Senate version, passed earlier, differed substantially. Influenced by the housing lobby headed by the NAHB, the Senate voted to reinstate the Section 235 and 236 programs with $500 million in new funds. The Banking Committee chair, Senator John Sparkman (D, Ala.), asserted that "much of the highly publicized criticism leveled at the subsidy programs did not stand up under deep scrutiny" and "the two subsidy programs had been revised to meet legitimate complaints" (*CQ Weekly Report* 1974d, 621).

In the summer of 1974, the imminent threat of impeachment led Nixon to rescind the moratorium, in one of several last-ditch attempts to salvage his presidency. The upcoming impeachment proceedings also spurred rapid action on the housing bill by the House-Senate conference committee, since its members felt that Congress' preoccupation with the Senate trial would kill the bill for that session. A compromise was reached on August 6, 1974, two days before Nixon's resignation. The conference committee report followed the House bill in adopting the administration's expanded version of the Section 23 program (Section 8 of the new law). However, House conferees agreed to continue Section 235 and Section 236, albeit with a drastically reduced authorization. To make up for this reduced new funding, the bill specifically authorized HUD to spend $400 million in prior contract authority which the moratorium had left unused (*CQ*

Almanac 1973b).The administration announced that the compromise was acceptable, and, nine days later, both houses cleared the conference version. It was signed into law as the Housing and Community Development Act of 1974 by the new president, Gerald Ford.

This new act was a large and complex piece of legislation. The impact of its community development provisions on housing policy will be explored in chapter 6, while our present focus will be on Section 8, which set a new course in housing assistance. This new program contained three subprograms—New Construction, Substantial Rehabilitation, and Existing Housing. A fourth, the Moderate Rehabilitation program, was added in 1978. Substantial Rehabilitation closely resembled New Construction, Moderate Rehabilitation resembled the Section 8 Existing program, and both were rather small in scale. Therefore, this discussion will deal mainly with the two larger subprograms. It will first outline their common elements, and then describe the unique features of each subprogram.

What these subprograms had in common was an emphasis on the direct subsidy of the tenant's rent as the basis for assistance. The widely accepted figure of 25 percent of income was chosen as a reasonable rent burden. The subsidy for each household was the difference between this percentage of income and an "economic rent" for the unit which HUD determined to be reasonable based on building costs, age, and amenities. However, the economic rent could not exceed the Fair Market Rent (FMR) for that particular size and type of unit in the project's geographic area, a figure determined by HUD on the basis of comparable units in the locality. FMRs ran substantially higher for New Construction than for the Existing Housing program. HUD officials could also set a project's rents as much as 20 percent higher than the FMR, if they believed that conditions warranted it.

Since Section 8 replaced both low and moderate income subsidy programs, eligibility requirements were fairly broad. The income maximum was set at 80 percent of the locality's median income for a family of four, with higher limits permitted for larger families. Further requirements were designed to avoid two extremes—the exclusion of very low income persons from the program (which many believed had occurred with Section 236) and the undue concentration of lower income people in projects (one of the shortcomings of public housing). On the one hand, the law required that 30 percent of those assisted must earn less than 50 percent of their local community's median income. On the other hand, the top limits were set high enough to include some of those previously considered to be moderate income, and new construction projects in which only a portion of the units were subsidized were given priority over projects consisting entirely of subsidized units (U.S. Congress, House Committee on Appropriations 1977, 28–30; Mandelker et al. 1981).

The total number of Section 8 units available was determined by the level of congressional appropriation. Unlike food stamps and other public assistance programs, housing assistance was never made an entitlement, that is, a benefit that was mandated to be available for all eligible households. From this pool, successive allocations were made to regional offices and from regional offices to area offices. The area office then determined the total number of units to be allocated to a community, and designated the proportions of units for new construction, rehabilitation, or existing housing, based on the Housing Assistance Plan submitted by each locality.

The requirement of the Housing Assistance Plan (HAP) was another innovation in the 1974 Act. Designed by congressional housing advocate Rep. Thomas Ashley, it was intended to make local governments take active responsibility for planning their communities' housing needs, thereby becoming more aware of the integral role of housing in community development. It was also hoped that the process would make the program more responsive to differences in local housing markets. In preparing their HAPs, localities were to gather data on the number, type, and condition of housing units in their community, and they were to determine the groups in the low income population (e.g., families, the elderly, the handicapped, etc.) most in need of assistance. Based on these data, they were to project housing needs for a three-year period, tabulate the extent to which housing currently under development would meet those needs, and request federally assisted units on the basis of remaining needs. HUD would, in turn, base its future requests for funds on HAP data (Struyk 1979).

The HAP process had a significant impact on the Section 8 program. However, HAPs were actually submitted as a part of each locality's Community Development Block Grant (CDBG) application. For this reason, and because the HAP process raised issues of federal-local relationships, which will be discussed more fully in chapter 6, a more complete discussion of its influence will be postponed until the CDBG process has been examined.

Around the core requirements just described, the two subprograms varied according to their distinct purposes. The New Construction program resembled Section 236 in that HUD reviewed and approved plans and cost data from each project and then signed a long-term rental assistance agreement. It also resembled Section 236 in the indirect subsidies associated with it. It was initially anticipated that the HUD approval and rental assistance contracts would be sufficient guarantees of project soundness to attract private mortgage money. However, private lenders proved reluctant to get involved on this basis alone, and the program was increasingly linked to other public subsidies and guarantees.

In addition to existing forms of government support, such as Ginnie Mae write-downs of mortgage costs and FHA insurance, two newer forms of subsidy were brought into play to support the program. One form took advantage of the ability of local housing authorities to issue tax exempt bonds. These authorities could themselves be developers of Section 8 New Construction units, but the use of tax exempt bonds (authorized for public housing under Section 11 b of the 1937 Housing Act) was also extended to private developers by the 1974 Act. Under this provision, the local authority usually formed a special entity to issue the bonds, and the proceeds were then lent to the private developer. Though not backed by the "full faith and credit" of the public entity, these bonds were seen by private developers as a relatively safe, inexpensive source of funds (U.S. Department of Housing and Urban Development 1978d 178).

Another form of subsidy for Section 8 New Construction came from state housing finance agencies. Created by state law to promote housing development, these agencies were empowered to issue tax exempt bonds to finance various types of housing, especially for lower income persons. States that had such agencies had utilized them to assist Section 236 projects. However, the Section 8 regulations actively encouraged state agency participation, and many more states were enticed to create such agencies by the prospect of easier participation. HUD created a special allocation of units for state agency–financed projects, permitted streamlined processing of applications, and allowed a forty-year contract (to match state agency bond terms). This was the beginning of substantial state involvement in assisted housing production, a role that would continue to be vital in the ensuing decades.

Finally, tax subsidies resulting from accelerated depreciation and the deductibility of mortgage interest continued to be available to Section 8 developers. Tax syndication was pushed vigorously, as it had been earlier, and many of the same specialized developers who had put together Section 236 projects continued to do so under Section 8. A 1978 HUD survey of one hundred Section 8 developers revealed that sixty-nine of them had been involved in some previous HUD program, and that nearly all planned to sell the tax benefits from their projects (U.S. Department of Housing and Urban Development 1978d, 168, 180).

In the end, the main differences between Section 8 New Construction and Section 236 were that the subsidy was couched in terms of a direct rent payment to tenants and that it was somewhat deeper than the earlier program had provided. It is ironic that the very features which had made President Johnson's rent supplement program so unpopular in the mid-1960s now *contributed* to the Section 8 program's appeal in the changed climate ten years later.

The Section 8 Existing Housing program more closely resembled the pure housing allowance concept, except that local housing agencies retained substantial administrative control. Such agencies applied to HUD for a certain number of units and, if approved, signed an Annual Contributions Contract permitting them to assist these units. Applications were then accepted from tenants, who had to be certified as eligible under the income guidelines. Eligible tenants then had sixty days to find a unit that met their needs and to secure the cooperation of the landlord. Or, they could request to remain in their current unit. In practice, agencies usually maintained lists of suitable units from which tenants were encouraged to choose. Once selected, the unit had to be inspected to determine compliance with minimum housing quality standards before occupancy was permitted. Having approved the unit, the agency then signed a contract with the landlord for up to fifteen years. The tenant also signed an agency-approved lease (Mandelker et al. 1981).

Despite the enactment of new legislation, the years 1974 and 1975 were the nadir of assisted housing production for the 1970s. This is clearly shown in Figure 5-1. There were enough units already in the pipeline to keep the moratorium from totally halting Sections 235 and 236, but the lack of new applications during that eighteen-month period was reflected in low levels of construction during the following two years. Meanwhile, Section 8 was very slow in starting. It took more than a year for HUD to develop regulations and for local agencies and developers to gain a clear enough understanding of the new rules to apply in large numbers. Thus, Section 8 did not make a major contribution until 1976.

However, Figure 5-1 also shows that, once the initial glitches were worked out, both the New Construction and the Existing Housing programs took off quickly. The Existing Housing program went into high gear first, since its approval process was much simpler. Yet, production of new units also began to rise rapidly after 1977, contributing an increasingly large proportion of the total assisted units. The Substantial and Moderate Rehabilitation programs began to have a visible role in 1977, but did not contribute large numbers of units. Overall production continued at high

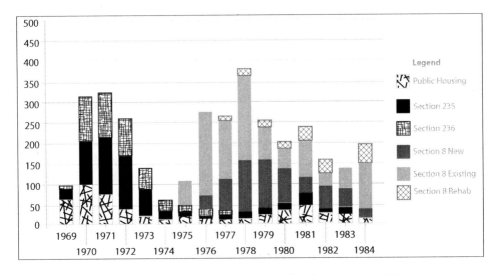

Figure 5-1 Assisted Housing Production: 1969–1984

Source: Pre–1975 data from U.S. Department of Housing and Urban Development, Statistical Yearbook, 1979. Post–1975 data compiled by National Low Income Housing Coalition from HUD sources.

levels into the early 1980s when Reagan's budget cuts and program changes began to have an impact.

This upsurge in production took place in an atmosphere of relatively low conflict surrounding housing policy. The administration of President Jimmy Carter, which took office in 1977, did not display the desire for large new social welfare initiatives that previous Democratic administrations had shown. Items such as energy and controlling inflation ranked ahead of these on Carter's policy agenda, and his desire to lower federal deficits limited his willingness to propose new expenditures. Furthermore, Carter proved unsuccessful in pushing through many of the modest proposals he did make. His welfare reform proposal stalled in Congress and was finally scrapped. He did succeed in enacting changes in CDBG funding rules and the new Urban Development Action Grant program; but several other parts of his urban package were defeated (*CQ Almanac* 1978, 1979).

Some responsibility for these failures must be laid at the feet of Carter and his advisors. As Edwards (1980) has documented, they displayed a notable lack of skill in dealing with Congress and on many occasions allowed potential support to dissipate through bad timing, bad communication, and poor personal relations with members of Congress. However,

Carter's difficulties were also due to the nature of the times. As noted in chapter 2, the optimism of the early 1960s had been replaced by widespread perceptions of economic stagnation and the notion that the nation was going to have to accept limits. In keeping with this mood, some former supporters of liberal programs moved toward the conservative view that government was becoming too large, too powerful, and too expensive, thereby gaining themselves the designation of "neo-conservative." One indication of this mood with regard to housing was Congress' failure to reestablish a housing production goal upon the expiration of the ten-year goals set in the Housing Act of 1968. Because the goal of six million federally assisted units had not been reached, there was pessimism that a new goal could actually influence policy and a desire not to commit the nation to large new efforts (*CQ Weekly Reports* 1978).

Nevertheless, in spite of the loss of support for social programs under Carter, existing housing programs reached high levels of production relative to previous years. The attention given to other issues helped to insulate them from scrutiny and debate, and the housing policy subsystem, finding after initial skepticism that many aspects of Section 8 were very congenial, continued to push for higher funding levels. Carter did call for and receive spending reductions in housing in the last year of his term, due to concerns with inflation and the federal deficit (*CQ Weekly Reports* 1979a,1979b, 1979c). However, his overall level of support was relatively high, compared to later years. It was only when Carter's ambivalent support was replaced by a new administration ideologically committed to retrenchment that these programs, too, came under attack.

Because of the lack of controversy during this period, evaluation studies of Section 8 are scarce in comparison to the extensive evaluations and critiques of programs of the early 1970s. However, available data permit a fairly detailed picture of Section 8 to be drawn. In addition, large amounts of data from EHAP became available during the late 1970s, data that were compared to ongoing, operational programs. All of these evaluation efforts were politically significant because some of their results were used by the Reagan administration to justify proposals for the reduction and redirection of federal housing assistance. These evaluations raise three key issues: cost and risk, the population served by the programs, and the geographical distribution of the housing produced.

With regard to Section 8 New Construction, the attention of policy analysts naturally turned to its cost, since this subprogram most closely resembled earlier programs believed by many to be too costly. Estimating the relative costs of Section 8 and other programs is a complex process for a number of reasons. First, actual construction and operating costs had to be accurately determined from data that varied widely within program types as well as between them. Second, the actual proportion of the total costs the government paid varied, depending on the clientele served and on the extent of indirect subsidy through tax shelters. Third, costs had to be projected for the entire twenty- to thirty-year life cycle of a project, a process that relied as much on estimates as on hard data.

However, studies of Section 8 program costs by the U.S. General Accounting Office (1980) and by HUD (1982b), found Section 8 New Construction to be comparable in costs and efficiency to Section 236. The two studies also reached similar conclusions concerning the relative costs of various forms of Section 8 financing (Ginnie Mae Tandem, Section 11b, or state housing finance agencies). Construction and operating costs varied less than 3 percent between various types of Section 8 New Construction, but there was a larger variation in subsidy costs to the federal government. Projects run by state housing finance agencies had more indirect costs because of the additional federal taxes foregone on their bonds, a point that led the GAO to question the cost effectiveness of this financing method. Units built under Section 236 were found to have cost slightly more than Section 8 units (in constant dollars). However, because of the somewhat higher income group served by Section 236, federal subsidies were lower.

Another important issue was the risk of project failure, since this issue had a major impact on the fate of the Section 235 and 236 programs. Due to the variety of financing mechanisms used in this program, there is no single, readily available source of data on foreclosures, such as exists for earlier, FHA-insured programs. Nevertheless, the GAO report showed striking differences in the development patterns of Section 8 and Section 236 which led to fewer problems in the former.

Table 5.1 contrasts the Section 8 New and Substantial Rehabilitation programs with Section 236 by type of sponsor and by the proportions of family and elderly units. If these data are compared with the data on the foreclosure rates of various types of Section 236 projects presented in Table 4.1 (chapter 4), it becomes clear that the distribution of projects shifted away from the higher-risk to lower-risk categories. The category with the lowest foreclosure rate, new construction for the elderly by for-profit sponsors, rose from 4 percent of Section 236 projects to 45.7 percent of Section 8 projects. In addition, in spite of the new emphasis placed on rehabilitation as a housing strategy in the late 1970s, a smaller percentage of Section 8 projects involved rehabilitation than had Section 236 develop-

Table 5.1 Characteristics of Section 8 and Section 236 Projects

Type of Sponsor and Program	Percentage of New Construction Units		Percentage of Substantial Rehabilitation Units	
	Family	Elderly	Family	Elderly
Limited dividend (for profit)				
Section 236	62.0	4.0	9.0	0.8
Section 8	39.2	45.7	3.5	0.4
Nonprofit				
Section 236	15.0	5.0	3.5	0.4
Section 8	1.3	4.5	—	0.3

Source: U.S. General Accounting Office, Evaluation of alternatives for financing low and moderate income rental housing, 180

ments. Since rehabilitation projects also had much higher foreclosure rates, this contributed to a lower probability of Section 8 failure.

Other factors were mentioned by the GAO as minimizing the risk of Section 8 financial failure. One was the cautious approach of state housing finance agencies. To a greater extent than federal agencies, state housing agencies were dependent upon a good financial track record for the continued salability of their bonds. This made them scrutinize their projects very closely. Second, financial failure was discouraged by the flexibility of the Section 8 subsidy mechanism. In Section 236, the subsidy was attached to financing costs. Though operating subsidies were eventually made available, these were seen by Congress as an excessive additional cost and were only reluctantly granted, as had been the case for public housing. Also, rising rents in Section 236 projects could force out the lower income tenants who originally occupied the units, thus reducing the market for the units. In Section 8, the subsidy was tied to the rents paid by the tenants, and the FMRs were expected to rise with inflation. Thus, the program could absorb cost increases and keep projects afloat. However, this flexibility also had a disadvantage in that rising costs contributed to criticism of the program as too costly. Why subsidized housing rents should be expected to be immune from the inflationary pressures affecting all other prices is not clear, but any social welfare program with rising costs seems to violate some conservatives' incremental criterion, regardless of the justification for the increases.

A second major issue that was raised in connection with Section 8 New Construction was the population served. The underlying irony of the risk reduction data just presented is that lower risks were achieved in part by shifting the population served in ways questionable on equity grounds. The most obvious shift was away from family units toward units for the elderly. Table 5.1, based on 1977 data, shows that just over 50 percent of new Section 8 units had been constructed for the elderly. By 1979, according to the HUD *Statistical Yearbook,* this proportion had risen to 74 percent. Many low income elderly persons had a genuine need for improved housing and could benefit from special security systems and other amenities. However, according to the GAO, the elderly represented only 23 percent of the total income-eligible population (U.S. General Accounting Office 1980, 77). Therefore, the dominance of Section 8 New Construction by elderly units can better be explained by their attractiveness to both builders and local officials than by need. First, the public tended to regard the elderly as the "deserving poor" and thus to be less hostile to housing for them than to family housing. Secondly, they were perceived as less likely to engage in antisocial behavior than families containing disadvantaged youth. This perception reduced neighborhood resistance and lessened the developer's sense of financial risk.

The geographic location of new Section 8 units also affected the population served. Here again, the program shifted its emphasis away from high-risk, inner city developments and toward construction in suburban and nonmetropolitan areas. The 1982 HUD study found that, whereas 56.5 percent of Section 236 developments were located in central cities (with 19.8 percent in suburbs and 23.7 percent outside SMSAs), the central city percentage of Section 8 developments varied from a low of 18.8 percent for state agency–financed projects to a high of 33.7 percent for GNMA-financed projects (U.S. Department of Housing and Urban Development 1982, 4–28). While there are legitimate housing needs in small communities, this trend also represented a movement away from the largest concentrations of the poor.

The large proportion of elderly and non–central city units also had a negative impact on the program's ability to serve minorities. A 1981 HUD study of the program's clientele found both African Americans and Latinos to be underrepresented. The concentration on elderly units contributed to this because a much smaller percentage of the elderly poor (23 percent) than of non-elderly poor (39 percent) were in these groups. But even among the elderly poor, minorities were underrepresented, constituting only 11 percent of those served. Those African Americans and Latinos who did participate often moved into neighborhoods with less minority concentration, shifting on the average from areas that were 54 percent minority to areas with 35 percent minority residence. Nevertheless, this advantage for a few participants was counteracted by the location of most projects outside central cities, since HUD also found that program participation was heavily influenced by the geographical proximity of a project. (U.S. Department of Housing and Urban Development 1981b)

The impact of program characteristics on the income distribution of those served is more ambiguous. The inclusion of large numbers of elderly tended to drive the income level of those served downward, since a larger number of elderly fit into HUD's Very Low Income category, which they defined as incomes of less than 50 percent of the median. Thus, the 1981 HUD study found that very low income persons were disproportionately represented among program beneficiaries. Yet, the 1980 GAO study found that Section 8 assistance was not as concentrated in the very low income brackets as public housing. According to GAO, families with incomes at 75 percent of the official poverty line were more than five times as likely to benefit from public housing as were families above the poverty line, whereas Section 8 benefits were much more evenly distributed between the very poor and the near poor (U.S. General Accounting Office 1980, 82–83).

In attempting to evaluate the total picture of the population served by Section 8 New Construction, one encounters the same complex tradeoffs that have bedeviled federal housing policy since the 1930s. This program was explicitly designed to give administrators the flexibility to serve a fairly wide range of lower income persons, from the destitute to the working poor. The GAO data suggest that this goal was met, while the HUD results suggest a marked, though not drastic, shift toward the lower end of the income scale. Either way, the results seem to violate a major criterion for policy success. Concentration on the lowest income persons satisfies the most straightforward principle of vertical equity (i.e., serve the neediest first). On the other hand, public housing suffered both administratively and politically from its concentration on an exclusively low income population, and it seemed unfair to penalize upward mobility by excluding people from participation when their incomes reached a certain level. In addition, Section 8 achieved its stress on very low income persons by concentrating on the elderly. Therefore, a shift away from the elderly would have meant an increase in the overall income level of Section 8 tenants. Although seemingly in violation of vertical equity, such a move might have actually made the program more equitable by restoring the flexibility to deal with the housing needs of poor working families closer to the eligibility cutoff.

Another trade-off was between financial risk and service to those in need. Risk and failure are labels that subject programs to political attack by opponents who attribute these to poor administration or the inherent shortcomings of nonmarket approaches. Yet, in reducing its risk factors, Section 8 New Construction moved away from large segments of the eligible population. Its projects had a better track record than either public housing or the earlier subsidy programs in terms of management and financial soundness, but they achieved this by serving more of those considered "safe" (i.e., elderly white poor in suburban communities).

Section 8 Existing Housing

The Existing Housing program involved lower costs and less financial risk than the New Construction program. The typically lower rents of older, existing units meant that Fair Market Rents were set much lower. According to a 1982 Congressional Budget Office study, the annual per unit subsidy was less than half that of the New Construction program (U.S. Congress, Budget Office 1982, 39). Also, because the units were already in place, the federal government did not have to share the financial risks of new construction in order to induce participation. However, despite these lower costs, some analysts raised questions about its cost effectiveness. These questions revolved around the complex relationship between rent levels, housing quality, and tenant needs. They can best be understood as a logical sequence in which each successive question generates the next.

The first question is whether or not the program induced increases in the rents of existing housing. One facet of this question is the issue raised by Hartman and others when the housing allowance was first proposed: Does the increase in real demand due to the subsidy push rents upward in areas where lower income persons are concentrated? The conclusion of both the EHAP study and of various studies of Section 8 Existing Housing was that this was not a serious problem. In most areas, the concentration of these units was not large enough to have an appreciable impact on aggregate demand for housing, yet even where large numbers of units were concentrated in modest sized communities, such as in the EHAP supply experiment, the introduction of the units was gradual enough not to have a major effect.

A second facet of this question is whether rents for participating units were pushed upward by the program. A 1978 HUD evaluation found that, while the subsidy reduced the tenants' average rent burden from 40 percent to 22 percent of income, the total rents paid on behalf of program beneficiaries went up substantially. Many tenants moved to more expensive quarters, causing the average total rent to be 70 percent greater than their rent prior to program participation. Those who stayed in the same units had a smaller, but nonetheless significant increase of 28 percent. Since the subsidy was based on the difference between a fixed 25 percent of the tenant's income and the rent actually charged, the landlord had an incentive to raise the rent to the FMR ceiling, while the tenant had no incentive to resist such an increase. Thus, the study found that the actual rents charged averaged from 92 to 96 percent of the FMR for the area, depending on unit size (U.S. Department of Housing and Urban Development 1978b, 33).

A second question, flowing from the first, is whether or not the increased rents actually improved housing conditions for the program's beneficiaries. The conclusion of the HUD study was that, while some of the increase could be attributed to the landlord's taking advantage of the FMR ceiling, much of it was related to improvement in the quality of the housing. Thirty-seven percent of all units received at least minor repairs in order to participate in the program, and movers reported their new units to be in better condition than their former ones. Moreover, tenants frequently reported that they had relieved overcrowding by moving to larger units or by separating families sharing the same quarters. Most of those who moved reported improvement in neighborhood environment.

The fact that housing quality improved for program participants raises, in turn, a third question, harking back to earlier arguments about the over-consumption allegedly resulting from in-kind subsidies. Was the Section 8 Existing Housing program paying for overconsumption of housing by a few while leaving a large number of eligible families without assistance? Clearly, this program served only a fraction of those eligible, so the heart of the question is really whether or not the level of housing services provided constituted overconsumption, in relation to some more limited level of services, which could be more broadly distributed within existing resource constraints. Expressed in this fashion, the question can, in turn, be divided into two parts: (1) Was there overconsumption relative to some reasonable objective standard of housing consumption? and (2) Was there overcon-sumption relative to the level of housing services the recipient would have chosen if given less constrained assistance?

The first part of the question was raised in a 1979 study by Olsen and Rasmussen. Building upon another study by Follain (1979), the authors argue that, early in the program, Fair Market Rents gradually moved beyond the levels required to obtain units meeting the absolute minimum standards set by HUD. The authors suggested tighter controls on the FMR so that the same amount of federal dollars would serve more households. However, their analysis did not take into account a fundamental problem associated with program implementation, namely, the variation in the quality of units selected on both sides of whatever physical standard is used. In such a program it is inevitable that substandard units will slip in through administrative laxity and/or through the inability of particular tenants to find units of the prescribed minimum quality. The 1981 HUD study found that, even with current FMRs, roughly 50 percent of the units sampled fell below the HUD minimum standard on at least one criterion. Therefore, if one wishes to assure that most tenants receive units at or above the minimum quality standards, it would seem poor policy to set a rent standard that will barely purchase the minimum unit.

The second part of the overconsumption question raised a more serious difficulty for the program, in light of the long debate over the value of in-kind subsidies to their recipients. The findings of the EHAP study, disseminated in the late 1970s, brought this question into clear focus. In EHAP's Demand Experiment, less constrained subsidy mechanisms were used than those incorporated in Section 8. The basic design involved a direct cash payment to the tenant, not the landlord. The payment was based on the difference between a percentage of the tenant's income and some rent level determined to be appropriate on the basis of comparable units in the area. However, unlike Section 8, the tenant did not actually have to pay this amount of rent to get the full subsidy payment but could choose how much of it to spend on improved housing and how much to allocate to other items of consumption. Given such a choice, EHAP participants usually chose to spend only a small portion of their grant on improved housing and to spend the rest on other items. Both tenants and landlords made only the minimum repairs needed to comply with the program's physical standards, and if repairs were too extensive, both tended to withdraw from the program rather than comply (Struyk and Bendick 1981). Thus, the study suggested that tenants might be satisfied with lower housing standards than those set by middle-class professionals and that subsidy levels could be lowered without sacrificing the perceived well-being of low income households.

Such a conclusion fit well with the conservative perception of the inappropriateness of active federal intervention on behalf of low income persons. It suggested that the priority on high quality new and rehabilitated units and even on consumption of improved existing housing was one shared by HUD officials, builders, and other housing advocates but not by the potential clients of their programs. As a result, this argument became a central feature of the Reagan administration's argument for its new *housing voucher* program, to be discussed in more detail in chapter 7.

In concluding this discussion of the Section 8 Existing Program, it is necessary to examine the population served, in order to compare this program with Section 8 New Construction. A conclusion supported by all the evaluations was that the Existing Housing program served a much more representative cross-section of the low income population than Section 8 New Construction. According to the 1981 HUD study, the households served were 26 percent elderly and 44 percent minority, proportions much closer to those in the eligible population. In addition, both the 1978 and 1981 HUD studies concluded that this program came much closer to balancing the desire of some minority and/or low income persons to move into available units in higher income, nonminority areas with the desire of others to have the program accessible in areas where they already lived. The 1978 study pointed out that, while only a small portion of participating families moved out of the area in which they currently lived, the probability of moving to a new area was strongly correlated with the extent of searching in those areas. Furthermore, moving or not moving into new areas was, to a significant degree, a matter of individual choice, although it was also recognized that units were not available in better neighborhoods for all who might want them, especially in the case of minority households.

While Section 8 was, in terms of numbers, the dominant program of the late 1970s, our picture of this period would be incomplete without noting the continued support enjoyed by public housing. Figure 5-1 shows a modest, but nonetheless constant level of public housing starts in the late 1970s. A portion of this was accounted for by units authorized earlier, but Congress continued to make new reservations of 35,000 to 50,000 units per year through the last Carter budget in 1981 (National Low Income Housing Coalition 1983a, 12). Also, substantial funds were provided for operating subsidies and for modernization of public housing units.

Why this continued support for public housing? Several reasons seem to be central. First, for all its faults, public housing was a tried and true program that could be counted on to produce units for low income persons. It had a constituency of local housing authorities that continued to press for more units. In the period of uncertainty following Nixon's moratorium, when it seemed Section 8 would never get moving, Congress decided to revive public housing and made a new appropriation for FY

1977. Out of frustration, they turned back to an established process of housing production (*CQ Weekly Report* 1976a).

Second, many housing advocates recognized that public housing served a segment of the low income population that it was difficult to induce the private sector to serve, even with deep subsidies. As has been shown, Section 8 New Construction drifted more and more toward serving the elderly. This meant that relatively few new units were made available to low income families. The Section 8 Existing Housing program served a better cross-section, but, according to Sternlieb (1980), there was a general tendency during this period for privately constructed units to move toward a standard size of two, or at the most three, bedrooms. This meant that large low income families were finding it increasingly difficult to find units in the subsidized or unsubsidized private market. In addition, both programs ameliorated but did not eliminate the market disadvantage suffered by minorities. For all these reasons, public housing remained the housing of last resort for the poorest and most desperate families.

A third basis for support was the efficiency argument, which could still be plausibly advanced on behalf of public housing. One argument for housing owned by the public sector was that the asset remained in the public domain, thereby allowing the initial investment to produce services to targeted groups over a long period of time. In contrast, (as the later resale crisis proved abundantly) there was no guarantee that new private housing built with public subsidies would remain available for low income housing, and subsidies to existing units involved simply the purchasing of a service, not a tangible public asset. The value of the assets already produced by the public housing program was tacitly recognized by Congress through its continued approval of operating and modernization subsidies for the 1.3 million units still in operation, although some members of Congress continued to object to the cost of these subsidies. Another efficiency argument was advanced in the 1980 GAO report cited earlier. GAO analysts argued that when costs related to the size and type of unit were held constant, the long-term subsidy costs for public housing units were less than for new, privately constructed units. Indirect tax subsidies, though included in public housing via the use of local tax exempt bonds were not as extensive as in privately built units. Also, the subsidy level in public housing was not as heavily influenced by rising rent levels in the private market.

Anyone who has raised house plants is familiar with the specimen that looks ragged most of the time but never seems to die. This seems an apt metaphor for the public housing program. The standard treatment of public housing in the media, and in academic texts on urban policy as well, suggests that it was the failure of this program that led to the development of new subsidy programs from 1968 on. Yet, for the reasons stated above, public housing continued to have its defenders, and the program's continued funding suggests that they were listened to by Congress. In addition, those who studied public housing more closely and comprehensively tended to find that its failure was far from total. For example, a 1983 study by the Congressional Budget Office found that approximately 15 percent of public housing units could be classified as seriously troubled, while most of the rest provided the poor with affordable housing which was in relatively good condition (U.S. Congress, Budget Office 1983, 15–16). While not an environment that many middle-class persons would find desirable, the majority of public housing units were providing a necessary service to the very poor in a reasonably adequate fashion.

CHAPTER 6

The Federal Role
in Community Development

Introduction

In this chapter, the major federal initiatives in community development between 1945 and 1980 will be explored, with particular attention to the close relationship between these efforts and federal housing policy. In chapter 2, it was argued that housing programs have often been viewed within the frame of reference of community development policy, since housing constitutes an important use of any community's physical space. Because of this close association, the policy subsystem that handles housing programs overlaps considerably with that which handles community development policy—the same subcommittees in Congress, the same federal agency (HUD), and, often, the same local agencies.

Nevertheless, as also suggested in chapter 2, there have always been powerful conservative groups interested in community development who have not shared with housing advocates a strong interest in utilizing community development programs to improve the housing conditions of the poor and who, in fact, have been willing to sacrifice low income housing quality in the name of other goals. Therefore, the alliance between housing advocates and community development advocates has always been uneasy, and liberals concerned with housing have had to push aggressively for the inclusion of housing goals in community development strategies.

In addition, a focal concern of community development policy has been the issue of intergovernmental power relationships. Though social welfare policies such as housing assistance have also been affected by intergovernmental relations, these issues have been raised more directly through the struggle over urban renewal and other community development strategies. The resolution of these intergovernmental issues has profoundly shaped community development programs, and this, in turn, has greatly affected their impact on housing.

In Part I of this chapter, the federal government's first major urban redevelopment effort, the urban renewal program, will be traced from its roots in the New Deal era to its demise in 1974. The struggle that occurred over the housing impact of this program will be given particular attention. In addition, the effects of urban renewal and other urban programs on federal/local relationships and local politics will be examined. Part II will explore the ways in which the local and national concerns raised by the impact of urban renewal and other federal categorical programs led to a shift in the nation's community development strategy. The Community Development Block Grant program which embodied this new approach will be discussed in some detail. Finally, it will be shown that this change had a major impact on housing by stimulating a shift from clearance to housing rehabilitation as the major focus of neighborhood renewal.

Part I—Urban Renewal as a Community Development Strategy

A major increase in federal involvement in the physical redevelopment of local communities was presaged by the emergency public works projects enacted early in the New Deal. The primary purpose of these projects was to create jobs for the legions of unemployed, but they also produced capital improvements which local governments that were nearly bankrupt could no longer afford. Significantly, federal construction of low income housing was initially a part of the Public Works Administration. The Roosevelt administration saw the replacement of slum dwellings with new, low-cost housing as a useful public purpose to be served by workers on the federal payroll.

However, it was also significant that local property owners successfully challenged in court the clearance aspect of this early federal housing effort, on the grounds that the goal of "removing blight" was not a legitimate public purpose of the federal government and thus could not justify the use of eminent domain to acquire property *(U.S. v. Certain Lands in the City of Louisville, Ky.)*. At the same time, the door was left open for the use of eminent domain by the local government for the same purpose, with proper state authorizing legislation. This led to a much more decentralized design for the public housing program, and this, in turn, helped to establish a more general pattern for federal programs—local planning and execution of projects utilizing federal dollars (Mandelker et al. 1981).

Early support for federal urban redevelopment arose in a seemingly unlikely quarter—the National Association of Real Estate Boards (NAREB). According to Gelfand, the drastic slowdown in urban growth brought about by the Depression aroused concern among real estate and business investors with a heavy financial stake in central city property. They feared that a spiral of decay would substantially reduce the value of their assets, and they accurately foresaw that prosperity would bring a renewal of the suburbanization which had begun in the 1920s. These investors defined blight not just as the existence of residential slums but as patterns of land use that blocked successful (i.e., profitable) redevelopment of central city land to "higher" uses, whether commercial, industrial, or residential. They came to believe that local government might, with federal financial backing, play a useful role in removing blight. First, it could use its power of eminent domain to overcome a major obstacle to redevelopment—the assembly of smaller parcels of land into larger ones. Second, using the justification of an increased tax base and a new, improved face for the central city, governments might be persuaded to write down high central city land acquisition and demolition costs that were also an obstacle to redevelopment.

Therefore, NAREB and its affiliated think tank, the Urban Land Institute, began in the late 1930s to generate proposals for federal involvement in urban redevelopment. NAREB's first proposal called for neighborhood associations of property owners to decide which properties to redevelop. This was later replaced with the idea of a community-wide redevelopment commission with broad condemnation powers. Eventually, their proposal was introduced as legislation in Congress in 1943. Although it never got out of committee, it was an important precursor to the redevelopment provisions of the Housing Act of 1949.

The advocacy of urban redevelopment by such a conservative group generated mixed reactions among academics and planners who had been urging the renewal of cities. Gelfand notes that "some took [it] . . . as a positive sign of a new civic awareness among realtors," and he goes on to quote Frederic Delano, who "considered it a matter of importance to find the real estate men taking an active interest in trying to solve the problems to which they have been somewhat indifferent and which, it seems to me, they have largely created" (Gelfand 1975, 117). In contrast, housing-oriented planners found it ironic that NAREB should propose federal subsidies to private developers while at the same time bitterly attacking the new public housing program as socialistic and un-American.

Nevertheless, as the 1940s progressed, liberal housing advocates began to see advantages to supporting urban redevelopment. The public housing program had taken a beating from NAREB and its conservative allies in Congress. Perhaps housing advocates could strengthen their position by agreeing to accept subsidies for private redevelopment in exchange for some units of public housing to re-house those displaced by redevelopment. Thus, there began an uneasy alliance between those who saw economic redevelopment as the main goal of such a program and those who wanted to make housing for the poor its central focus.

In the end, the two purposes were firmly linked together in the bill, introduced in 1945 by Senators Wagner, Ellender, and Taft, which became the Housing Act of 1949. Much to the chagrin of NAREB leaders, the bill emphasized housing as its main goal. It required that redevelopment take place primarily in residential areas and that decent housing for those displaced be provided. The law also authorized 810,000 units of public housing to replace and supplement the housing destroyed. This housing emphasis was a short-term political liability in that the public housing provisions sparked a bitter debate which held up passage for four years. Yet, in the long run, the urban redevelopment proposal benefited from its attachment to housing goals. First, it made the bill more appealing to liberals than urban redevelopment alone would have been, especially in light of the housing shortages after World War II. Second, the controversy surrounding public housing deflected critical attention from the redevelopment provisions. On the other side of the coin, private real estate and business interests found the bitter pill of public housing easier to swallow when sweetened with the prospect of federal subsidies for economic development. Of the diverse coalition that supported the Housing Act of 1949, long-time housing advocate Catherine Bauer commented, "Seldom has such a variegated crew of would-be angels tried to sit on the same pin at the same time" (quoted in Gelfand 1975, 153).

The implementation of urban redevelopment under Title I of the Housing Act of 1949 raised a number of complex housing issues. However, before exploring these issues, a brief overview of the design and impact of the program is in order. Title I provided federal funding for property acquisition, demolition of structures, and site preparation in redevelopment areas. However, it also required that the local government support one-third of program costs, a share usually provided in the form of "non-cash grants-in-aid" (i.e., various public works carried out in support of the redevelopment project). Proceeds from the sale of land were used to repay as much of the federal costs as possible, but because the cost of acquiring and demolishing existing structures was much greater than the price at which the land was sold, the program provided a substantial federal subsidy to encourage private redevelopment.

Another attractive feature of the program was that eminent domain could be used to assemble large parcels of land for redevelopment. Private land assembly in central cities was difficult because of multiple owners and often clouded titles. Compulsory public acquisition eliminated these problems. Unlike the federal use of eminent domain for clearance, its use by local authorities passed muster with the courts, as long as proper state authorizing legislation was in place. The removal of "blight" and the conversion of land to "higher and better" uses were considered legitimate public purposes for state and local governments.

As with any new and complex program, initial implementation was slow. By 1953, only $105 million out of the original $500 million in grants had actually been committed. However, economic and political pressures brewing in the early 1950s contributed to the program's expansion. Suburbia was exploding with new housing and commercial activity, which reduced the central cities' share of total metropolitan retail trade from 68 percent in 1948 to 58 percent in 1954 (Gelfand 1975, 158). This suburban development was profitable to many business interests, but for many others, it was a major threat to their huge investments in the central city and to their civic pride. These central city–oriented business leaders made common cause with a new group of progressive big city majors who saw redevelopment as a source of long-term political support. Pittsburgh under David Lawrence and New Haven under Richard Lee provided models to other cities in this regard. Initially, much of this work was done with private and local government funds, but the federal urban redevelopment program proved an increasingly attractive supplement to local efforts. Therefore, applications increased in the late 1950s, in spite of complex federal requirements (Mollenkopf 1983).

Meanwhile, legislative changes made the program more attractive to localities. The Housing Act of 1954 changed the program's name from *urban redevelopment* to *urban renewal,* and, to encourage comprehensive planning, required each city to submit a Workable Program showing how it planned to attack urban decay. Though this requirement imposed more red tape on localities, the Housing and Home Finance Administration (HHFA) left the real planning initiative to local governments, restricting itself to a technical and financial review of applications. More importantly, the new law shifted the program's emphasis away from housing by allowing a larger percentage of projects to be nonresidential.

By 1959, when Eisenhower tried to cut back the program as a budget reduction measure, it enjoyed strong enough support that the Democratic Congress blocked his effort. When Kennedy took office in 1961, he showed the same favorable attitude toward urban renewal as toward other urban-oriented programs, and funding was increased substantially. More and more cities applied during the early 1960s, so that, by the end of the decade, there were few large cities that did not have at least one urban renewal project planned or underway.

Yet, as projects multiplied, so, too, did the controversy surrounding the program. Some critics were laissez-faire conservatives, such as Martin Anderson (1964). He argued that federal funds should not be used to selectively subsidize private developers to carry out projects that would not be feasible or profitable within the natural workings of the market system. This criticism reemerged in later years as it became increasingly clear that urban renewal could not reverse the suburbanization of the U.S. metropolis. In 1974, Irving Welfeld, writing for the American Enterprise Institute, questioned the cost effectiveness of what he saw as a government financed attempt to "buck the tide" of polycentric urban settlement (Welfeld 1974).

However, many urban leaders believed there was something vital to be preserved for the community as a whole by maintaining a viable central business district and a viable central city community. The new central business districts that emerged in the 1950s and 1960s were administrative, governmental, and cultural centers rather than the dominant commercial hubs they had once been. Yet, economic leaders and government professionals shared the view that a positive image and function for downtown were worthy of public support.

Liberals concerned with ameliorating the plight of the poor also recognized a close association between the fate of the central cities and the fate of the poor. In general, urban aid and aid to the poor continued to be closely linked, and any move to withdraw funds from community development altogether would have been resisted as contrary to their interests. Although civil rights advocates began to talk about opening up the suburbs and although the Fair Housing Act of 1968 gave them a new tool to do this, the central city was realistically seen as the main point at which housing and other services would continue to be delivered to the poor.

Nevertheless, the urban renewal program itself became the target of increasing criticism from liberals. While accepting the need to aid the central cities, liberal critics became concerned with the housing and neighborhood impact of the program. Since this is the facet of urban renewal that is of most importance to the present work, these liberal concerns will be discussed in some detail. These problems may be grouped into three basic categories: (1) Problems of project delays; (2) Problems of relocation; and, (3) Problems of neighborhood impact.

Project Delays

On a late spring day in 1970, a group of about one hundred demonstrators (of which this author was one) marched from downtown Louisville, Kentucky, south to an urban renewal site adjacent to the University of Louisville. To protest the fact that this land, which had once contained low income housing, had lain vacant for several years, we planted a Poor People's Garden among the remaining rubble, asserting that if the land couldn't house the poor, at least it could feed them. This protest symbolized the hostility which the long delay between clearance and rebuilding engendered in many citizens. The site we cultivated was part of dozens of acres of cleared land adjacent to Louisville's central business district, which lay vacant for periods of five to ten years before any new construction was begun.

Five years later, as an urban renewal administrator in Richmond, Virginia, I obtained an insider's view of the causes of such delays. Richmond's renewal efforts were much more oriented to replacing demolished housing with low to moderate income housing than were Louisville's, yet delays still detracted from the program's image and impact. One of Richmond's typical projects, Fulton, had been designated in the city's Community Renewal Program in 1966. After three years of planning and community organizing, property acquisition finally began in 1969. One site within the project had been designated for Section 236 housing, to provide at least some low and moderate income replacement units. Acquisition and condemnation of property, relocation of its occupants, and demolition of structures on that site took at least two more years. Then, the site was graded and filled to raise it out of the James River's hundred-year flood plain, which proved to be more expensive and time consuming than anticipated.

Meanwhile, Richmond ran afoul of HUD's site selection criteria which, as noted earlier, sought to avoid excessive concentration of new subsidized units in low income areas. In a classic federal Catch-22, the agency was halted by one set of regulations while trying to comply with another set— namely, urban renewal regulations (to be discussed below) requiring that redevelopment of cleared residential areas include a substantial proportion of low to moderate income housing. The agency was eventually able to show that private developers had constructed enough comparable units in outlying areas to satisfy HUD's requirements, but not before an additional delay had occurred. Still another year's delay resulted from the inability of HUD, the developer, and the Virginia Housing Development Authority (which was providing low interest financing) to agree on various cost and design issues. Finally, ground was broken in 1976, with occupancy beginning eighteen months later, more than ten years after the project began.

A national survey of program impact by Heywood Sanders showed that the delays encountered in Louisville and Richmond were very typical. Some could be attributed to local agency errors, but the sheer complexity of the process was the fundamental reason. Problems of planning and political organization; legal problems with the acquisition of property; problems of coordination between the renewal agency, other local government agencies, private developers, HUD, or other federal programs—none were amenable to quick resolution. However, as Sanders suggests, delay was a major enemy of public acceptance of the program, intensifying other criticisms. The years of further decay and destruction in project areas which elapsed before renewal began created a negative image which it was hard for the eventual new development to erase (Sanders 1980).

Relocation

Of all the issues raised in connection with urban renewal, the issue of the displacement of low income residents was the most powerful catalyst for opposition. The scene in which an elderly person is evicted from his/her home of thirty years while the bulldozer operator revs his engine outside had become a staple of television and movies, and the villain was usually labeled "urban renewal" regardless of the private or public nature of the redevelopment causing the eviction. Yet, on a less emotional level, data began to accumulate during the first fifteen years of the urban renewal program's operation which showed a severe problem of housing destruction and displacement. With the public housing component reduced and the emphasis on commercial redevelopment increased in the late 1950s, the program quickly destroyed many more units of low income housing than it replaced. To be sure, many of the units destroyed were far below prevailing standards of decent habitation, but they did provide shelter for persons with few other housing choices. And, to representatives of the poor and minorities who were becoming increasingly politically active in the 1960s, this massive physical assault on their neighborhoods was the ultimate indignity. Coupled with extensive displacement due to highway construction and to private redevelopment, urban renewal was one more way the poor were being shoved aside to meet the needs of upper income groups.

In 1971, Chester Hartman summarized a decade of studies of the impact of displacement on the poor. These studies found the impact to be largely negative, in both economic and psychological terms. In most cases, persons displaced had to occupy more expensive units in only marginally better structures as a result of their move. Homeowners, though compensated for their dwellings at market value, were often forced to become tenants, because the prices paid for their substandard homes were too low to permit the purchase of even modest replacement units (Hartman 1971). Equally harmful, in many cases, were the psychological effects of being uprooted from a home and a neighborhood that the family had occupied for many years. Marc Fried titled his study of the effects of relocation from a Boston neighborhood, "Grieving for a Lost Home," because he found that the distress suffered by those displaced resembled that associated with the death of a close friend or relative (Fried 1966).

Moreover, many displaced households sought shelter in neighborhoods adjacent to their previous area of residence. In many cases, this was an attempt to maintain old community ties, while in others it signaled a perceived or actual lack of choice of alternative areas in which to live. Economic constraints limited their choices, and for the disproportionate share of those relocated who were African American, racial discrimination was also a limiting factor. Of course, the rapid influx of low income tenants into areas near urban renewal sites, areas which themselves were often physically and economically marginal, usually tipped the balance in favor of rapid deterioration, thus creating a new slum to replace the one federal funds had demolished.

The response of federal and local officials to the problems of relocation was limited and slow in coming. The local business/government coalitions pushing for urban renewal, to the extent that they were concerned about the poor at all, tended to accept the traditional view of the slums as primarily a physical problem. They believed that if the physical blight could be removed, the problems of the poor inhabitants would somehow disappear, as they were dispersed into other areas. In addition, local officials were reluctant to add the cost of adequate relocation benefits to the direct costs of the program, and they found little community acceptance of large-scale subsidized replacement housing to aid those who were displaced. The business interests backing urban renewal were interested in converting cleared land into more profitable uses, not in using cleared sites for low income housing. Other neighborhoods, of course, displayed their usual reluctance to have low income housing thrust into their midst.

The federal government was, formally, the watchdog over the displacement and re-housing of existing residents of urban renewal areas. The

1949 Act required that localities guarantee an adequate supply of "decent, safe, and sanitary" replacement housing, "[available] . . . at rents or prices within the financial means of the families displaced" (quoted from the statute by Hartman 1971). However, federal officials had little incentive to further slow down an already lengthy process by requiring effective relocation planning. They, like local officials, wanted to demonstrate results by getting more cities to participate and by completing projects faster. Therefore, relocation planning became little more than a paper exercise (Hartman 1971; see also, Greer 1965).

Perhaps of greater importance than the apathy of federal and local administrators was the lack of federal resources directed at re-housing the poor, for not even conscientious relocation planning could work in the absence of suitable replacement units. This lack of resources had two dimensions. First, throughout most of the first twenty years of urban renewal, new units of assisted housing were being produced in numbers far too small to replace those demolished. Second, direct relocation payments to displaced households were either nonexistent or inadequate to fully compensate them for their losses. Both of these dimensions of the problem require further examination.

The ebb and flow of subsidized housing programs from 1950 to 1973, described in chapter 4, had an obvious impact on replacement housing. In the case of the very poor, public housing was virtually the only housing that could meet the 1949 Act's criterion of "decent, safe and sanitary housing within their ability to pay." Thus, the abandonment of the Act's commitment to 810,000 units of public housing meant the loss of relocation resources. Only as public housing construction increased in the 1960s and as new programs came on line in 1968 were enough units being produced to have a positive impact on relocation.

Moreover, since land and resources for low income housing were already in short supply before urban renewal got underway, it was recognized early by many urban planners that a general commitment to new low income housing was not enough. Housing plans and commitments tied specifically to urban renewal were also necessary. However, the federal and local response to this need was sluggish, due to the fundamental drift of the program away from its original housing thrust. Various provisions were added to the 1949 Act, such as special FHA financing of housing in urban renewal areas (Section 220) and rehabilitation loans and grants (Sections 312 and 115), designed to create incentives to construct or rehabilitate replacement housing. However, these additions stimulated little residential reuse.

It was only in the late 1960s, when the Johnson administration began to respond to pressure for a change in the priorities of urban renewal that this re-housing element changed substantially. In 1966, the 1949 Act was amended to *require* that, in predominantly residential projects, a "substantial" number of low to moderate income replacement units be constructed (Hartman 1971, 751). Then, in 1967, HUD Secretary Robert Weaver announced that "the conservation and expansion of the housing supply for low and moderate income families" would be a central goal of the urban renewal program (quoted in Sanders 1980, 1081). In further pursuit of this goal, the 1968 and 1969 Housing Acts strengthened the vague language of the 1966 amendment, making it clear that "renewal projects . . . must replace any occupied low or moderate income . . . units demolished . . . with at least an equivalent number of units . . . to be constructed or rehabilitated somewhere within the jurisdiction of the local public agency" (Hartman 1971, 751).

Hartman notes that this language still allowed local agencies to avoid replacement housing that was strictly for low income persons. Nevertheless, data presented by Sanders show a marked shift toward residential reuse in programs which were begun in the late 1960s. The *average* amount of project land designated for residential reuse rose from less than 25 percent before 1968 to nearly 50 percent after that date. Meanwhile, the average amount of land devoted to residential rehabilitation rose from less than 15 percent to between 25 and 30 percent (Sanders 1980, 111). Furthermore, well over half the residential reuse was designated as housing for low to moderate income people. Sanders suggests that the characterization of urban renewal as a destroyer of low income housing which has prevailed in much of the academic literature was much more accurate during its early years than in the years from 1968 until its demise in the mid-1970s.

The other facet of the replacement housing issue was direct compensation for those displaced. During the early years, compensation for tenants was limited to a small reimbursement for moving expenses. The agency was required to assist in finding replacement housing, but studies showed that only a small proportion of those affected took advantage of these services. In 1964, Congress added a Relocation Adjustment Payment of up to $500 to cover the difference between old and new rent, which was expanded to $1,000 in 1965. But the problem of the family's inability to remain in a higher priced unit after one or two years was not dealt with (Hartman 1971, 749–50). Payments to homeowners were limited to the prices offered for their home plus moving expenses. Moreover, until the late 1960s, when HUD insisted on a single offer based on the appraised price, local agencies were permitted to offer less than their own appraised value and to bargain hard for this low figure. Owners could appeal in condemnation court, but few had the knowledge or resources to pursue this remedy.

It was not until 1970 that Congress saw fit to increase relocation payments to levels that might truly begin to compensate for the losses incurred and even to improve substantially the household's living conditions. This legislation, the Uniform Relocation Assistance and Real Property Acquisition Policies Act, covered those displaced from highways and other federal projects, as well as urban renewal. For tenants, this act increased benefits to include moving expenses plus a rental assistance payment based on the difference between the tenant's rent before and after relocation for a period of forty-eight months up to a maximum of $4,000. Tenants with some savings could also qualify for down payment assistance, in which their savings would he matched up to $2,000 for a down payment on a new home. Homeowners received a maximum of $15,000 over and above the purchase price of their old property, plus moving expenses.

For a piece of legislation involving the expenditure of large sums of money to benefit lower income persons, this measure passed Congress with very little debate or public attention (*CQ Almanac* 1970b). Given the opposition to urban renewal generated by the displacement issue, greater compensation for those affected seemed prudent. . Also, persons displaced through no fault of their own could more easily be placed in the category of the deserving poor than low income persons in general.

Very little research on the impact of the Uniform Relocation Act on the fortunes of those displaced has been done. However, along with Christopher Silver, I examined urban renewal relocation in Richmond, Virginia, most of which was done after the passage of the Uniform Relocation Act. We found that displaced persons fared considerably better with its financial support than was typical prior to the act. First, most displacees moved into neighborhoods that were in substantially better physical condition than those they left, and most were living among persons of higher income than themselves. Second, because of the homeowner payments and the down payment assistance, there was actually an increase in the percentage of owners in our sample from 28.4 to 39.1 percent. Third, those displaced were scattered over relatively wide areas of the city, rather than concentrated in areas immediately adjacent to clearance areas (Hays and Silver 1980).

Nevertheless, there were continuing problems with relocation. First, the $15,000 payment to homeowners was greatly reduced in value by the housing price inflation of the 1970s. This was a special problem because most displaced owners were elderly with small fixed incomes and, thus, were limited to houses for which they could pay cash. In Richmond, the average price received for their homes was $6,700, giving them a total of $21,700 to purchase a new one (Hays and Silver 1980). In the early 1970s this could still buy a modest but decent home. Later, this was not the case. (Ultimately, the assistance payment was changed to a flexible one based on the gap between the appraised price of the old house and the price of a comparable replacement house in standard condition.)

Second, the issue of racial discrimination was not resolved by the economic support provided by the Uniform Relocation Act. Our Richmond study found that approximately 40 percent of displaced African Americans moved into predominately white census tracts, a not insignificant pattern of dispersal given the high level of segregation typical of U.S. housing markets. However, some of this apparent dispersal was to areas of considerable white flight, thus making it likely that these areas would become resegregated in the future. Sanders (1980) notes that the label of "Negro removal," which was given to urban renewal by civil rights activists, was somewhat exaggerated in that, on a national scale, the majority displaced were whites. However, other studies indicate that because of the dual housing market in most U.S. cities, African Americans had much greater difficulty finding decent replacement housing than whites.

Finally, the substantial cost of relocation may have contributed to the program's demise, by raising substantially the total cost of each project. For example, unpublished data from the Richmond Redevelopment and Housing Authority show that tenants received an average payment of $2,500 and that virtually every homeowner received the full $15,000 payment. As a result, relocation was the largest single item in the Richmond Authority's clearance budget, much larger than the cost of buying the property. Such payments represented the project's true costs, in that the burdens of displacement were no longer externalities borne by the current residents. Nevertheless, they contributed to the impression that urban renewal was excessively costly and thus buttressed Nixon's arguments for change.

Neighborhood Impact

The struggles surrounding relocation tended to focus on the individual problems of displaced households in finding a new place to live. Yet these individual struggles often took place in the context of a neighborhood that was being destroyed by the renewal process. Not only were specific families uprooted, but a whole fabric of economic, social, and political relationships was permanently disrupted. Families reacted differently to separation from their neighborhood. Some grieved in the manner described by Marc Fried. Others were glad to escape to better areas. But regardless of individual reactions, the urban renewal program was increasingly confronted with neighborhoods as organized entities fighting for their collective existence.

According to Christopher Silver, the idea of a neighborhood as a consciously planned or organized unit has been central to urban life since the beginning of U.S. cities (Silver 1982; Rohe 1985). Neighbors have recognized that they are economically and socially interdependent and that they receive a common package of government services, the quality of which is dependent on their socioeconomic status and political clout. This has led to neighborhood political organizations aimed at improving existing conditions, keeping "undesirables" out, and pressuring City Hall for a bigger share of services.

Though the importance of neighborhoods in general has long been recognized, the types of neighborhoods labeled "slums" have frequently been characterized as pathological in nature. From nineteenth-century moralistic tracts denouncing the slums as human cesspools to seemingly more sophisticated twentieth-century discussions of the culture of poverty, the physical concentration of the poor has been seen as reinforcing and enhancing their alienation from the rest of society. Dilapidated housing; poor sanitation; the temptations of crime and drugs; inferior schools; and a street culture that discourages normal (i.e., middle-class) achievement—all of these neighborhood factors have been seen as barriers to the individual's escape from poverty. This analysis has at times been used to support the conclusion that if the physical concentrations of the poor are broken up, some of their pathologies may also be reduced.

However, two alternative views emerged in the 1950s and 1960s which helped generate opposition to urban renewal. One view emphasized that whatever pathology exists in low income neighborhoods arises primarily from the economic and social deprivations of poverty and the inability of individuals to change their situation. Therefore, even though neighborhood influences may be the proximate causes of an individual's failure to advance, the underlying causes relate to the economic structure of the society. Unless more dignity and material well-being are brought to those in low-status occupations and unless more opportunities for upward mobility are created, people will continue to adapt in terms of some version of the culture of poverty, no matter how self-defeating it might appear to an outsider (Waxman 1983). This view supports the conclusion that displacement of the poor out of one area will simply lead to their absorption into another slum environment or to the creation of a similar environment in an adjacent area (Judd and Swanstrom 2010).

The second view emphasized the positive aspects of the culture of poor and working class urban neighborhoods. Scholars such as Herbert Gans (1962), Jane Jacobs(1961), and Gerald Suttles (1968) stressed the intricate and often supportive social relationships that exist beneath the drab and sometimes violent exterior of these areas. Many of the poor live out their entire lives in a single neighborhood, and, though it symbolizes to them their deprivation, it is also familiar territory. Forcible relocation means cutting people loose from the support networks that they have been able to establish in an unfriendly world.

These reevaluations of the nature and causes of low income living patterns coincided with an increasing amount of political organization by low income neighborhoods. Much of this organization was spontaneous, stimulated, particularly in African American areas, by the civil rights movement and modeled after the tactics used by Saul Alinsky in Chicago's working-class areas (Alinsky 1971). However, the organization of these neighborhoods was also greatly encouraged by the federal government's own new solution to the problems of low income areas—the War on Poverty. Far from trying to eliminate these neighborhoods and convert the land to "higher" uses, Community Action Agencies were designed to protect them from neglect, abuse, and encroachment by City Hall or the private sector.

The Community Action Program was, in its own way, as narrow in its approach to poverty as was physical renewal. As several critics have noted, it attributed poverty to the powerlessness of the poor and tried to cure it by political organization, while devoting few resources to correcting the underlying mal-distribution of skills and income. Yet, in many cities, the Community Action Agencies did help to create new political leverage for low income neighborhoods, leverage that was used to tackle concrete problems confronting them. This was particularly true for African American neighborhoods, whose leaders had been the most thoroughly excluded from local political structures (Donovan 1967; Moynihan 1969; Piven and Cloward 1971).

To the residents of low income areas, the prospect of massive displacement due to urban renewal was a problem requiring action. Thus, urban renewal agencies began to encounter organized, articulate opposition where once they could have expected passivity or only mild protest. The economic and political interests behind urban renewal still held most of the high cards and could often win the game anyway, but the political costs of redevelopment were raised considerably. In addition, the federal government was, in effect, put on both sides of the fence. On the one hand, it was encouraging grand schemes for economic redevelopment which involved major changes in the face of the city, particularly in areas outsiders considered blighted. On the other hand, through the War on Poverty and other participatory programs such as Model Cities, it was encouraging the empowerment of those groups most likely to suffer the direct costs of such schemes.

In response to these pressures, HUD began to require local renewal agencies to do their own community organization. After 1968, local agencies had to set up a Project Area Committee (PAC) during the early stages of each project, made up of elected representatives from the target area. These committees were consulted on plans for the area and often suggested both major and minor changes in direction. Though the authority to approve the Redevelopment Plan lay ultimately with the local governing body and with HUD, agencies found it very advantageous to secure solid PAC approval before approaching higher authorities. A supportive PAC could, for example, mobilize area residents to fill City Council chambers on the night the plan was to be approved. A hostile PAC could, in contrast, make trouble for the agency throughout the process.

Counter-pressures from low income neighborhood organizations also contributed to the passage of the various measures aimed at softening and redirecting the program's impact. Offering rehabilitation as an alternative to clearance could mollify opposition, especially when accompanied by low-interest loans and grants to area property owners. Promising to replace a portion of the demolished housing with new units for low and moderate income persons was also a way to reduce opposition. Finally, after the passage of the Uniform Relocation Act, the prospect of its rather substantial financial benefits stimulated many less-committed residents to "take the money and run" rather than to support efforts to save the area. If, as Heywood Sanders suggests, urban renewal was a somewhat different program in the early 1970s than in the early 1960s, the influence of aroused urban neighborhoods can be credited with some of these changes.

Federal Expansion and Intergovernmental Relations

It has been suggested here that a gradual evolution of urban renewal took place, changing it from a program that simply brushed aside low income individuals and neighborhoods (in favor of uses more suitable to local political and economic elites) to a device at least partly targeted at improving the physical environment of the poor, either through conservation of their existing housing or through re-housing them in new units. This change in the direction of physical renewal did not, however, resolve the even more fundamental issue of the relationship between physical improvement of neighborhoods and the total improvement in the lives of the persons affected. Even if an area could be physically renewed with a minimum of displacement, there still remained the question of how the area's residents had really benefited from such renewal. Unless their fundamental lack of resources and opportunities were improved, or, at the very least, they received services that improved their social as well as physical environment, had the quality of their lives been genuinely improved? Conversely, would the physical improvements themselves last if other social problems contributing to physical decay were not dealt with?

The answer among those knowledgeable and active in urban policy was, increasingly, "No!" The longer that poverty remained in the public eye, the more apparent became its multifaceted nature. The causes and solutions to the problems of the poor raised issues of physical health, mental health, employment, education, crime, transportation, recreation, and many others besides housing and community development. Each of these issues touched, in turn, on the basic quality of life of all urban residents, not just the poor. Those concerned with a particular problem constantly found themselves blocked by a nearly seamless web of related problems which seemed to prevent a totally satisfactory solution to that problem alone.

For this reason, the overall increase in government concern about the poor and about urban areas which characterized the late 1960s stimulated new programs in all the areas just mentioned. After years of debate as to whether or not the federal government should get involved, the prevailing liberal consensus seemed to dictate federal action on as many of the problems as possible. This multifaceted approach also enhanced support for the total effort in the short run, in that many different groups in society were eager to get a piece of the action in solving urban ills.

Yet, in the long run, the effort to attack so many problems at once inevitably led to confusion and conflict. Each program spawned a complex set of relationships between executive, legislative, administrative, and citizen centers of power at all levels of government. As programs multiplied they challenged the prerogatives of various political leaders, administrators, and interest groups. No single program could be expanded or redirected without affecting and being affected by the total size and complexity of the federal effort. Moreover, while it was possible as an intellectual exercise to devise ways to consolidate or coordinate related programs, it was much more difficult as a political exercise. When push came to shove, few actors were willing to give up power in order to make the total system more rational.

Thus, by the late 1960s the number and complexity of federal programs had become a political issue in its own right. Liberals became concerned about the effect of chaos and duplication on the ultimate efficacy of programs, while conservatives saw this problem as one more bit of evidence that government efforts on behalf of the poor could never succeed. The continued passage of a variety of programs also triggered conservative concerns about the growth in the total amount of resources being devoted to such purposes.

Therefore, in order to understand why community development policy underwent a major transformation in the early 1970s it is not only necessary to understand earlier community development efforts and the problems they spawned. It is also necessary to examine the issue of programmatic complexity and its political expression in the form of demands for program consolidation. It was in the context of this broader issue that the Community Development Block Grant (CDBG) program emerged and became the centerpiece of federal community development strategy. Thus, the discussion of the CDBG program in Part II will begin with a look at this issue.

Part II—Community Development Block Grants

The Creation of Community Development Block Grants

As a framework for discussing the problems that led to the movement toward grant consolidation and decentralization in the early 1970s, it is useful to review the pattern of involvement of all types and levels of public bodies in formulation, administration, and review which characterized many categorical programs developed during the 1960s. Typically, a problem was perceived and a program formulated at the federal level, often at the initiative of the president and his advisors. Nationally organized interest groups often had input into presidential decisions or helped shape the revisions made in Congress. The administrative responsibility was conferred on whatever federal agency seemed most appropriate to the members of the national coalition backing the program, and the agency then developed regulations to implement the program. Two slightly different coalitions dealing with related areas could generate two programs with fairly similar objectives, which, in retrospect, would appear duplicative. Yet, each agency might make a legitimate argument for its responsibility for the problem and might fear their concerns would be ignored if their program were eliminated or consolidated.

The political commitments behind specific programs and administrative procedures became solidified further as authority passed down through state and local channels. Programs involving an area of traditional state responsibility, such as welfare administration, might rely on state agencies and their local offices for administration. Or, as was more frequently the case, authority might be delegated to mayors, city agencies, local independent commissions, or even nonprofit corporations.

This process contained the seeds of conflict in that federal objectives, procedures, and timetables usually differed from those of the local or state administrative units. Conflicts over objectives reflected differences in political values between levels of government (such as the federal government's greater commitment to enforcing equal opportunity statutes), but there were also numerous conflicts over the complexity of federal procedures and the slowness of federal reviews and approvals (Ingram 1977). For the political reasons mentioned in chapter 2, it was easier for the federal government to *initiate* such programs. However, once the program was in place, it was the local agency delivering the service that was under the most pressure to produce results. The federal government was now in the monitoring and reviewing role, and, though federal agencies were reluctant to totally block local action, they did attempt to gain leverage by imposing complex technical requirements and by holding projects to their own timetable.

Despite these conflicts, specialized local agencies learned the procedures and worked out a *modus vivendi* with their federal counterparts. Also, as federal money began to flow, these local units developed a strong stake in preserving and expanding programs in their charge. Thus was created the vertical, functional integration of categorical areas of governmental activity to which former North Carolina governor Terry Sanford gave the name "picket fence federalism." Each program represented not only a coalition at the federal level, but an alliance between agencies and interest groups at all levels of government.

These alliances were highly resistant to coordination by political executives, no matter which level of government attempted it. When Kennedy's advisors formulated an attack on poverty and, later, when Johnson took a new look at neighborhood development in low income areas, the desirability of coordinating the efforts of various federal agencies was readily apparent. Yet, the mere creation of an umbrella agency, such as the Office of Economic Opportunity (OEO) or the Model Cities Administration, was not enough to ensure successful coordination. The resistance of the political and administrative alliance around each program was so strong that only constant, strong, presidential intervention could compel cooperation, and, given the broad responsibilities of the presidency, such constant pressure was unlikely. Thus, according to Peterson and Greenstone (1977), the OEO embarked on a program of political organization of the poor in order to develop its own constituency, after its initial efforts at coordination on the federal level foundered on agency resistance. Similarly, according to Frieden and Kaplan (1977), the Model Cities program, designed to coordinate services in distressed neighborhoods, was weakened by lack of cooperation at the federal level, even before it began to administer the program locally.

If presidential plans and initiatives had difficulty in changing existing administrative patterns, it is easy to see why governors and mayors soon became frustrated at their lack of control. Both were engaged in building political support behind their own priorities, and they found that the acceptance of much-needed federal funds often brought with it conflicting priorities. Ironically, the whole system of grants-in-aid to state and local governments was designed to allow these governments to shape their own programs. Yet, because program control was conferred on separate agencies, rather than on state or local executives, the latter had a sense of losing, rather than gaining, control over programs in their jurisdiction.

The extension of funds to neighborhood-based organizations created further conflicts. These organizations often had less success in taking on established agencies and programs than did the political executives just mentioned. Procedural changes were difficult enough to obtain, but, more importantly, the extension of federal funds to OEO or Model Cities was not accompanied, in most cases, by sufficient additions to the funding of categorical programs to enable them to respond on a large scale to the problems of a given neighborhood. Meanwhile, federally funded neighborhood groups were putting political heat on local executives and councils, who could not effectively control the direction of the programs they were being asked to change. Where local government did respond, it was inclined to spread benefits among a number of neighborhoods in order to maximize political influence. This pattern did not sit well with the federally organized poor, who felt that resources should be concentrated in their areas. The local *pork barrel* also violated federal criteria for eligibility for specific programs. Thus, local officials felt encircled by demands they could not or did not want to meet.

Finally, there was competition between localities for federal largesse. Some local governments, particularly in larger cities, had years of experience soliciting federal funds. They had developed the staff, the expertise, and the political contacts to successfully push for federal dollars. As the range of federal activities expanded, communities previously too cautious or too conservative to get involved began to feel pressure to bring in federal money. Since they entered the game later, these communities perceived themselves as at a disadvantage. They complained that federal dollars were being handed out on the basis of grantsmanship rather than real needs (Hale and Paley 1981).

It was in the context of these many conflicts that the concept of revenue sharing took root and flowered. Liberal economist Walter Heller, the first to set forth this concept in rigorous form, argued that the expansive and flexible nature of the federal tax base, in contrast to the relatively inflexible tax mechanisms available to state and local governments, necessitated a continuing federal role in aiding these governments. However, he also saw a need to give states and localities greater flexibility in administering federal dollars. He felt the continued use of categorical grants for certain basic federal purposes was necessary, but that, if given extra dollars beyond this, local governments could be encouraged to demonstrate creativity in meeting local needs (Reagan 1972).

This idea received increasing attention throughout the 1960s. Johnson appointed a commission to study it, but because he was cool to the idea, he did not even publish the commission's report, let alone implement its recommendation that revenue sharing be tried. Nevertheless, the bipartisan Advisory Commission on Intergovernmental Relations strongly endorsed the idea in 1967, and various versions of revenue sharing were introduced in Congress. By 1969, when Richard Nixon took office, the idea had been endorsed by the National Governors Association, the U.S. Conference of Mayors, the National Conference of State Legislators, and the National Association of Counties (Reagan 1972, 90).

This broad-based support showed the potential appeal of revenue sharing to both liberals and conservatives, especially at the local level. However, it generally fit more comfortably in a conservative than a liberal agenda. Paul Dommel, in one of the clearest treatments of the history of revenue sharing, points out that the majority of the revenue sharing bills before Congress in the late 1960s were introduced by political conservatives, and it was not until an administration that was basically conservative, despite its pragmatism, came into power in 1969 that the idea moved to the top of the agenda (Dommel 1974, 55). In examining the way Nixon's supportive rhetoric attached revenue sharing to conservatives' focal concerns, the reasons become apparent.

There were three interrelated themes in Nixon's approach to the issue. First, echoing the long-term conservative concern with the total resources going to aid disadvantaged groups, he decried as excessive the expansion of federal activity represented by categorical grants. In his 1969 message proposing the "New Federalism" of which revenue sharing was a part, he asserted that "a majority of Americans no longer support the continued extension of federal services. The momentum for federal expansion has passed its peak; a process of deceleration has set in."

Second, he linked revenue sharing to an attack on the competence and responsiveness of the federal bureaucracy, another conservative theme of his administration. Later in the 1969 speech just cited, he said that "the problems of the cities and the countryside [have] stubbornly resisted the solutions of Washington" (Reagan 1972, 97), thereby suggesting that the federal bureaucracy was incapable of understanding what the people really needed. During his 1972 campaign, he intensified his attack. In one speech he asked, "Do we want to turn more power over to the bureaucrats in Washington in the hope that they will do what is best for all the people? Or do we want to return more power to the people and to their state and local governments, so that the people can decide what is best for themselves?" (Nixon's remarks quoted in Lilley, Clark, and Igelhart 1973, 76–79; see also Nixon 1971).

Such statements identified the federal government entirely with the bureaucracy, as if agencies and programs were *sui generis* rather than created by a popularly elected president and Congress. They reflected Nixon's intense desire to curtail bureaucratic power, thereby reversing the liberal momentum which he and his advisors felt had been built into its structure by two previous administrations. A study of the attitudes of federal civil servants in 1970 by Aberbach and Rockman quotes a "manual" prepared by the Nixon White House for its political appointees to various agencies: "Because of the rape of the career service by the Kennedy and Johnson Administrations this Administration has been left a legacy of finding disloyalty and obstruction at high levels while those incumbents rest comfortably on career civil service status" (Aberbach and Rockman 1976, 456). The study goes on to show that Nixon's image of career civil servants as much more liberal than himself was essentially accurate, especially for those in social service departments such as HUD and HEW.

Third, he linked revenue sharing to a shift in power at the state and local level. Revenue sharing would not only reduce the influence of federal agencies; it would also reduce the influence of local agencies with direct ties to them and enhance the influence of local elected officials. Nixon's advisor, Daniel Patrick Moynihan voiced the administration's criticism of what he called "para-governments" (i.e., nonprofit organizations set up outside the local political structure to receive federal funds directly). In his view, top elected officials at each level of government should set local priorities and disburse federal funds (Lilley, Clark, and Iglehart 1973).

It was within this ideological framework that Nixon developed his revenue sharing proposals. However, these proposals also showed the pragmatic orientation of his administration, in that they were designed to attract the broadest possible support. He proposed two basic types of revenue sharing; general revenue sharing, in which a virtually unrestricted grant would be dispersed to states and localities, and special revenue sharing, or block grants, in which groups of related categorical programs would be replaced by grants covering broad functional areas, within which states and localities could allocate funds to programs they felt could best serve the overall function. The six functional areas selected for block grants by Nixon were health, education, police, manpower, medical care, transportation, and community development (Clark, Iglehart, and Lilley 1972, 1927). General revenue sharing was expected to appeal to liberals because it was extra money on top of categorical programs, as in Heller's original proposal. The block grants were the heart of Nixon's attempt to curb federal influence in that they actually replaced existing programs.

Not surprisingly, the general revenue sharing proposal had a much easier time in Congress than the grant consolidation measures, even though Wilbur Mills (D, Arkansas), the powerful chair of the House Ways and Means Committee, led the opposition. In his view, revenue sharing led to a loss of accountability on both the federal and the local level. On the one hand, the federal government was simply handing over billions of dollars to the states and localities with no control over how it was to be spent. On the other hand, state and local governments were spending funds that they had not taxed their own citizens to obtain, thereby giving them less incentive to spend it wisely. For a time, Mills delayed the legislation, but, under intense pressure from the White House and from others in Congress, he eventually agreed to report it. The State and Local Fiscal Assistance Act became law early in 1972, with Nixon adding a heavy dose of symbolism by signing it in front of Independence Hall in Philadelphia (Reagan 1972).

When special revenue sharing proposals were considered by Congress, opposition was much stronger, and this time the debate focused directly on who would benefit and who would lose. Opponents felt that the poor and minorities would be the big losers if spending priorities were allowed to be set locally. Walter Hundley, head of the Seattle Model Cities program, put their argument very forcefully:

> I am convinced that the only real salvation for the disadvantaged, and for poor blacks in particular, is the direct intervention of the federal government. Local political pressures militate against giving to blacks any priority for public monies, as the federal special impact programs do now. That's why local government is not ready for the burdens which Nixon wants to give it. (Clark, Iglehart, and Lilley 1972,1923)

Wilbur Cohen, former HEW Secretary under Lyndon Johnson, broadened the argument from concern for the poor and minorities to a defense of the federal government's need to clearly and precisely set national priorities. He pointed out that targeting money for a program to deal with a specific problem, rather than lumping a variety of related programs into block grants, involves a clear federal commitment to solving that problem It builds a constituency of those concerned with that problem that would not exist for a broader area, and the federal commitment backed by dollars induces communities to become concerned that would otherwise have ignored the problem. In addition, he argued that the very specificity of categorical programs enabled faster action on social problems. "If [Nixon aide] Ehrlichman's criteria is, solve the problems slower, and maybe a little more cheaply, with more local people," Cohen said, "that's one statement of the problem. But I wouldn't state the problem that way . . . in the kind of society we have . . . we've got a lot of social problems, and we've got to deal with them through strong, federal action" (Clark, Iglehart, and Lilley 1972, 1921).

These arguments enjoyed wide support in the Democratic Congress and, bolstered by organized groups with a stake in existing programs, they blocked much of what Nixon proposed. In transportation, health, and education, where beneficiaries of existing programs were most numerous and well organized, block grant proposals died quickly. In law enforcement, the existing Law Enforcement Assistance Agency (LEAA) program was widely seen as providing sufficient state and local latitude. Only in manpower and community development did legislative movement take place.

The reasons why community development revenue sharing made progress, while proposals in other policy areas did not, revolved around the nature of these programs' constituency. Local government officials had, by this time, become a potent lobby in Washington, represented by several organizations (Farkas 1971; Hays 2001). Whereas other categorical grants had been funneled through groups specializing in those issues, local chief executives had traditionally had a greater say in policies of physical development. Many had succeeded in the grantsmanship game, but many others had failed, and virtually all were attracted to the idea of greater discretion in the handling of federal funds. Though they had fought hard since the New Deal to gain federal attention to community development needs, they were naturally attracted to the possibility of getting the money with fewer controls.

Nixon also appealed indirectly to another constituency, consisting of middle-class residents of central cities, suburban communities, and smaller cities and towns who were little concerned or affected by the problems of the poor. The Democrats felt it essential to appeal to the disadvantaged as well as the middle class to build a winning coalition. Nixon, on the other hand, believed he had little to lose and much to gain politically by redirecting federal dollars toward those whose definition of urban problems revolved around public works, services, and amenities for their own neighborhoods (Mollenkopf 1983). During the debate on revenue sharing, public awareness of this policy change and its implications was not high, but Nixon could anticipate favorable responses when federal funds began to flow to this group.

The broad outlines of the legislative struggle over the Housing and Community Development Act of 1974, which included the CDBG program, have already been presented. However, having emphasized the housing aspects of the bill earlier, it is now necessary to review in more detail the struggle over its community development provisions.

Nixon's proposal for community development revenue sharing included the consolidation of the urban renewal, model cities, and neighborhood facilities programs, replacement of the categorical grant application process by a statutory formula for allocating funds to each community, a reduction in federal administrative requirements, and the transfer of decision making to general purpose local governments from specialized agencies (HUD 1977, 38).

This proposal made no progress in 1971 or 1972 (*CQ Almanac* 1971, 1972). Instead, the housing subcommittees of both chambers each drafted their own legislation, retaining much more federal oversight. The battle was resumed in 1973. After having shown his determination by declaring the moratorium in January, Nixon introduced the Better Communities Act in March. This contained modifications designed to answer some of the objections raised in Congress. It included three more programs in the block grant—open spaces, water and sewer grants, and public facilities loans—but it contained a *hold harmless* provision to protect the funding levels of communities already receiving large amounts of aid. Nevertheless, this bill again stalled for most of 1973 (*CQ Almanac* 1973a).

One reason for the delay, according to Nathan, was the moratorium itself. As noted earlier, Nixon had instituted it, in part, to pressure Congress into action on housing and community development. In the long run, this strategy proved effective. However, in the short run, many pro-housing legislators did not want to approve a major community development initiative without positive housing action on Nixon's part. Therefore, they waited until the fall of 1973, when Nixon put his housing proposal on the table, before they were willing to move on the block grant proposal. Thus, the close relationship between housing and community development measures which had characterized the debates of the 1940s reasserted itself in the 1970s. Supported by slightly different coalitions, they needed to be combined into the same legislation in order to command sufficient support (U.S. Department of Housing and Urban Development 1977, 36).

The other reason for delay was the need to work out multiple disagreements concerning the provisions of the new program. Seeing that some kind of block grant was inevitable, supporters of categorical programs shifted their strategy to working for as limited and controlled a program as they could obtain. They were eventually able to exact compromises on most of the major points Nixon had originally outlined in his 1971 proposal.

First, the concept of a formula distribution system was attacked as unfair. The Senate's housing subcommittee concluded that, due to the complexity and variety of urban problems, *no* formula could accurately determine whether one city had a greater need for community development funds than another (Magida 1974, 1372). Backed by most of the housing and urban development interest groups, the Senate did not include such a formula in its version, and only reluctantly agreed to it in conference committee. The approved formula utilized population, number of overcrowded housing units, and the amount of poverty, with the last factor weighted twice.

Second, criticism was directed at the U.S. Census data used in the formula. Its accuracy had already been questioned in connection with general revenue sharing, and the prospect of millions more dollars riding on population and poverty counts reignited the controversy. The main criticism was that the Census systematically undercounted African Americans and other urban minorities, a point supported by the Census Bureau's own admission that it had undercounted blacks by 7.7 percent in 1970, in contrast to a 1.9 percent undercount for whites (Magida 1974, 1373). In response, Representative Thomas Ashley, (D, Ohio), a long-time housing advocate, supported the data used and said of the formula's critics, "The formula will be practical and feasible. Those complaining . . . are those who have had grants far in excess of equity and more than they can use" (quoted in Magida 1974, 1373). A majority of Congress agreed, and these objections did not block passage of the formula entitlement.

Third, protests were raised about the immediate impact of conversion to the formula on cities currently enjoying much higher levels of funding under categorical programs. Such communities, which tended to be larger, older urban areas, were unhappy about the whole formula idea, but they were especially dismayed by the prospect of a sudden drop in funding. Once having resigned themselves to the formula, they concentrated on strengthening the hold harmless provision that would gradually reduce funding to formula levels. The Nixon administration was very reluctant to provide such a cushion because of its impact on program costs, but it found a great deal of support for these communities' predicament in Congress. As a result, the final bill included a gradual, six-year phase-in of the formula entitlements. During the first three years of the CDBG program, cities currently utilizing categorical grants would be allowed a hold harmless grant, calculated on the basis of their prior level of activity. During the following three years, this would be phased down by thirds, until the formula entitlement level was reached in the sixth program year.

This debate over the use of formula entitlements highlights an ironic twist taken by the struggle over local versus federal discretion in community development. One of Nixon's main criticisms of the categorical grant system was its inflexibility. He objected to the fact that both the purpose for which federal dollars could be used and the way in which funds could be applied to each purpose were specified by federal decision makers (Lilley,

Clark, and Inglehart 1973). However, the block grant system, while giving cities flexibility in *how* to spend federal money, imposed a new rigidity by utilizing a predetermined formula to determine *how much* a community would receive. This system gave less money to those communities that had shown the most interest in community development, while it rewarded those that had shown little interest in the past. Advocates of the old system pointed out that under it, a community containing a political coalition demanding solutions to its problems and/or activist leaders wanting to deal positively with them could respond with aggressive pursuit of federal funds in the areas it thought most vital. This was a clear indication of a felt need for those funds, which might be a more accurate reflection of true needs than an automatic formula.

Another major struggle surrounding the passage of CDBG concerned the degree of administrative control to be retained by HUD. The original Nixon proposal called for no review of locally devised programs—the funds would simply be passed along with no strings, as in general revenue sharing. However, this degree of local discretion was unacceptable to the housing subcommittees and to other Democratic congressional leaders. They wanted to maintain general federal oversight, to ensure that the money was spent for legitimate purposes. The administration held out longer on this issue than on any other and was accused of "more Watergate arrogance" for its refusal to compromise. However, as 1974 progressed, the administration showed more flexibility. The final bill required localities to submit annual applications for CDBG funds, but the HUD review process was drastically shortened. HUD was given seventy-five days to review an application after which it would automatically be considered approved unless objections had been raised; and HUD was only to disapprove those that included clearly impermissible or inappropriate activities or where "the needs and objectives described in the plan are 'plainly inconsistent' with available facts and data" (U.S. Department of Housing and Urban Development 1977, 55).

Nevertheless, HUD was left with some basis for critical review and even rejection of applications. The Act incorporated the following broad, national objectives toward which CDBG expenditures were to be directed:

1. The elimination of slums and blight and the prevention of blighting influences and the deterioration of property and neighborhood and community facilities;
2. The elimination of conditions which are detrimental to health, safety,

and public welfare, through code enforcement, demolition, interim rehabilitation assistance, and related activities;

3. The conservation and expansion of the Nation's housing stock in order to provide a decent home and suitable living environment for all persons;

4. The expansion and improvement of the quantity and quality of community services . . . essential for sound community development;

5. A more rational utilization of land and other natural resources and the better arrangement of residential, commercial, industrial, recreational, and other . . . [uses];

6. The reduction of the isolation of income groups within communities . . . and the promotion of an increase in the diversity and vitality of neighborhoods;

7. The restoration and preservation of properties of special value for historic, architectural, or aesthetic reasons. (Act summarized in U.S. Department of Housing and Urban Development 1977)

Moreover, the Act specified that the needs of low to moderate income people were to be given the highest priority. These goals were vague enough to allow localities plenty of latitude; but, continuity was maintained by echoing themes established in earlier housing and community development legislation (see also Nathan and Dommel 1978; Bekowitz 1977).

Another significant administrative requirement, designed to preserve a strong linkage between community development and housing, was the Housing Assistance Plan (HAP) mentioned in chapter 5. This plan required that all participating jurisdictions: (1) survey the conditions of their existing housing stock; (2) determine the extent and character of present housing needs and estimate the housing needs of those persons "expected to reside" in the jurisdiction; and (3) establish a realistic annual goal of the amount and kind of housing assistance to be provided (U.S. Department of Housing and Urban Development 1977, 56). In defending this provision, Thomas Ashley argued that "if there is anything we have learned in the last few years, it is that we cannot have effective housing programs without local governments providing . . . a healthy community environment for housing" (quoted in U.S. Department of Housing and Urban Development 1977, 55–56).

The passage of the Housing and Community Development Act in August 1974 set a new direction in community development policy (*CQ Weekly Reports* 1974a). The federal government would not be totally uninvolved in urban areas, yet the influence of political and administrative judgments at the national level would be reduced. HUD would retain broad oversight, as a safeguard against gross misuse of federal funds, but detailed planning and decision making would shift to localities. Local officials had complained that the typical urban renewal application was two and one-half feet thick and took two years to process. Now, the review would be much more streamlined.

Yet, in another sense, CDBG did not represent a totally new direction as much as a restoration of an earlier relationship. Despite all the paperwork, urban renewal had, in the 1950s and 1960s, basically underwritten projects conceived by local political and economic elites. It provided a way to legally displace land uses and people that were considered to be "undesirable" in favor of improvements to the local tax base and private investment opportunities. Other physical development programs added in the 1960s, such as grants for sewers and water, open space, and neighborhood facilities also served very broad improvement purposes which both economic elites and middle income voters supported.

However, as the 1960s progressed, the direction of federal involvement changed. At first it was a new program, the War on Poverty, which signaled that federal dollars would support new political involvement by disadvantaged groups. This new approach, while distinct from traditional community development efforts, eventually helped to stimulate change in the community development process itself. The social services approach of Model Cities, plus changes in urban renewal that moved it toward benefiting, rather than merely displacing, the urban poor, were the products of these pressures. Simultaneously, other categorical programs for the poor burgeoned rapidly.

All these activities were stimulated by presidents who adhered to the liberal ideology more intensely than any others since the New Deal. Kennedy, Johnson, and their advisors believed that active federal problem solving in urban areas was essential to system survival, for all the social cost reasons outlined in earlier chapters. Since many political leaders and interest groups at all levels of government shared their concerns, they enjoyed considerable support for the enactment of categorical programs.

However, within the framework of the liberal thrust provided by presidential leadership, the process of program enactment was essentially incremental. No one planned out in advance the cost or administrative structure required to solve all the problems of urban areas or even to solve one particular set of problems thoroughly. Kennedy and Johnson deliberately pursued this incremental strategy because it was easier to build coalitions around specific issues that to sell a comprehensive attack on a whole range of problems. Those hostile to government intervention in general could often be persuaded to support programs dealing with a problem of sufficient personal concern.

This piecemeal accumulation of programs was politically successful in the short run, but in the long run, it left the Great Society vulnerable, once the cumulative impact of all these programs began to be felt. State and local officials who had initially welcomed federal funding began to feel frustrated and limited by the multiplicity of federal goals and administrative requirements. More importantly, they began to find the direction of federal involvement increasingly troublesome. Federal agencies were pushing them toward provision of services to, and political recognition of, groups whose needs had not been reflected in the local policy process before. The para-governments about which Moynihan complained so bitterly were making life more complicated by increasing the number of organized groups they had to please. In short, although federal money was still seen as a useful tool, it was also increasingly seen as an obstacle to their political control.

The conversion to Community Development Block Grants may, thus, be seen as a correction of the balance of power in favor of those groups who had traditionally set the direction of community development. To be sure, African Americans and other disadvantaged groups would never be as underrepresented as they had been before the 1960s. However, with CDBG it was anticipated that local elected officials, and the popular and elite coalitions surrounding them, would once again be firmly in control.

The situation was further complicated by the issue of fund distribution between communities. Nixon was politically beholden to white, middle-class suburbs, not to ethnically diverse central cities. He was also more beholden to the South and West than to the Northeast and North Central regions of the United States. He wanted an urban aid formula that would increase these areas' share of federal largesse without appearing to abandon traditional grant recipients. The struggle over the hold harmless provision made it apparent that many who supported block grants did not support this intercity redistribution, and the issue would arise again during implementation. Nevertheless, a new middle-class constituency was written into urban aid by CDBG.

In light of these considerations, the rhetoric with which Nixon and others justified these changes cannot be taken at face value. Nixon talked a great deal about the "distortion of local priorities" due to categorical grants. However, while the federal bureaucracy is often a blunt and inflexible instrument, there is nothing inherently illegitimate about the national government setting priorities for all its citizens and then trying to ensure that these priorities are carried out. One can, in fact, make a strong argument that it is unfair to allow local political forces to fundamentally alter benefits that should be available nationally to all persons in certain categories. This distortion is only a serious problem if, like Nixon, one disagrees ideologically with federal priorities and expects local priorities to be better.

Nixon's rhetoric also emphasized the confusion and complexity of federal programs, as if this were an ultimate moral evil to be corrected at all costs. Certainly, efficiency and order are important values, but one may legitimately ask what other values should be sacrificed in order to achieve them. When the political mood of the country favors the solution of a certain set of problems, it is to be expected that a variety of actors will get involved, and that programs dealing with a wide variety of problems will be put forward. The resulting programs may duplicate and conflict with one another, but collectively they represent momentum toward solving the problem. In a world where perfect efficiency and coordination are unattainable, perhaps it is better to have government agencies tripping over each other in their eagerness to solve important national problems than to allow the problems to be ignored.

Was Nixon primarily concerned with the duplication and waste in categorical programs or with the overall policy directions they represented? Based on an overview of the revenue sharing debate, the latter concern seems much more prominent. Many ways could have been devised to eliminate waste and inefficiency short of wholesale combinations into block grants. Here, as in the case of housing assistance, Nixon seized on the shortcomings of existing programs as a political weapon to bring about changes in the underlying direction of federal involvement.

The Implementation of Community Development Block Grants

In the following pages, four aspects of CDBG implementation will be examined. The first is the overall impact of the program on the level of federal spending for community development. The second is its impact on the distribution of funds between cities. The third is its impact on the distribution of funds among projects and claimants within local communities, along with the political struggles these issues engendered in the late 1970s. Finally, the impact of the CDBG program on housing in urban areas will be assessed, with particular attention to the shift toward housing rehabilitation as the main strategy the CDBG program helped to engender.

When CDBG was enacted, fears were expressed by some community development advocates that the change in program structure would serve as a smokescreen for reducing federal involvement. Certainly, Nixon had encouraged such fears by suggesting that a block grant structure would weaken the competitive push of national constituencies for funds directed at special problems. However, an analysis of the program's impact on federal spending shows a more complex picture.

Figure 6-1 shows the total federal outlays for community development activities for Fiscal Years 1962 to 2007, as reported by the OMB. It should be kept in mind that there is often a lag between appropriations (budget authority) and program outlays due to the time needed for implementation. This figure reveals a steady increase in outlays during the 1960s, followed by a rapid increase (over 100 percent) between 1969 and 1972, reflecting the spending initiatives of the late Johnson years and Nixon's initial reluctance to cut back in this area. The dip in expenditures during 1973 and 1974 reflects the moratorium, followed by an increase after the 1974 Act went into effect. CDBG spending leveled off in 1978, after an initial burst of activity, but outlays grew rapidly after that to a 1981 peak of more than $5 billion. The sharp drop after that reflects the large Reagan cutbacks in all types of federal grants-in-aid. Since the

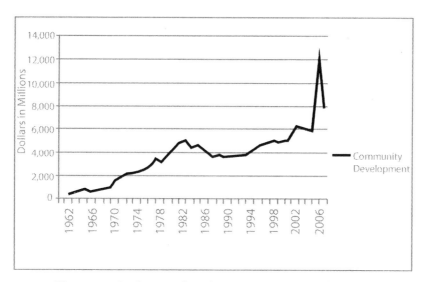

**Figure 6-1 Budget Outlays for Community Development
in Current Dollars**

Source: U.S. Office of Management and Budget, Federal Budget, Historical Tables.

1980s, outlays have steadily increased when measured in current dollars. The spike in outlays in 2005 and 2006 reflects special assistance for the areas struck by Hurricane Katrina.

This trend in the absolute amount of community development spending must, of course, be looked at in relation to inflation and to total federal expenditures. Figure 6-2 includes both these factors by showing community development outlays as a percentage of total outlays during the same period. One striking characteristic of these expenditures is that they have never exceeded 1 percent of total outlays. This fact gives conservative rhetoric about a "massive" commitment of federal funds to urban development a slightly hollow ring. Secondly, the steady rise in absolute dollar amounts shown in Figure 6-1 actually represents a steady, if fluctuating, proportion of total expenditures. The rapid increases between 1969 and 1972 did represent a substantial proportional increase, but after a peak of just over 0.9 percent in 1972, expenditures fluctuated between 0.7 and 0.85 percent. The moratorium caused a sharp dip, while a rapid rise in other federal expenditures not matched by community development expenditures caused the 1978 dip. Of course, Reagan's cuts after 1981 represented a large proportional as well as absolute decline, and the levels set in the Reagan era have remained pretty much constant since then.

Although these data give some idea of the resources committed to community development, they conceal two other sources of retrenchment within the block grant program. First, it should be recalled that the

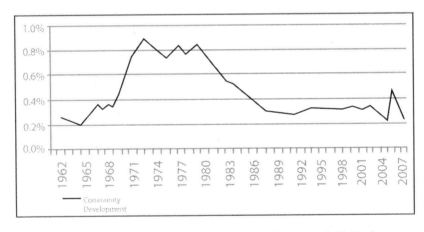

Figure 6-2 Community Development as a Percent of all Outlays

Source: U.S. Office of Managment and Budget, Federal Budget, Historical Tables

urban renewal program had required a one-third matching expenditure by localities. Under the new program, this match was not required, and communities spent federal funds on the physical improvements they had previously funded themselves in order to earn federal dollars. A precise analysis of this change is beyond the scope of this book. Nevertheless, given the size of the local commitment formerly required, it is likely that a noticeable shrinkage in the impact of community development expenditures occurred.

Secondly, retrenchment occurred as a result of the splitting of the community development pie among a larger number of communities. The increased funding after 1974 was not directed at the same universe of problems, but was accommodating many new claimants while avoiding sudden cutbacks in communities already using these funds. This distributional impact of CDBG must now be explored.

The effects of CDBG on the distribution of funds among communities were, in general, those that could have been predicted from the program's design. Under categorical programs, funds flowed to the central city more than to suburban areas. Under CDBG, suburbs received more, despite the double weighting of the poverty factor (Hirshen and Le Gates 1975). Under categorical programs, older central cities of the Northeast, North Central, and Midwest received the largest share of funds. Under CDBG there was a shift toward the South and West. Under categorical grants, metropolitan areas (SMSAs) received almost all the funds. Under CDBG, they continued to receive the lion's share, but 20 percent of the dollars were set aside in a discretionary fund for smaller, nonmetropolitan communities. However, analysis of these trends is made more complicated by the fact that additional political struggles took place during implementation, resulting in significant midcourse changes in direction. Therefore, it is necessary to look at the original direction the program would have taken, in contrast to the direction it actually took and in contrast to the direction taken by the categorical grants it replaced.

For the first two years of CDBG implementation, its impact on large central cities that had been active in categorical programs was muted by the hold harmless provision. The total amount of community development funds was increased by Congress, and larger cities shared the increment with metropolitan and nonmetropolitan areas, but since their individual funding levels were not reduced, this was only mildly troublesome. However, as the full implementation of formula entitlements loomed closer, their substantial redistributive impact became apparent. The first two columns of Table 6.1 contrast what various jurisdictions received

Table 6.1 CDBG Dollar Shares by Type of Recipient

Type of Recipient	Hold Harmless Allocation*	Allocation Under 1974 Formula	Allocation Under 1977 Dual Formula
MSA Total	87.5	80.0	81.3
Entitlement Jurisdictions	74.0	48.0	62.5
Central Cities	69.6	42.4	55.5
Satellite Cities	4.4	5.6	7.0
Urban Counties	—	11.0	12.0
Non-Entitlement Jurisdictions	—	21.0	6.8
Non-MSA Jurisdictions	12.5	20.0	18.7

*Based on amount received under categorical programs

Source: *Department of Housing and Urban Development, City need and community development funding. 1979.*

under the categorical system (as reflected in their hold harmless share) with what they would have received had the original CDBG allocation system gone into effect.

These data reveal the precipitous decline that would have occurred in the share of funding received by central cities in SMSAs in the sixth year of the program, fiscal 1980. Funds would have been redistributed from these traditional beneficiaries of categorical grants to virtually every other type of jurisdiction. In spite of the protection that was supposed to be afforded to large urban areas by the double weighting of the poverty factor in the formula, many of these areas would have seen funds flowing into the prosperous suburban communities surrounding them.

It also became apparent that a regional redistribution of funds would occur. Table 6.2 shows projections made by the Brookings Institution's first-year CDBG evaluation as to its regional impact. It shows the percentage of funds received by each of the nine U.S. Census subregions under the categorical programs, in contrast to the percentage they would have received under the 1974 formula. It also shows per capita expenditures as a proportion of the national average before and after the change. Clearly, the New England, Middle Atlantic, and North Central regions would have lost from one-fourth to one-half of their funds and would have dropped from relatively high per capita expenditures to levels well below the national average. In contrast, much of the South and West would have gained in their share of funds. The Brookings study went on

Table 6.2 Regional Distribution of CDBG Funds

Region	Hold Harmless		CDBG Formula	
	Percent	Per Capita*	Percent	Per Capita*
New England (ME, NH, VT, MA, CT, RI)	9.9	170	4.7	80
Mid-Atlantic (NY, PA, NJ)	22.7	124	17.4	95
South Atlantic (WV, MD, DE, VA, NC, SC, GA, FL)	15.0	99	16.5	109
E. South Central (MS, LA, TN, KY)	6.0	95	7.9	126
E. North Central (OH, IN, IL, MI, WI)	15.9	80	17.2	87
W. South Central (LA, TX, AR, OK)	8.2	80	12.4	130
W. North Central (MO, KS, NE, IA, MN, ND, SD)	7.7	96	6.7	84
Mountain (AZ, NM, CO, UT, NV, WY, ID, MT)	3.6	80	3.9	96
Pacific (CA, OR, WA, AK, HI)	11.0	84	13.3	101

*Proportional per capita share (national per capita share = 100)

Source: U.S. Department of Housing and Urban Development, Block grants for community development 1977.

to show that the cumulative result of both redistributions would have been a drastic loss of funds by some of the most distressed cities in the United States. The metropolitan areas measuring highest on their index of the economic disparity between central cities and suburbs were some of the biggest losers of funds.

The Brookings evaluation team recommended a new formula to reduce the flow of funds away from these distressed areas. The two indicators they found to be most closely correlated with distress were the age of a city's housing stock and the extent of population decline. They suggested that these factors be included in a new formula, in lieu of the overcrowded housing factor previously used. However, to prevent too drastic a reduction in the newer cities' share, they suggested a dual formula system, in which each city would get the larger of the amounts computed with both formulas. Under increasing pressure from representatives of larger urban areas, the outgoing Ford administration recommended the dual formula in 1977.

President Jimmy Carter had even more reason to be enthusiastic about the dual formula than President Gerald Ford, since the traditional Democratic urban coalition had contributed greatly to his election. Therefore, the Carter administration retained the idea in its proposed housing and community development legislation, and expanded its impact by substituting a measure of growth lag for population loss. This meant that cities with growth rates lower than the national average would receive increased funding, as well as cities actually losing population.

Although the dual formula did not directly cut the funding of any entitlement city, the measure precipitated an intense debate in the House, dividing its members along regional lines. Representatives from the South and West denounced the age of housing factor as discriminatory against more recently settled parts of the country. As Representative Jerry Patterson (D, California) put it, "The real issue here is: Do we want to address poverty or do we want to address old houses?" (Quoted in HUD 1978a, 24). Northeastern and Midwestern representatives argued, on the other hand, that the poverty factor alone would not prevent rapidly growing Sunbelt cities from receiving funds more desperately needed by declining cities in the Frostbelt. The dual formula survived an attempt to delete it from the law by a vote of 261 to 149. Representatives from the East voted 110 to 1 in favor of the dual formula and members from the Midwest supported it by a 105 to 7 margin. Those from the South and West voted to delete it 132 to 18 (HUD 1978a, 25).

The impact of the new formula is clearly shown in the third column of Table 6.2. Entitlement cities retained a 62.5 percent share of CDBG funds, substantially less than under categorical grants but a marked improvement over the original 1974 formula. Most of this gain was allocated to central cities, at the expense of the smaller, suburban communities. The regional distribution was also affected, in that the Northeast and North Central regions regained some of the share they enjoyed under categorical grants.

In addition to the formula change, the Carter administration successfully initiated in 1977 a new program designed to further correct the shift of funds away from the older, more distressed cities. This program, the Urban Development Action Grant (UDAG), enabled economically declining central cities to support large redevelopment projects of a commercial, industrial, or residential nature that were beyond the scope of CDBG but which would offer improvements in employment and tax base. Although the projects envisioned for UDAG were similar to urban renewal projects of an earlier era, the new program reflected the caution of the 1970s in that it required prior commitment of funds by private investors in an amount five or six times that of the federal investment. The program reflected a renewed interest in leveraging private central city investment through direct cash subsidies, low interest loans, or public financing of land assembly or public improvements needed to make a project economically viable. UDAG added $500 million per year to community development coffers during the late 1970s and early 1980s.

The political struggle over the CDBG formula showed the ability of representatives of older, larger urban areas in general and of central cities in particular to mount effective political pressure. The way this issue was resolved again illustrates the complexity of community development issues in political and ideological terms. In one sense, aid to declining urban areas was the type of government intervention liberals tended to favor and conservatives questioned. The cumulative effect of market decisions was to favor some cities over others and, within cities, some areas over others. Conservatives lean toward enhancement of or, at the least, noninterference with these trends. This outlook was reflected in the 1974 Act in that it broadened the set of legitimate targets for community development aid to include better-off communities as well as declining central cities.

Yet, this redistributive pattern also triggered opposition, which cut across ideological lines. Economic and political elites in many cities were negatively affected by the formula, and loyalty to their own communities did not permit acquiescence to a drastic reallocation of funds. Each community's power structure remained committed to its economic viability, even though national economic criteria might classify the area as declining. Thus, the formula struggle pitted region against region and central city against suburb, rather than liberal against conservative. To the extent that the poor were concentrated in declining areas, they benefited from the dual formula; but their actual level of benefits depended more on another struggle—the struggle over the use of funds within urban areas.

The CDBG guidelines established by Congress and by HUD gave local officials something less than carte blanche in using federal dollars, yet their control over planning and executing specific projects increased substantially. As a result, each city had to create its own mechanism for allocating funds. According to the 1978 Brookings evaluation (HUD 1978a), most of these new mechanisms reflected the desire of local chief executives for more direct involvement. During the first two years, many cities spent CDBG funds to finish out existing urban renewal and model cities commitments. This perpetuated the influence of existing agencies and maintained the direction they had set. However, most chief executives tried to place CDBG administration much closer to their own office. Some urban renewal agencies were abolished and some had their staffs absorbed by new community development offices headed by a deputy to the mayor or city manager. Others survived but had to deal directly with city, rather than federal, officials.

In addition to greater involvement by local chief executives, the Brookings study notes the importance of citizen involvement. HUD required as a minimum that public hearings be held to inform local citizens of the availability of the money, but most communities also created citizen advisory boards, representing both community leaders and people in targeted neighborhoods. The term *advisory* is important, since most executives maintained ultimate control, yet these groups did provide a means by which the needs of various neighborhoods could be heard.

Citizen's groups tended to gain influence as the program matured. During the first year, local citizens knew very little about the flexibility of the program. As the application procedure became routinized and as more community groups became aware of the relatively unrestricted funds it provided, demands for CDBG funds increased. At this point, participatory mechanisms became one means of resolving conflicting citizen pressures. In addition, members of local legislative bodies became more active in reviewing individual projects. They, too, saw the block grant as a source of funding for projects important to their districts.

Increased involvement by both chief executives and citizens encouraged the spreading of funds, which many had predicted. Mayors, city managers, and councils were anxious to please as many local constituents as possible. Categorical program guidelines might have enabled or compelled them to concentrate millions of dollars in a single urban renewal or model cities area. Now, with these constraints removed, their attention turned to projects benefiting the entire community or to smaller-scale projects enabling them to spread funds among many neighborhoods (Kettl 1979).

This spreading effect led to two major conflicts between HUD and local officials—the conflict over socioeconomic targeting and the conflict over geographic targeting. With regard to socioeconomic targeting, the 1974 Act specified that "maximum feasible priority" be given to low and moderate income persons in utilizing block grant funds. Since "maximum feasible priority" was as vague as "maximum feasible participation" had been in the War on Poverty, this was a rather flexible guideline. Yet, despite a few well-publicized cases of suburban golf courses or tennis courts being built with CDBG funds, there was no wholesale abandonment of community development in lower income areas. What concerned HUD officials, and a number of liberal interest groups, was a slow drift of funds away from low income projects. HUD saw its role as preserving the original legislative intent by insisting on continued concentration of effort in low to moderate income areas, while local officials felt that the flexibility accorded them by the 1974 Act was being negated by HUD.

Although HUD officials took this position from the beginning, their emphasis on targeting was strengthened by the appointment of Patricia Roberts Harris as HUD Secretary by President Jimmy Carter in 1977. In testimony before the House Subcommittee on Housing and Community Development she said, "We will expect communities to direct development and housing programs toward low- and moderate-income citizens. I do not consider this to be just an objective of the block grant program—it is the highest priority of the program and we in the federal government must see to it that the thrust of the program serves that objective" (Quoted in Dommel 1980, 466). HUD immediately proposed regulations requiring that 75 percent of all CDBG funds be used to directly benefit low and moderate income persons, while 25 percent could go to other projects.

This proposal met stiff opposition from Representative Thomas Ashley and other community development specialists who felt that aid to the poor was only one of several important goals of the 1974 Act. Therefore, HUD's final regulations acceded to congressional pressure by allowing more flexibility. However, the department continued to push localities to spend as much of their grant on low and moderate income areas as possible, and the Brookings evaluation team concluded that they were partially successful. In the cities sampled by Brookings, spending directed at low to moderate income persons increased from 54 percent to 62 percent over the first four years of CDBG (Dommel 1980, 469).

HUD also stressed a second form of targeting—geographical—which ran counter to the local spreading of funds. Federal officials believed that sound community development strategy involved concentrating funds and activities in well-defined areas, rather than spending funds on a community-wide basis. They felt this would make the effects of various programs mutually reinforcing, and that permanent improvement in neighborhood conditions, rather than piecemeal solutions to immediate problems, would more likely result. In pursuit of this goal, which of course was similar to that of Model Cities and the War on Poverty, they pushed localities to concentrate on specific census tracts and even disapproved some applications on the grounds that activities were too widely dispersed. This concern overlapped with their concern with socioeconomic targeting, since it was in lower income areas that, in their view, intensive activity should take place.

The HUD push for geographic targeting culminated in a series of new regulations in 1977 and 1978 which formally designated areas of concentrated activities as Neighborhood Strategy Areas (NSA). Communities were required to show that these areas were mainly residential and that enough resources were being committed to meet major community development needs. Communities were pressured to designate areas as NSA and to shift resources away from city-wide projects (HUD 1981a). The reaction of local officials was skeptical. The Brookings team quotes one local official that "if HUD wants to play NSA, we'll play NSA" (HUD 1981a, 91). However, the Brookings evaluators found that, in their sample, there had been a noticeable shift toward neighborhood targeting. In the fourth and fifth program years, benefits were more concentrated in fewer census tracts, and the boundaries of target areas tended to contain fewer people. Interestingly enough, it was cities with the worst problems that had the least geographic targeting, while economically advantaged communities targeted more. This suggests that even scattered projects were directed at serious needs rather than dissipated on nonessential services (U.S Department of Housing and Urban Development 1981a).

Table 6.3 summarizes the general categories of activities funded by Community Development Block Grants for selected fiscal years between

Table 6.3 Uses of CDBG Funds

Type of Activity	Fiscal Year				
	1979	1982	1984	1986	1989
Redevelopment	17.9	9.0	8.0	7.0	7.0
Housing	34.1	35.1	36.0	38.0	36.0
Public facilities and improvements	29.8	26.1	22.0	18.0	23.0
Economic development	4.5	9.0	12.0	13.0	10.0
Public services	9.7	8.0	8.0	11.0	10.0
Administration and planning	4.0	13.0	14.0	14.0	14.0

Source: U.S. Department of Housing and Urban Development, Community block grant report. 1982–1990.

1979 and 1989. Public works, redevelopment activities, and related public services stand out as major activities. However, the most striking feature is the large concentration of funds in the area of housing rehabilitation, which represented about one-third of CDBG expenditures in FY 1979 and grew to 40 percent in FY 1981. These data suggest that the importance of housing as a community development goal had increased greatly as a result of the shift to CDBG, continuing the trend noticeable in urban renewal during the early 1970s. The reasons for this lie both in a changed concept of proper housing strategy and in the political dynamics of CDBG program implementation just described. Both these factors will be explored in examining the impact of CDBG on housing policy.

Community Development Block Grants and Housing Policy

The close political linkage between housing and community development, which had existed since the 1940s and which reemerged in the passage of the 1974 Act, has already been discussed. In this section, the implementation linkages between the two will be explored. A general link may be found in the use of CDBG funds to provide physical improvements in neighborhoods. Since the neighborhood is part of the housing package a family purchases, improvements in the area can enhance the quality of their housing. For both budgetary and political reasons, communities tended to do much less clearance under CDBG than under urban renewal. Thus, physical development could be directed at making existing neighborhoods viable.

In addition, there existed two more specific ways in which the CDBG program shaped the direction of housing policy. One was the incorporation of the Housing Assistance Plan (HAP) into the CDBG application. The HAP set a precedent for HUD housing planning requirements that have continued to the present day, first through the Comprehensive Housing Affordability Strategy (CHAS) and later through the Consolidated Plan which is now required of all cities receiving CDBG funds. The other was the extensive development of housing rehabilitation programs as a major object of CDBG expenditures. Each of these relationships deserves further exploration.

THE HOUSING ASSISTANCE PLAN

As discussed earlier, the 1974 Act required each locality to submit a Housing Assistance Plan as part of its CDBG application. The plan was to be followed by HUD in allocating units of assisted housing to that community. The immediate impact of this requirement was to encourage communities to be conscious of housing needs when planning their CDBG strategies and to compel them to collect more detailed information on their housing stock. The data they gathered varied in quality. Some communities hired consultants to carry out sophisticated surveys. Others merely manipulated 1970 Census data to produce numbers they hoped HUD would find plausible. Yet, Raymond Struyk suggests that regardless of variations in the accuracy of the data collected, the HAP had a positive impact on local political leaders' awareness of housing needs, since it was debated and approved along with the rest of the CDBG application (Struyk 1979).

At the same time, the HAP process demonstrated the difficulty of federal-local relationships. Although the HAP was intended to encourage local planning of housing strategies, HUD was required to assess the reasonableness of local plans. In order to do this, HUD Area Offices obtained their own, independent data on the housing stock of the communities in their jurisdiction. This led local officials to complain that area offices often attached little credibility to local data and, instead, substituted their own figures. An internal HUD memorandum reported that "[m]ost . . . [local officials] said that they take what the Area Office gives them. First you submit a set of numbers and 'then you play games'; you put down the bottom numbers and the Area Office divides them up" (quoted in Struyk 1979, 14).

Another factor that detracted from full utilization of the HAP was that the units actually funded by Congress were usually only a small percentage of any community's total need. Therefore, there was a tendency not to take the total need figures seriously, since the actual units built would never come near that level. Nevertheless, Struyk concluded that the HAP's enhancement of local housing planning was a good reason for continuing the requirement (Struyk 1979, 20–22).

HOUSING REHABILITATION

Throughout most of the history of U.S. housing policy, the idea of utilizing rehabilitation to improve the housing stock existed mostly as an afterthought. While lip service was paid to the notion that rescuing existing structures might be an economically desirable alternative to new construction, this activity was given low priority. FHA financing of rehabilitation was available, but the number of units rehabilitated was dwarfed by the agency's massive commitment to new construction. The Housing Act of

1954 included rehabilitation as an eligible urban renewal activity, but the dominant strategy was still clearance and rebuilding.

This de-emphasis on rehabilitation was in keeping with the spirit of the postwar era. The emphasis then was on the new—new factories, new commercial developments, and new suburban housing reached by new cars on newly built freeways. Progress was measured by the degree to which open countryside could be filled with crisp, clean new dwellings equipped with the modern conveniences that were now within financial reach of middle-class families. Central cities tried to compete with suburban development with sleek new office towers and other new uses of blighted areas. The idea of converting an old warehouse into shops or restaurants, so typical of the plans that captivate contemporary urban dwellers, would have seemed eccentric to all but a few in the 1950s.

In the case of housing rehabilitation, the negative impact of the general cultural emphasis on newness was reinforced by concrete economic and administrative problems. As a planned, public activity, rehabilitation has typically been slower and much more difficult than new construction. There are several reasons for this.

First, mass production has proven difficult in rehabilitation. Whereas a new development can be erected with a limited number of floor plans, and large-scale purchase of materials, existing houses and neighborhoods contain numerous variations in design and condition. Therefore, each rehabilitation job must be tailored to the needs of a specific structure and family, a process requiring considerable administrative, as well as construction, time and discouraging economies of scale. Moreover, the economic structure of the housing rehabilitation industry reflects its technical characteristics, in that firms specializing in rehabilitation tend to be smaller operations than those doing new construction. Agencies experimenting with large-scale rehabilitation have, therefore, found it difficult to recruit private firms willing to carry out their plans (National Commission on Urban Problems 1969; Hartman 1975).

Second, housing rehabilitation requires a very different set of relationships between government agencies and citizens than does suburban new construction or clearance of older areas. During the first fifteen years of the urban renewal program, agencies bent on clearance and armed with the power of eminent domain could relatively easily overcome neighborhood resistance, especially when the target area's citizens were poor, inarticulate, and unorganized. The process required little cooperation from the areas affected. In contrast, rehabilitation requires cooperation from the very beginning, at both the neighborhood and the individual level.

At the neighborhood level, agencies must work with existing property owners to reverse the "prisoner's dilemma" situation described by Davis and Whinston (1966). In their model, property owners in older areas are reluctant to invest in repairs for fear that other property owners will not match their investment. Since property values in a given area are interdependent, the owner will be worse off if he/she invests while others do not than if no one invests or if others invest while he or she does not. A program targeted at a specific neighborhood must, therefore, engage in extensive neighborhood organization (or work to strengthen existing organizations) in order to convince individual property owners that their investment will pay off. Coercion (i.e., the ability to condemn property that does not comply with standards) may be used to back up persuasion, but if it is not used extremely sparingly, it will intensify, rather than weaken, resistance.

Cooperation must also be secured during the rehabilitation process. In order to encourage participation in the program, the property owner must be allowed some choice as to the type of work to be done. This requires negotiations between the owner and the agency, and it may also require the inclusion of visible amenities the property owner can enjoy, as well as basic structural repairs, such as new plumbing and heating. This lengthens the process and increases the cost of each dwelling. It is not, of course, absolutely necessary to utilize existing property owners as vehicles for rehabilitation. Several federal programs have purchased and rehabilitated small numbers of dwellings. However, it has, in general, been more difficult to justify politically the coerced purchase of a dwelling and the displacement of its occupants if it needs modest repairs and is in a moderately deteriorating area than if it is dilapidated and located in an area that is seen as in need of clearance. The notion of leaving a neighborhood physically intact has seemed to fit, in the minds of most policy makers, with the utilization of existing owners, although displacement has also occurred.

In addition to the technical problems of construction and the sociopolitical problems of securing neighborhood cooperation, rehabilitation has also encountered a third set of problems—those associated with finances. Rehabilitation of existing structures in older, declining areas is a best a risky venture, as evidenced by the higher foreclosure rates among Section 236 and Section 221(d)(3) rehabilitation units than among newly constructed units. Unless the whole area is substantially upgraded, owners often have difficulty attracting tenants at rents that will support even subsidized borrowing for rehabilitation.

Finally, rehabilitation programs have encountered opposition in some communities on ideological grounds. Though clearance has been resisted by doctrinaire conservatives, the notion of removing blight for beneficial reuse of land has appealed to a broad political spectrum as a legitimate public purpose justifying interference with private property rights. In contrast, rehabilitation of structures that remain in private hands has met resistance on dual grounds: (1) that forced inspection and rehabilitation violates the property rights of landlords and homeowners; or (2) that direct subsidies to private owners that enhance the value of an asset they hold represent an unfair benefit to a few at the expense of others. The first attitude has shown up in the rulings of local judges, who are extremely reluctant to convict or punish landlords for code violations. According to Chester Hartman, "Few judges take housing violations as seriously as they take other types of cases, nor do they have sufficient background in housing or knowledge of the particular defendant and his patterns of operation to make a sound judgment" (Hartman 1975, 66). The second attitude has shown up in protests by property owners in other sections of a city when a specific geographic area is designated for rehabilitation. This has made local officials reluctant to assist any but the lowest income owners.

None of these fundamental problems disappeared during the 1970s, yet rehabilitation grew rapidly into the most popular community development strategy. This may be accounted for by cultural, economic, and political factors, which overrode traditional obstacles to the utilization of this strategy.

On the cultural level, the American belief that "new is better" was, if not eliminated, at least chastened by the events of the 1970s. First, the environmental movement raised public consciousness of the heavy costs of growth in general, and new suburban development, in particular, in terms of air and water pollution and in terms of lost open space and farm land. Second, the energy shortages of the 1970s led many to the growing conviction that resources were finite and that the continued consumption of more fuel, more raw materials, and more land for new products might eventually lead to disaster. Both of these movements stressed the desirability of reuse and recycling of existing resources, and the reuse of existing neighborhoods and structures fell naturally within this area of interest. Also, these movements called attention to older technologies and lifestyles which were less wasteful of natural resources. Mass transit and intensive urban land uses such as row houses, which had seemed destined for the trash heap in the early postwar decades, were now more attractive.

These changes also helped bring into sharper focus the social and aesthetic critique of suburbia that had always been an intellectual current in the United States (Elazar 1966). Malvina Reynolds's song about "little boxes made of ticky-tacky," whose inhabitants allegedly acted in blind conformity, had earlier expressed intellectuals' association of suburbia with middle-class philistinism (Reynolds 1964). Now these "little boxes" were seen as wasteful and environmentally damaging, as well as aesthetically and socially distasteful.

To these aesthetic arguments were added practical economic disincentives to suburban life as well. Many suburbs were becoming increasingly congested and were suffering from some of the same problems of crime and social alienation as the central cities. Moreover, the energy costs of long commuting distances were beginning to hit the pocketbooks, as well as the social consciences of middle- and upper-class persons.

In this atmosphere, the "back to the city" movement took hold and flourished among a segment of the middle and upper-middle classes. In an oft-described pattern, a few middle-class families would renovate older structures in neighborhoods filled with rooming houses and lower income apartments. These "pioneers" (it is interesting to note that terms from the early frontier such as "pioneer" and "homesteading" brought another set of symbols to play in this process) would discover that these older houses, many built by the well-to-do of the nineteenth century, had design and aesthetic elements not available at any reasonable price in the suburbs—large rooms, parquet floors, stained glass, carved woodwork, etc. By restoring these elements (and modifying them to modern tastes) these early renovators attracted others, with the result that the filtering process which had seemingly doomed the area was suddenly reversed. Property values rose; rental property became owner occupied; low income persons were forced to move elsewhere; and the area became, in the new terminology of the decade, gentrified (Black 1975; Zukin 1982).

Since the writers and intellectuals who shape the direction of the media and academic research were in the social stratum most involved in this process, the phenomenon of gentrification quickly captured public and academic attention. Features on upper-middle-class couples fixing up old townhouses became a staple of Sunday newspaper supplements and national magazines. Urban policy researchers began to explore the dynamics and implications of reverse filtering. Judging from the intensity of interest, it was easy to conclude that a major national trend was occurring.

In addition, some hard data indicated a change in patterns of urban housing investment and ownership. James reported that the middle 1970s saw a modest increase in the proportion of central city dwellers owning their own homes and a proportionally faster increase in the value of central city housing than in suburban housing. He also reported a significant increase in the level of investment in existing housing, as measured by the U.S. Census' Survey of Residential Alternations and Repairs (James 1980,131–35).

Doubts were soon raised, however, about the scope and direction of the back to the city movement by more intensive and critical demographic research. One fact that quickly became clear was that this new flow of people back to the city was really a trickle. Even the most sanguine estimates showed a relatively few families and a relatively few neighborhoods involved. Moreover, this trickle was largely counteracted by the continued exodus of other middle-class families (especially white) to the suburbs (Sternlieb et al., 1980; Palen and London 1984). In addition, much evidence indicated that it was more a "stay in the city" than a back to the city movement. Young, single, or recently married persons, a group traditionally attracted to the central city, were the main ones who chose to invest in older areas, rather than move to the suburbs as their economic status improved. While this trend in itself was not insignificant, it did not represent a choice of the central city over the suburbs by middle-class persons of child-rearing age who had traditionally lived in outlying areas. Also, analyses by Philip Clay and others showed that considerable reinvestment was being made by families of more modest means who already lived in the central cities (Clay 1980). Such "incumbent upgrading" was less likely to make the newspaper's Sunday supplement and so did not attract as much attention as gentrification.

At the same time, it was clear that the impact of the back to the city movement was greater than could be measured by the numbers of people involved. First, the revitalization that did take place was generally spread out over highly visible and strategically located neighborhoods close to downtown. A few hundred families occupying as many units in a previously decaying section had a major visual and psychological impact, and often turned the area into a showcase for the entire central city. Second, the fact that it was so striking a reversal of a decades-old exodus of the white middle and upper-middle classes gave it added psychological significance. Planners, policy makers, and other interested urban dwellers anticipated (and hoped) that these families might be the "thin edge of the wedge."

Finally, and most importantly for the present analysis, the back to the city movement gave added respectability and impetus to the use of housing rehabilitation in community development (Laska and Spain 1980). Its growth coincided with an increasing desire among planners and policy makers to find a less costly and disruptive mechanism of urban revitalization than total clearance, a desire reflected in the growing use of rehabilitation in urban renewal (Sanders 1980).

Analyses such as Grigsby's study of filtering (1965) had focused attention on the long-term process of physical and social decay which turned neighborhoods into slums. These suggested that it would be less costly to intervene in the process *before* it had advanced to the point where total clearance was necessary. While neighborhoods undergoing gentrification were generally those with special architectural or historical appeal, the fact that private individuals could, virtually unaided, turn a neighborhood around suggested that planned, public intervention might be successful in other declining neighborhoods.

Even though housing rehabilitation had played a minimal role in earlier housing programs, there were several programs that contributed administrative models and implementation experience to the rehabilitation push of the 1970s. Most important were the Section 312 and Section 115 programs. The Housing Act of 1954 enabled localities to utilize urban renewal funds for housing rehabilitation, but for all the reasons mentioned, it was difficult to get either public or private agencies excited about renovation. Therefore, pressure developed for more concrete incentives, particularly as the destruction of housing by urban renewal became widespread. The Section 312 program was part of the Housing Act of 1964, while the Section 115 program was enacted a year later, but they were so closely linked in implementation as to be, in effect, one program (Hartman 1975, 73). In addition to urban renewal areas, localities used them in areas designated for concentrated code enforcement. This came to be known as the FACE (Federally Assisted Code Enforcement) program.

The Section 312 program provided loans of up to $15,000 to property owners at 3 percent interest for twenty years. At first, this was only a small subsidy in relation to market rates, and the main benefits of the loans were; (1) that they were available in areas where private banks would not extend credit; and (2) that they were an alternative to demolition for property owners in the path of urban renewal. However, as private market interest rates gradually increased, the subsidy increased until, by the late 1970s, a 3 percent loan seemed almost like free money in comparison to double digit private rates. As an added incentive, these loans could be used to refinance existing mortgages, if necessary to make the rehabilitation financially feasible for the owner. Hartman notes that this sometimes made the monthly payment after rehabilitation less than it was before (Hartman 1975, 73).

The Section 115 program made grants of up to $3,500 available to owners with incomes too low to support a loan, and grants of up to $3,000 were available as supplements to Section 312 loans. The three types of aid—grants, loans, and loan/grant combinations—could thus span a wide range of incomes, mostly at the lower end of the scale. The impact of these programs, measured in terms of total units upgraded, was limited during their first decade. According to HUD's 1979 Statistical Yearbook, 66,045 units had been rehabilitated under Section 312 by 1974. Nevertheless, certain administrative patterns were set which carried over into CDBG.

One pattern established by Section 312 was a strong preference for loans to homeowners over loans to investor owners. Homeowners were seen as a stable, responsible element in the community, a perception similar to that which stimulated Section 235. To encourage owners to reinvest in their homes was to aid residents who would continue to care about the overall condition of the area in order to preserve their investment. This perception was borne out by the experience of many agencies, which generally found homeowners the most eager to organize and to participate in the program.

In contract, investor owners were viewed, especially on the local level, as "slumlords" undeserving of aid. They were often, though not always, higher income individuals residing outside the target area, and the prospect of subsidizing them was unappealing, despite the fact that low income tenants were the intended beneficiaries. Added to this were serious practical problems with their inclusion. Contrary to the popular stereotype of profiteering, many operated their properties on a slim margin (Stegman 1979). This meant that additional financing costs were hard to sustain while maintaining a minimal return on investment. This made investor owners reluctant to participate, to the point that some would demolish their units rather than bring them up to code, even when low interest loans were available. Their participation also often led to increased rents for improved units. Hartman, Kessler, and LeGates (1974) found that FACE programs in San Francisco and elsewhere led to considerable displacement of low income tenants, either due to demolition or to rent increases.

The targeting of housing rehabilitation at homeowners influenced, in turn, the segment of the low income population served. Deteriorating areas of rental housing in which many of the poor lived were passed over. U. S. Census data show that, in 1978, 51 percent of those with incomes under $10,000 owned their own homes (Hays 1982a). This ownership was concentrated among one type of poor person—the elderly. Many elderly persons had high enough incomes during their working lives to purchase a modest home, but their fixed retirement incomes did not permit them to maintain it. In contrast, other poor families tended not to have the resources even to begin to purchase a home, especially as home prices escalated during the 1970s.

Another characteristic of housing rehabilitation which emerged from the Section 312/115 program was the emphasis on neighborhoods with modest levels of decay (i.e., with structures in what HUD called "deteriorating" rather than "dilapidated" condition). Many dilapidated dwellings were structurally unsound or obsolete to a degree that would make any rehabilitation investment of dubious value. But, beyond this, the program's heavy reliance on a financial contribution from property owners limited the amount that could be spent on each structure. Thus, the program only worked in less seriously deteriorated areas where costs were affordable by residents. Such a strategy was justified as avoiding excessive per structure costs and as preventive medicine for neighborhoods that had not yet become slums. Nevertheless, it further narrowed the segment of low income persons served.

When the CDBG program was enacted, Section 115 was folded into the block grant, but Section 312 continued to be funded separately, due to its great political popularity. Therefore, rehabilitation programs using CDBG funds tended to closely parallel or to consciously supplement this older program. Grant programs were established to replace Section 115, and loan programs with slightly higher or lower interest rates than Section 312 were set up, in order to reach a broader segment of property owners within affected neighborhoods. Though the amount of Section 312 funds available from HUD fluctuated greatly during the 1970s, my 1980 survey of rehabilitation programs in a national sample of 154 communities revealed that it was still the single largest source of funds for these localities (Hays 1982b). The Reagan administration succeeded in reducing funding of new loans to the proceeds of previous Section 312 loans, but the program continued to play a role in a number of communities (U.S. Department of Urban Development1992).

One significant way in which CDBG programs differed from earlier efforts was in their greater emphasis on the *leveraging* of private loan funds through the use of limited CDBG subsidies. In most such arrangements, a local bank made market rate loans, while CDBG funds were used either as a grant to lower the principal or as an interest subsidy. The public agency might further protect and subsidize the private lender by depositing public funds as security against defaults. This arrangement was advantageous to the public sector because the number of units served was greater than if CDBG funds were loaned out directly. It was also advantageous to private lenders who had come under increasing pressure during the 1970s to make more credit available in lower income, central city, and minority areas. Neighborhood groups were increasingly critical of redlining, and Congress attempted to limit this practice by requiring financial institutions to publicly report loans made by geographic areas through the Home Mortgage Disclosure Act (HMDA). In 1975, Congress also enacted the Community Reinvestment Act, in which banks had to report to federal regulators their efforts to reinvest in disadvantaged neighborhoods (*CQ Weekly Reports* 1975a, 1975b; Sidney 2003). Cooperation in a CDBG program was one way they could increase lending in central city areas, with some protection from risk (Agelasto and Listokin 1975).

Despite such changes, the direction, impact, and structure of CDBG loan programs remained very similar to Section 312 and Section 115. Most communities kept their upper income limits low so as to keep the program targeted at lower income groups. However, they also continued to exclude, or give lower priority to, investor owners, and they targeted neighborhoods with modest levels of decay. Thus, these programs still served only a limited segment of the low income population.

Having shown how long-term cultural and economic trends encouraged a new emphasis on housing rehabilitation, it is now necessary to highlight the relationship between this particular community development strategy and the political dynamics of CDBG implementation. Housing rehabilitation appealed strongly to CDBG decision makers in so many localities for several reasons. One was, of course, steadily increasing federal pressure. However, there were also strong elements within local political arenas that pushed CDBG policy in this direction.

First, cities traditionally active in urban renewal were generally receiving less money than before and, therefore, could not afford the massive investment in acquisition, relocation, and demolition required by clearance. Richmond, Virginia, for example, spent more than $30 million in federal and local funds over a ten-year period in a single urban renewal project. In contrast, the city's entire hold harmless allocation was approximately $10 million for each of the first three years of CDBG, and it dropped to $4.5 million in 1980, when the formula allocation took full effect. Rehabilitation was attractive to that city because it promised to make a substantial impact in many neighborhoods with the limited funds available.

Second, rehabilitation fit the need of localities to spread out the dollars among a larger number of claimants. Whereas clearance lent itself to concentrated efforts in the worst neighborhoods, rehabilitation lent itself to modest efforts in several, less deteriorated neighborhoods. The fact that numerous well-organized neighborhood groups existed in many localities also enhanced the normal desire of local political leaders to please as many citizens as possible with a given expenditure of funds. Many cities made housing rehabilitation loans available on a citywide basis, but HUD's pressure for geographic targeting discouraged this. Therefore, the more common pattern was to select a few declining areas and to combine rehabilitation loans and grants with modest public improvements so as to provide at least the image of a long-term commitment to upgrading those neighborhoods. In this way, the demands of groups whose needs had been neglected in the past could be satisfied.

Interestingly enough, there is little evidence of direct support for gentrification by CDBG loan and grant programs. While the income ceilings on these programs generally included moderate as well as low income recipients, these ceilings were too low to permit aid to upper-middle-class renovators. One federal program, urban homesteading, was established separately from CDBG by the 1974 Act. Under it, repossessed FHA houses were sold to new owners at a nominal cost in exchange for substantial investment in rehabilitation on their part (Hughes and Bleakly 1975). The high cost of rehabilitating these structures limited this program mainly to middle and upper-middle income families, but, while CDBG funds were used to defray urban homesteading costs in some areas, this was not a major form of rehabilitation activity. CDBG programs, to the extent that they did aid those returning to or remaining in the city, assisted mainly to those more modest areas in which incumbent upgrading was taking place.

In light of the excitement generated by the back to the city movement this low level of CDBG involvement might seem surprising. One might expect that communities would be eager to use funds to attract and retain higher-status residents. Yet, the constituency for such support was not large in most communities, and the residents of most successful gentrification areas were making it on their own, without government aid or guidance. Also, local governments could have become targets for the critics of displacement by the new gentry. Such criticism became more prominent during the late 1970s, although a relatively small number of low income families were actually displaced in this fashion (Palen and London 1984).

A third reason why rehabilitation fit into the political environment of CDBG was that it was less disruptive of existing neighborhoods. Though concerns continued to be raised about displacement, it was, for obvious reasons, less likely than earlier strategies to cause massive dislocation. Unlike clearance, rehabilitation did not involve direct transfer of the use of a geographical area from one group to another. This was appealing to communities that had not previously had extensive community development activities and where housing problems were not severe enough to create pressure for clearance. It was also appealing to previously active cities that had encountered increased neighborhood resistance to massive change. The negotiation and cooperation involved in rehabilitation fit better in a political environment containing many organized constituencies than did earlier slum removal strategies.

Finally, housing rehabilitation was compatible with the generally lowered expectations of federal involvement in urban problems which characterized the 1970s. In the 1950s and 1960s, both liberal reformers and conservative business interests hoped that federal dollars could transform their decaying central cities into new, more hospitable environments. Urban renewal succeeded in transforming parts of the central city but with high dollar costs in relation to the objectives achieved, and with the added human costs of the destruction of low income neighborhoods. In contrast, rehabilitation promised steady, rather than dramatic, improvements, and it concentrated on delivering them as a service to property owners already in place. As such, it was a gentler form of government intervention but also one containing lower expectations for radical change in the urban environment.

Housing and Community Development Under CDBG: An Overview

This chapter has described a complex relationship between housing and community development policy. In some respects the two have been closely interdependent. In terms of impact, housing is undeniably an important aspect of community development. It is hard to imagine any other single factor that has more effect on the appearance and livability of a community than the condition of its housing stock. In political terms, legislators and interest groups concerned with housing have found it necessary to band together with those whose main concern was other types of community development in order to push through crucial pieces of legislation such as the Housing Act of 1949 and the Housing and Community Development Act of 1974.

Yet, in other respects, the thrust toward community development and the thrust toward housing improvements have worked at cross-purposes. Economic and political elites pushing for major physical changes in their communities were concerned mainly with economic development and civic pride. Housing, especially for the poor, was at best an afterthought and at worst an end to be sacrificed to the goal of civic betterment. Urban renewal, the centerpiece of community development policy for many years, was first proposed by NAREB, a group unalterably opposed to public sector provision of low income housing; and, true to the thrust of NAREB's initial proposals, urban renewal destroyed more housing than it erected during its first fifteen years. Only under intense pressure from those negatively affected did urban renewal begin to evolve into a program that could contribute to the housing quality of lower income persons, and shortly after the tools were in place to make it a pro-housing effort, the program was abolished.

In light of this complex relationship, how may the housing impact of CDBG be judged? On the positive side, the upgrading of housing in low to moderate income areas via rehabilitation did move to center stage in the CDBG process. Communities found it a popular and useful way to spend their grants, one that pleased both HUD and local constituencies. If one compares the typical CDBG program with the early urban renewal projects, in which thousands of units were destroyed and their inhabitants left to fend for themselves, one may conclude that CDBG was a much more pro-housing community development strategy. If, on the other hand, one compares CDBG to the strategy that seemed to be evolving out of the categorical programs in the late 1960s, the comparison becomes more troubling. There are at least two points of concern.

First, CDBG housing efforts bypassed the most desperate slums, and the low income persons inhabiting them. *Some* public housing was refurbished and some land was cleared for new low income housing construction; but, for the most part, CDBG programs were aimed at areas where decay was less advanced. Severely dilapidated and/or abandoned slum properties generally require clearance—they cannot be economically restored to meet modern definitions of standard housing. Clearance is expensive, and it disrupts the lives of some low income people in ways that dollars or new housing cannot totally compensate. But if clearance is undertaken with improved housing as its ultimate goal, it can pay off for the low income population as a whole. Dangerous or unhealthy units can be replaced by publicly assisted housing which, while not without problems of its own, generally provides quarters much superior to those it replaces. Many communities had begun to use their urban renewal funds in this way during the last years of the program, and CDBG did little to replace this commitment to the positive aspects of slum clearance.

Second, CDBG rehabilitation is essentially a slow, gradual approach. Because of its complexity and the limited funds available, it has not produced massive numbers of upgraded units. Data from my national survey revealed an average output of four to five rehabilitated units per month in the responding cities, and rates of output increased only slightly with the size of the community (Hays 1982a). As an alternative measure of output, national yearly CDBG rehabilitation expenditures were divided by $10,000, the average per unit rehabilitation amount reported in the survey. Again, the result was just under 100,000 units per year, far fewer than subsidized new construction was producing during the same period (Hays 1982b). These findings were further confirmed in a 1983 GAO report on CDBG housing rehabilitation programs (U.S. GAO 1983). This is not to deny that rehabilitation is an essential part of an urban housing strategy. However, sole or primary reliance on rehabilitation is unlikely to produce large numbers of upgraded units within a reasonable time period. Only new construction will generate *volume*. In addition, unless it is backed up by deep subsidies, rehabilitation is unlikely to benefit those with the very lowest incomes.

Third, under CDBG, housing rehabilitation has had to compete for funds with other legitimate community development needs. In addition to the public works and public facilities, there has been an increasing concern with economic development. Without a stable economic base that provides employment at adequate wages, no community can expect the housing improvements it makes to last. Thus, communities in economic decline have diverted funds from other purposes in an effort to revive their economic base. Though economic development still consumed a smaller percentage of CDBG funds than housing rehabilitation, it is difficult for most communities to fund both activities adequately out of the same pool. Thus, a special commitment to each is needed in order for federal funds to have a greater impact.

Positions on community development policy do not sort themselves out as clearly along the liberal/conservative dimension as do positions on housing assistance to the poor. Most major community development programs have drawn support from both liberals and all but the most doctrinaire conservatives. Nevertheless, such efforts have enjoyed the most enthusiastic support among liberal administrations while undergoing curtailments during more conservative administrations. Also, liberals have pushed community development in the direction of providing more direct benefits to low and moderate income persons. These positions are consistent with the definitions of these ideologies given in chapter 2. Both liberals and conservatives tend to support government interventions in the market that enhance the position of market winners. Certainly, a community development strategy aimed at upgrading central business districts is just such an intervention. Liberals, however, support additional interventions to modify market outcomes in ways they feel will stabilize the entire system, particularly on behalf of groups severely disadvantaged by market outcomes. Thus, they have pushed community development in the direction of upgrading the housing and neighborhood environments of those lower on the economic scale.

The CDBG program was developed and pushed through by a moderately conservative administration. It represented a long-term disengagement of the federal government from urban problems, particularly from the problems of those distressed cities that had competed most vigorously for categorical community development funds. The more modest kinds of housing and neighborhood upgrading typical of CDBG programs reflect this underlying spirit of disengagement. At the same time, liberals were strong enough during the period when CDBG was being formulated to exact restrictions on its direction as the price for the program's existence. The establishment of national goals for the program, the subsequent emphasis on the low to moderate income goal during implementation, and the softening (via the dual formula) of the redistribution away from large, decaying cities were the most important restrictions imposed. The influence of these restrictions is apparent in the types of programs funded by CDBG. Housing rehabilitation programs, though slow and limited, are still housing programs and are still, for the most part, directed at low to moderate income residents. Public improvements, too, have been directed to support the upgrading of declining areas.

In sum, CDBG was in harmony with the lowered expectations Richard Nixon envisioned for the 1970s, yet it was far from the total retrenchment liberals feared and some conservatives wanted. It remains to be discussed, in the next chapter, how the Reagan administration tried to turn this modest disengagement into a rapid federal withdrawal from all urban problems.

CHAPTER 7

Retrenchment and Recovery:
Reagan and George H. W. Bush

Part I—A Change of Direction: The Early Reagan Administration

The 1980 election, in which Ronald Reagan defeated the incumbent president, Jimmy Carter, brought to power the most ideologically conservative administration since the 1920s. This set the stage for a major shift in expenditures and in philosophy at the federal level, and housing programs could hardly avoid the effects of this shift. President Reagan's overall economic and budgetary goals were discussed in chapter 2. The present discussion will focus on the impact of these changes on housing policy.

Budgetary Retrenchment

Based on the strength of his electoral victory and on the appeal of his plan for economic recovery, Reagan was able to push through Congress a package of substantial cuts in virtually all areas of domestic spending except entitlements, amounting to approximately $40 billion in FY 1982 (Pechman 1981, 1982). In achieving such cuts, the Reagan administration utilized its political resources skillfully to influence Congress.

The administration used the procedures of the 1974 Budget Act as its principle tool, an act passed, ironically, to give Congress more leverage in budgetary decisions relative to the president. Building on his Republican majority in the Senate and on considerable support from conservative Democrats in the House, he worked with congressional leaders in 1981 to produce a budget resolution reflecting his priorities. He then pushed through a reconciliation bill, which forced program authorizations by individual committees to conform strictly to the limits set in the budget resolution. In doing so, he overrode substantive committees tied to agencies and program clientele, the traditional centers of support for domestic programs. With equal skill, Reagan also pushed through drastic tax cuts, including the most restrictive measure of all with regard to revenues—the indexing of tax rates to prevent their automatic rise with inflation (so-called bracket creep).

In Reagan's second year, congressional support for his initiatives weakened, and defenders of various domestic programs were better prepared for his onslaught. As a result, the additional deep cuts in nonentitlement domestic spending that Reagan requested encountered stiffer opposition. Nevertheless, the overall decline in such expenditures was maintained because earlier decisions proved difficult to reverse. Many in Congress feared that backtracking on defense increases would make them vulnerable to charges of undermining national security. To enact major tax increases or to cut entitlements were also unacceptable political risks. Therefore, restoration of funding for other domestic programs would inevitably result in increased deficits, leaving Reagan the opportunity to blame Congress for the sea of red ink. Thus emerged the stalemate over budget priorities which would dominate national politics into the 1990s (Reischauer 1984).

One other major impact the Reagan administration had on the course of domestic programming came through its control of the federal bureaucracy. His cabinet and subcabinet appointees generally came from the most conservative end of the political spectrum, and they brought to domestic agencies a mandate to curtail their activities. In symbolic recognition of one of HUD's main constituencies, Reagan appointed an African American, Samuel Pierce, as Secretary of HUD. However, Pierce was one of the least aggressive advocates of housing for the poor to be found in the African American community (Stanfield 1983c). He also proved to be an ineffective administrator with only a distant relationship to the White House. In addition, budget cuts and reorganizations led to Reductions in Force (RIFs), which demoralized the remaining administrators. To the extent allowed by administrative discretion, agencies were pushed to reduce regulation of local governments and private businesses and to tighten eligibility for social programs.

The Reagan administration was not immune to the frequently observed tendency of presidential appointees to "go native" and protect their agencies from White House cuts. Even Pierce went to bat for the CDBG program in the face of OMB Director, David Stockman's budgetary axe. However, the extreme disparity between the conservative ideology of appointees and the liberal purposes of the agencies they headed minimized this tendency.

The continued evolution of housing policy in the first Reagan term was, as shall be shown, influenced by the ongoing policy dilemmas described in earlier chapters. However, the influence of the overall policy environment just described was also very powerful. A group of political leaders with ideological assumptions deeply at odds with the existing course of policy were striving to redirect its course. The ideas of balancing the budget and reducing federal spending were important from their point of view, but they soon gave way to two higher priorities; cutting taxes and redirecting federal spending toward defense and away from social programs. They found it politically impossible to reduce the largest welfare state programs, those affecting millions of working and middle-class citizens. Therefore, they focused their attacks on programs directed at the weaker constituency of the disadvantaged. This having been done, they seemed willing to accept large deficits resulting from their other priorities. Housing programs were among the primary targets for cuts. Housing efforts carried out under Community Development Block Grants were also affected, though they proved somewhat less vulnerable.

The major features of housing proposals and actions during Reagan's first term may be divided into two categories. First were the extensive budget cuts for these programs alluded to above. Second were recommended structural changes in housing assistance programs. These two aspects are best treated as analytically distinct, though they were closely intertwined in the political struggle.

In his budget "coup" of 1981, Reagan succeeded in cutting new budget authority for Section 8 and public housing in the FY 1982 budget to approximately $17.5 billion, just over half the $30 billion appropriated under Carter's FY 1981 budget. (The reader will recall that actual expenditures [outlays] from this budget authority are spread out over many years in the form of contracted subsidy payments.) In addition, he pushed through a rescission of approximately $4 billion in budget authority left over from previous years (*CQ Almanac* 1981a, 1981b). However, these cuts were small in comparison to those requested in 1982 for the FY 1983 budget. For that year, Reagan asked for what was, in effect, a negative appropriation; that is, no additional budget authority for new units, plus a rescission of $2.5 billion in budget authority from previous years (National Low Income Housing Coalition 1983b, 10).

Reflecting its new willingness to give at least a qualified "no" to the Reagan administration, Congress balked at such deep cuts. In the House, the defenders of housing assistance had a strong advocate, Representative Henry Gonzalez (D, Texas), as chair of the Housing and Community Development Subcommittee of the Banking and Urban Affairs Committee. He regarded such cuts as unacceptable and gained enough support from his colleagues to battle the administration to a stalemate on new authorizing legislation for housing programs. The result of the lack of authorizing legislation was an initial HUD appropriations bill containing no new budget authority and no rescissions. However, in a later compromise, $8.6 billion in new budget authority for FY 1983 was added through a continuing resolution.

In 1983, Reagan again tried to cut new budget authority to the bone, asking for $500 million for FY 1984. Congress again proved determined to keep some new housing efforts going, and just over $12 billion was appropriated (*CQ Weekly Reports* 1983). By 1984, the administration was seeking to soften its image of hostility to social welfare programs, and its FY 1985 budget request of $6.3 billion was much closer to what Congress had appropriated in the previous two years. In contrast to the prolonged battles of earlier years, the HUD appropriations bill was one of the first approved in 1984, including $7.9 billion for new housing assistance (Hays 1990).

Looked at from one perspective, the appropriations of FY 1983–85 may be seen as a testimony to the powers of resistance of congressional housing advocates. However, from another angle, this battle confirms the ability of ideological changes in the presidency to shape the terms of the debate. Housing advocates did not suffer total defeat, yet they were clearly fighting a rearguard action. The amounts approved represented a reduction in budget authority from pre-Reagan levels of more than two-thirds. The full impact of this reduction was not felt immediately, due to the extended time frame of housing expenditures. But this was clearly a drastic change in the order of magnitude of the federal effort.

Meanwhile, the Reagan administration sought administrative changes in the Section 8 program designed to directly affect outlays. First, they received congressional approval of a gradual increase from 25 to 30 percent in the percentage of income families in Section 8 units had to pay in rent. Second, they proposed that the cash value of food stamps received by Section 8 tenants be counted as income in computing their rent, a measure that Congress rejected. Finally, they succeeded in lowering the levels to which Fair Market Rents would normally have risen; first by delaying the publication of new FMRs for two years and, second, by instituting a new FMR formula, based on the fortieth percentile of area rents, rather than the median. Protest from local housing agencies was muted by a hold harmless provision, which prevented any area's current FMR from being reduced.

Programmatic Changes

During the same period that the Reagan administration was pushing hard for reductions in the level of federal housing assistance, it was also reviewing the structure of housing programs. Early in the administration, key officials indicated that a new form of housing allowance, "housing vouchers," would be a central concept. However, in order to elaborate and justify program options, the President's Commission on Housing was appointed in 1981. According to Rochelle Stanfield, appointees largely shared Reagan's conservative political outlook, rather than representing a broad spectrum of opinion as had previous commissions. The administration wanted concrete proposals that matched its desired direction, rather than broad statements upon which a diverse commission could agree (Stanfield 1982b).

In keeping with the affinity of Reagan and his advisors for housing vouchers, the central recommendation of the commission was a Housing Payments Program. The following summarizes its major features:

1. It would be administered by the agencies currently administering Section 8 Existing Housing, and they would continue to enforce minimum housing standards.
2. Eligibility would be restricted to those below 50 percent of the local median income, rather than 80 percent as in Section 8, so that the program would, in the commission's words "be directed to those most in need."
3. A "payment standard" would be substituted for the Fair Market Rent. Like the FMR, this would be calculated on the basis of the cost of a typical unit of that size in the community, with the subsidy computed as the difference between 30 percent of income and the standard. However, *the actual rent of the unit could be more or less than the payment standard*, and households would be "rewarded" with extra cash income for other purposes if they found a less costly unit. Also, households could choose to spend more than 30 percent of their income on housing and still receive assistance.

4. The government should "move toward" direct payment of the subsidy to the tenant, but local agencies could, if they wished, maintain their current practice of paying the landlord (U.S. President's Commission on Housing 1982, 23–30).

The principal arguments used by the commission to justify this new program were similar to those raised on behalf of a voucher approach throughout the 1970s. First, they reiterated the argument that the chief housing problem experienced by the poor is excessive cost, not poor housing conditions Using American Housing Survey data, they calculated that "[o]f the 10.5 million very low-income renters [less than 50 percent of median income] identified in the 1977 Annual Housing Survey, 6.5 million paid more than 30 percent of their incomes for rent, while 2 million lived in inadequate housing" (U.S. President's Commission on Housing 1982, 12). On this basis, they concluded that the provision of cash rent supplements was much more urgent than the construction of new, standard, assisted units.

Second, they relied upon the reduced cost argument used in Nixon's report, *Housing in the Seventies.* They provided data showing the substantially lower per unit cost for Section 8 Existing Housing than for Section 8 New Construction, and they argued that less constrained cash payments to tenants would push costs even lower. They cited evidence from the EHAP Demand Experiment that tenants would use only part of an unconstrained cash grant for housing, while spending the rest on other goods. They also noted the tendency of rents in the Existing Housing program to be pulled upward toward the Fair Market Rent ceiling.

Third, they took pains to refute the notion that cash subsidies would cause the poor to pay more for less by driving up prices within the restricted housing market available to them. Again, they cited the results of EHAP, in this case the Supply Experiment, which showed that even a fairly extensive program did not increase rents in the communities affected (Bradbury and Downs 1981). With regard to minorities, they recommended strict enforcement of fair housing laws, but they noted favorably the HUD findings (discussed in chapter 6) that: (1) minorities were better represented in the Section 8 Existing Housing program than in Section 8 New Construction; and (2), a significant number of minority households used their subsidy to shop for housing in physically better, more racially integrated areas.

In spite of its strong advocacy of concentrating federal subsidies on existing units, the commission's report did express concern that the overall supply of standard, low income units might not be adequate, especially in localities with very tight housing markets. Their proposal for dealing with this problem was a radical decentralization of new construction programs. They recommended that new construction be included as an eligible activity under the Community Development Block Grant program. Extra funds would be added to the grants, using a separate formula based on the extent of local housing needs. However, the commission recommended that the ultimate decision to spend these extra funds on new construction be left to local governments. In support of this proposal, the commission praised the willingness of localities to utilize CDBG funds for housing purposes, and they praised local creativity in leveraging private investment with federal dollars.

In many respects, the political atmosphere was propitious for acceptance of the types of programmatic changes recommended by Reagan's Housing Commission. The same conservative coalition in Congress that had supported Reagan's budget cuts was receptive to alternative program designs that promised lower costs and less active governmental intervention in market transactions between tenants and landlords. In addition, a decade of debate and experimentation had brought many liberal housing advocates to the position that it was necessary for programs utilizing existing units to shoulder an increasing share of the task of housing the poor. Nevertheless, proposed structural changes ran into much stronger opposition than budget cuts.

Contemporary accounts of the housing debate in the *Congressional Quarterly* and the *National Journal* suggest two basic reasons for the stalemate over programmatic change during the first three years of the Reagan administration. The first was disagreement over the composition of the federal effort. Throughout most of the debate, Reagan and his advisors were intransigent in insisting that no units whatsoever be allocated to new construction. Not only were allocations to Section 8 New Construction cut to zero, but also the Housing Commission's proposal for a housing block grant was modified to include only rehabilitation of existing rental units. According to the *National Journal,* Reagan's HUD Secretary Samuel Pierce, as well as a number of congressional Republicans, urged the inclusion of a modest amount of new construction as a compromise essential to the passage of a bill containing the new voucher program. Liberal lobbyists such as Cushing Dolbeare, president of the National Low Income Housing Coalition, stated their willingness to endorse housing vouchers, as long as they were supplemented by some new construction, in order to maintain an adequate supply of low income housing, and many in Congress supported their position. Within the administration, however, David Stockman's concern with the long-term costs of new construction subsidies prevailed, and Reagan opted for stalemate with Congress over housing legislation rather than compromise on this issue (Stanfield 1983a).

The second source of opposition to Reagan's program was the relationship between his proposals for program changes and his push to drastically reduce total housing assistance costs. Several actions by the Reagan administration led housing advocates to believe that his new programs were a smokescreen for emasculating the federal effort. First, Reagan proposed to pay for his voucher plan with funds recaptured from prior budget authority for Section 8 units, rather than with new funds. This was totally unacceptable to housing proponents in Congress. Second, Reagan coupled vouchers with administrative efforts, described above, to cut deeply the subsidy going to each household. Again, this made an otherwise acceptable concept unacceptable to many housing advocates. They supported the cost savings inherent in vouchers as a legitimate way to spread benefits to a larger group of recipients. However, additional subsidy cuts were seen as punitive, and as more evidence that the Reagan administration's real concern was saving money, not serving the poor. In an interview with the *National Journal*, Cushing Dolbeare complained that "Reagan is giving housing vouchers a bad name" (Stanfield 1983a, 843).

Secondly, the level of funding provided for the proposed housing block grant was very low, in addition to being directed only at rehabilitation. The total amount proposed in the FY 1983 budget was $150 million, and the Section 312 program, a major supplement to CDBG rehabilitation, was virtually eliminated. This suggested the use of block grants to cover reductions in funding, a maneuver widely perceived by liberals to be the basis for Reagan's block grant proposals in other social service areas. There was also concern among housing advocates that localities lacked the technical capacity to carry out new construction. Thus, the block grant proposal generated as little enthusiasm as the housing voucher program.

Eventually, Reagan succeeded in substantially changing the direction, as well as the scope of housing programs. Congress refused to approve housing vouchers except on an experimental level, yet the proportion of units going to Section 8 Existing Housing was greatly increased, and new construction was funded only in conjunction with Section 202 housing for the elderly and handicapped. Yet, the preservation of this small effort, plus continued appropriations for some new public housing units, indicated that Congress was unwilling to abandon new construction altogether. Also, the Housing Development Action Grant (HODAG) program, modeled after the UDAG program, was authorized.

Housing and the Tax System

Another housing program emerged in the mid-1980s which, at first, appeared to have only a minor impact but which would come to be a major underpinning of low income housing construction from the 1990s on. This was the Low Income Housing Tax Credit (LIHTC), enacted as part of the Tax Reform Act of 1986. The 1986 Act had eliminated the ability of individual investors to claim "passive losses" (i.e., the depreciation of the value of assets) as a deduction against regular income. Since this had been a major financial prop for previous housing construction programs, there was great concern that investment in such programs would drop. Also, many wealthy investors in lower income housing were outraged that the government had "broken its contract" with them by removing one of the main financial benefits of their previous investments.

The LIHTC was enacted as a substitute for the loss of these tax breaks. It provided a dollar for dollar tax credit for investment in low to moderate income housing. Advocates for low income families joined forces with representatives of the housing industry to lobby for this new tax credit, because they believed that private housing production for low and moderate income families would come to a standstill without some form of tax subsidy (U.S. Congress, Senate 1985). The tax credits could be spread out across the first sixteen years of the project's existence, as long as low/moderate income occupancy was maintained during that time. (More details on this program will be provided in a later section.) Investors were slow to respond to the new program, fearing that the federal government would cancel its benefits at a later date as it had done to the passive loss provision. Therefore, it had little impact on housing production in the 1980s. However, in the 1990s its role began to increase to the point that it would eventually become the nation's largest subsidy program for the construction of low and moderate income housing (Guthrie and Mc Quarrie 2010; Schwartz 2006).

One other provision of the Tax Reform Act of 1986 would also prove to be important for future housing production. During the late 1970s and early 1980s, state and local governments were increasingly using their capacity to issue tax exempt bonds to subsidize not only housing, but a variety of other economic development activities, such as restaurants and retail outlets. The proliferation of Industrial Development Bonds (IDBs) was criticized by some federal policy makers as an abuse of the states' and localities' federal tax exemption, which was originally intended to lower the costs of public capital projects such as roads, sewers, and schools. The result was that the 1986 Act put a cap on the issuance of tax exempt bonds that was based on a per capita amount for the citizens of the state. This cap initially produced fears that low and moderate income housing production would be sacrificed to economic development pressures, but states maintained a strong commitment to utilizing bonding for housing purposes. Under pressure from state and local government lobbyists, Congress raised the per capita limit several times after 1986 and eventually indexed it to inflation in 2002 (Schwartz and Melendez 2008).

CDBG under Reagan

The fate of CDBG under Reagan was not nearly as grim as that of housing assistance. One reason was that the design of the program fit Reagan's ideological predisposition toward consolidation of categorical programs and a return of federal dollars to state and local control. In fact, CDBG served as a model for the reorganization of other federal social programs into block grants. Reagan's ideology also predisposed him favorably to UDAG, with its use of federal seed money to promote private investment in the central city.

Another reason was the popularity of these programs among local political and economic elites. As discussed in chapter 6, community development has generally enjoyed a broader political base than housing programs. Although groups representing mayors and other local officials lobby for both, community development programs gain additional support from local and national business interests. The pool of money channeled into CDBG is largely under local control and can be used in ways that do not disturb local political arrangements. Also important is the fact that CDBG money is available for general community improvement and for various kinds of subsidies to market winners. This last point was even more applicable to UDAG, which aided numerous private investors in profitable involvement in downtown revitalization.

To say that community development programs were relatively better off is not to say, however, that they emerged unscathed. According to the National Journal, OMB Director Stockman initially recommended drastically reducing CDBG. Backed by local government lobbyists, HUD Secretary Pierce fought successfully to preserve CDBG, but funding fell sharply from the levels reached in the late 1970s. UDAG, too, followed a twisting course that led ultimately to its demise. In the early budget fights, Stanfield notes that "wealthy private interests, such as the hotel chains that take advantage of action grants...talked convincingly to presidential counselor Edwin Meese III and White House chief of staff James A. Baker III," and their intervention helped to ensure that UDAG also escaped the axe (Stanfield 1983b, 1645–46). However, the program lost popularity in the mid to late 1980s because it was seen as selectively subsidizing businesses in certain areas, while similar businesses received no assistance. Also, the cost effectiveness of some UDAG investments came to be seriously questioned, and the program was effectively ended in 1988 (*CQ Weekly Reports* 1988).

A number of structural changes in community development were also proposed, with varying degrees of success, by the Reagan administration. First, the administration of CDBG funds for small, nonentitlement cities was shifted from HUD to state governments. Some community development officials predicted that this devolution of authority would lead to the same spreading effect that occurred in some communities with regard to CDBG projects. That is, state political leaders would give small amounts to as many communities as possible, rather than concentrating on large projects in a few cities. A HUD report cited by Mary K. Nenno confirmed that the average number of recipients in each state increased by 75 percent, and that the average grant per recipient declined from $485,000 to $219,000 under state administration (Nenno 1983, 146). The report also noted an increased emphasis on economic development and public facilities and a decreased use of these nonentitlement CDBG funds for housing.

Second, HUD reopened the debate on targeting CDBG funds by announcing a new interpretation of the Housing and Community Development Act of 1974. Rather than insist that the primary beneficiaries of CDBG funds be low and moderate income persons, HUD stated that the other two broad goals of the 1974 Act, "the elimination of slums and blight" and "meeting urgent community needs," would be treated as coequal. This gave localities more flexibility in the activities they could fund with block grants. Such a move was not well received in the housing and community development subcommittees in Congress, and bills were proposed that would change the 1974 Act to more explicitly target funds to low and moderate income persons. In the HUD reauthorization bill of 1983, a compromise was reached in which 51 percent of CDBG funds had to be thus targeted.

Third, the Reagan administration offered, as its only new urban aid proposal, a program implementing the concept of "enterprise zones," which Reagan had proposed in his 1980 campaign. This program would have designated certain areas of cities as distressed and then granted relief from federal taxes and regulations to private firms engaging in economic development within these areas. State and local governments would also have been urged to grant tax relief. This proposal made it through the Senate in 1983 and was added to the bill repealing tax withholding on interest and dividends. However, it was deleted in conference committee.

In addition to proposed changes in community development programs, Reagan proposed an ambitious "New Federalism" plan. (It really should have been called the New New Federalism, to distinguish it from Nixon's initiatives in the early 1970s.) Under this plan, many federal domestic responsibilities would have been turned over to states and localities, with a gradual phase-in of financial responsibility over several years. As part of implementing this plan, CDBG would have been merged with General Revenue Sharing and turned over to the Treasury Department to administer. The New Federalism proposal stirred widespread opposition among state and local officials, who protested their own fiscal incapacity to handle many of the large federal programs. As a result, the effort was abandoned by Reagan.

Reagan's Second Term—New Problems and New Directions

Hard numbers do not indicate much change in housing policy from Reagan's first term to his second term. The administration continued to push for a minimal federal effort, while actual appropriations emerging from the stalemate with Congress stayed at about the levels to which they had fallen in 1983. Nevertheless, a series of developments, some dramatic and some quiet, gradually changed the perceptions of the public and decision makers concerning the seriousness of housing problems, and placed Reagan increasingly on the defensive in arguing for a low level of federal effort. The four to be discussed here are: the growing perception of a shortage of rental housing; the emergence of homelessness; the prospective loss of existing assisted units; and local housing initiatives.

HOUSING SUPPLY

Data on growing housing problems came from credible sources such as the Congressional Budget Office (1989) and the Harvard-MIT Joint Center on Housing (Joint Center 1989, 1990). Both homeowners and renters were having an increasingly difficult time obtaining affordable housing, but the problem appeared especially acute for renters. Although a big part of the "shortage" still involved affordability rather than a lack of physical structures, the soothing rhetoric of the 1970s concerning the gradual improvement in housing conditions which Reagan had used to justify cutbacks increasingly lost credibility. Thus, in Congress, the mood subtly shifted in favor of seeking more government action, rather than fighting to retain a minimum effort. The recapture of the Senate by the Democrats in 1986 also made the political atmosphere more hospitable to new housing initiatives. However, Kingdon suggests that an issue needs both a gradual increase in awareness within a policy community and some dramatic event(s) to move on to the policy agenda (Kingdon 1984). The dramatic issue of homelessness provided the latter ingredient.

HOMELESSNESS

The term *homelessness* was not prominent in the vocabulary used to discuss housing problems before the late 1980s. Most of the informed policy debate focused on families in housing that was inadequate or too costly, not on individuals cut loose from social moorings and totally without shelter. And, as Redburn and Buss (1986) point out, those individuals without permanent shelter were seen by the public either in a romantic light as "vagabonds," or in a negative light as "bums" and "winos" who had fallen into homelessness through irresponsible actions. The entry of this term into public discourse can be traced to increases in the numbers, visibility, and variety of people in this condition.

Documenting trends in the numbers of homeless with precise, quantitative data has proved extremely difficult, so difficult, in fact, that methods for counting the homeless became the subject of vigorous debate during the 1980s. Nevertheless, it is clear that in many cities, the numbers of people visibly living on the streets or in places not intended for human habitation grew substantially in the early 1980s. Those places offering temporary shelter were overwhelmed with new demand, and a need for additional temporary lodging became apparent. In addition, the composition of the group changed from overwhelmingly single males to include substantial numbers of single women and families with children (Redburn and Buss 1986).

Visibility was also increased by early efforts to organize the homeless. In Washington, D.C., Mitch Snyder utilized nonviolent protests to highlight homelessness, and to force the federal government to make available a vacant building for a shelter (Imig 1996). The media began to focus both its news and its entertainment wings on dramatic stories about people suffering on the streets. For many liberals, the growth in homelessness epitomized the callousness of the Reagan era toward the disadvantaged.

The underlying causes of this increase in homelessness have been as much in dispute as the exact numbers involved, but it is clear that a combination of factors, rather than any single factor, led to this problem. The number of citizens living below the poverty line increased in the 1980s, after two decades of steady decline. This reflected an overall increase in the degree of inequality. The income share earned by the two lowest income quintiles decreased, while the income share of the highest quintile rose dramatically, and the Gini Index, which measures income inequality, also rose dramatically (Mischel and Bernstein 2009). The combination of steadily rising rents, declining incomes, and the demolition of housing units led to an overall loss of affordable rental units which occurred in the 1980s, despite modest increases in the number of assisted units (National Low Income Housing Coalition 1983a). Both of these trends created conditions under which homelessness was more likely to result from a variety of crises overtaking a family or individual.

Most homeless households consist of single individuals without children, in spite of increases in the number of homeless families (Burt 1992). Single, non-elderly and non-handicapped adults are often excluded from federal housing programs and other welfare benefits, leaving them without the normal safety net. In addition, the form of housing on which many low income singles depended, Single Room Occupancy (SRO) structures consisting of cheap rooming houses and hotels, increasingly fell victim to downtown revitalization and gentrification. Hoch and Slayton (1989) report losses ranging from 20 percent to 60 percent in many of the nation's large cities.

Still other data point to the interaction of poverty with other social problems such as mental illness and drug abuse as a critical factor in homelessness. In the 1970s, advocates of deinstitutionalization of the mentally ill anticipated that community-based services would be created to meet the support needs of those formerly warehoused in state hospitals. When funding for such services was not forthcoming in many areas, chronically mentally ill persons were left to wander the streets as an increasingly visible segment of the homeless. In addition, drug and alcohol abuse continued to drive a wedge between individuals (most frequently single males) and their normal social networks. Martha Burt notes that, despite the increasing number of households who are homeless simply because of economic deprivation, the proportions of the homeless who abuse drugs or alcohol or who are mentally ill still far exceed the proportions in the general population, or even among the poor as a whole (Burt 1992, 109–10).

The Reagan administration responded to growing public concern over homelessness by trying to minimize the problem and by raising various objections to proposed federal programs to meet their needs. Nevertheless, the extent of public concern made legislative action inevitable, and the administration stopped short of threatening to veto programs for the homeless. Mitch Snyder's Coalition for Creative Non-Violence camped on the steps of the Capitol, and a number of members of Congress, along with other celebrities, spent a night on a steam grate two blocks from the Capitol in the *"Grate" American Sleep-Out* orchestrated by Snyder and the actor who played him in a TV movie, Martin Sheen *(CQ Almanac* 1987, 506–507). A bill made its way through Congress in 1987 which would ultimately be named the Steward B. McKinney Homeless Assistance Act, after a prominent Republican congressman from Connecticut who was an advocate for the homeless and who died of AIDS.

The complexity of homelessness, and the range of services needed to deal with it, was shown by the fact that four congressional committees had to approve various parts of the bill. Under normal circumstances, this might have led to paralysis, but in the atmosphere of urgency, the bill moved forward quickly. As signed into law on July 22, 1987, the McKinney Act:

- Expanded emergency food and shelter grants administered by the Federal Emergency Management Agency (FEMA);
- Funded Emergency Shelter Grants and other programs for creating new shelter space, administered by HUD;
- Provided for community-based health care and services for the homeless mentally ill and substance abusers;
- Expanded job training programs;
- Provided additional funding for emergency food programs in the Department of Agriculture *(CQ Almanac* 1987, 509–10).

However, the funding for each of these components was not large in comparison to the need.

Public concern with homelessness contributed greatly to a more positive atmosphere in the late 1980s for consideration of housing needs, yet some of the traditional housing interest groups were not on the cutting edge of leadership in this area. The focus of the major housing assistance programs on families drew their attention away from the needs of solitary adults, while the services needed by these persons, such as treatment for mental illness and alcoholism, were outside the boundaries of traditional housing agency responsibilities. Once the issue had been raised, these groups vigorously supported new programs, as well as modification of existing programs such as Section 8 to allow construction or rehabilitation of SRO facilities and shelters. Special programs for the homeless became standard components of housing legislation from the late 1980s on.

THE REPAYMENT CRISIS

In the early years of the Reagan presidency, the main focus of concern and debate was appropriations for additional units of assisted housing. Because long-term contracts established during earlier administrations maintained prior commitments, and because Congress insisted on funding a small number of additional units each year, the total number of assisted units actually increased during Reagan's first term. This fact cushioned the blow of Reagan's shift in priorities, since families were not directly being thrown into the street as the result of budget cuts (despite their indirect link to homelessness, as noted above).

However, in the late 1980s, a number of private developers holding long-term contracts with HUD under Section 221 (d)(3) and Section 236 began to prepay their mortgages and to convert their units into condominiums or higher rent apartments. As noted in chapter 4, projects carried out under these programs yielded their maximum tax benefits to investors during the first sixteen years of ownership, and HUD contracts allowed for prepayment after twenty years. The trend toward prepayment aroused considerable concern within the housing policy community, since it threatened not only incremental units but the units already part of the assisted stock. In 1989, the General Accounting Office estimated that as many as 233,000 HUD-insured units were subject to prepayment by 1995, and another 173,000 by 2005 (U.S. General Accounting Office 1986, 24). In addition, thousands of Section 8 certificates that had been issued to older projects in order to keep them financially afloat were due to expire during the 1990s, leaving the owners little choice between sale and bankruptcy (see also Center on Budget and Policy Priorities and National Low Income Housing Information Service 1991).

The Housing Act of 1987 reflected concern with the prepayment problem. It contained language restricting prepayment unless the owner could prove "that tenants' economic hardship would not be increased and that any shortage of low-rent housing in the area would not be exacerbated" (*CQ Weekly Reports* 1989a, 1043). Many owners found these conditions impossible to meet, and a few sued HUD for breach of contract. Some congressional housing leaders, such as Rep. Henry Gonzalez, advocated a "get tough" approach to developers, while others, such as Senator Alan

Cranston, favored tax incentives not to prepay, rather than a restrictive approach. All clearly recognized that the 1987 restrictions were not a permanent solution.

Nevertheless, the restrictions remained in force between 1987 and 1990, while Congress debated a permanent solution, to be incorporated in the omnibus housing act then being fashioned. This proved to be such a contentious issue that it was not resolved until the final conference committee on the National Affordable Housing Act of 1990. The solution finally enacted included a complex set of procedures that attempted to protect the owners' return on investment while requiring the maximum possible effort to retain units for low income occupancy. Among other things, the legislation provided for tenants whose rent would be increased by conversion to receive vouchers that they could use either to remain in the property or to move elsewhere (*CQ Weekly Reports* 1989a, 1043; *CQ Almanac* 1990, 652–53).

In 1998, Abt Associates conducted a case study of twelve projects that had undergone prepayment of mortgages or opting out of Section 8 contracts. This study provides a perspective on the longer term consequences of the pre-payment crisis. The study covered properties that were originally assisted by Section 221d3, Section 236, Section 8, or a combination of these programs. The result of prepayment of the mortgages or opting out of the Section 8 contracts was usually an immediate increase in rents, because a major reason for an owner's termination of the relationship with HUD was the anticipation of being able to rent the units to more affluent tenants at market rates. Households who met income guidelines and whose rent burden would exceed 30 percent of their income were eligible to receive vouchers, but a significant number did not receive them, either because they were spooked by the announcement of the conversion into moving before they could sign up or because they were ineligible for other reasons. As might be expected, satisfaction or dissatisfaction with their current unit greatly affected tenants' decision to remain in place or use the voucher to seek lodging elsewhere. Most of the tenants who moved ended up in census tracts with the same or lower concentrations of poverty and the same or lower proportions of minority residents (U.S. Department of Housing and Urban Development 2000).

The prepayment issue highlighted two underlying policy problems. First, it revealed an inherent limitation of utilizing private for-profit providers of assisted housing; namely, that the government is not in complete control of the fate of properties in which it has a considerable amount invested. Unlike public housing, which is a more or less permanent public stock of units, privately owned housing is subject to future market pressures toward removal from the assisted stock. Trying to force investors to hold on to unprofitable properties is, at best, an uphill battle. This trade-off was not fully considered in the initial shift to private sector subsidies in the 1960s, but some participants in the debate of the late 1980s took note of it. Rep. Bruce Vento (D, Minn.) commented, "It points out the problem when you don't have public housing" (*CQ Weekly Reports* 1989a, 1042).

The second problem the crisis highlighted was the long-term impact of cuts in incremental expenditures for housing assistance. In the debate of the early 1980s, assistance commitments made earlier were tacitly regarded as a more or less permanent base against which incremental expenditures could be weighed and argued. In the late 1980s, the fact that these prior commitments would not last forever was forcefully brought to the attention of policy makers. Existing tenants of assisted units might be protected from rent increases through vouchers, but the long-term supply of assisted units would be reduced because once these tenants moved, owners could rent their units at market rates. From this point on, it was clear that substantial additional appropriations would be needed just to stay in the same place with regard to assisted units. This would increase the pressure on Congress to make housing a higher priority within its limited discretionary spending.

LOCAL AND NONPROFIT INITIATIVES

There are times when the old cliché that "crisis is just another word for opportunity" rings true, and the local response to federal cutbacks in housing assistance is one of those instances. As the impact of the loss of federal housing funds became apparent in the mid-1980s, localities with serious housing problems began to search for alternative sources of funding. To lower the financing costs of housing, they turned to state housing finance authorities and to their own bonding power in order to take advantage of the tax subsidy on public borrowing that was still available. In order to build and manage housing for low or moderate income persons, they increasingly turned to nonprofit, neighborhood-based housing development corporations. In the absence of federal assistance, profit-making developers found investment in low income housing much less attractive, and it was left to community-based entities to pick up the slack. (These efforts will be discussed in more detail in chapter 8.)

There were also increased efforts on the part of the private, voluntary sector to deal with housing problems. Programs for the homeless were frequently supported by churches, the United Way, or other nonprofit organizations. Habitat for Humanity International was founded in Georgia by millionaire businessman turned social crusader Millard Fuller, who used Christian symbolism to call attention to a moral obligation to help those without decent housing. (A favorite slogan: "Once again, God's people can use a good carpenter.") In part due to the publicity garnered by the participation of former president Jimmy Carter and his wife Rosalyn, Habitat attracted support across the nation for its program, which involves constructing houses with volunteer donations and labor (including "sweat equity" contributed by future owners) and then selling them to low income families with a zero-interest mortgage. By 1994, Habitat had constructed nearly fifteen thousand units and was listed by *USA Today* as the seventeenth-largest private builder in the United States (Hays 2002).

The political impact of the numerous local government and private volunteer efforts is hard to gauge precisely, but it seems clear that they contributed to the overall revival in interest in housing policy questions. Localities demonstrated that their concern for housing went beyond just sitting back and absorbing federal resources. Private volunteer efforts such as Habitat articulated and mobilized the compassionate strain in the American belief system that frequently helps soften the anti-poor and antigovernment strains with which it coexists. Of course, neither local governments nor private charities can mobilize resources on a scale sufficient to solve a community's (let alone the nation's) housing problems (Dreier and Keating 1990). Nevertheless, the commitment they demonstrated, in combination with the other factors just discussed, encouraged federal policy makers again to devote more of their attention to housing problems.

Part II—The First Bush Administration

U.S. history records few vice presidents who have succeeded the president under whom they served, except through his death. In trying to get elected on their own, they face blame for the shortcomings of the administration of which they were a part, before they have the chance to gain the popular support enjoyed by a sitting president, or to establish their own clear identity in the minds of voters. In 1988, George Herbert Walker Bush beat these odds, assisted by a well-orchestrated campaign in which he avoided attacking the Reagan administration while at the same time successfully distancing himself from some of its policies. He was also assisted by a healthy economy and by the inept campaigning of his opponent, Michael Dukakis.

Nowhere was Bush's balancing act more clearly revealed than in the area of social policy. While he was in basic philosophical agreement with Reagan's "minimum government involvement" stance toward social policy, he was not as rigidly ideological as many on the Reagan team. Moreover, his strategists accurately perceived that many voters were turned off by the image of callousness toward human needs acquired by the Reagan administration. Therefore, the promise of a "kinder, gentler nation" was included in his campaign rhetoric, along with the assurance that he would not raise taxes in order to pursue a slightly more expansive social agenda. This strategy was successful in deflating Dukakis's claim to the moral high ground in this area, especially since, because of the deficit, Dukakis could not credibly promise large social spending increases. In retrospect, the George H. W. Bush administration proved to be the last in which Republicans and Democrats were able to work together to craft moderately progressive social policies.

Bush's broader thrust toward less ideological hostility toward social spending set the stage for the appointment of former representative Jack Kemp as Secretary of Housing and Urban Development. As Bush's unsuccessful competitor for the Republican presidential nomination, Kemp had set forth what was widely labeled a "populist conservative" message. He asserted a belief in government action to assist the disadvantaged, but he criticized traditional liberal approaches to assistance as "paternalistic" and, therefore, counterproductive. He believed that conservatives should design programs that foster self-sufficiency and independence on the part of the poor (i.e., that wean them as quickly as possible from dependence on public "handouts"). Like Reagan, he believed that government was the major villain in creating and perpetuating poverty, but he believed that with proper redesign of programs, the government's role could be positive. Kemp entered office with a clear agenda for housing, of which the centerpiece was the sale of public housing to its tenants. However, before he could pursue this agenda, he was faced with a crisis at HUD, which resulted from the negligent, and in some instances, criminal behavior of his predecessor, Samuel Pierce, and other HUD political appointees. This episode put a final black mark on the housing record of the Reagan administration.

The HUD Scandal

The scandal involved the Section 8 Moderate Rehabilitation Program. For most of Reagan's two terms, his administration pushed for the abolition of this program, yet Congress continued to allocate modest funding for it.

Since the number of units funded was so small, they were not apportioned geographically like other HUD funds, but left in a discretionary fund, under the direct control of HUD Secretary Samuel Pierce. On April 26, 1989, the HUD Inspector General released a report suggesting that contracts utilizing these funds had been awarded on the basis of political influence, not need. Secretary Kemp immediately froze the program, while the House Government Operations Committee, chaired by Rep. Tom Lantos (D, Calif.) began a series of hearings (*CQ Weekly Report* 1989b, 1127).

As it emerged from testimony by the Inspector General, and by various developers, the scam ran something like this. A developer with an idea for a project would contact a former Reagan administration official, such as, in one instance, former interior secretary James Watt. For a hefty consulting fee (in Watt's case, $300,000), the official would call Pierce, or his top assistant, Deborah Dean, who would promise approval of the project. Then, the developer would advise the city in which the project was to be located to apply for units through HUD's nominally merit-based application procedure. Within a few months, the city would be allocated a number of units which "coincidentally" corresponded to the exact number needed for the developer's project.

Over the next six months, the hearings took on a tragicomic air, as witness after witness tried to deny or evade responsibility for her or his actions (U.S. House, Committee on Government Operations 1989; *CQ Weekly Reports* 1989c). Pierce testified on May 25, 1989, and, in often heated exchanges with the committee, he relied on the "I don't recall" strategy utilized so effectively by the principals in the Iran-Contra scandal. He asserted that any influence peddling was done by his subordinates without his knowledge, evidently preferring to appear incompetent rather than corrupt. When the committee called him back in September, to explore contradictions between his earlier testimony and that of other witnesses, he pleaded the Fifth Amendment, as did several other top HUD officials.

Jack Kemp showed great political skill in immediately and aggressively attacking the problem. In addition to freezing the program, he instituted an administrative review and drafted reform legislation for consideration by Congress. These actions won him wide praise by both Democrats and Republicans, and reinforced the impression that he was a "breath of fresh air" after eight years of stagnation. Thus, he ended up in a stronger position to make his mark on the new housing legislation that was eagerly anticipated within the housing policy community.

From the fall of 1989 onward, congressional action followed two parallel paths. First, HUD reform legislation began to move through both houses. Following the general outlines of Kemp's proposal, the legislation restricted the HUD Secretary's control over discretionary funds, restricted the use of waivers of regulations, and put limits on consulting fees for HUD projects (*CQ Weekly Reports* 1989d, 3193). The progress of the bill was, at first, delayed by the insistence of House and Senate Democrats that HUD reform be part of a broad new housing authorization bill. Through this strategy, they hoped to gain leverage on the Bush administration not to veto some of the housing policy changes they sought. However, as the year progressed, Democrats such as Rep. Barney Frank (D, Mass.) began to fear being labeled "anti-reform" if they continued to hold the reform bill hostage to a larger housing measure. Therefore, they "decoupled" the two efforts, and the reform bill cleared Congress on November 22, 1989 (*CQ Weekly Reports* 1989e, 3242).

Meanwhile, various members of Congress called for the appointment of a special prosecutor to conduct a criminal investigation of the principals in the HUD scandal. In contrast to Kemp's quick action, Bush's attorney general, Dick Thornburg, appeared reluctant to pursue the matter, but upon receiving a formal request from the Democratic members of the House Judiciary Committee in November 1989, he agreed to investigate the need for a special prosecutor (*CQ Weekly Reports* 1989g, 3371). Arlin Adams was appointed special prosecutor in January 1990. His efforts yielded four guilty pleas and three convictions. Three more top HUD officials, including Thomas Demery and Deborah Dean, were eventually convicted (*New York Times* 1993a, A15). However, Pierce himself was never indicted, although he later admitted failure to competently administer the office (Shenon 2000).

In accounting for this scandal, one may look to both short-term and long-term factors. In the short term, the atmosphere at the top levels of HUD during the Reagan administration did not encourage respect for the real purposes of HUD's programs. Many of Reagan's appointees apparently saw nothing inconsistent in simultaneously urging the termination of a program while milking it for maximum benefits for their political cronies. In the long term, a certain level of risk of this type of corruption is inherent in the use of private, profit-seeking developers to provide assisted housing. Private contractors serving all facets of government have historically shown an inclination to use any available political leverage in their competition for contracts.

The endemic nature of political manipulation by private contractors in alliance with government officials was shown by the questionable relationships between some members of the housing subcommittees in Congress and contractors, which came to light at about the same time as the HUD scandal. Senator Alfonse D'Amato (R, New York), the ranking Republican on the Senate's subcommittee, was accused of demanding campaign contributions in exchange for exerting his influence on behalf of some housing contractors in his state, although he was not held account-able for this either in court, in the Senate, or by the voters in 1992 (*CQ Weekly Reports* 1989c, 2947). In a different, but related, policy area under the committee's jurisdiction, Senator Alan Cranston (D, California), the committee chair, was found to have sought special treatment for savings and loan owner Charles Keating, in exchange for campaign contributions. Finally, members of the appropriations subcommittee covering housing and community development were roundly criticized by Kemp, and others, for the practice of earmarking funds for specific projects for their districts in appropriations bills. While not illegal, such a practice suggested cozy relationships between members of Congress and the particular groups pushing these projects (*CQ Weekly Reports* 1989f, 3315).

THE HOUSING ACT OF 1990

There are times when scandal in an agency blocks congressional consider-ation of legislation in the agency's policy area, since members do not want to be associated with giving more power or money to an organization that is tainted in the public eye. However, since Kemp's aggressive action clearly disassociated the "new HUD" from the "old HUD," this particular scandal did not put the brakes on congressional consideration of new housing legislation. The force generated by the rising consciousness of housing problems discussed in the last few pages was still there, and the Bush administration was receptive to some action in keeping with its "kinder, gentler" image. Thus, 1990 became a year dominated by consideration of several versions of a new, omnibus housing authorization bill, the first major revision of housing programs to be considered in many years. After several apparent deadlocks were broken by key compromises, the Cran-ston-Gonzalez National Affordable Housing Act became law on November 28, 1990 (*CQ Almanac* 1990, 531).

The new act reflected a new paradigm for federal involvement in housing which had evolved over the sixteen years since the 1974 Act was passed, a paradigm on which a considerable degree of consensus existed among liberals and conservatives. The major elements of this new paradigm are as follows:

1. Primary reliance on tenant-based assistance through vouchers and certificates, utilizing existing standard housing;
2. Local control of those production programs that do exist, exercised either through local government or through local nonprofit community development corporations;
3. Home ownership as a central strategy for assisting low income households;
4. Integration of other social services with housing.

Let us review some of the major features of the Act, showing how it reflected the basic elements of the paradigm.

Assisted Housing. The Act authorized a modest number of additional units of Section 8 certificates and vouchers, as well as units to replace some of those lost through prepayment. However, it did not attempt to restart federal efforts to assist the poor through new construction. Gonzalez and other Democrats originally wanted a limited new construction program, and their proposal stimulated a strategy debate over new versus existing units reminiscent of the 1970s. But, even these liberal Democrats did not advocate a shift back to the predominantly new construction orientation of earlier years. Rather, they were concerned with keeping the new construction option available for areas where the market was not producing enough moderately priced units to meet the needs of assisted households. Thus, the Act codified the reliance on vouchers that had emerged, de facto, from the appropriations process and from less sweeping amendments to housing legislation during the 1980s.

The HOME Program. Despite its emphasis on vouchers, the Act provided for the production of new and rehabilitated units through the HOME program. However, in keeping with the second element in the paradigm, HOME placed production firmly under local control by providing block grants that could be used for various housing development strategies. While the main production strategy was rehabilitation of existing units, the Act permitted HOME funds to be used for new construction, if the community could demonstrate a shortage of affordable housing suitable for rehabilitation. HOME funds were to be distributed to larger cities via a formula, while funds were given to the states to allocate to smaller cities.

HOME also required that 15 percent of a locality's funds be set aside for use by community housing development organizations (CHODOs). These are nonprofit neighborhood development corporations or alliances of local nonprofit groups formed for the purpose of providing affordable housing. Nonprofit groups were involved in housing programs during the 1960s, but, as noted in chapter 4, their involvement had been limited, and frequently unsuccessful. In the 1980s, a new breed of nonprofit organization arose, stimulated by communities' desperate search for ways to make up for dwindling federal housing funds. These new non profits showed they could address the social and neighborhood concerns often ignored by for-profit developers, while avoiding the management problems of publicly owned housing (Rasey 1993). For this reason, Congress wanted to ensure nonprofits an important role in HOME and to encourage communities without an active nonprofit housing sector to form one.

Homeownership. The Act included the top priority of HUD Secretary Jack Kemp, the HOPE program. (HOPE stands for "Housing Opportunities for People Everywhere.") This embodied his strong belief that home ownership was a central element in self-sufficiency and pride for low income persons, particularly those residing in public housing. As discussed in chapter 4, the Section 235 program had also rested on this assumption, and the broad perception that it was a failure had discredited the idea in the 1970s. However, in the early 1980s, renewed discussion of the idea was stimulated by large scale sales of British public housing units to their tenants by the government of Prime Minister Margaret Thatcher. Kemp, at the time a congressman from New York, eagerly embraced it as part of his populist conservatism.

Due in large part to Kemp's vigorous advocacy in Congress, a public housing sales demonstration project was established by HUD in 1984. Seventeen housing authorities were selected to participate, and they put forward plans to offer 1,315 units for sale. An evaluation of the program, published in April 1990, revealed mixed results. First, many housing authorities lacked the will or expertise to participate effectively. Second, for the most part, only units in lower density or single family detached projects were deemed suitable for sale, since sales in high rise complexes raised issues related to the quality and value of the units, as well as the issue of displacement of tenants who could not or would not purchase. This meant that the "cream" of the housing authority's units were sold off, with a net loss of publicly assisted units. Finally, many tenants' incomes were simply too low to afford ownership, even at the substantially discounted sales prices offered by the authorities. Again, only the "best" tenants in terms of income and family stability were able to participate, leaving questions as to the relevance of the program for the vast majority of public housing residents (U.S. Department of Housing and Urban Development 1990).

Undeterred by these problems, Kemp continued to advocate public housing sales vigorously, using the rhetoric of independence and self-reliance for the poor, and pointing to successful pilot projects such as Kenilworth-Parkside in Washington, D.C. In the 1990 Act, the "HOPE I" program dealt specifically with public housing. It envisioned the sale of projects to tenant management organizations. However, in contrast to the tenant management schemes of the 1960s that emphasized ongoing collective responsibility for the units, tenant management was seen as an intermediate step toward ownership by individual tenants. "HOPE II" allowed for a similar process in privately owned projects receiving federal assistance, while "HOPE III" enabled nonprofit organizations to build or rehabilitate units for purchase by low income persons.

The consensus behind the homeownership strategy appeared not to be as broad or deep as that supporting other aspects of the paradigm, since both positive and negative aspects of this strategy were apparent. On the positive side, both the experience of public agencies and of nonprofit groups such as Habitat for Humanity International showed that homeownership can be an empowering experience for low income families who are relatively stable financially and are otherwise predisposed to move toward middle-class status. Also, since homeownership is the desired state for middle-class persons, one that they associate with many positive values, their support for housing aid to the poor can often be better mobilized for this goal than for other forms of assistance.

On the negative side, many low income households lacked the stability and resources to benefit from ownership. Heavily subsidized rental units were the only practical means to provide them with physically adequate, affordable housing. Whether or not the HOPE programs benefit low income households in general depends on whether they reduce the net supply of rental housing or serve as an additional resource for those in a position to take advantage of them. The HOPE programs contained provisions protecting nonpurchasing tenants from displacement and providing vouchers to replace the units sold. However, whether or not these programs supplement, rather than supplant, other commitments depends more on the overall level of national resources committed to housing than on specific program designs.

Integration of Social Services. The 1990 Act called for coordination of other social services with the provision of housing assistance. It was noted earlier that, due to its historical linkage with physical, rather than personal or social development, housing assistance has tended to be administered in isolation from other social services, by persons with different backgrounds than the traditional "helping" professions. Many observers have long recognized that this separation is not only artificial, but counterproductive. On the one hand, many of the problems of assisted housing are related to unresolved economic, social, and familial issues, not the nature of the housing itself. On the other hand, if the impact of a household's physical surroundings on its ability to solve problems is ignored when helping them shape solutions, intervention is less likely to succeed. Nevertheless, only recently have programs been designed to incorporate housing into an integrated attack on the problems of particular households.

The Act included one type of integrated approach to household problems in its Family Self-Sufficiency program. The goal of this program was to gradually wean families from all forms of public assistance. The family received public support for housing and other needs, while also receiving assistance for the education or job training necessary to upward mobility. The program was somewhat coercive, in that the household signed a contract making continued assistance contingent on progress in its self-sufficiency plan, but intensive case management was also considered essential to a successful transition. In HOPE III, the prospect of homeownership was included in a similar self-sufficiency plan, as an incentive toward greater economic stability and responsibility.

As critics on the Left might readily point out, this program is based on the assumption that barriers to a decent, middle-class existence are primarily individual in nature, rather than built into the opportunity structure of the economy. The current service-based economy contains reduced opportunities for those without advanced education to earn decent incomes, in comparison to the manufacturing-based economy of thirty years ago, and unless this situation improves, upward mobility will continue to be difficult, no matter how motivated the individual. Nevertheless, such programs do recognize the interrelatedness of family problems and can remove those very real individual barriers, which prevent individuals from taking advantage of opportunities that do exist. As is the case with home ownership, they serve that segment of the poor already inclined toward upward mobility.

Improvements in the social environment have also been linked to housing improvement through various efforts to deal with severe social problems in public housing or in assisted private housing developments. Earlier in the 1980s, some funding was made available to housing authorities to deal with drug trafficking, which is perhaps the major source of violence in low income areas, and the 1990 Act continued various forms of special antidrug funding. Authorities were also allowed to expedite eviction for those suspected of drug involvement. Of course, driving drug dealers out of public housing simply moves the problem elsewhere, while federal programs for drug treatment remain grossly underfunded. However, as long as public resources are being utilized to provide families with housing, it was reasonable to expend additional resources to make at least that housing a safe haven against violence. Not to do so would delegitimize the entire federal housing effort in the eyes of the public.

Comprehensive Planning. One final aspect of the 1990 Act bears some discussion—the requirement that communities prepare a Comprehensive Housing Affordability Strategy (CHAS). This strategy replaced the Housing Assistance Plan (HAP), and involved an even more comprehensive planning process than the HAP. Communities were required to conduct a comprehensive analysis of market conditions, the conditions of their housing inventory, their housing needs, and the resources currently available to meet the needs. They were also required to establish five-year priorities and an annual plan showing what actions would be taken to address those priorities. In preparing this plan, they were encouraged to form a task force consisting of all relevant governmental, nonprofit, and private housing actors, and they were required to solicit public comments.

Fair Housing

The issue of racial discrimination in the sale and rental of housing also bears some discussion here, since it was raised more forcefully in the 1980s than it had been for fifteen years. As discussed in chapters 4 and 5, this issue has entered into the policy debate over housing assistance at various points, but as a distinct policy, governmental efforts to prevent housing discrimination have stayed somewhat on the fringe. The Civil Rights Act of 1968 set the goal of nondiscrimination in housing, but provided relatively ineffective enforcement tools. The Johnson administration left office before having to enforce the Act, and the Ford and Nixon administrations showed little inclination to enhance enforcement or even to use what tools they had vigorously (Lamb 1992, 4–6).

According to data collected by Charles Lamb, enforcement became more vigorous during the Carter years, as measured by the ratio of cases brought to HUD's Office of Fair Housing and Equal Opportunity to the number of cases closed. When Ronald Reagan took office, most observers assumed that enforcement would decline, since Reagan had been an opponent of fair housing legislation in California when he was governor of that state. In fact, Lamb's data show that the rate of closed federal cases did decline during the Reagan years to levels below those of all other administrations (Lamb 1992, 11).

Nevertheless, the Reagan administration did agree to two important measures that resulted in strengthened enforcement of fair housing. First, the Fair Housing Amendments of 1988 put more teeth in HUD's enforcement powers, including mechanisms making it easier to award actual damages to complainants. Second, the Reagan administration encouraged states to strengthen their fair housing enforcement mechanisms, in an effort to devolve more responsibility away from the federal government. State civil rights agencies responded with a rapid increase in cases considered and closed. Lamb attributes the first move to Reagan's desire to deflect criticism that he was anti-civil rights, based on his actions with regard to busing and affirmative action. Also, HUD Secretary Samuel Pierce is given credit for pushing this issue, in spite of his dubious record in other areas (Lamb 1992, 7). The second move was related to Reagan's general belief in decentralization. Although states had not been known for vigorous civil rights enforcement in the past, state agencies appeared to tackle their new role much more vigorously than HUD had pursued its enforcement role.

CHAPTER 8

Stagnation and Progress: The Clinton Era

Compared to the 1980s, the 1990s began more auspiciously for the federal effort to address the housing needs of low and moderate income families and to revitalize communities. In 1990, a moderate Republican administration had worked with a Democratic Congress to produce a bold redesign of the federal housing effort. Two years later, the Democrats regained control of the White House for the first time since 1980. An informed observer might reasonably have anticipated that, even though the production levels of the 1960s were unlikely to be restored, federal housing efforts would be expanded considerably, Instead, federal efforts stagnated during the 1990s, while the real revolution in low and moderate income housing programs occurred at the state and local levels. In Part I of this chapter, the causes and consequences of federal stagnation under Clinton will be explored. In Part II, the revolution at the state and local level will be addressed.

Part I—The Clinton Administration

The presidential election of 1992 displayed volatility typical of recent national elections. President Bush began the year with such great popularity (based on the American victory in the first Iraq war) that it seemed quixotic for any Democrat to challenge him, and several potential contenders sat out the election. Then, as Bush's popularity began to slide, the independent candidacy of Ross Perot seemed to be the major beneficiary. In the early summer of 1992, the possibility that the Democratic candidate might come in third loomed briefly in the polls. It was only when Perot withdrew, and Clinton was able to defuse some of the personal criticism leveled at him, that the Democrats began to gain advantage from public discontent with the economy and to pull ahead. Perot's later reentry helped prevent Bush from regaining momentum by giving some of his former supporters an alternative to Clinton, but the 19 percent of the vote Perot received also left Clinton with the weak mandate of a plurality victory (*CQ Weekly Reports 1993a*).

The Clinton candidacy emerged within a party engaged in internal debate and self-examination that stemmed from sound defeats in five of the six previous presidential elections. In 1984, Reverend Jesse Jackson had argued, during his campaign for the Democratic presidential nomination, that a Democratic majority could be built on the basis of a "Rainbow Coalition," consisting of the growing minority populations along with disaffected poor and working-class white voters. This strategy would have, in effect, revived in a slightly different form the New Deal Coalition that was the traditional basis of Democratic electoral strength. However, potential members of this coalition did not vote consistently or in enough numbers to counter the massive shifts of white, middle-class voters to Republican candidates in the 1980s. Therefore, Democrats began to listen to the counsel of those who said the party should move toward the political center, in order to draw mainstream voters back in.

Prior to his presidential bid, Bill Clinton had been a leader in one of the groups arguing this position—the Democratic Leadership Council. He also drew inspiration from a book by David Kusnet entitled, *Speaking American: How the Democrats Can Win In the '90s*. Although centrists were accused of abandoning the party's historical commitment to social justice, Kusnet took a more sophisticated approach. He argued that the party should continue to strongly advocate the use of government to improve the lives of ordinary citizens, including many of the core social programs they have always defended, because this basic stance is still supported by a large majority of the electorate. However, Democrats must also deliver a clear message that they support the core values of hard work, family, and public civility that are cherished by the middle class. If they appear to be "soft" on crime, or unwilling to require some effort from the poor in return for government benefits, the Republicans will turn these "values" issues to their advantage (Kusnet 1992).

Another strain of new Democratic thought came from such analysts as Robert Reich, who wrote extensively on the economic problems of the 1980s. Reich was strongly critical of the Reagan administration's "hands-off" strategy for promoting economic growth, and he envisioned an active partnership between business and government to foster wise investments and accelerate growth (Reich 1983). These arguments appealed to centrist Democrats, because they enabled them to position themselves as strong supporters of economic growth. In the 1980s, Republicans had undermined the public's New Deal faith in the Democrats as the party of prosperity by successfully labeling them as the party willing to sacrifice growth to ever more burdensome redistributive programs. Many Democrats believed Reich's approach could help restore their positive image.

Clinton's campaign strategy showed that he had taken both kinds of advice to heart. He took a tough stance on welfare, promising to "end welfare as we know it" and replace it with strict requirements for work or job training. He emphasized job creation strategies and programs such as health care reform that would deliver benefits to broad segments of the population. He also distanced himself from prominent African American leaders such as Reverend Jesse Jackson, whom voters associated with the "old" Democratic attitudes (although, ironically, Jackson was as outspoken as anyone on the need for pride, initiative, and personal responsibility among the poor). Clinton created an image of a leader committed to economic development and change, not one whose primary goal was to redistribute resources to the poor.

The results of the 1992 election provided mixed evidence as to the success of this strategy. On the one hand, Clinton drew his core support from traditional Democratic strongholds in the central cities. An analysis of the vote by *Congressional Quarterly* shows that most of the ninety-eight congressional districts that Clinton won with a majority of the three-way vote were urban districts where minority voters were in the majority (*Congressional Quarterly* 1993k, 2176–77). On the other hand, he also built his plurality by making serious inroads into youth groups, urban white ethnic voters, independents, and suburban voters, all of whom had previously supported Reagan and Bush. Many of the remaining 158 congressional districts he carried encompassed smaller cities in the Midwest; and while he did not win a majority in the South, he carried more Southern states than other recent Democratic candidates.

The coalition he built was shaky, according to many analysts. To maintain it, he had to walk a fine line between rewarding his traditional Democratic supporters in the central cities and maintaining his image as a "New Democrat" to his other supporters (*Congressional Quarterly* 1993i, 1828). Upon taking office, he further weakened his political support by his failed initiative to permit gays and lesbians to serve openly in the military, controversies surrounding several of his appointments, and responses to foreign policy crises such as Somalia, Bosnia, and Haiti that were widely perceived as weak and ambivalent (Hamilton 2007). He also failed to get a major stimulus package enacted by Congress that was directed at urban areas (*CQ Weekly Reports* 1993 b through 1993f).

His position on a tightrope was fully reflected in the kinds of initiatives Clinton sponsored upon entering office.

The problem of housing was not attractive to the Clinton administration as an area in which they could make a significant policy impact. At first glance, this might seem surprising, in light of the worsening housing problems and the growing public concern documented in chapter 7. However, there are several important reasons why this issue lacked appeal. First, vigorous pursuit of housing equality could be a divisive policy for Clinton's centrist coalition. While inadequate housing is seen as a problem worth solving by many middle income persons, their views tend quickly to become negative if housing programs are seen as having a detrimental impact on their own neighborhoods. An aggressive policy to expand the supply of affordable housing could have led to such impacts, especially if the suburbs were asked to absorb a larger share of assisted housing.

Second, even if potential opposition were seen as a surmountable obstacle, the resources for seriously addressing housing needs were lacking in the budgetary environment of the early 1990s. To provide serious relief of the housing burdens experienced by lower income households would have required: (1) upgrading the current housing voucher program to an entitlement available to all eligible persons, like food stamps; (2) expanding programs to assist local governments and nonprofit organizations in financing the additional production of housing needed to meet the demand generated by the expanded voucher program. The Congressional Budget Office (1989) estimated that the first element alone would more than double the current $17–18 billion in yearly outlays for housing assistance.

While $35 billion to guarantee decent housing was not a huge commitment in a $5 trillion economy, the politics of the budget deficit were such that a proposal of this magnitude would not receive serious consideration. A logical way to partially pay for such a commitment would be to cap the tax deductions given to middle and upper income homeowners for mortgage interest and property taxes, so that they would only be available to those who really needed them to make homeownership affordable. However, these deductions were another political "sacred cow" that Congress was unlikely to disturb.

A third reason for a lack of emphasis on housing issues by the Clinton administration is that an innovative blueprint for current approaches to housing had already been set by the National Affordable Housing Act of 1990, and many of the programs authorized by this act were barely under way. In many respects, this act represented state of the art thinking with regard to the structure of housing programs, if not the appropriate level of resources. Thus, unlike welfare reform, the administration could not position itself as an innovator by bringing the federal government's approach in line with current consensual perceptions of the problem.

Finally, many housing programs did not immediately present themselves as the kind of "human resource development" policies typically embraced by Clinton. Clinton promised policies that would do more than maintain the poor at a minimum standard of living. This "new Democrat" offered, instead, a renewed promise of transforming the poor, and moving them from their current deprived, dependent state to one of independence and material well-being. While a strong case can be made that decent housing is as essential to household and neighborhood development as any other social factor, its linkage is not as self-evident as that of employment, training, and health programs.

Despite its relatively low priority, action in housing policy was not totally absent under Clinton. He picked a strong leader for the Department of Housing and Urban Development (HUD) in Henry Cisneros, former mayor of San Antonio. However, the housing themes struck by Clinton and Cisneros were procedural in nature, rather than promises of substantially increased resources or activities. In fact, the Administration even proposed cuts in certain housing programs (such as public housing) to pay for higher priority programs (such as vouchers), eliciting strong protests from supporters of federal housing assistance (National Association of Housing and Redevelopment Officials 1994). There are four themes that predominated in the Clinton administration's approach.

First, Cisneros repeatedly stressed the need to reform HUD itself. In the face of budget cuts, followed by a major scandal, HUD's morale and reputation fell to an all-time low in the 1980s. As noted earlier, Jack Kemp received praise for vigorous action to correct some of the organizational problems that helped foster corruption. However, Cisneros still criticized the agency for losing sight of its primary goals and becoming absorbed in "paper pushing" (*Washington Post* 1993a, F1). He called for the elimination of one thousand jobs in order to remove a "layer of bureaucracy," even though HUD had already shrunk considerably during the 1980s (*Washington Post* 1993j, A19). He also searched for ways to simplify the planning documents required by HUD from local communities.

He also tackled the agency's troubling financial problems, such as the numerous bankrupt private housing projects under its control. A negative side effect of efforts to control the loss of federally assisted private rental units through sale and conversion to middle income units was the financial failure of some projects, leaving HUD to dispose of the units. In the fall of 1993, at the urging of the administration, Congress enacted legislation giving HUD more flexibility in disposing of these projects, as well as others that had come into HUD ownership (*Washington Post* 1993i, A16).

A second, related theme was the need to remove tight bureaucratic controls on local public housing authorities (PHAs). The report on "Reinventing Government" prepared by Vice President Al Gore's task force devoted considerable attention to the public housing program. They portrayed it as the epitome of the smothering of local flexibility and inno-vation by excessive "top-down" regulation, which they saw as prevalent throughout the federal government. The task force advocated allowing local PHAs the freedom to run their own show, subject only to evaluation according to clear performance criteria (*Washington Post* 1993j, A19).

Like many such "efficiency" reports, this analysis reflected a certain amnesia concerning the history of the regulations that stifle local initia-tive. As documented in earlier chapters, public housing is an unpopular program which, while more successful in many locations than its popular image suggests, is studded with spectacular failures. Efforts to "fix" it have resulted in constant battles between the federal government and local housing authorities—each blaming the other for the program's difficul-ties. Many elaborate federal regulations have been directed at what was perceived as lax management and maintenance by local PHAs—a percep-tion that is a combination of reality and blame shifting. It was likely that, given additional discretion, some PHAs would improve management while others would stay the same or get worse. Whether Congress would become so dissatisfied with the "worst cases" that it began another cycle of reim-posing regulations remained for the future to determine.

Despite its dissatisfaction with the current state of public housing, the Clinton administration quietly scaled back some of the HOPE programs included in the 1990 Housing Act at Kemp's insistence (*New York Times* 1993b, A16). Funding for HOPE I and HOPE II, programs designed to sell public housing units and federally subsidized private rental units to their tenants, was cut deeply in Clinton's first budget proposal. Funding for HOPE III, a program to build or rehabilitate additional units for low income homeownership, was limited to those projects that had already received planning grants. Homeownership for the poor would seem to be in keeping with the administration's emphasis on self-reliance among the poor, yet they shared the skepticism of many experts as to whether selling off public housing to its *extremely* low income tenants was the proper strategy to achieve self-reliance (*Congressional Quarterly* 1993g, 919).

A third major theme stressed by Secretary Cisneros was a renewed emphasis on fair housing. One part of this emphasis might be labeled an "integrationist" strategy (i.e., one trying to provide more housing opportunities for minorities in predominantly white areas). Cisneros expressed the view that racial segregation is one of the most serious barriers to the advancement of minorities. He criticized discrimination in the private market, and he promised tough enforcement of fair housing laws. He also criticized the perpetuation of racial and ethnic segregation through site selection of federal projects, and he promised a new emphasis on wider distribution of units across jurisdictions, as well as trying to settle some of the outstanding discrimination suits against public housing authorities (*Washington Post* 1993k, AZ9).

HUD also initiated an experimental program called "Move to Opportunity" (MTO), modeled after local experimental programs in Chicago and other cities. This program encouraged and supported families receiving housing vouchers (including some current tenants of public housing) to move to neighborhoods where their race was underrepresented. Particularly encouraged were minority moves to majority areas, since it was felt that this would enhance job and educational opportunities for these families (Turner 1994). The Chicago program was initiated in response to the lengthy *Gautreaux* litigation, and it was regarded as having been reasonably successful in "de-concentrating" about six thousand minority families away from traditional minority areas (Peterman 1994).

The other part of the Clinton administration strategy was aimed at upgrading existing low income and minority areas. Cisneros promised a vigorous attack on redlining of inner city neighborhoods both by lending institutions and by companies providing property insurance. Some banks were already induced to cooperate with government and nonprofit agencies in special lending programs for lower income homeowners or neighborhoods, because they feared that approval of mergers and other business transactions by banking regulators might be delayed if their Community Reinvestment Act profile was not acceptable. Since public funds for housing rehabilitation were limited, these were vital to maintaining or upgrading neighborhoods in which disinvestment had occurred.

A fourth theme of the Clinton administration was the need to commit more resources to assisting the homeless (*New York Times* 1993c). An administration report on homelessness asserted that the problem had been greatly understated by previous administrations. In particular, the fact that the approximately half-million people to be found homeless on a given night is surrounded by a "penumbra" of millions of others, who move in and out of homelessness, had been ignored. It stressed that, while problems such as those of mental illness contribute to homelessness, the shortage of affordable housing was a central factor in its continued existence. The report was largely written by Andrew Cuomo (who later became governor of New York), who had worked extensively with homelessness in New York City before being appointed to HUD by the Clinton administration (*New York Times* 1994b, A1).

The report was critical of the federal resources going to support housing for the affluent, in the form of taxes forgone on mortgage interest and property taxes. It also advocated greatly increased resources for housing assistance and expanded programs for the mentally ill, including aggressive outreach (*New York Times* 1994b, A1). However, there was a large gap between the scale of effort advocated in this report and the actual expenditures recommended by the Clinton administration. Spending for the homeless was increased in the FY 1995 budget recommendations, but only by taking away funds from other housing programs. As noted above, a serious attack on this problem would have required spending far beyond that which the current budget situation permitted.

As in other areas, they advocated a coordinated approach, in which multiple services are directed at getting the homeless into permanent shelter. A HUD initiative for the Washington, D.C., area was based on a "continuum of care" system, in which all the barriers to independent living experienced by the homeless, including mental illness and lack of job training, are dealt with. They proposed consolidation of five separate programs authorized under the McKinney Act into a single, streamlined program (U.S. Department of Housing and Urban Development 1993, 6). This proposal failed to pass as part of comprehensive housing bill in 1994. However, as shall be discussed in chapter 8, the model was later revived as a guide to HUD administration of programs for the homeless.

Two of the Clinton administration's policy initiatives spoke directly to the overall development of cities. Since such developmental policies have a direct impact on housing and neighborhood improvement, they bear some discussion here. They also illustrate the large political obstacles that confronted even modest initiatives by Clinton to help disadvantaged areas. One was the economic stimulus package, which went down to defeat in April 1993. The other was the proposal to establish "Urban Empowerment Zones," signed into law in August 1993.

In February 1993, President Clinton unveiled an economic stimulus package intended to exemplify his emphasis on economic growth. Totaling $16.3 billion, its aim was to boost the economy and create jobs through an assortment of job training and public works programs. Though the package was sold in terms of its benefit to the whole economy, urban areas were the direct targets of much of its spending. Approximately $2.5 billion was to be added to the popular Community Development Block Grant program for job producing projects; $3.2 billion was for transportation projects; and $5 billion was for job training and unemployment benefits (*Congressional Quarterly* 1993b, 581).

The bill sailed quickly through the House of Representatives. Clinton carefully marshaled Democratic votes, and he tailored the bill to convince liberal, urban representatives that he cared about their problems, in spite of his centrist rhetoric. He felt no need to compromise with House Republicans and conservative Democrats, who questioned whether the stimulus was needed in a recovering economy and bitterly attacked the increased deficit that would result from the measure. However, this strategy backfired in the Senate, where the ability to delay action through a filibuster gives the minority party more leverage than in the House. Once having passed a very liberal bill, without Republican consultation, Clinton felt he could not compromise in the Senate without cries of "betrayal" from his liberal supporters in the House. However, without such a compromise, he could not lure enough Republican votes to achieve the sixty votes necessary to block the filibuster. Meanwhile, Senate Minority Leader Robert Dole (R, Kansas) rallied his Republican troops by stressing the bill's impact on the deficit and by his argument that Republicans had to stand firm or be totally ignored by the Clinton administration. Unable to close off debate, Senate Majority Leader George Mitchell (D, Maine) was forced to withdraw the bill on April 21, 1993 (*Congressional Quarterly* 1993h, 1001).

Clinton hoped, and the Republicans feared, that the latter might be viewed as obstructionist by the public for blocking Clinton's plan. However, public opinion was not seriously aroused on this issue. The kinds of jobs created by the stimulus package could easily be dismissed by voters as temporary and not really relevant to their underlying economic problems. Most Republicans could be counted upon to oppose it, given the affluent, nonurban nature of their constituencies, as well as their high priority on not increasing the deficit. However, crucial defectors might have been attracted to the fold had Clinton convinced the public that a sufficient emergency existed to justify such spending measures. Without this broader support, the enthusiastic backing of traditional urban constituencies was insufficient to secure passage.

The empowerment zone program did not stir the same dramatic, partisan confrontation as the stimulus package, in part because it was much smaller in scope. As noted earlier, Congress repeatedly rebuffed the Reagan administration's proposal to create "urban enterprise zones" in economically distressed urban areas during the 1980s. Many in Congress never accepted the premise, popular with conservatives, that government regulations and taxes, not the numerous other problems of these areas, were the major obstacle to private investment, and they were reluctant to increase the deficit through further business tax cuts. A very limited program was approved by Congress in 1988; however, President Bush's HUD Secretary, Jack Kemp, felt the program was flawed and refused to approve any zones, despite the fact that applications had been taken. Meanwhile, forty states adopted enterprise zone statutes, and the thirty most active states designated eight hundred zones (*Congressional Quarterly* 1993j, 1881–82).

Clinton's proposal incorporated the tax incentives and regulatory relief of the Republican proposals, but it also included federal funding for various community needs and a much more active role for the federal government in approving local strategies and supervising their implementation. This indicated a lack of confidence in the capacity of tax breaks alone to revitalize distressed areas. Clinton's advisors were very critical of the rigidity of federal program requirements and stressed that coordination and flexibility in the delivery of federal funds was essential to their approach. Nevertheless, the conservative author of the enterprise zone idea, Stuart Butler of the Heritage Foundation, bitterly criticized Clinton's proposal for reintroducing the "meddlesome" government he wanted to get rid of (*Congressional Quarterly* 1993j, 1882).

As finally approved by Congress, as part of the Omnibus Budget Reconciliation Act of 1993, Clinton's program designated six urban and three rural empowerment zones, utilizing a competitive application process. Empowerment Zones (EZs) were required to have substantial concentrations of poverty. Applications included a "Strategic Plan" emphasizing sustainable economic development through job creation and coordination of related social and community services, from housing, to education, to drug abuse prevention, to policing. Among the benefits these zones received were:

- Tax-Exempt Facility Bonds for certain private business activities;
- Social Service Block Grant funds, passed through the state, for activities identified m their Strategic Plan;
- Special consideration in the competition for funding in numerous federal programs;

• An Employer Wage Credit to employers for hiring zone residents, plus special tax treatment of expensing and depreciation.

Another sixty cities and thirty-five rural areas were to be designated as Enterprise Communities. The emphasis on coordination of programs dealing with the multiple problems of economically depressed areas was reminiscent of the Model Cities Program of the late 1960s. However, unlike Model Cities, which was changed from a pilot program to a widely available program prior to implementation (Frieden and Kaplan 1977), this program initially (in Round I of the designations) retained its pilot status. On the negative side, this pilot status frustrated many cities desiring the benefits of the program, and it revealed the limited commitment of resources to urban problems that either Clinton or Congress was willing to make. On the positive side, the design of empowerment zones was so complex that testing the approach thoroughly before attempting it on a larger scale was desirable.

The Taxpayer Relief Act of 1997 authorized Round II of the program, which included another five urban and fifteen enterprise zones, plus two additional Round I enterprise zones. During Round II, eligibility standards were changed slightly to increase localities' flexibility with regard to the number of high poverty census tracts that were to be included in the zones. In 2000, the Community Renewal Tax Relief Act of 2000 created an additional program, the Renewal Community (RC) program, which focused more exclusively on tax relief for companies investing in seriously disadvantaged communities. It authorized forty RC sites, of which twelve were reserved for rural areas (US General Accounting Office 2004).

Throughout the program, an emphasis was also placed on "regulatory relief" for businesses operating in EZ or RC areas. This enshrined the conservative belief that economic development is inhibited by "excessive" fees and regulations. The RC program, in particular, required a specific commitment on the part of local governments to reduce or streamline regulations within the designated zones (U.S. General Accounting Office 2004, 12). By 2004, when the General Accounting Office (later renamed the Government Accountability Office) conducted an evaluation of the EZ, EC, and RZ programs, they provided the following data on its impact:

• A total of 33 urban and 3 rural EZs had been designated.
• A total of 53 urban and rural Enterprise Communities had been designated.

- A total of 28 RC areas had been designated, although some of these were EZs that had been converted to the new program.
- The poverty rates in these areas averaged over 40 percent, while unemployment rates were in the 13 percent range for rural zones and in the 15 to 20 percent range for urban zones.
- A total of $1 billion in Social Services Block Grants had been designated for EZs and ECs, of which $711 million had been drawn down.
- A total of $300 million in Economic Development Initiative Grants had been appropriated, of which $163 million had been spent.
- An additional $434 million in direct HUD appropriations had been designated for EZs and ECS, of which $183 million had been spent.
- State and local governments had issued $300 million in tax exempt bonds designated for EZs. They were encouraged to do so by the fact that these "Facility Bonds" were not counted toward the per capita ceiling on tax exempt bonds imposed by the 1986 tax reform law.
- Corporations and individuals had claimed an estimated $251 million in EZ employment credits. (The GAO found it impossible to estimate the value of other tax breaks because the data were not easily separable from other deductions on tax returns.)

In short, this seemingly minor program had turned into a fairly significant federal investment in disadvantaged areas over the course of its implementation. Maps provided by the GAO show that the designated areas were widely distributed across the United States (U.S. GAO 2004, 25–31).

As with so many complex and decentralized federal programs, evaluating the actual impact of the program on the targeted areas has proved very difficult. An interim report prepared for HUD in 2001 indicated that employment had increased in five of the six original EZ areas, but there was no way to know if this was due to the program's impact or other factors. The report attempted to compare EZ growth with adjacent neighborhoods but it was not clear that these other areas had been precisely matched with the target areas (Hebert 2001). In addition, two other factors made a comprehensive evaluation difficult: (1) the variety of approaches utilized within the EZs, and (2) the fact that data on the use of tax breaks provided by the IRS could not be disaggregated to individual zones to see what direct impact these tax expenditures had made on employment. The fact that more than three thousand businesses had claimed the tax credit by 2004 indicates that there was substantial private investment in these areas but the assessment of how much of it "trickled down" to the residents would require a rigorous analysis of the program that, so far, has not been done.

The political factors that shaped the election of Bill Clinton in 1992 contributed to a record of action toward the problems of housing and community development in urban areas that was both weak and contradictory. He could not afford to ignore his strong urban base altogether, yet he went out of his way to demonstrate he was not beholden to them. The development of a strategy such as Empowerment Zones that mixed traditionally liberal and traditionally conservative ideas enabled Clinton to show a commitment to dealing with urban problems, while at the same time signaling that he was a "new Democrat" who thought that more federal spending was not the sole solution. Yet, some of Clinton's problems did not stem entirely from his electoral non-mandate. The limitations imposed by the federal government's fiscal dilemma meant that he was unable to initiate any large new flow of resources. The huge deficit proved a more effective brake on governmental activism than any other policy development during the Reagan era. Even if Clinton had been the most dedicated "urbanist" since Lyndon Johnson, he would not have been in a position to launch expensive programs.

Republican Counterattacks and Clinton's Responses

During the Clinton administration, a seesaw battle between increasingly polarized political parties began which has characterized American politics ever since. Just as one side scores a resounding victory, and seems to be in a position to enact its policy goals, the other side counterattacks and is able to neutralize the victory. Analysts of public opinion disagree on the extent to which the general public shares this polarization. The scholarly consensus seems to be that each party has a core of supporters who are as ideologically committed as its leaders, but that there is another large group of voters that are "in the middle" and who are discontented with both parties for their perceived lack of leadership (Patterson 2003; Fleisher and Bond 2001). The situation is exacerbated by the nature of American political institutions, which are designed to prevent strong government by majority coalitions. The separation of powers in the Constitution is reinforced by antimajoritarian traditions such as the filibuster in the Senate, so that even a party with a clear congressional majority often has difficulty enacting its policies.

Beginning late in 1993, President Clinton decided to take on the thorniest issue in American social policy, health care reform. Reform seemed urgent, given rising costs, the fact that the current health care system left millions of people uninsured, and the fact that the United States measured much lower on many measures of collective health than other industrialized countries, despite spending a much larger share of its GDP on health care than any of these other countries. However, the current system was very profitable to drug companies, hospitals, and insurance companies, and these entities had millions of dollars to spend to influence members of Congress. In a manner typical of Clinton's centrist approach, his advisors (led by First Lady Hillary Clinton) devised an incredibly complex reform proposal, designed to correct the flaws of the current system without fundamentally changing it. The proposal was so complex that few voters (or members of Congress for that matter) fully understood it, so that it became easy for opponents to paint it in any negative way they wished. The proposal foundered in Congress, and Clinton came away with a major domestic policy defeat (Skocpol 1996).

Meanwhile, conservative Republicans had come up with an effective strategy for regaining the power they had lost in the election of 1992. Even though they had played a major role in blocking the Democrats' agenda, they campaigned against Democratic incumbents in Congress as an entrenched, do-nothing bloc of ineffective leaders. In addition, they appealed to conservative antitax sentiments and to voters who remained concerned about social issues, such as abortion. The result was a smashing victory in the 1994 congressional election that gave Republicans control of both houses of Congress for the first time since the 1950s.

Another element contributing to the Republican victory was that they had outlined a set of clear proposals for moving public policy in a conservative direction, known as the Contract with America. Within the tradition of American political parties as loose coalitions hammering out incremental policy through compromise, it was an unusual move for a congressional party to commit itself in advance to a specific set of measures. Voters may not have agreed with all the specifics of the plan, but it conveyed an image of positive leadership to a public disillusioned with congressional inaction. This Contract also coincided with the transformation of the Republican Party into a cohesive and ideologically uniform coalition that was strongly committed to reducing taxes, cutting social programs, and enacting the agenda of social conservatives. Republican moderates were becoming a rare breed. House Speaker Newt Gingrich had helped engineer this transformation by promoting conservative candidates throughout the nation, and he provided leadership in the House of Representatives.

However, in the end, very little of the Contract was enacted into law.

With a president of the opposite party, and with congressional Democrats able to block some measures, the legislative results were limited. Moreover, in 1995, the Republicans became locked into an extended budget battle with Clinton that threatened to shut down large sections of the government because appropriations bills had not been passed. In response to his previous failures in moving Congress and convincing the public to support him, Clinton had hired Dick Morris, a sophisticated political strategist, to help rescue his presidency. With Morris's help, Clinton was able to skillfully shift the blame for the budgetary stalemate to the Republicans, so that it was they whom the public perceived as being obstructionist. The party that had gained public support by promising leadership ended up with a more negative public image.

Following the 1994 Republican victory, a number of conservatives had intensified their calls for the abolition of the Department of Housing and Urban Development, and they introduced bills to that effect. Moderate Republicans, such as Rep. Rick Lazio (R, N.Y.) and Senator Christopher Bond (R, Mo.), who remained as chairs of the House and Senate Banking Committees, believed that this was not feasible, and they helped to ensure that the HUD abolition bills got nowhere in Congress (*CQ Almanac* 1995, 1996). However, these moderates, along with the Clinton administration, believed that HUD needed a serious overhaul. The administration continued to push for radical decentralization of the administration of public housing, including loosening of income rules and the conversion of public housing subsidies to portable vouchers for tenants.

The voucher idea was not supported by Bond or Lazio, but their committees reported a HUD reauthorization bill that included many of Clinton's proposals, including consolidation of programs serving the homeless. It also included provisions that would have encouraged the "working poor" to live in public housing by reducing the required percentage of public housing that had to be allocated to "very low income" households, i.e., those at 30 percent of the median income or below and by relaxing the Brooke Amendment requirement that all tenants pay 30 percent of their income in rent. (This meant that increases in income due to working led to rent increases to bring the rent burden up to 30 percent—considered a work disincentive by many.) Finally, it included provisions that liberals considered punitive, such as requiring eight hours per week of "community service" as a condition for the receipt of public housing assistance. However, no housing reform bill emerged during the mid-1990s, as the opposition of Congressional liberals and the threat of a veto prevented the drastic overhaul that many Republicans wanted. In 1995, a reform bill was passed by the House, but failed in the Senate (*CQ Almanac* 1995). In 1996, the House and Senate passed different versions of a reform bill but were unable to reconcile their differences (*CQ Almanac* 1996, 7-21 to 7-23) A similar stalemate between the two chambers occurred in 1997 (*CQ Almanac* 1997, 7-12 to 7-16).

Meanwhile, the HUD appropriations process took a slightly different path. In 1995, the FY 1996 appropriations bill cut funding for housing programs by 21.5 percent, and because of this and cuts to other agencies such as EPA in the bill, it was vetoed by President Clinton. Eventually, as a result of the slow working out of the budgetary stalemate, Clinton was still forced to accept serious HUD budget cuts, so that, as Figure 8-1 shows, appropriations dropped from $24.6 billion in FY 1995 to $19.1 billion in FY 1996. However, after that, HUD funding began a slow recovery, so that by FY 1999, the $24.08 billion appropriated was close to the FY 1995 level.

In addition, many of the provisions of the two HUD overhaul bills that

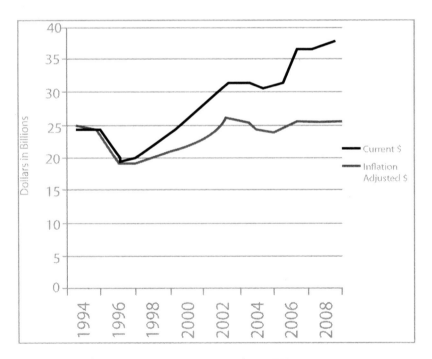

Figure 8-1 HUD Approproations: FY 1994–2008

Source: U.S. Department of Housing and Urban Development Budget Documents

Inflation adjustment based on Consumer Price Index: 1994 = 100

failed in the authorization process were successfully attached as a rider to the FY 1999 appropriations bill (*CQ Almanac* 1998, 20-7 to 20-13). Among the most significant programmatic features attached to the appropriations bill were the following, as outlined in the *CQ Almanac*:

- Conversion of the Brooke Amendment limit on the percentage of income that can be charged as rent by public housing authorities from a floor to a ceiling, so that many tenants would have to pay at least some minimum monthly rent (no more than $50) even if their incomes were near zero;
- Formal abolition of the federal occupancy preference rules, although requirements as to the percentage of units that must be allocated to very low income families (<30% of median income) were left in place. By a complex formula, public housing authorities were allowed to increase the number of somewhat higher income families that they could rent to, as long as they preserved 75 percent of the units for very low income families;
- A requirement of eight hours per month of community service for adult tenants who were not working or participating in job training programs;
- Elimination of the requirement that public housing authorities replace every unit of obsolete or dilapidated public housing demolished with an equivalent unit or voucher. This provision would prove critical to the implementation of the HOPE VI program, which was also reauthorized in this measure.

The derailment of the Contract for America and the successful labeling of Republicans as obstructionists helped to set the stage for Clinton's reelection in 1996. The economy was in good shape, and the Republicans' nominee, Senator Robert Dole, proved to be a less than effective campaigner. Clinton, whose political fortunes had been at low ebb just over a year earlier, won a resounding victory. However, as part of the price of that victory, he felt compelled to sign a welfare reform bill that reflected, in large part, the Republican philosophy. It abolished the AFDC program, put a five-year lifetime limit on the receipt of welfare benefits by any individual, and it required recipients to be seeking work or training for work as a condition of their benefits. In 1992, Clinton had promised to "end welfare as we know it." Even though the bill was more conservative than he would have liked, he knew that failing to sign it would lead to accusations of failure to follow through on his promise.

Frustrated in their attempts first to render President Clinton powerless and then to prevent his reelection, Republicans turned to what Ginsburg and Schefter (1999) have referred to as "politics by other means." Kenneth Starr, a special prosecutor appointed to investigate alleged improprieties associated with the Whitewater land deal that Bill and Hillary Clinton had been involved with prior to Clinton's presidency, changed direction and began to investigate reports he'd received concerning an affair between President Clinton and a White House intern, Monica Lewinsky. In 1997, House Republicans brought impeachment charges against Clinton based on his alleged perjury before a grand jury concerning the affair. Even though the Republicans insisted that they were trying him for perjury, not adultery, a majority of the public did not see it that way, and polls showed a lack of support for the impeachment. The Senate acquitted Clinton, failing to find that he had engaged in the "high crimes and misdemeanors" that the Constitution says are grounds for impeachment. Once again, Clinton was still standing after a Republican onslaught.

Despite the bitter impeachment confrontation between Clinton and Congress, they continued to hammer out compromises on appropriations bills, and this process resulted in increasing HUD appropriations during the last two years of the Clinton Administration. In 2000, a very generous HUD/VA/NASA appropriations bill passed. During negotiations Clinton beat back Republican attempts to kill his pet program, AmeriCorps, and, with the support of some moderate Republicans, he was able to increase funding for housing vouchers. Passage of the bill was also greased by $360 million in congressional earmarks (CQ Almanac. 2000a, 2-148 to 2-158) As Figure 8-1 shows, HUD appropriations continued their steady climb out of the trough of 1994–95 during 1999 and 2000, even though adjusting appropriations for inflation shows that, in terms of real dollars, they were only holding their own, rather than increasing. This history suggests that, even in a situation of deeply polarized parties, the pressure to keep the government running and to meet basic human needs can sometimes produce compromises.

Another housing bill was approved by Congress in 2000 that illustrated the ambiguity that frequently emerges when policy makers try to identify critical housing needs and the populations that should be targeted for assistance. The housing market was booming in 2000, and even though home ownership had increased to a record level of 67.7 percent of households, members of Congress were concerned that low to middle income families were being priced out of the home ownership market. Supported by lobbyists from the housing industry, the bill included provisions that allowed some Section 8 vouchers to apply to home purchases and enabled localities to loosen regulatory barriers to the creation of affordable housing. However, the AARP and the National Low Income Housing Coalition did not endorse the bill, arguing that it did not target the families most in need of housing assistance. In earlier versions of the bill there was a provision to assist police officers and firefighters to acquire homes in disadvantaged neighborhoods, but this was eliminated in the final bill at the behest of Senator Phil Gramm (R, Texas) a strong opponent of any nonmarket solutions for disadvantaged neighborhoods (*CQ Almanac* 2000b 17-18 to 17-22).

Hope VI

Out of the maelstrom of attack and defense that characterized housing policy in the first half of the 1990s emerged another program that was to have a profound impact on the federal role in housing. Even though its name links it to the language of the 1990 Act, it was, in fact created in 1993, under the original title of "Urban Revitalization Demonstration," as part of the Department of Veterans Affairs and Housing and Urban Development and Independent Agencies Appropriations Act of 1993 (U.S. Department of Housing and Urban Development 2003). As was the case with subsequent legislative battles, its passage reflected the growing consensus among both Democrats and Republicans that certain aspects of the public housing program were fundamentally broken. The immediate impetus was a report on troubled public housing units issued by the National Commission on Severely Distressed Public Housing in 1992 (U.S. Department of Housing and Urban Development 1992). The report identified 86,000 units of public housing across the United States that were grossly unfit for human habitation, many of which were sitting vacant and abandoned. While these units represented only 6 percent of the total of 1.4 million public housing units, they tended to be highly visible because of their concentration in large urban areas and because they exerted a powerful negative impact on both their residents and those living in surrounding neighborhoods. An explicit goal of the Clinton administration in implementing this program was to improve the public's image of public housing (Smith 2006, 31–32).

Although HOPE VI was originally enacted as part of an appropriations bill, it was given firmer legislative authorization through the Quality Housing and Work Responsibility Act of 1998 (Smith 2006). This act also enabled the program to proceed more vigorously by eliminating the "one for one replacement rule" which had compelled local authorities to replace any public housing unit demolished with another comparable one. The units eliminated by HOPE VI could now be replaced with vouchers, giving localities a great deal more flexibility in developing HOPE VI plans.

During the eighteen years that the program has operated, 96,200 units of public housing have been demolished. They have been replaced by 107,800 new or renovated housing units, of which 56,800 are affordable to the lowest income families. This net loss of low income units was counter-balanced by the issuance of 78,000 vouchers (U.S. Department of Housing and Urban Development 2010, 20). Whether or not these vouchers would have been available to other low income families if not used for HOPE VI is not clear; certainly, Congress' extreme reluctance to fund new vouchers suggests that they might not have been.

As has been discussed throughout this work, concern with the intense concentration of extremely low income households in public housing has been a recurring theme throughout the history of the program, and this concern has generated a variety of programs to deal with this concentration. However, previous programs, from Section 23 in the 1960s to Move To Opportunity in the 1990s, were directed at finding *alternative* places for some of the poor to live, while leaving large public housing projects more or less intact. In contrast, the aim of HOPE VI was to obliterate these concentrated units and replace them with alternative land use patterns and structures that were considered more desirable by housing planners.

The criterion for desirability that became central to the HOPE VI program was the idea of *mixed income* neighborhoods. The large high rises that concentrated thousands of very low income households in relatively small geographic areas were to be replaced with lower density units that would be occupied by higher income households as well as by former public housing tenants. Tenure would also be mixed, with units for sale existing side by side with rental units, either within the same structures or on adjacent blocks. This lowering of density and infusion of higher income households would, of course, displace a substantial portion of the existing public housing tenants, but these displaced households were to be either moved to other public housing units or provided with vouchers so that they could secure decent housing in other neighborhoods.

Because the "mixed income" concept is so central to HOPE VI, it is important to consider the various arguments that have been advanced to support the desirability of mixed income neighborhoods and the various criticisms that have been raised to counter these arguments. Table 8.1 briefly summarizes both the basics supportive arguments and their critical counterpoints.

Table 8.1 The Pros and Cons of the Hope VI "Mixed Income" Strategy

Supporting arguments	Critical rejoinders
Concentration of low income families in single developments exacerbates all of the problems associated with poverty.	The concentration argument "blames the victims," rather than focusing on gross mismanagement and neglect by those charged with providing public housing.
Low income households that live alongside higher income households will have better physical access to jobs and schools, which will enhance the opportunities of both adults and children.	These benefits are merely assumed by planners, without sufficient support by empirical evidence.
Living in better neighborhoods will enable low income families to develop better social capital that will help them be more successful in breaking the cycle of poverty and dependence.	Public housing tenants have dense, supportive networks of social capital within their existing neighborhoods that are disrupted by displacement.
Households with relatively higher incomes will provide positive role models for public housing tenants who live among them.	How many individuals really utilize their neighbors as important role models in making decisions about their lives?
Mixed income developments improve both the reality and the perceptions of the neighborhoods that public housing tenants inhabit, thereby improving their living conditions and removing the stigma that comes from living in "the projects."	Public housing tenants are merely displaced to other disadvantaged neighborhoods, where they are equally segregated by race and class.

Because of the controversy concerning the HOPE VI strategy, public housing tenants affected by these projects have been fairly extensively studied. Therefore, it is possible to review considerable empirical evidence to determine whether the arguments of either supporters or opponents are supported by experience with the program over eighteen years that it has been in existence. Edward Goetz (2010) has provided a clear and comprehensive review of the literature relevant to the impact HOPE VI on displaced public housing tenants. He presents the following conclusions:

• Those households displaced by HOPE VI have moved to neighborhoods with lower concentrations of poverty than the public housing projects they formerly inhabited. However, there is little evidence to support an improvement in employment opportunities for adults or educational achievement in children as a result of displacement to these slightly higher income neighborhoods. Factors such as lack of human capital, discrimination, family, and health problems are much more powerful determinants of success than the location of one's residence.

- While tenants displaced by HOPE VI report significant increases in physical safety, there is little evidence for a correlation between this and improvements in physical or mental health.
- The social networks formed by displaced households in their new neighborhoods are often weaker than those that they had in their former dwellings. Neighboring behavior between these households and the higher income households among whom they live has been found by several studies to be limited and superficial.

An article by Alexandra Curley (2010) published in the same issue of *Cityscape* as Goetz's literature view reports a more detailed study of the issue of social capital formation by displaced households. Utilizing both quantitative and qualitative data on displaced households from the Maverick Gardens public housing project in Boston, she finds that many households have experienced a loss of the regular interactions with neighbors that they had in Maverick Gardens. Whereas the density and common entryways of the old project made such interactions virtually mandatory and led to lots of informal socializing between neighbors, displaced households report a greater sense of isolation because the enhanced private spaces of their "improved" neighborhoods encourage people to stay within their houses and to ignore their neighbors. The key variable determining whether social capital is improved or detracted from by their moves was whether or not common spaces such as neighborhood centers had been created in the new neighborhoods to which they had moved.

In sharp contrast to the critical perspectives just presented, a comprehensive study of HOPE VI conducted for the Urban Institute in 2004 emphasizes the concrete benefits that public housing tenants have received as a result of HOPE VI (Popkin et al., 2004). They begin their analysis with data showing the abysmal physical and social conditions of the public housing that they left. In many projects, years of neglect and incompetent management by public housing authorities had exposed tenants to serious health and safety threats from their units. Many units were vacant, and new families would often refuse to move in, even after finally coming to the top of a years-long waiting list for public housing.

Vacant units were magnets for illegal activity by squatters. The authors acknowledge that the neighborhoods to which displaced tenants moved are often only slightly less poor than the projects they left and that racial segregation has been largely perpetuated by the moves, but they stress the improved physical condition of the housing these households now occupy and their improved sense of safety in their new neighborhoods. They also highlight the vastly improved appearance and atmosphere of the new, lower density housing that has replaced the grim, massive public housing blocks in which thousands of desperately poor people were crammed together. Similar positive outcomes for both the tenants displaced and the revitalized public housing neighborhoods created were reported in a study conducted for HUD in 2003 by Abt Associates (U.S. Department of Housing and Urban Development 2003).

The debate over HOPE VI gets to the heart of the issues of housing needs raised in chapter 3. Decent housing and neighborhood conditions clearly make an important contribution to people's overall quality of life. It is difficult to argue that the isolation, stigmatization, danger, and physical deterioration associated with the type of distressed public housing demolished by HOPE VI could have anything but a negative effect on the lives of the poor people living there, despite the networks of mutual support which residents often formed to cope with these difficult conditions. However, in analyzing the problems of impoverished public housing tenants, it is easy to move beyond this obvious but limited relationship to an argument that rests on physical determinism. The empirical evidence fails to support the expectations of some HOPE VI advocates that simply changing the addresses of public housing tenants would create dramatic improvements in their lives. Given all the other negative factors that affect low income households, it is not surprising that such expectations would prove unrealistic.

In addition, critics have, accurately, called attention to the negative consequences of the coercive element in HOPE VI displacement. They point out that the move to "better" neighborhoods was not something chosen by public housing tenants but something imposed on them by planners and decision makers from more privileged groups. Despite the provisions in the HOPE VI legislation for the involvement of residents in the transformation of their housing, there was often little consultation or effective involvement of public housing residents in the process (Smith 2006). Moreover, embedded in the argument for forced dispersal of concentrations of poor people is continued stigmatization and "victim blaming." While HOPE VI has aggressively addressed the poor federal and local management of public housing that contributed to its problems, the stigmatizing notion that "too many" poor people in one place is a "bad" thing is still implicit in its approach.

Homelessness

Programs directly addressing homelessness found a fairly stable funding niche during the 1990s, albeit at lower levels than many advocates believed were necessary to effectively address the problem. Two key developments in the design of homeless assistance reflect two different images of the homeless problem that can sometimes come into conflict. One image emphasizes the multiple personal and social problems faced by homeless people, such as alcohol or drug abuse, mental health issues, domestic violence, or employment issues as the drivers of homelessness that must be addressed before the individual or family can acquire stable housing (National Coalition for the Homeless 2009a). The second view sees homelessness as, first and foremost, a housing problem and seeks to establish stable shelter for the household before other services. These images are not mutually incompatible and, over the course of time, have been combined by many communities into a holistic strategy for addressing homelessness (Burt and Spellman 2007). However, they represent two polarities that may pull programs for the homeless in different directions.

During the late 1990s and early 2000s, the first view was the most influential in guiding federal policy. From the early 1990s on, local communities were required to establish local homeless coordinating boards, which would bring providers together to adopt a common understanding of how each could contribute to alleviating homelessness. Beginning in 1995, HUD distributed funds based on the Continuum of Care model, in which a homeless family or individual would be guided toward a coordinated set of services that would address their multiple problems. The providers involved typically included mental health, drug treatment, social service, and job training agencies (Burt and Spellman 2007). Veterans' service organizations were also included to address the special problems of this important subgroup among the homeless, which, according to the National Coalition for the Homeless (2009) may represent between one-fifth and one-fourth of all homeless people.

However, as localities continued to address the needs of the homeless, the second view began to gain greater influence, as expressed the in "housing first" programs adopted by many localities (National Alliance to End Homelessness 2010). In these programs, the first priority was to place the household in stable housing, which was required to be more permanent than shelters or transitional housing. A continuum of care was still provided, but the idea guiding these programs is that the household will be better able to take advantage of these services once their anxiety about having a roof over their heads is reduced. It was also increasingly recognized that some homeless persons would need Permanent Supportive Housing, in which services would continue to be provided to them in their units.

Homeless policy was also guided by an increasingly sophisticated model of homelessness, in which the homeless are seen not as a uniform group but as composed of distinct subgroups. One is the chronically homeless, who typically consume a great deal of the resources devoted to homelessness because of their multiple problems. It is this group at which Permanent Supportive Housing is directed. Even though this might seem to require a large amount of resources, it often saves money by preventing multiple crisis incidents with service providers and the police. Another group consists of the transitional homeless, whose homelessness is occasioned by a short-term crisis of one sort or another. For example, a woman fleeing domestic abuse with her children may find herself without the resources to secure alternative housing, and she needs temporary help until she can get herself on a sounder financial footing. (The National Coalition for the Homeless [2009a] reports that an estimated 63% of homeless women have experienced domestic violence in their adult lives.) Economics also plays a big role in transitional homelessness. The general effects of the 2007–2010 recession have added to this population, and housing foreclosures, in particular, have increased the risk of homelessness for both lower income homeowners and tenants who are evicted from foreclosed rental properties (National Coalition for the Homeless 2009b). A third group consists of persons whose chronically low income, or other personal problems, makes them subject to periodic homelessness. They may require intensive services, but not on the level required by the chronically homeless (Burt and Spellman 2007).

As housing and service providers continued to seek creative ways to serve the homeless, another uglier strain in local politics had a negative impact on this population. Many communities became committed to removing the homeless from public places by criminalizing such behaviors as sleeping in public places or carrying one's belongings in a grocery cart. These measures were ostensibly to "restore public order" along the lines of George Kelling's "broken windows" theory of crime reduction (Kelling

1996). While it is certainly true that certain elements of the homeless population exhibited behavior such as aggressive panhandling and public urination that made public areas much less attractive and pleasant, one can argue that the main purpose of these punitive measures was to get the homeless out of the sight of higher income citizens and to stigmatize them as a "criminal element" that was responsible for their own problems. A few communities went so far as to prohibit charitable organizations from serving meals to the homeless on the grounds that it "promoted" the homeless lifestyle! (National Coalition for the Homeless and National Law Center on Homelessness and Poverty 2010). If there is a positive side to this trend, it is that, as Burt and Spellman (2007) report, the threat of such punitive measures caused a number of communities to intensify their efforts to provide effective services.

Part II—State and Local Leadership in Housing

There was no single decision point during the 1990s at which state and local governments stepped forward to become the leading actors in housing production for low and moderate income households. Rather, their role emerged gradually, as the federal government continued the reduced level of support for housing that had been established during the 1980s. A series of federal actions had created the tools that states and localities would use to fulfill their new role, but the creative leadership would come from a partnership between state government, local government, nonprofit housing corporations, and for-profit developers. These networks were also supported by national nonprofit organizations, such as the Local Initiative Support Corporation (LISC) and the Enterprise Foundation, which provided both credit and technical assistance (Erikson 2009).

As has been shown in earlier chapters, state and local governments have come down on both sides of the liberal versus conservative values divide, depending on the circumstances. As Molotch (1987) has argued, much of local politics revolves around land use, with different groups competing for control of land either as an investment or as a place of residence or both. Where lower income households, particularly people of color, have tried to compete (or even been perceived as competing) with higher income households for desirable locations, then local government has often been utilized as a tool for massive, reactionary resistance. Where local elites decided that land should be converted to a "higher and better" use, that is, one that protected or enhanced their investments, poor people have been displaced, either through massive removal (as in the case of urban renewal) or through gradual pricing out of the market (as in the case of gentrification).

On the other side of the coin, local communities are directly confronted with the daily problems of declining neighborhoods, homelessness, and other negative effects of a lack of affordable housing. Therefore, they are often encouraged by circumstances to take a more pragmatic approach to these problems, in contrast to the ideological posturing that often dominates the national politics surrounding housing assistance and other social policies. Local business and political elites can often be convinced that the creation of decent, affordable housing is in the best interests of their community, in that it may reduce the negative externalities associated with deprivation and with declining neighborhoods. In addition, local private developers have found that, with the proper subsidies, the production of low to moderate income housing can be quite profitable.

Neighborhood organizations have also played an important role in generating local support for housing initiatives. Many of the stronger ones have created CDCs to rehabilitate or construct housing, piecing together funding from a variety of sources (Vidal 1992). Randy Stoecker (2001) has argued that when a neighborhood association becomes a housing developer, it blunts the edge of their militant protests against overall conditions of inequality, because they have to please multiple, powerful actors in order to keep their often meager flow of housing investment coming in. However, this has been an acceptable trade-off for many neighborhood leaders, because of the immediate positive effect that improved housing has on the quality of life in their neighborhoods.

The emerging role of state governments in housing provision has been discussed earlier. The issuance of tax-free bonds for investors provided a way in which states could support housing development without a large, immediate impact on their expenditures. This form of financing for low to moderate income housing continued to be important, even after the large federal production programs of the 1960s and 1970s were phased out. Because of their already established role in housing, states were given the important responsibility of allocating Low Income Housing Tax Credits among communities and projects when that program was established in 1986. This guaranteed that they would be a vital part of the support network for local initiatives.

David Erickson (2009) argues that the functioning of this state/local system of low income housing depends on a network of relationships between public and private actors. Local projects rarely rely on a single source of financing or subsidy but, rather, combine multiple sources to create financially viable projects. Thus, government, nonprofit, and for-profit entities have been compelled to work together cooperatively in order to produce the units.

Federal subsidies play a large role in making these projects work, but they come in indirect forms that leave much of the control in the hands of state and local officials. Part of the financing is usually provided by Low Income Housing Tax Credits. These are syndicated by project developers, in order to attract a variety of investors. The federal government thus becomes part of the network, but through tax expenditures administered by the IRS, rather than through direct federal subsidies administered by HUD. Additional federal funds enter the mix, through the CDBG and HOME programs that are largely controlled by local governments. Finally, state governments utilize a portion of the tax exempt bonding capacity that is allowed to them on a per capita basis by the federal government. In return, they can maintain much lower interest rates for their bonds than would be necessary if they were not exempt from federal taxes, and these lower borrowing costs help make lower income housing projects financially viable. In the end, most housing projects borrow only a limited portion of their project capital from regular commercial sources (Erickson 2009).

During the 1990s, the rapid growth in nonprofit community development corporations that had started in the 1980s placed these organizations in the role of major housing providers. The National Congress for Community Economic Development, an advocacy group for CDCs, periodically conducts a "census" of housing units produced by these entities. According to NCCED data, there were 2,000 CDCs in the nation in 1991, which had, as of that date produced 320,000 housing units and 17 million square feet of commercial/industrial space. By 2005, the number of CDCs had doubled, to 4,000, and their cumulative production had risen to 1,252,000 housing units and 126 million square feet of commercial/industrial space (NCCED 2005). These data indicate that they had assumed a major role in housing production, but also that they are broad-gauged organizations interested in the economic and social development of neighborhoods.

CDCs vary in size from small, storefront operations to large organizations with hundreds of employees. For many years, they engaged in constant struggles to cobble together multiple financing sources for relatively small-scale projects (Vidal 1992). However, Erickson (2009) suggests that in recent years, they have become integrated into the more stable networks of support for low income housing production that he documents. They have routinely been supported by set asides in state and federal housing programs. For example, states are required to reserve 10 percent of LIHTC support for nonprofit housing developers. They are widely viewed as more integrated into the neighborhoods they serve than other types of providers and as more willing to risk developments in seriously deteriorated neighborhoods. However, Stoecker (2003) has documented their struggles to reconcile their role as neighborhood advocates with their role as landlords, as well as their need to be responsive to external funding sources.

Without state, local, and nonprofit providers, there would have been little or no housing produced for low and moderate income families in the 1990s and 2000s. Their flexibility and their sensitivity to local needs and conditions meant that, in many cases, they could provide housing in a better managed and less stigmatizing form than earlier federal programs relying either on public ownership/management or private, for-profit ownership/management. Nevertheless, their projects could not fail to be affected by ongoing divisions between class and race and the pervasive neighborhood segregation that results from these divisions. A number of studies have suggested that state and local projects have resulted in less concentration of lower income households in areas where their neighbors are of the same class and color. Because of their smaller scale, these developments did not have the intense segregating impact on neighborhoods that earlier projects had. However, Julian and McCain (2010) found that many projects funded from a combination of the LIHTC and state/local sources were located in such a way as to perpetuate class and racial segregation, rather than to diversify neighborhoods.

Again one encounters the complex trade-offs that bedevil the creation of housing for low and moderate income people, especially those in stigmatized racial and ethnic groups. In many communities, the price of not conforming to neighborhood types and boundaries in siting new multifamily developments created by state/local/private partnerships would probably have been that no housing would have been built, because community controlled institutions would not be allowed to challenge community norms that support segregation. Also, as shown in connection with HOPE VI, the benefits to lower income families of scattering them among middle-class neighbors have been overstated in many cases. On the other hand, the deleterious effects of housing segregation in the areas of education, economic opportunity, and wealth accumulation are still strongly in evidence.

Conclusion

This chapter has shown that the 1990s were a basically a period of stagnation on the federal level. The major innovations in the Housing Act of 1990 were maintained, but few new programs or resources were directed at the housing problems of low income households. While HUD appropriations grew, they were mainly directed at maintaining prior commitments to project-based housing or housing vouchers. Homeless programs continued to be funded, and some programmatic innovations occurred, but the level of funding directed at homelessness grew very little. The decade's most innovative program, HOPE VI, was directed at the very serious problem of public housing developments that, in many cases, were barely habitable, but its impact on the residents of those projects was decidedly mixed. Again, no large new infusion of resources accompanied this program.

In the face of this stagnation, states and localities stepped forward to create new additions to the supply of affordable housing. Nonprofit housing organizations also played a major role in this innovative culture. Without their collective efforts, virtually no new units of affordable housing would have been created during the 1990s. However, these state/local/nonprofit networks were still dependent on key tools supplied by the federal government, including tax subsidies through the Low Income Housing Tax Credit and tax exemption for state bonds, direct funding through CDBG and HOME, and vouchers supplied to tenants who could not afford even the reduced rents of these projects. Therefore, the limited commitment of the federal government also limited the efforts of states, localities, and nonprofits. State and local tax bases simply cannot provide the revenues that would be necessary to address the entire national problem of housing deprivation.

In the next chapter, we will review housing policy in the first decade of the twenty-first century. Late in this decade a major housing crisis emerged which affected people of all classes. However, unlike the Great Depression, this crisis has not, so far, produced bold new policy initiatives.

CHAPTER 9

Housing in the Twenty-first Century

Part I—The First Decade

The Administration of George W. Bush

The long-term result of the contested election of 2000 was another significant rightward shift in American politics, but the will of the voters was decidedly murky at the time, given the extreme closeness of the vote. The most important effect of the Electoral College system for electing presidents is to divide the national election into fifty separate state elections. The perverse math that is built into this system always contains the risk that the winner of the popular vote will not win a majority in the Electoral College, especially when support for the candidates is evenly divided. The election of 2000 represented the first time that this had happened since the late nineteenth century, although Patterson (2003) points out that there have been several other "close calls." The combination of two polarized wings of the electorate with a critical swing vote in the middle produced razor-thin majorities for either Al Gore or George W. Bush in a number of states, of which Florida received the most attention since its electoral votes would determine the final outcome. With the victory ultimately determined by a Supreme Court decision on the Florida recount (*Bush v. Gore*) that many viewed as politically motivated, George W. Bush entered office with a very shaky mandate, although Republican control of both houses of Congress provided him with the opportunity to pursue his conservative agenda.

As has been well documented, the destruction of the World Trade Center and the attack on the Pentagon by terrorists on September 11, 2001, transformed the Bush presidency by placing him in a leadership position during a severe national crisis. Bush's popularity soared, as he responded to the crisis with the Patriot Act, which was designed to enhance the government's intelligence-gathering powers, and the invasion of Afghanistan to eliminate a key operating base of Al Qaeda, the group that was responsible for the 9/11 attack. Key neoconservative advisers within the Bush administration were already committed to pushing U.S. foreign policy toward a more aggressive, nationalist stance, and the 9/11 crisis gave them that opportunity (Mann 2004). In the spring of 2003, they utilized popular support of any strong military action to engineer the American invasion of Iraq, despite the absence of any evidence linking the regime of Saddam Hussein to terrorism.

The result of these events was that most of the Bush presidency was focused on foreign policy and national security issues, rather than domestic policy. However, this did not prevent the Bush administration from having a significant impact on domestic policy. The measure that had the most profound impact was the extensive tax cut legislation that was pushed through Congress early in his presidency. Thanks to the booming economy in the late 1990s and to the modest tax increases on higher income households that were enacted during the Clinton administration, the last two years of that administration saw the first federal budget surpluses that the nation had experienced since the late 1960s. The Bush tax cuts eliminated higher rates on the wealthy, as well as providing across the board tax cuts for other households. (The benefits of these tax cuts were concentrated in the highest income brackets—see Mishel, Bernstein, and Allegretto 2009.) As a result of these tax cuts, plus the increased spending necessary to fight two wars and a slowing of economic growth, Clinton's budget surplus was quickly converted to large structural federal deficits, the largest since the Reagan Administration (U.S. Office of Management and the Budget 2011).

The effect of large deficits is to discourage additional discretionary domestic spending, which, as was noted in chapter 7, may not be an entirely accidental outcome of Republican budgetary strategy. However, during both of George W. Bush's terms housing programs were not the targets of intensive efforts to cut them, as they had been during the Reagan administration and during the early years of Republican Congressional majorities during the Clinton administration. Both Republicans and Democrats on the relevant congressional committees continued to advocate for these programs, and a large portion of the funds were utilized just to maintain the status quo in federally assisted housing, rather than make bold new initiatives. Although many Republicans continued to be hostile to housing assistance programs and to HUD in general, the potential displacement of millions of families who were already receiving federal assistance made drastic cuts politically risky.

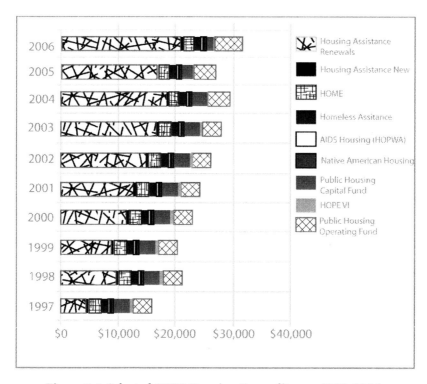

Figure 9-1 Selected HUD Housing Expenditures: 1997–2006

Source: U.S. Department of Housing and Urban Development Budget Documents

Figure 9-1shows the "status quo" nature of housing assistance during this period. Renewals of existing housing vouchers and Section 8 contracts consumed the lion's share of HUD's housing expenditures, with only very small amounts being allocated to new vouchers. Another large portion of HUD's housing budget went to capital and operating subsidies for existing public housing units. Compared to these expenditures, appropriations for the HOPE VI program were miniscule, despite all the attention that this program had received. President Bush tried to eliminate the program altogether during the last three years of his term, but Congress kept it minimally funded at $100 to $150 million a year (*CQ Almanac* 2007).

The only programs aimed explicitly at production were the HOME program and the Native American Housing Block Grants, both of which were under local or tribal control. Of course, CDBG funding, not shown here but averaging $4 to $5 billion a year, was also partly used for housing.

In addition, tax expenditures for housing production through the LIHTC are not reflected in the HUD budget. As noted in chapter 8, these modest sources of federal production support were a vital ingredient in the success of the housing production network created by states, localities, and nonprofit housing providers.

The fact that housing expenditures remained steady and even grew slightly during this period does not mean that there was not considerable hostility toward housing assistance programs within the administration of George W. Bush. Bush appointed Mel Martinez, a Florida political ally of himself and his brother Jeb Bush (then governor of Florida), as HUD Secretary. The *National Journal*, a publication that follows housing issues on a regular basis, gave Martinez a C+ for leadership, saying that he did not argue vigorously for HUD programs or exert careful control over HUD's various divisions ("A Bush Favorite Goes with the Flow" 2003). Bush's only new housing proposal was a program to promote homeownership among low income families, which was part of his "ownership society" initiative that also included the privatization of Social Security. It would have provided down payment assistance grants, reflecting the fact that the down payment is often a bigger obstacle to low income home ownership than are the monthly payments. The program was touted as particularly helpful to minority households, whose lack of home ownership contributes to the huge wealth gap between them and white households. However, this program never got very far in Congress. Many housing advocates were skeptical of this program because they viewed it as a "Trojan Horse" that would lead to deep cuts in rental assistance, to which Bush's team had expressed great hostility. In addition, many stressed the risks involved in extending credit to people of very low incomes, even with an upfront grant (Kosterlitz 2004). In light of the subprime meltdown to be described in the next section, their concerns seem prescient. Such a program might very well have added fuel to the fire of irresponsible lending and borrowing that was already occurring in low income areas.

The Mortgage Collapse

The central housing story of the 2000s was the collapse of the housing market during the latter half of that decade. As Dan Immergluck (2009) documents, many of the problems that precipitated this collapse were readily apparent earlier in the decade, but the warning signals were either totally ignored or not acted upon by either Congress or the president. The Federal Reserve set interest rates low, to encourage economic growth, but of course the most dramatic impact of low interest rates tends to be on the housing market. Meanwhile, credit was extended to an ever riskier set of borrowers by means of subprime lending. The availability of easy credit increased the demand for housing, thereby putting upward pressure on prices, while the prospect of escalating housing prices encouraged both borrowers and lenders to take more risks. This mutually reinforcing cycle produced a "housing bubble" that most observers predicted would eventually collapse. Some prominent economic leaders, such as Federal Reserve Board Chairman Alan Greenspan, minimized the possibility that such a collapse would have negative effects for the whole economy, emphasizing the "self-corrective" elements of the free market (Kosterlitz 2007). Other economists were more concerned about the collapse, but, in any case, few decision makers in either party were willing to take action to address it.

Charging a more risky "subprime" borrower a somewhat higher interest rate is not, in and of itself, necessarily destructive. For some borrowers, paying a higher rate is preferable to getting no loan at all. However, the type of loans that were being made in the subprime market involved not just higher rates but terms and conditions that many would argue were deceptive. Most of these loans offered a low, teaser interest rate that provided the buyer with payments he or she could afford, and they also often included a zero down payment and limited or no income or credit checks. However, after two to five years, a balloon note would come due. Since there were also substantial prepayment fees, the borrower had little choice but to refinance at a much higher interest rate. There were also several other types of substantial charges and fees that were hidden in the fine print of lengthy origination documents. Loan payments could more than double under many of these arrangements, leaving the buyer unable to pay and faced with foreclosure. It was these features that earned many subprime lenders the label of "predatory lenders" (Immergluck 2009).

The key to easier credit was the ability of lenders to pass on some of the risk to an increasingly complex layer of secondary investors. Mortgages were sold by the originators to various types of intermediaries, who would then bundle them together to create the basis for issuing mortgage-backed securities. Investors could choose from securities backed by several "tranches" of loans, distinguished from one another by the degree of risk that they represented. Many major financial institutions invested large amounts of their capital in these mortgage-backed securities, on the assumption that risk would be distributed over a collection of mortgages and that the booming housing market would protect them from serious losses due to foreclosures on the underlying mortgages. Key bond rating companies such as Moody's and Standard and Poor's often gave these instruments high ratings that would later prove questionable and would draw attention to the conflict of interest inherent in the fact that the bond evaluators are paid by those who issue the bonds.

Meanwhile, on the front end of these transactions, the incentive structure for brokers encouraged achieving a high volume of loans, rather than ensuring that the loans were sound. Non-bank mortgage originators, who dominated the subprime market, made most of their money on origination fees, not on the return of the mortgage as a longer-term investment. Their agents were given bonuses based on the number of loans they originated, not the soundness of those mortgages, so they had a powerful incentive to use aggressive selling techniques to push a household into a mortgage, regardless of whether they could afford it. By the time the borrower defaulted on the payments, forcing the house into foreclosure, the originators had passed on much of the risk to other investors.

Defenders of this system would later argue that it put home ownership within reach of families who could otherwise not afford it or would not qualify for a regular mortgage due to credit problems (Clemmitt 2007). Aside from the fact that pushing a household into a loan they couldn't afford and setting them up for later foreclosure was not exactly doing them a favor, the notion that all subprime borrowers couldn't qualify for regular loans was largely a myth. Many of the households that were pushed into more expensive, subprime loans by aggressive brokers could have qualified for more conventional loans but were told that they couldn't. Particularly vulnerable to this kind of hard sell were minority households, who often distrusted regular banks based on their own past experience, or the past experience of members of their group, of being denied credit despite their qualifications. Rather than risk the stress of applying for a regular loan and being rejected, many such households were willing to listen to promises of easy, no-questions-asked access to credit to purchase the home they had always wanted.

One of the most pernicious myths about the subprime lending crisis, one that was promulgated by some bankers and by conservative ideologues, was that it was precipitated by pressure on banks to make loans in low income areas resulting from the Community Reinvestment Act. Immergluck has clearly shown that this version of events is fallacious for at least two reasons:

- Many of the non-bank mortgage lenders who were most aggressive in pushing subprime loans were not subject to CRA regulations, which apply only to depository institutions.
- The community-based organizations that were working with banks to extend credit to previously redlined areas had a strong interest in making sure that the loans they made were sound. Loan defaults would not only harm individual buyers and neighborhoods but discourage banks from making additional loans. Therefore, their loan programs were the opposite of the high risk lending that was being foisted on low income households by deceptive sales practices. In fact, one can argue that even greater availability of responsible credit through CRA processes would have *discouraged* predatory lending.

Delinquency and foreclosure rates were, of course, much higher among subprime mortgages than among conventional loans, but the high numbers of households losing their homes put strong downward pressure on housing prices and cast a pall of uncertainty over the entire housing market. In 2008, Congress passed a housing finance overhaul bill, which included a first-time homebuyer tax credit, loan guarantees, and extra CDBG funds to buy abandoned and foreclosed homes (*CQ Almanac* 2008). The homeowner assistance program was expanded in 2009. While in effect, this provided a temporary boost to home sales, once it expired in April 2010 home sales dropped quickly to a level 18 percent below the 2009 rate (Clark 2010, 36). According to information provided to the *CQ Reporter* by the National Consumer Law Center, by the summer of 2010, one in twelve mortgages was seriously delinquent and one in ten was past due (Clark 2010, 35). Clearly, federal action had been insufficient to improve the longer-term health of the housing market.

The Mortgage Crisis and the Recession

During the latter half of 2008, a number of very large banks and financial institutions were facing bankruptcy, due to their extensive investments in mortgage-backed securities and other real estate–based derivatives. Congress had already passed legislation to bail out Fannie Mae and Freddie Mac, because their financial soundness had been seriously undermined by the crisis (*CQ Almanac* 2008). However, both liberals and conservatives came to believe that the collapse of large private financial institutions would have strong cascading effects throughout the economy, possibly including triggering another Great Depression. Therefore, both parties united behind a financial institution bailout proposal, costing in excess of $700 billion, which was proposed by the Bush administration. This legislation provided funds to keep banks and insurance companies afloat while they tried to clear their books of nearly worthless real estate investments. The fact that many executives of these large institutions were receiving huge bonuses at the same time that they were poorly managing their institutions became an emotional public issue. Much of the debate over the bailout centered on how many restrictions to put on executive compensation, with the Bush administration favoring a less restrictive approach. The bill eventually passed, with strong bipartisan support. However, it would be left to the next administration to administer the program.

The Obama Administration

The election of Barack Obama as the nation's first African American president in 2008 appeared to presage a significant liberal shift in American politics. Despite a bruising primary fight with Senator Hillary Clinton, he mobilized a vigorous campaign that attracted enthusiastic support from a wide range of voters. Voter turnout achieved levels not seen since the early 1960s (McDonald 2008). He carried states such as Virginia, which had not gone for a Democrat in several decades. Moreover, he brought in with him the largest Congressional majorities that the Democrats had owned since the 1960s. However, in spite of this overall liberal shift, millions of polarized voters on the right were bitterly opposed to Obama's candidacy, and there was an ugly undercurrent of racism in some of this opposition. Several analysts have concluded that had it not been for the deepening recession, which influenced swing voters in his direction, John McCain would have defeated him (Campbell 2008).

Having been swept into office on a wave of economic discontent, President Obama would find himself and his agenda engulfed by the same wave during his first two years in office. Several factors converged that would fuel subsequent criticism of his economic management. First, he had to manage the bailout of financial institutions, which he had inherited from the previous administration. He tightened restrictions on the affected institutions, and some of them began to pay back the large sums they had borrowed from the government in order to avoid further restrictions. Nevertheless, in the minds of many conservatives, particularly white middle-class members of the "Tea Party" movement, the measure became "Obama's Wall Street Bailout." These individuals basically rewrote history in order to justify their general distrust and rejection of the Obama administration.

Secondly, soon after taking office, Obama was faced with a difficult decision concerning the American automobile industry, which was also on the verge of collapse due to sales declines during the recession and due to their reliance on the production of large, fuel-inefficient cars that became less popular as gasoline prices increased. The collapse of these large corporations would throw hundreds of thousands of people out of work, both in the automobile companies and in the many other companies that were their suppliers. Therefore, the Obama administration decided to provide additional federal bailouts to these firms, as well. This measure, too, was used by his conservative opponents to portray him as favoring big corporations rather than "the little guy," even though conservative politicians have historically supported government interventions to rescue market winners who are in trouble.

Third, the Obama administration secured the enactment of a large federal stimulus package, consisting of public works and public services spending, in order to jump start the slumping economy. There was nothing radical about this measure. It was a pretty much standard Keynesian intervention. However, it occurred against a backdrop consisting of the large structural deficits inherited from the Bush era plus the large bailout expenditures already incurred. Therefore, federal deficits shot up to extremely high levels, generating concerns from a variety of economists about their potential impact on the country's economic health. These rapidly increasing deficits provided the basis for further conservative attacks on Obama for his perceived "fiscal irresponsibility."

The final nail in the coffin for Obama's image as a fiscal manager came from the fact that the economy did not respond rapidly to his stimulus efforts. There were several reasons for this lack of response:

- Despite the fact that many banks had received federal bailouts and were turning back toward profitability, they were still extremely reluctant to lend money. The resulting tight credit made it difficult for businesses to expand, even in the face of renewed demand for their products.
- Much of the economic impact of the stimulus package was blunted by drastic cutbacks in spending by state and local governments, due to lowered tax revenues. In many states, stimulus money went to preserve existing public sector jobs, rather than to create new public or private sector employment.

- The housing market continued to be extremely weak, with foreclosure sales absorbing much of the housing demand that remained, and tight credit making home purchases more difficult. In addition, faulty underwriting procedures had exposed many foreclosures to legal challenge, creating even greater sluggishness and uncertainty in the housing market.
- Millions of families were still in economic crisis due to layoffs and/or foreclosures, so that consumer demand remained weak.

During his first two years in office, Obama utilized his substantial congressional majorities to secure passage of two major pieces of domestic legislation. One was the enactment of major health care reform, a goal that had eluded progressive presidents since the 1960s. The second was the enactment of reforms to the regulation of financial institutions, which restored, to a limited degree, some of the regulatory authority that had been so drastically eroded since the 1980s. Both of these accomplishments would appear to have had the potential to gain considerable public support, but a number of analysts suggest that Obama made an important political miscalculation in underestimating the strength and virulence of the conservative counterattack against his policies (Bromwich 2010).

As noted in chapter 2, conservatives had developed a number of effective propaganda tools during the 1980s and 1990s. They again utilized these tools to frame the debate around Obama's legislative agenda. These included talk radio hosts such as Rush Limbaugh, a blatantly partisan Fox News Network, and numerous Internet sources that disseminated the most scurrilous of rumors about Obama's character and intentions as if they were established facts. Their messages found a receptive audience among groups of white, middle- and working-class voters who had constructed a political identity around a profound distrust of any government efforts to assist people in need and of government regulation of the economy. Obama was portrayed as an elitist who was out of touch with ordinary people and who wanted to institute socialist controls over the economy. Some commentators have also pointed out the thinly veiled racist messages imbedded in conservative propaganda. Their overt messages questioning Obama's citizenship and his religion were, in reality, aimed at portraying him as a dangerous outsider because of his race and because of his unusual background (Bromwich 2010).

The ongoing economic crisis, plus these effective conservative attacks, combined to produce a stunning reversal of party fortunes in the 2010 midterm elections. Republicans gained more than sixty congressional seats, retaking control of the House of Representatives (Tomasky 2010). They also made gains in the Senate, although Democrats held on to their majority there. This restored the pattern of divided party control of Congress and the presidency, which has been the norm since 1970. Although many commentators assume that divided control equals gridlock, a more detailed analysis by David Mayhew (2005) showed that major legislation has often passed in spite of divided party government. However, the ideological polarization of the parties continues to get more extreme, making gridlock a more likely outcome in the future. Although candidates supported by the extreme, "Tea Party" wing of the Republican Party had mixed success in the 2010 election, the movement still exerts a strong rightward pull on the party, an influence that is enhanced by its wealthy corporate backers. Tea Party followers not only disagree with Democrats on policy outcomes but they appear to have constructed an alternative view of reality, based on their own set of "facts." To the extent that members of Congress disagree with the president on their basic versions of reality, compromise becomes ever more difficult (Lilla 2010).

As the United States moves into the second decade of the twenty-first century, one is forced to draw the ironic conclusion that housing policy may actually benefit from not being at the top of the national agenda. Issues at the center of the agenda trigger intense, emotional debate that frequently produces less than optimal policy outcomes. Policy areas that are more on the periphery may be dealt with in less extreme and emotional terms. During the George W. Bush administration, housing programs were preserved and, to a limited degree expanded, despite Republican majorities in both houses of Congress. This was due to low key advocacy by moderate Republicans on the committees that deal with housing policy and a presidential administration that, while proposing cuts in housing programs at various times, did not commit serious political capital to enacting these cuts. The divided Congress that was produced by the 2010 election is even less likely to agree on severe cutbacks to existing housing programs, even though the Obama administration has not attached a high priority to housing issues.

Nevertheless, while deep retrenchment is unlikely, a serious expansion of federal housing efforts is even more unlikely. In 2009, the Obama administration had begun to work with Congressional Democrats to modestly ramp up federal housing efforts, with HUD Secretary Shaun Donovan, a former New York City housing official, providing leadership (Calmes 2008). They expressed caution about tearing down more public housing units through HOPE VI without increasing funds for replacement units.

Increased spending for housing vouchers and CDBG were included in the stimulus bill. In addition, the Obama administration supported efforts to capitalize the Federal Housing Trust Fund. This fund, modeled after the housing trust funds created by several states, had been a long-term goal of low income housing advocates, and it was finally created as part of the mortgage finance reform measure passed in 2008. However, Congress had been unable to agree on providing actual funds to capitalize it, so a push from the White House would have been very helpful in creating the long-term, stable source of financing for low income housing construction (Benson 2009).

However, in 2011, deep deficits, plus intense Republican opposition, will prevent most domestic programs from doing more than holding their own. The current level of funding for housing vouchers and other federal assistance is far below the level needed to fully address the housing needs of low and moderate income households. Only by making housing vouchers an entitlement will an adequate level of support be achieved, and this is extremely unlikely to happen. Thus, millions of low income households will continue to spend large percentages of their income on housing, which tends to crowd out other needs and which makes them vulnerable to homelessness should their limited incomes be interrupted. In the absence of a strong federal commitment local governments, in partnership with nonprofit and for-profit builders, have shown incredible creativity in producing decent, affordable housing with limited resources. Without a substantial new infusion of federal funds, these efforts will continue to address only a portion of the need.

Part II—Lessons and Recommendations
for the Future

In examining the eighty-year overview of federal housing policy that this work has provided, strong elements of change and strong elements of continuity both become readily apparent. Programmatic changes have been frequent, as policy makers have attempted to correct what they perceived as the mistakes of previous policies and to respond to new problems. Levels of federal commitment to addressing housing problems have varied considerably, from the highs of the 1930s and 1960s to the lows of the mid-1980s. However, though programs and funding may vary, federal housing policies of all eras can be seen to address a common set of issues and to be confronted by a common set of dilemmas and trade-offs. The definition of these issues is strongly affected by the differences in social and political values that are subsumed under the liberal-conservative ideo-logical split. The overall tenor of the debate has shifted from left to right and back over this eighty-year period, but the fundamental nature of the polarity remains the same.

As a summary and conclusion to this work, I begin with a review of the role of government in society as a whole. Within the context of this review, I then present a series of questions concerning the design and impact of housing policies that are critical to shaping decent and humane policy responses.

The Role of Government

A strong lesson of history is that capitalism *depends* on an active and effective public sector, which acts to maintain economic stability and to promote citizen well-being. The public sector serves the common good when it invests in goods and services that are essential to economic and social well-being that would not be provided, or would be inadequately provided, by the market system in the absence of government action. Clear and consensual targets of such investment include public and quasi-public goods such as infrastructure. More controversial, but no less essential, are investments in *human capital*. Providing people with access to a good education, adequate health care, adequate nutrition, and adequate shelter can be justified in terms of justice and compassion, but it is also an invest-ment in their capacity to be productive citizens that pays off for the whole society.

Ignoring this clear historical record, the Republican Party has shifted, during the last three decades, towards an ever more extreme antigovern-ment ideology. They posit a "free market" that operates in the absence of "burdensome" government regulations or redistribution. Such a system never has and never will exist. This ideology serves the interests of corpora-tions who want to pursue profit in the absence of any effective protection of their workers and the larger community from the negative effects of this pursuit. These same corporations will eagerly seek government protection and subsidy when it suits their interests.

The well-financed appeals of ultraconservative organizations have persuaded a significant number of white, middle-class voters to embrace their antigovernment ideology. Independence and self-reliance have always been important American values, and, when exercised within the proper context, pursuit of these values creates positive results for the society as a whole. However, when people become convinced that the government is the most important threat to these values, it leads them to ignore the numerous ways in which corporate action constrains and disrupts the very freedom and independence they are seeking. A corporate health care system robs people of benefits that they were conscientiously paying to receive. Corporations move jobs to locations with the lowest production costs, with total disregard for the lives and livelihoods that are destroyed as a result. Corporations seek to block or subvert regulations designed to protect the earth's resources and livability for future generations. Neoliberal economists assure us that this is all for the best in the long run, but this is cold comfort to those immediately affected. And yet, many citizens' distrust of government is so profound that they are blind to the ways that government could be used to protect their interests.

Housing policy clearly illustrates the vital role that government can and must play in order to assure the minimally decent standards of habitation that are so central to satisfying basic human needs. There are three basic reasons why the housing needs of low and moderate income persons will never be successfully addressed without a strong role played by government.

1. The gap between incomes at the lower end of the distribution and housing costs is simply too great. Incomes can be improved in a number of ways: by better education and training for individuals, by economic development that creates better jobs, and by policies that seek to promote living wages. However, it is unlikely that this income/housing cost gap could ever be closed to the extent that direct housing assistance would not be required for millions of households.

2. Construction of good quality low and moderate income housing has never produced a sufficient return on investment to attract private developers without some form of public subsidy, either directly through funds flowing to owners or tenants or indirectly through the tax system. Thus, even if such housing could be provided at a profit, the unsubsidized returns will always be lower than are obtained from producing higher income housing or by alternative investments.

3. The main process by which low and moderate income households obtain housing is through the filtering down to them of older units that have been vacated by higher income households. If this process was accompanied by sufficient levels of private investment to maintain the quality of these dwellings, then it might serve as an economically valid way to supply their housing needs. However, filtering is more typically accompanied by significant disinvestment. Individual property owners may disinvest in order to increase their profit margin in renting to

lower income households. This disinvestment, in turn, produces a downward spiral in the neighborhoods surrounding their units, which interferes with future investment by others. In most cases, it is only significant government intervention, utilizing both regulations and assistance, that can reverse this spiral.

Strategies for Government Intervention

Having established the necessity of some form of government intervention in the private economy in order to assure the availability of decent, affordable housing for all, one is still left with the task of examining and evaluating the multiple strategies for government intervention that have been proposed and utilized over the past eighty years. This has been the major purpose of this book. The best way to summarize the conclusions and recommendations to be drawn from this examination is to ask and answer a series of fundamental questions about housing strategies.

Question 1: What is the best mechanism for direct housing assistance for low and moderate income households?

Direct public ownership and operation of housing units was a successful post–World War II strategy in a number of European countries (although most have now moved away from it). However, in the United States since World War II, publicly owned housing has always been marginalized to serve only the most desperately poor households and, thus, it has always carried a heavy stigma associated with the nature of its residents. Class stigma was intensified by racial stigma, and as such housing was deliberately utilized to maintain racial segregation in many communities. As a result, even though public housing continues to provide decent, affordable housing for hundreds of thousands of households, it will, in all likelihood, never play a central role in future efforts to assist low and moderate income families.

Direct subsidies to reduce the cost of private construction of low income housing were provided in the 1960s and early 1970s, but these programs suffered a number of problems, including insufficient cost reduction, continuing stigmatization of the projects, and longer-term disinvestment by owners. Therefore, these programs were discontinued. However, indirect tax subsidies have continued, albeit in the altered form of the Low Income Housing Tax Credit. Units produced with these subsidies currently have a fairly good track record, but that is due to the fact that they are embedded in a complex intergovernmental network, to be discussed below. Also, the tax subsidies alone still do not produce housing that is affordable to the lowest income households, without additional direct subsidies.

From the late 1970s on, tenant-based assistance became the strategy of choice for providing low to moderate income housing needs. Initially, a significant portion of these tenant-based subsidies was tied to construction, through the Section 8 New Construction and Moderate Rehabilitation programs. However, assistance to households in securing existing housing units gradually replaced construction programs altogether in the early 1980s. Tenant-based assistance clearly has many advantages over project-based assistance; it is more direct and efficient in producing housing cost reductions and it results in somewhat greater dispersal of low income households than occurs in project-based assistance. However, this approach still has not overcome the racial and class stigmatization that bedevils all forms of housing assistance. Landlords can exclude "Section 8" tenants as an indirect and legal way of excluding households of a different color. Also, despite efforts to maintain the quality of units, many assisted households still find themselves in substandard units and neighborhoods. Therefore, while tenant-based assistance will clearly remain the central strategy for addressing the housing needs of low income housing for the foreseeable future, its efficacy depends on careful design and implementation. Also, as noted above, it will never fully serve the need for affordable housing unless it becomes a federal entitlement that is available to all eligible households.

Question 2: What are the proper roles for the various levels of government in the provision of housing?

The idea of direct federal ownership and management of assisted housing experienced an early death during the Great Depression, replaced by federally assisted local management of public housing. The legal and political obstacles to a more direct federal role were simply too great. In many instances of public housing development, the federal/local partnership operated to the detriment of low income households. Local governments were more concerned with warehousing the poor, particularly the black poor, at a safe distance from white, middle-class neighborhoods than they were with providing them with the "decent home and suitable living environment" called for in the Housing Act of 1949. Over its entire history, the program has oscillated between tighter federal regulations and greater local autonomy, with each level of government blaming the other for its problems. This debate has often obscured the deeper question of whom the program is really intended to benefit—the poor themselves or middle-class constituencies seeking to avoid contact with the poor. The failure to resolve this deeper question has contributed more to troubles experienced by the program than any particular management or financing strategies.

The widely perceived failure of public housing shaped the role of the federal government in all subsequent housing efforts. The federal role increasingly became that of financier, with management delegated to the private, for-profit sector or to the nonprofit sector, with local government playing an active role in shaping how and where units were developed or utilized. Clearly, only the federal government has the revenue-raising capacity to provide deep subsidies to individual households, but it exercises somewhat limited control over how and where those subsidies are utilized. Local markets, zoning regulations, and neighborhood boundaries still serve to minimize the "threat" of low income families moving into higher income neighborhoods in significant numbers.

In recent years, the federal-local-nonprofit-for-profit partnership has continued to produce new units for low and moderate income households, even as the federal government has abandoned its direct production role. Any future housing assistance strategy will necessarily be based on this partnership. However, advocates for households that are in need of assistance will have to aggressively monitor both concentration and quality issues in the units thus created.

During the 1970s, state governments overcame their traditional disregard for the problems of urban housing and became important players in producing housing for low and moderate income households. They did this by utilizing an indirect federal subsidy—their capacity to issue bonds with interest that is not subject to federal taxation. This form of state support will remain an important element in the package of assistance that localities utilize to produce affordable units.

Question 3: What are the continuing effects of racial inequality on the provision of housing to all citizens?

Today, in 2011, most Americans still live in neighborhoods where all or most of their neighbors are of the same race. Living in a white neighborhood is a racial privilege because property values are higher and appreciate faster than in neighborhoods of color, regardless of the socioeconomic status of the inhabitants. This disparity is largely responsible for the huge disparity in net worth between white households and others. It is also a privilege because white neighborhoods and communities generally have access to higher quality services, including the quality education that is necessary for economic success. As has been discussed earlier in this work, enforcement of fair housing laws has been weak and spotty since the passage of the 1968 Act. Even where African Americans and Latinos can utilize anti-discrimination laws to obtain housing in better neighborhoods, these laws cannot prevent the white flight that, within a few years, will turn many of these neighborhoods into largely minority areas. Only the most vigorous enforcement of antidiscrimination laws in the purchase and rental of housing and in obtaining housing credit can even make a dent in this problem.

Housing and neighborhood segregation intersects with the criminal justice system to produce even more severe problems for those who live in neighborhoods of color. Even though numerous surveys show that drug usage is roughly equivalent among whites, blacks, and Latinos (U.S. Department of Health and Human Services 2010), drug enforcement is highly concentrated in minority neighborhoods. The result is that an African American male is more than four times more likely to be arrested and imprisoned for a nonviolent drug offense than a white male (Mauer 2009). The arrest and imprisonment of a large percentage of African American and Latino males has devastating consequences for their neighborhoods. Regardless of the length of the sentence, a felony conviction is a life sentence in terms of its negative effects on an individual's job and educational opportunities. Economic failure contributes to recidivism, and it also contributes to the creation of impoverished households headed by a female parent, since prison frequently renders males to be unreliable economic contributors to the family.

Housing segregation produces difficult tradeoffs for housing assistance programs. As one example, HOPE VI has attempted to break up the overwhelming concentration of very low income minority families in large public housing projects, only to find that families use the vouchers they issue to settle in only slightly less segregated neighborhoods, because their other housing opportunities are limited. As another example, developers of affordable housing are often forced to choose between locating affordable housing within already disadvantaged neighborhoods and building no housing at all, given the political constraints on dispersal imposed by racial and class privilege.

Reversing the negative impact of racial segregation requires not only the strict enforcement of fair housing statutes but a comprehensive attack on all forms of racial privilege. Educational opportunities must be equalized by substantial investment in inner city schools, accompanied by high standards for school and teacher performance. There must also be a radical reconsideration of the War on Drugs, both because of its disparate impact on minorities and because of its general lack of efficacy. Otherwise, this source of inequality will continue to exert an extremely negative impact on neighborhoods of color.

Question 4: What should be the role of the tax system in enhancing housing opportunities for American households?

The federal tax deduction for mortgage interest and local property taxes started as a minor provision in the original income tax law and grew into a major tax expenditure, as home ownership spread and as housing costs increased. It remains the largest single expenditure that the federal government makes in support of housing (Dolbeare, Saraf, and Crowley 2005). It is clear that encouraging home ownership is generally good public policy, although it is not the panacea that is often claimed, and decent affordable rental housing should never be written out of the picture. However, the current tax deductions form an inverted pyramid in terms of the level of benefits households receive as they move up the income scale, namely, the larger the income, the higher the benefits. Higher income households are given an incentive to do what most would already do without the tax benefits, that is, become home owners. Meanwhile, households of modest income gain few benefits and suffer the negative consequences of reduced federal revenue on programs designed to benefit them. If the nation truly wants to encourage home ownership at the margin—that is, among households who might not otherwise be able to afford it—then the pyramid of benefits should be flipped over, so that the most significant tax breaks go to those with lower incomes and the deductions are gradually reduced as income increases. Such a change is unlikely to happen soon, given the strong resistance of middle income taxpayers reinforced by the strong lobbying of the real estate and construction industries.

Tax benefits for firms that construct and operate housing for low and moderate income people were initially criticized as producing, through syndication, a set of investors who had little concern for the overall viability of a project, just as long as they could extract the tax benefits in order to offset other income. However, developments utilizing the current major form of tax subsidy, the Low Income Housing Tax Credit, have accumulated a decent track record in most localities. In addition, tax subsidies have the huge political advantage of being a less visible form of federal assistance than direct federal expenditures. Given that private investment in such housing is generally not sufficiently profitable without such benefits, these benefits will, as noted above, continue to be an important element in housing creation. The advantage of the Low Income Housing Tax Credit over earlier tax assistance is that it is generally utilized within a network of public and private entities that can act to ensure that the credit is used to support viable projects that provide needed benefits to households with a range of reduced incomes.

The federal subsidy to state and local governments that occurs through the exemption of interest on their bonds from federal taxation provides a vital form of indirect assistance to many of their important activities. In the 1970s, the use of tax-exempt bonds expanded from financing traditional public improvements to providing subsidized financing for private development through Industrial Development Bonds (IDBs) This form of assistance was similar to the issuing of state tax-exempt bonds for low and moderate income housing, and, in some states, both programs were administered by the same state agency. The rapid growth of IDBs, accompanied by questions about the targeting of this benefit, led the federal government to establish, through the Tax Reform Act of 1986, per capita limits on state bonding for private purposes, and these limits had the potential to negatively affect state commitments to this form of housing assistance. However, despite these limitations (which are now routinely adjusted for inflation), states continue to regard housing assistance as a valid and important use of these bonds, so that such bonding has remained an important source of support for affordable housing development.

Question 5: How can the housing credit system be regulated so as to ensure fair access to affordable credit for American households seeking to purchase homes or improve their existing homes?

The recently enacted banking reform legislation provides for some consumer protection through greater disclosure and the creation of a separate regulatory agency to address lending abuses. Observers disagree as to whether or not these measures are strong enough to discourage or prevent deceptive lending practices in the future. Only after a few years of implementation will this question be fully answered. The strength of the banking lobby makes the passage of strong consumer protections a difficult struggle, and people desiring quick profits have always proved very clever in circumventing any regulatory system. Therefore, unfortunately, various forms of predatory lending will continue to be a fact of life.

By far the best way to counteract predatory lending is to make sure that affordable loans with reasonable and transparent terms are available to the groups most vulnerable to predatory practices, namely, households living in less desirable neighborhoods and all households of color. These groups have historically experienced discrimination by regular credit sources. As Immergluck (2006, 2009) documents, until the mortgage crisis hit, slow progress was being made in increasing access to credit for these groups. Under pressure from the Community Reinvestment Act (CRA), banks were entering into agreements with nonprofit neighborhood groups to provide secure and affordable loans in areas that had previously been redlined. It will be the worst sort of tragedy for neighborhoods and households if the mortgage lending crisis is allowed to permanently disrupt these relationships, or if false claims about the CRA by conservatives result in its weakening or elimination. Far from being eliminated, the CRA, and its companion measure, the Home Mortgage Disclosure Act (HMDA) should be expanded to cover *all* housing lenders, not just depository institutions of a certain minimum size, as is currently the case.

Consumer education can play a role in preventing future mortgage meltdowns. Individuals often receive little or no formal education on financial management, and, thus are left to figure things out on their own. Also, households are under pressure to spend a lot of money on the constantly changing array of consumer goods that are promoted by advertising as keys to "the good life." Lenders and credit card issuers conceal interest rates that in past generations were correctly labeled "usury" through an array of fees and minimum monthly payments. Consumers must learn to understand the long-term consequences of credit cards, and other forms of high interest borrowing. In addition, consumers must be taught to resist the temptation to milk the equity in their homes in order to finance short-term consumer purchases. They must also be taught to read and understand the complex terms of mortgage lending. Otherwise, additional disclosure requirements will have little impact. Of course, in stressing consumer education, one must also recognize that households may knowingly take risks because they believe that it is the only possible way to secure a decent home.

The development of the secondary mortgage market in the 1930s made an important contribution to the availability of home ownership to a larger segment of the population, by allowing for the greater circulation of lending capital. Securitization of mortgages further enhanced the circulation of capital. However, from the 1990s on, this system developed into a mechanism for transferring risk to other investors, thereby encouraging ever more risky loan initiations at the front end. Over the years, large private firms, such as Moody's and Standard and Poor's, developed to provide risk ratings for these and other debt instruments. However, their independence was compromised by the fact that they were being paid by the issuers of these debt instruments, and they contributed to the crisis by providing grossly inaccurate assessments of risks for mortgage-backed securities. While it may be unfeasible to have a public takeover of bond rating companies, there should be effective regulations that minimize the conflict of interest that is inherent in their role. Also, further disclosure requirements for all mortgage-backed securities can protect both investors and the households that pay the ultimate price for their folly.

In the 1980s, the lessons of the 1920s were forgotten, as many of the regulations designed to restrain speculative investment by depository institutions were abolished. In a capitalist economic system, there is probably no way to prevent the expansion and collapse of speculative bubbles, whether it is in high tech industries or housing. However, effective regulation can minimize the spillover effects of such bubbles on the rest of the economy and can prevent the type of expensive government bailout that was necessary in 2008 in order to forestall a recurrence of the Great Depression.

Conclusion

In their recording of the late 1960s, "Gimme Shelter," the Rolling Stones sang the following lyrics: "Ooh the storm is threatenin' my very life today. If I don't get some shelter, girl, I'm gonna fade away." They may have been talking primarily about emotional, rather than physical shelter, but their refrain can easily provide a mantra that expresses the vital importance of housing to human existence. The need for safe and adequate shelter against the storms of life is one of the most fundamental human needs. If it is not satisfied, many other aspects of life are negatively affected. In addition, if households spend a disproportionate share of their income to obtain housing, then their ability to address other needs, such as health, nutrition, and education, may be seriously impaired.

During the eighty years that have passed since the Great Depression of the 1930s, our nation has struggled greatly over what role the government should play in providing this need to those who are unable to supply it themselves through private market transactions. Many reasons for not providing it have been put forward: they lack character and don't deserve it, it's too expensive, the government is incapable of managing housing, or it will force middle-class people to live alongside the poor. These arguments generally boil down to one central argument—that the more privileged members of society should be allowed to maintain their status, while the needs of others are ignored. Housing inequality reflects the general inequality that exists in society, and conservatives basically believe that such inequality is just and should be maintained.

A broader conception of both morality and self-interest suggests that the well-being of all humans is interdependent. When one person in a society is denied the opportunity to live a dignified, worthwhile existence, the effects of that denial ripple out to all other members of that society. This view does not deny the importance of self-reliance and independence, because the long-term dependency of one person on another eventually erodes that person's sense of self-worth. However, it does suggest that a community in which people reach out and provide mutual aid to one another is essential to achieving the full potential of all of its members. Of course, the market mechanism provides one way for people to establish mutually beneficial relationships that don't rely on altruism. But history has shown over and over again that the unrestrained operation of this mechanism leaves millions of people without the wherewithal to achieve a decent and rewarding life. There is no substitute for compassion in maintaining the mutual well-being of all, and the government is a key instrument of that collective compassion.

Trying to respond to the cries of our fellow citizens to "Gimme shelter!" is a complex and difficult process. Programs that solve one set of housing problems often trigger unanticipated consequences that must be dealt with by constant modification. Efficiency in providing the greatest assistance to the greatest possible number is often elusive. However, there has been a learning curve over the eighty years of federal housing programs, and we, as a nation, must continue to experiment and learn. We have a much more varied toolbox to deal with housing problems than we did eighty years ago, so that each tool, or combination of tools, can be applied where it is most appropriate. The important element in applying these tools is the will and the compassion to make improvements in the lives of others, so that the lives of all will be better. That will has ebbed and flowed over the past eight decades. Hopefully, progressive citizens can work together to maximize the will to act on housing programs over the coming decades of the twenty-first century.

REFERENCES

Aaron, Henry J. 1972. *Shelter and subsidies: Who benefits from federal housing policies?* Washington, DC: The Brookings Institute.

———.1981. Policy implications: A progress report. In *Do housing allowances work?,* ed. Katharine L. Bradbury and Anthony Downs, 67–98. Washington, DC: The Brookings Institution.

Aberbach, Joel D., and Bert A. Rockman. 1976. Clashing beliefs within the executive branch: The Nixon administration bureaucracy. *American Political Science Review* 70: 456–68.

Agelasto, Michael, and David Listokin. 1977. Redlining in perspective: An evaluation of approaches to the urban mortgage dilemma. In *A decent home and environment: Housing urban America,* ed. Donald A. Phares. Cambridge, MA: Ballinger.

Agid, Shana. 2007. Locked and loaded: The prison industrial complex and the response to Hurricane Katrina. In K. A. Bates and R. S. Swan, *Through the eye of Katrina: Social justice in the United States,* 55–76. Durham, NC, Carolina Academic Press.

Alexander, Michelle. 2010. *The new Jim Crow: Mass incarceration in the age of colorblindness.* New York: The New Press.

Alinsky, Saul D. 1971. *Rules for radicals: A practical primer for realistic radicals.* New York: Random House.

Allen, Theodore W. 1994. *The invention of the white race.* New York: Verso.

Anderson, Martin. 1964. *The federal bulldozer: An analysis of urban renewal 1949–1962.* Cambridge: The MIT Press.

Bachrach, Peter, and Morton S. Baratz. 1962. Two faces of power. *American Political Science Review* 56 (December): 947–52.

Bates, K. A., and R. S. Swan. 2007. *Through the eye of Katrina: Social justice in the United States.* Durham, NC, Carolina Academic Press.

Bauman, J. F., R. Biles, and K. M. Szylvian, eds. 2000. *From the tenements to the Taylor homes: In search of an urban housing policy in twentieth century America.* University Park, PA; Pennsylvania State University Press.

Baumgartner, Frank R., and Bryan D. Jones. 1993. *Agendas and instability in American politics.* Chicago: University of Chicago Press.

Baxandall, Rosalyn. 2005. The new politics of participatory democracy viewed through a feminist lens. In *The Great Society and the high tide of liberalism,* ed. Stanley M. Milikis and J. M. Mileur, 270–89. Amherst: University of Massachusetts Press.

Beer, Samuel H. 1978. In search of a new public philosophy. In *The new American political system,* ed. Anthony King, 5–49. Washington, DC: American Enterprise Institute for Public Policy Research.

Bekowitz, Marti Anne. 1977. National problems and local control tension in Title I of the housing and community development act of 1974. *Columbia Journal of Law and Social Problems* 13(3/4): 409–63.

Bell, Daniel. 1965. *The end of ideology: On the exhaustion of political ideas in the fifties.* New York: Free Press.

Bennett, L., J. L. Smith, and P. A. Wright, eds. 2006. *Where are poor people to live? Transforming public housing communities.* Armonk, NY: M. E. Sharp.

Benson, Clea. 2009. Beyond the bulldozer: The surging demand for public housing has advocates looking for alternatives to a decade of teardowns. *Congressional Quarterly Weekly Report* (July 13), 1629–34.

Berger, Curtis J. 1969. Homeownership for low-income families: The 1968 housing act's "cruel hoax." *Connecticut Law Review* 2: 30–36.

Berger, P. L., and T. Luckman. 1966. *The social construction of reality: A treatise in the sociology of knowledge.* Garden City, NY: Doubleday.

Bernstein, E. 1961. *Evolutionary socialism: A criticism and affirmation.* Trans. Edith C. Harvey. New York: Schocken Books.

Bertram, E., M. Blachman, K. Sharpe, and P. Andreas. 1996. *Drug war politics: The price of denial.* Berkeley: University of California Press.

Black, J. T. 1975. Private market renovation in central cities. *Urban Land* 34 (November): 3–9.

Boyer, Brian D. 1973. *Cities destroyed for cash.* Chicago: Follet Books.

Bradbury, Katherine L., and Anthony Downs. 1981. *Do housing allowances work?* Washington, DC: The Brookings Institute.

Bradford, Calvin. 1979. Financing home ownership: The federal role in neighborhood decline. *Urban Affairs Quarterly* 14 (March): 313–36.

Bromwich, David. 2010. The rebel germ. *New York Review of Books.* November 25. www.nybooks.com/archives.

Brown, D. A. 1971. *Bury my heart at Wounded Knee: An Indian history of the American west.* New York: Holt.

Bryce, Herrington J., ed. 1979. *Revitalizing cities.* Lexington, MA: D. C. Heath.

Bullard, Robert D. 2008. Toxic wastes and race at twenty: Why race still matters after all these years. *Environmental Law* 38(2): 371.

Buenker, John D. 1973. *Urban liberalism and progressive reform.* New York: Scribner's.

Buron, L., D. K. Levy, and M. Gallagher. 2007. *Housing choice vouchers: How HOPE VI families fared in the private market.* Metropolitan Housing and Communities Center, The Urban Institute, Brief No. 3, June. Washington, DC: The Urban Institute.

Burt, Martha R. 1992. *Over the edge: The growth of homelessness in the 1980s.*

New York and Washington, DC: The Russell Sage Foundation and The Urban Institute Press.

————, and Brooke E. Spellman. 2007. Changing homeless and mainstream service systems: essential approaches to ending homelessness. Published in *Toward understanding homelessness: the 2007 National Symposium on Homelessness Research.* Conducted by Abt Associates, Inc. and Policy Research Associates, Inc. under contract with the Office of the Assistant Secretary for Planning and Evaluation of the U.S. Department of Health and Human Services and the Office of Policy Development and Research, U.S. Department of Housing and Urban Development. Retrieved from www.aspe.hhs.gov.

Butler, Stuart. 1980. Urban renewal: A modest proposal. *Policy Review* 13 (Summer): 95–107.

Calmes, Jackie. 2008. New York's housing chief is chosen for cabinet. *New York Times,* December 19. Retrieved from www.nytimes.com.

Campbell, A., P. E. Converse, W.E. Miller, and D. E. and Stokes. 1964. *The American voter.* New York: John Wiley and Sons.

Campbell, James E. 2008. An exceptional election: performance, values, and crisis in the 2008 presidential election. *The Forum* 6(4) Article # 7 Berkeley Electronic Press, www.bepress.org.

Caputo, David, and Richard L. Cole. 1974. *Urban politics and decentralization.* Lexington, MA: D. C. Heath.

Caraley, Demetrios. 1976. Congressional politics and urban aid. *Political Science Quarterly* 91 (Spring): 19–45.

————.1989. Elections and dilemmas of American democratic governance. *Political Science Quarterly* 104(1): 19–40.

Center on Budget and Policy Priorities and National Low Income Housing Information Service. 1991. *A place to call home: The crisis in housing for the poor.*

Chudacoff, Howard P., and Judith E. Smith. 2000. *The evolution of American urban society.* Upper Saddle River, NJ: Prentice-Hall.

Clark , Charles S. 2010. Key events since the *CQ Researcher* report on Nov. 2, 2007. (See Clemmitt 2007) Retrieved from *CQ Researcher Online,* library. cqpress.com/cqresearcher.

Clark, Timothy B., John K. Iglehart, and William Lilley. 1972. New federalism report. *National Journal* 4 (December 16). 1907–40.

Clay, Philip L. 1980. The urban Neighborhood in the 1980s: Towards a New Definition of Housing Opportunity. Paper presented to the 1980 Annual Meeting. Urban Affairs Association.

Clemmitt, Marcia. 2007. Mortgage crisis: Should the government bail out borrowers in trouble? *CQ Researcher* 17(39) (Nov. 2). Retrieved from *CQ Researcher Online,* library.cqpress.com/cqresearcher. (Updated August 9, 2010—see Clark 2010).

Cobb, Robert W., and Charles D. Elder. 1981. Communication and public policy. In *The handbook of political communication,* ed. Dan D. Nimmo and Keith R. Sanders. Beverly Hills: Sage.

Cohen, J. E., R. Fleisher, and P. Kantor, eds. 2001. *American political parties: Decline or resurgence?* Washington, DC: Congressional Quarterly Press.

Congress for the New Urbanism. 2000. *Charter of the new urbanism.* New York: McGraw-Hill.

Congressional Quarterly, Inc. *Almanac (CQ Almanac).* 1965. Major Housing Legislation Enacted, 21: 358–87.

———. 1966. Restricted rent supplements funded by bare margin. 22: 245–46.

———.1968. Housing bill provides home-buying, riot, other aid. 24: 313–35.

———. 1970b. Relocation assistance. 26: 761–63.

———. 1971. Community development: Senate, house hold hearings. 27: 841–49.

———. 1972. Rules committee kills housing-urban development Act. 28: 628–35.

———. 1973a. Housing and urban development. 29: 421–23.

———. 1973b. Housing program authority extended to Oct. 1, 1974. 29: 425–32.

———. 1978. Housing authorization. 34: 303–11.

———. 1979. Housing authorization. 35: 315–21.

———. 1981a. Reagan housing plans generally approved. 37: 111–13.

———. 1981b. HUD, agencies funds. 37: 34–35.

———. 1987. $443 million homeless aid bill authorized. 43: 506–11.

———. 1990. U.S. housing programs overhauled. 46: 631–68.

———. 1995. Housing bill cleared at session's end. 367–75.

———. 1996. Public housing overhaul bill dies. 7-21 to 7-23.

———. 1997. No consensus on housing overhaul. 7-12 to 7-18.

———. 1998. Three years of negotiations yield a housing bill that compromise built. 20-7 to 20-15.

———. 2000a. More than 1,000 earmarks adorn VA-HUD bill; housing gets a big boost. 20-148 to 20-158.

———. 2000b. Lawmakers clear legislation aimed at helping more families afford housing. 17-18 to 17-22.

———. 2007. Some hits for Transportation-HUD. 2-49 to 2-52.

———. 2008. Treasury gets the keys to Fannie, Freddie. 7-9 to 7-16.

———. 2005. *Presidential Elections.* Washington, DC.

Congressional Quarterly, Inc. *Weekly Reports (CQ Weekly Reports).*1972a. Federal low-income housing programs under scrutiny. 30 (May 13): 1100.

———. 1973a. Housing: First battle in the war over spending? 31 (January 1): 40.

———. 1973b. Housing: Nixon likes cash payments, but not yet. 31 (September 22): 251–54.

———. 1973c. Housing funds: The nation seems unconcerned. 31 (November 10): 2969–72.

———. 1973d. Housing programs: Administration-congress clash. 31 (January 27): 139–41.

———. 1974a. Congress clears omnibus housing bill. 32 (August 17): 2253–66.

———. 1974b. House passes omnibus housing bill. 32 (June 29): 1702–06.

———. 1974c. Housing, urban development. 32 (February 2): 222.

———. 1974d. Senate committee reports omnibus housing bill. 32 (March 9): 621–25.

———. 1975a. Congress clears "redlining" legislation. 33 (December 20): 2779–81.

———. 1975b. Neighborhood decay: Is "redlining" a factor? 33 (May 17): 1041–43.

———. 1976a. Conferees agree to revive public housing. 34 (June 19): 1587–90.

———. 1976b. Housing: Continuation of existing programs. 34 (January 24): 129.

———. 1976c. Housing: Ford proposal, democratic criticism. 34 (September 25).

———. 1976d. Panels want more variety in housing efforts. 34 (April 10): 829–31.

———. 1976e. Senate panel seeks changes in housing policy. 34 (April 24): 979–80.

———. 1976f. Suburban public housing orders upheld. 34 (April 24): 958.

———. 1978. Congress cool to renewal of 10-year housing goals. 36 (July 15): 1801–1804.

———. 1979a. Carter proposes cutbacks in housing, urban programs. 37 (January 27): 145–56.

———. 1979b. Housing bills reflect budgetary concern. 37 (June 2): 1055–56.

———. 1979c. Senate approves cutbacks in federal housing programs. 37 (July 21): 1455–57.

———. 1983. House approves HUD bill after funding is slashed. 41 (July 16): 1983.

———. 1988. Space station survives money-tight HUD bills: UDAG bites the dust. 46 (June 25): 1754–55.

———. 1989a. Expiring federal subsidies raise a policy dilemma. 47 (May 6): 1041–45.

———. 1989b. Members of congress deplore influence-peddling at HUD. 47 (May 13): 1127.

———. 1989c. Inquiry into HUD scandal entering new stage. 47 (November 4): 2946–50.

———. 1989d. House OKs HUD "reform" plan; Senate proposal in works. 47 (November 18): 3193–95.

———. 1989e. HUD reform package clears on edge of adjournment. 47 (November 25): 3242–43.

———. 1989f. Kemp targets hill earmarks in HUD's new spending bill. 47 (December 2): 3315.

———. 1989g. Former HUD Secretary Pierce may face special prosecutor. 47 (December 9): 3371.

———. 1993a. Clinton climbs to power on broad, shaky base. (January 23): 188–91.

———. 1993b. Clinton's stimulus plan is picking up speed. (March 13): 579–82.

———. 1993c. Stimulus bill prevails in house, but senate battle awaits. (March 20): 649–52.

———. 1993d. Even foes predict some version of stimulus plan will pass. (March 27): 737–38.

———. 1993e. Republicans slam the brakes on economic stimulus plan. (April 3): 817–20.

———. 1993f. Clinton now must sell urgency of stimulus bill's jobs. (April 100: 907–909.

———. 1993g. Rooms for improvement: Can Cisneros fix HUD? (April 10): 915–20.

———. 1993h. Democrats look to salvage part of stimulus plan. (April 24): 1001–1004.

———. 1993i. Study says Clinton must use "new Democrat" themes. (July 10): 1828.

———. 1993j. Enterprise zones struggle to make their mark. (July 17): 1880–83.

———. 1993k. Clinton struggles to meld a governing coalition. (August 7): 2175–79.

———. 1993l. Special report: Issue-enterprise zones. (December 11): 3391.

Conover, Pamela J., and Stanley Feldman. 1984. How people organize the political world: A schematic model. *American Journal of Political Science* 28(1): 95–126.

Converse, Philip E., et al. 1969. Continuity and change in American politics: Parties and issues in the 1968 election. *American Political Science Review* 63 (December): 1092–1115.

Cooke, Jacob E., ed. 1961. *The federalist.* Cleveland: The World Publishing Company.

Curley, Alexandra M. 2010. Neighborhood institutions, facilities, and public space: A missing link for HOPE VI residents' development of social capital? *Cityscape: A Journal of Policy Development and Research* 12, no. 1. 33–63.

Dahl, Robert A. 1971. *Polyarchy: Participation and opposition.* New Haven: Yale University Press.

Daniels, M. 1988. The myth of self-actualization. *Journal of Humanistic Psychology* 28(1): 7–38.

Danziger, Sheldon H., and Robert H. Haveman, eds. 2001. *Understanding poverty.* New York: Russell Sage Foundation.

Dolbeare, Cushing N., Irene B. Saraf, and Sheila Crowley. 2005. *Changing priorities: The federal budget and housing assistance.* Washington, DC: National Low Income Housing Coalition. Retrieved on line at www.nlihc. org.

Dolbeare, Kenneth M., and Patricia Dolbeare. 1971. *American ideologies: The competing political beliefs of the 1970s.* Markham Political Science Series. Chicago: Markham.

Dommel, Paul R. 1974. *The politics of revenue sharing.* Bloomington: Indiana University Press.

———. 1980. Social targeting in community development. *Political Science Quarterly* 95 (Fall): 465–78.

Donovan, John C. 1967. *The politics of poverty.* New York: Pegasus.

Dovey, K. 1985. *Home and homelessness.* In I. Altman and C. M. Werner, *Home Environments,* 33–64. New York: Plenum.

Downs, Anthony. 1973. *Federal housing subsidies: How are they working?* Lexington, MA: D. C. Heath, Lexington Books.

Dreier, Peter, and W. Dennis Keating. 1990. The limits of localism: Progressive housing policies in Boston, 1984–1989. *Urban Affairs Quarterly* 26(2): 191–216.

Dye, Thomas R., and L. Harmon Zeigler. 1981. *The irony of democracy: An uncommon introduction to American politics.* 5th ed. Belmont, CA: Wadsworth, Duxbury Press.

Edelman, Murray. 1964. *The symbolic uses of politics.* Urbana, IL: University of Chicago Press.

Edsall, Thomas B. and Mary D. Edsall. 1991. *Chain reaction: the impact of race, rights, and taxes on American politics.* NY: Norton.

Elazar, Daniel J., et al., eds. 1969. *Cooperation and conflict: Readings in American federalism.* Itasca, IL: F. E. Peacock.

———. 1966. Are we a nation of cities? *The Public Interest* (Summer): 42–58.

Erikson, D. J. 2009. *The housing policy revolution: Networks and neighborhoods.* Washington, DC: The Urban Institute Press.

Evans, Rowland, and Robert D. Novak. 1971. *Nixon in the White House: The frustration of power.* New York: Random House.

Farkas, Suzanne. 1971. *Urban lobbying: Mayors in the federal arena.* New York: New York University Press.

Fleisher, R., and J. R. Bond. 2001. Evidence of increasing polarization among ordinary citizens. In J. E. Cohen et al., *American Political Parties: Decline or Resurgence?,* 55–78. Washington, DC: CQ Press.

Follain, J. R., Jr. 1979. How well do Section 8 FMRS (Fair Market Rent) match the cost of rental housing? Data from 39 large cities. *American Real Estate and Urban Economics Association Journal* 7 (Winter): 466–81.

Frank, Thomas. 2004. *What's the matter with Kansas?* New York: Henry Holt (Owl Books).

Free, Lloyd A., and Hadley Cantril. 1967. *The political beliefs of Americans:A study of public opinion.* New Brunswick: Rutgers University Press.

Freedman, Leonard. 1969. *Public housing: The politics of poverty.* New York: Holt, Rinehart, and Winston.

Freeman, J. Leiper. 1965. *The political process: Executive bureau-legislative committee relations.* New York: Random House.

Frej, William, and Harry Specht. 1976. The housing and community development act of 1974: Implications for policy and planning. *The Social Service Review* 50 (June): 275–92.

Freund, D. 2007. *Colored property: State policy and white racial politics in suburban America.* Chicago: University of Chicago Press.

Fried, Marc. 1966. Grieving for a lost home: Psychological costs of relocation. In *Urban renewal: The record and the controversy,* ed. James Q. Wilson, 359–79. Cambridge: The MIT Press; Chicago: University of Chicago Press.

Friedan, Betty. 1983. *The Feminine mystique.* New York: W. W. Norton.

Friedman, Milton. 1962. *Capitalism and freedom.* Chicago: University of Chicago Press.

Frieden, Bernard J., and Marshall Kaplan. 1977. *The politics of neglect: Urban aid from model cities to revenue sharing.* Cambridge: The MIT Press.

Frieden, Bernard J., and Arthur P. Solomon. 1977. *The nation's housing:1975 to 1985.* Cambridge: Joint Center for Urban Studies of the Massachusetts Institute of Technology and Harvard University.

Friedman, Lawrence M. 1968. *The government and slum housing: A century of frustration.* Chicago: Rand McNally.

Friedman, Milton. 1962. *Capitalism and freedom.* Chicago: University of Chicago Press.

Gans, Herbert J. 1962. *The urban villagers: Group and class in the life of Italian-Americans.* New York: The Free Press.

Gelfand, Mark I. 1975. *A nation of cities: The federal government and urban America.* New York: Oxford University Press.

Geller, Leonard. 1982. The failure of self-actualization theory: A critique of Carl Rogers and Abraham Maslow. *Journal of Humanistic Psychology* 22(2): 56–73.

Gifford, Robert. 1997. *Environmental psychology: Principles and practice.* 2nd Ed. Boston: Allyn and Bacon.

Ginsberg, Benjamin, and M. Schefter. 1999. *Politics by other means.* New York: W. W. Norton.

Glazer, Nathan. 1967. Housing problems and housing policies. *The Public Interest* 7 (Spring): 21–51.

Goering, John M. 1979. The national neighborhood movement: A preliminary analysis and critique. *American Planning Association Journal* 45 (October): 506–14.

Goetz, Edward. 2010. Better neighborhoods, better outcomes? Explaining relocation outcomes in HOPE VI. *Cityscape: A Journal of Policy Development and Research* 12(1): 5–31. Published by the U.S. Department of Housing and Urban Development, Office of Policy Development and Research.

Goldfield, Michael. 1987. *The decline of organized labor in the United States.* Chicago: University of Chicago Press.

Goldstein, G., R. Novick, and M. Schaefer. 1990. Housing, health, and well-being: An International perspective. *Journal of Sociology and Social Welfare* 18(1): 161–81.

Goodwin, Doris K. 2005. *Team of rivals: The political genius of Abraham Lincoln.* New York: Simon and Schuster.

Greenbaum, R., and J. Engberg.2000. An evaluation of state enterprise zone policies. *Policy Studies Review* 17(2/3): 29–46.

Greer, Scott. 1965. *Urban renewal and American cities: The dilemma of democratic intervention.* Indianapolis; New York: Bobbs-Merrill.

Greider, William. 1981. The education of David Stockman. *Atlantic Monthly* (December): 27–54.

Grigsby, William C. 1965. *Housing markets and public policy.* Philadelphia: University of Pennsylvania Press.

Guthrie, Doug, and Michael McQuarrie. 2010. Privatization and the social contract: Corporate welfare and low income housing in the United States since 1986. Forthcoming in *Research in Political Sociology.*

Haas, Peter J., and J. Fred Springer. 1998.*Applied policy research: Concepts and cases.* New York: Garland.

Hale, George E., and Marian L. Palley. 1981. *The politics of federal grants.* Washington, DC: Congressional Quarterly.

Hamill, Ruth C., Milton Lodge, and Frederick Blake. 1985. The breadth, depth, and utility of class, partisan, and ideological schemata. *American Journal of Political Science* 29(4): 850–70.

Hamilton, Nigel. 2007. *Bill Clinton: Mastering the presidency.* New York: BBS Public Affairs.

Harrington, Michael. 1971. *The other America.* Baltimore: Penguin.

Hartman, Chester W. 1971. Relocation: Illusory promises and no relief. *Virginia Law Review* 57 (June): 745–817.

———. 1975. *Housing and social policy.* Englewood Cliffs, NJ: Prentice-Hall.

Hartman, Chester W., and Dennis Keating. 1974. The housing allowance delusion. *Social Policy* 4 (January/February): 31–37.

Hartman, Chester W., and Gregory D. Squires. 2010. *The Integration debate: Competing futures for American cities.* New York: Routledge.

Hartman, Chester W., Robert P. Kessler, and Richard T. LeGates. 1974. Municipal housing code enforcement and low income tenants. *American Institute of Planners Journal* 40 (March): 90–114.

Haveman, Robert H., ed. 1977. *A decade of federal anti-poverty programs: Achievements, failures, and lessons.* Institute for Research of Poverty, Poverty Policy Analysis Series. New York: Academic Press.

Hays, R. Allen. 1982a. Housing rehabilitation as an urban policy alternative. *Journal of Urban Affairs* 4 (Spring): 39–54.

———. 1982b. Public sector housing rehabilitation: A survey of program impact. *The Urban Interest* 4 (Spring): 70–86.

———. 1986. Perceptions of success or failure in program implementation: The "feedback loop" in public policy decisions. *Policy Studies Review* 5(1): 51–68.

———.1993. *Ownership, control, find the future of housing policy.* Westport, CT: Greenwood.

———. 2001. *Who speaks for the poor?* New York: Routledge.

———. 2002 Housing America's poor: Conflicting values and failed policies. *Journal of Urban History* 28(3): 369–81.

———. 2002. Habitat for Humanity: Building social capital through faith based service. *Journal of Urban Affairs* 24(3).

———, and Christopher Silver. 1980. Can you compensate for a lost home? An assessment of the 1970 uniform relocation act. *Urban Affairs Papers* 2 (Winter): 33–49.

Heclo, Hugh. 1978. Issue networks and the executive establishment. In *The New American Political System,* ed. Anthony King, 87–125. Washington, DC: American Enterprise Institute for Public Policy Research.

Hetherington, Marc J., and Bruce A. Larson. 2010. *Parties, politics, and public policy in America. 11th Edition.* Washington, DC: CQ Press.

Hirshen, Al, and Richard T. LeGates. 1975. HUD's bonanza for suburbia. *Progressive* 39 (April): 32–34.

Hoch, Charles, and Robert A. Slayton. 1989. *New homeless and old: Community and the skidrow hotel.* Philadelphia: Temple University Press.

Hughes, James W., and Kenneth D. Bleakly Jr. 1975. *Urban homesteading.* New Brunswick: Center For Urban Policy Research, Rutgers University.

Imig, Douglas. 1996. *Poverty and power: The political representation of poor Americans.* Lincoln: University of Nebraska Press.

Immergluck, Daniel. 2006. *Credit to the community: Community reinvestment and fair lending policy in the United States.* Armonk, NY: M. E. Sharpe.

———. 2009. *Foreclosed: High risk lending, deregulation, and the undermining of America's mortgage market.* Ithaca: Cornell University Press.

Ingram, Helen. 1977. Policy implementation through bargaining: The case of federal grants-in-aid. *Public Policy* 25 (Fall): 499–526.

Jacobs, Jane. 1961. *The death and life of great American cities.* New York: Vintage Books.

James, Franklin J. 1980. *Back to the city: An appraisal of housing reinvestment and population change in urban America.* Washington, DC: Urban Institute.

Joint Center for Housing Studies of Harvard University. 1989,1990. *The state of the nation's housing* (yearly report). Cambridge.

Judd, Dennis R., and Todd Swanstrom. 2010. *City Politics.* 7th Ed. New York: Longman.

Julian, Elizabeth K., and Demetria McCain. 2010. Housing mobility: A civil right. In Chester Hartman and Gregory D. Squires, *The integration debate: Competing futures for American cities.* New York: Routledge. 85–98.

Keith, Nathaniel S. 1973. *Politics and the housing crisis since 1930.* New York: Universe Books.

Kelling, George L., and Catherine M. Coles. 1996. *Fixing broken windows: Restoring order and reducing crime in our communities.* New York: Touchstone.

Kern, C. R. 1981. Upper-income renaissance in the city: Its sources and implications for the city's future. *Journal of Urban Economics* 9 (January): 106–24.

Kettl, D. F. 1979. Can the cities be trusted?: The community development experience. *Political Science Quarterly* 94 (Fall): 437–54.

Kingdon, John W. 1984. *Agendas, alternatives, and public policies.* Boston: Little Brown.

Koebel, C. Theodore, ed. 1998. *Shelter and society: Theory, research, and policy for nonprofit housing.* Albany: State University of New York Press.

Kolko, Gabriel. 1962. *Wealth and power in America.* New York: Praeger.

Koltko-Rivera, M. E. 2006. Rediscovering the later version of Maslow's hierarchy of needs: Self-transcendence and opportunities for theory, research, and unification. *Review of General Psychology* 10(4): 302–17.

Kosterlitz, Julie.2004. Home sweet home? *National Journal* 36, 10. 712–15.

———. 2007. Bubble watch. *National Journal* 39,16. 53–56.

Kozol, Jonathan. 2006. *Rachel and her children: Homeless families in America.* New York: Three Rivers Press.

Kusnet, David. 1992. *Speaking American: How the Democrats can win in the nineties.* New York: Thunder's Mouth Press.

Ladd, Everett Carl. 1993. The 1992 vote for President Clinton: Another brittle mandate? *Political Science Quarterly* 108(1): 1–28.

Lamb, Charles M. 1992. Fair housing implementation from Nixon to Reagan. Robert A. LaFollette Institute of Public Affairs, Working Paper No. 11. Madison: University of Wisconsin.

Laska, Shirley B., and Daphne Spain, eds. 1980. *Back to the city: Issues in neighborhood renovation.* New York: Pergamon Press.

Lazin, Frederick A. 1976. Federal low-income housing assistance programs and racial segregation: Leased public housing. *Public Policy* 24 (Summer): 337–60.

Levy, J. M. 1995. *Essential microeconomics for public policy analysis.* Westport, CT: Praeger.

Lewis, Michael. 1978. *The culture of inequality.* Amherst: University of Massachusetts Press.

Liechty, Joseph, and Cecelia Clegg. 2001. Moving beyond sectarianism: Religion, conflict, and reconciliation in Northern Ireland. Dublin: The Columba Press.

Lilla, Mark .2010. The Tea Party Jacobins. *New York Review of Books* May 27. www.nybooks.com/articles/archives.

Lilley, William III. 1972. Cities and suburbs/Chicago case shows courts hold key to mandatory housing desegregation. *National Journal* 4 (September 16): 1459–65.

————. 1972b. Urban report/federal programs spur abandonment of housing in major cities. *National Journal* 4 (January 1): 26–33.

————. 1972c. Urban report/immense costs, scandals, social ills plague low-income housing programs. *National Journal* 4 (July 1): 1075–83.

Lilley, William Ill, Timothy B. Clark, and John K. Iglehart. 1973. New federalism report: Nixon attack on grant programs aims to simplify structure, give greater local control. *National Journal* 5 (January 20): 76–88.

Lindblom, Charles E. 1977. *Politics and markets: The world's political/economic systems.* New York: Basic Books.

Lipsitz, George. 2006. *The possessive investment in whiteness: How white people profit from identity politics.* Philadelphia: Temple University Press.

Listokin, David. 1973. *The dynamics of housing rehabilitation.* New Brunswick: Center for Urban Policy Research, Rutgers University.

Lowi, Theodore J. 1964. American business, public policy, case studies, and political theory. *World Politics* 16 (July): 677–715.

————. 1979. *The End of liberalism: Ideology, policy, and the crisis of public authority.* 2nd Ed. New York: W. W. Norton.

Maas, Arthur. 1951. *Muddy waters.* Cambridge: Harvard University Press.

Magida, Arthur J. 1974. Housing report/major programs revised to stress community control. *National Journal* 6 (September 14): 1369–79.

Mandelker, Daniel R 1973. *Housing subsidies in the U.S. and England.* Indianapolis, New York: Bobbs-Merrill.

————, et al. 1981. *Housing and community development: Cases and materials.* Contemporary Legal Education Series. New York: Bobbs-Merrill.

Mann, James. 2004. *Rise of the Vulcans: The history of Bush's war cabinet.* New York: Viking.

Marcus, C.C. 1992. Environmental memories. In *Place Attachment,* ed. I. Altman and S. Low, 87–112. New York: Plenum.

Mare, Robert D., and Christopher Winship. 1991. Socioeconomic change and the decline of marriage for blacks and whites. In *The Urban Underclass,* ed. Christopher Jencks and Paul K. Peterson. Washington, DC: The Brookings Institution.

Maslow, Abraham. 1970. *Motivation and personality.* New York: Harper and Row.

Massey, Douglas S., and Nancy A. Denton. 1993. *American apartheid: Segregation and the making of the underclass.* Cambridge: Harvard University Press.

Mauer, M. 2009. *The changing racial dynamics of the war on drugs.* Report prepared for The Sentencing Project, www.sentencingproject.org.

Mayhew, David. 2005. *Divided we govern: Party control, lawmaking, and investigations.* New Haven: Yale University Press.

McClaughry, John. 1975. The troubled dream: The life and times of Section 235 of the National Housing Act. *Loyola University Law Journal* 6 (Winter): 1–45.

McConnell, Grant. 1966. *Private power and American democracy.* New York: Random House, Vintage Books.

McDonald, Michael P. 2008. The return of the voter: Voter turnout in the 2008 presidential election. *The Forum* 6(4), Article # 4. Berkeley Electronic Press, www.bepress.org.

McGuire, Chester C. 1981. *International housing policies: A comparative analysis.* Lexington, MA: D. C. Heath, Lexington Books.

Meehan, Eugene. 1979. *The quality of federal policymaking: Programmed failure in public housing.* Columbia: University of Missouri Press.

Meyerson, Martin, and Edward C. Banfield. 1955. *Politics, planning, and the public interest.* Glencoe, IL: The Free Press.

Milikis, Sidney M., and Jerome M. Mileur, eds. 2005. *The great society and the high tide of liberalism.* Amherst: University of Massachusetts Press.

Mills, C. Wright. 1959. *The power elite.* New York: Oxford University Press.

Mills, Gregory B., and John L. Palmer, eds. 1984. *Federal budget policy* in *the 1980s.* Washington, DC: The Urban Institute Press.

Mishel, L., J. Bernstein, and S. Allegretto. 2009. *The state of working America.* Ithaca: ILR Press (Cornell University).

Mitchell, James K 1974. *Pennsylvania vs. Lynn:* The rest of the iceberg. *University of Detroit Journal of Urban Law* 52: 421–58.

Mohl, Raymond A., and James F. Richardson, eds. 1973. *The urban experience: Themes in American history.* Belmont, CA: Wadsworth.

Mollenkopf, John H. 1983. *The contested city.* Princeton: Princeton University Press.

Molotch, Harvey. 1987. *Urban fortunes: The political economy of place* (with John Logan). Berkeley and Los Angeles: University of California Press.

Monti, Daniel. 1993. People in control: A comparison of residents in two U.S. housing developments. In *Ownership, Control, and the Future of Housing Policy,* ed. R. Allen Hays. Westport, CT: Greenwood Press.

Moynihan, Daniel P. 1969. *Maximum feasible misunderstanding.* New York: Free Press.

Murphy, P. and Cunningham, J. 2003. *Organizing for community controlled development.* Thousand Oaks, CA: Sage.

Murray, Charles. 1984. *Losing ground: American social policy, 1950–1980.* New York: Basic Books.

Nakamura, Robert T., and Frank Smallwood. 1980. *The politics of policy implementation.* New York: St. Martin's.

Nathan, Richard P., and Paul R. Dommel. 1978. Federal-local relations under block grants. *Political Science Quarterly* 93 (Fall): 421–42.

National Alliance to End Homelessness. 2010. Solutions: Housing first. www.endhomelessness.org.

National Association of Housing and Redevelopment Officials (NAHRO). 1994. From the President. *NAHRO Monitor* 16(2) (January 31): 3.

National Coalition for the Homeless. 2009a. Fact sheets on homelessness. www.nationalhomeless.org.

————. 2009b. *Foreclosure to homelessness, 2009: The forgotten victims of the subprime crisis*. Report co-sponsored by the National Health Care for the Homeless Council, the National Alliance to End Homelessness, the National Association for the Education of Homeless Children and Youth, the National Law Center on Homelessness and Poverty, the National Low Income Housing Coalition, and the National Policy and Advocacy Council on the Homeless. www.nlihc.org.

————, and National Law Center on Homelessness and Poverty. 2010. A place at the table: Prohibitions on sharing food with people experiencing homelessness. Joint Report. www.nationalhomeless.org.

National Commission on Urban Problems. 1969. *Building the American city: Report of the national commission*. Praeger Special Studies in U.S. Economic, Social and Political Issues. New York: Praeger.

National Congress for Community and Economic Development (NCCED). 2005. *Reaching new heights: Trends and achievements of community-based development organizations*. NCCED: Washington DC (downloaded from www.ncced.org).

National Low Income Housing Coalition. 1983a. The 1984 Reagan budget and low income housing. Special Memorandum No. 18 from the Low Income Housing Information Service (February).

————. 1983b. Low Income Housing Appropriations for 1984. Statement of Cushing N. Dolbeare, President, Before Subcommittee on HUD-Independent Agencies, Senate Committee on Appropriations, May 24,1983. Copy supplied to author.

————. 1988. *Out of Reach.*

————. 2011. *Advocate's guide.* www.nlihc.org.

Nenno, Mary K. 1983. The Reagan housing, CD record: A negative rating. *Journal of Housing* 40(5) (September/October): 135–41.

Neustadt, Richard E. 1980. *Presidential power: The politics of leadership from FDR to Carter*. New York: John Wiley.

Newman, Oscar. 1972. *Defensible space: Crime prevention through urban design*. New York: MacMillan.

————. 1995. Defensible space. *Journal of the American Planning Association* 61(2): 149–60.

The New York Times. 1993a. Three found guilty in HUD influence peddling Case. January 6: A16.

————. 1993b. The new presidency: Confirmation roundup: HUD choice wary of selling public housing. January 13:A16.

————. 1993c. Housing Secretary Cisneros declared homelessness "a highest priority." January 30.

————. 1994a. Clinton proposing $30 billion shift in federal budget. February 6: A1.

————. 1994b. Report to Clinton sees vast extent of homelessness. February 17: A1.

Nivola, P. S., and D. W. Brady, eds. 2008. *Red and blue nation? Consequences and correction of America's polarized politics.* Volume 2. Washington, DC: Brookings Institution Press.

Nixon, Richard M. 1971. *Nixon: His second year in office.* Washington, DC: Congressional Quarterly.

Olsen, Edgar O. and David W. Rasmussen. See: U.S. Dept. of HUD, 1979b.

Palen, J. John, and Bruce L. London. 1984. *Gentrification, displacement, and neighborhood revitalization.* Albany: State University of New York Press.

Patterson, Thomas. 2003. *The vanishing voter.* New York: Knopf.

Peabody, Malcolm E., Jr. 1974. Housing allowances: A new way to abuse the poor. *New Republic* 170 (March 9): 20–23.

Pechman, Joseph, ed. 1981. *Setting national priorities: The 1982 budget.* Washington, DC: The Brookings Institute.

———.1982. *Setting national priorities: The 1983 budget.* Washington, DC: The Brookings Institute.

Peterman, William. 1993. Resident management and other approaches to tenant control of public housing. In *Ownership, control, and the future of housing policy,* ed. R. Allen Hays. Westport, CT: Greenwood Press.

———. 1994. Deconcentrating Chicago's public housing residents. Paper presented at the Urban Affairs Association Annual Meeting, New Orleans, La. (March).

Peterson, Paul K. 1981. *City limits.* Chicago: University of Chicago Press.

———, and J. David Greenstone. 1977. Racial change and citizen participation: The mobilization of low income communities through community action. In *A decade of federal anti poverty programs,* ed. Robert H. Haveman, 241–78. New York: Academic Press.

Phillips, James G. 1973a. Housing report/HUD proposes cash allowance as link to broad plan for welfare reform. *National Journal* 5 (August 25): 1225–61.

Pierson, P., and T. Skocpol. 2007. *The transformation of American politics: Activist government and the rise of conservatism.* Princeton: Princeton University Press.

Piven, Frances Fox, and Richard A. Cloward. 1966. Desegregated housing? Who pays for the reformers' ideal? *New Republic* 155 (December 27): 17–21.

———. 1971. *Regulating the poor: The functions of public welfare.* New York: Pantheon Books.

Pomper, Gerald M. 1981. *The election of 1980: Reports and interpretations.* Chatham, NJ: Chatham House.

Popkin, Susan J. 2006. The HOPE VI program: What happened to the residents? In *Where are Poor People to Live? Transforming Public Housing Communities,* ed. L. Bennett, J. L. Smith, and P. A. Wright, 68–90. Armonk, NY: M. E. Sharpe.

Putnam, R. D. 2000. *Bowling alone: The collapse and revival of American community.* New York: Simon and Schuster.

Radford, Gail. 1996. *Modern housing for America: Policy struggles in the New Deal era.* Chicago: University of Chicago Press.

Rasey, Keith P. 1993. The role of neighborhood-based housing nonprofits in the ownership and control of housing in the U.S. In *Ownership, Control, and the Future of Housing Policy,* ed. R. Allen Hays, 195–224. Westport, CT: Greenwood Press.

Reagan, Michael D. 1972. *The new federalism.* New York: Oxford University Press.

Redburn, F. Stevens, and Terry F. Buss. 1986. *Responding to America's homeless: Public policy alternatives.* New York: Praeger.

Reed, Richard Ernie. 1979. *Return to the city: How to restore old buildings and ourselves in America's historic urban neighborhoods.* Garden City, NY: Doubleday.

Reich, Robert B. 1983. *The next American frontier.* New York: Penguin.

Reischauer, Robert D. 1984. The congressional budget process. In *Federal budget policy in the 1980s,* ed. Gregory B. Mills and John L. Palmer. Washington, DC: The Urban Institute Press.

Reynolds, Malvina. 1964. Little boxes. In *Little boxes and other handmade songs.* New York: Oak Publishing Co.

Ripley, Randall B., and Grace A. Franklin.1991. *Congress, the bureaucracy, and public policy.* 5th Ed. Pacific Grove, CA: Brooks/Cole Publishing Company.

Riposa, Gerry. 1996. From enterprise zones to empowerment zones: the community context of urban economic development. *American Behavioral Scientist* 39(5) (March-April): 536–52.

Rohe, William, and L. Gates. 1985. *Planning with neighborhoods.* Chapel Hill: University of North Carolina Press.

Rose-Ackerman, S. 1977. The political economy of a racist housing market, *Journal of Urban Economics* 4 (April): 150–69.

Roszak, Theodore. 1995. *The making of a counterculture: Reflections on the technocratic society and its youthful opposition.* Berkeley: University of California Press.

Ryan, William. 1976. *Blaming the victim.* Rev., updated ed. New York: Vintage Books.

Saegert, S. J., J. Thompson, and M. Warren, eds. 2001. *Social capital and poor communities.* New York: Russell Sage Foundation.

Safire, William. 1975. *Before the fall: An inside view of the pre-Watergate White House.* Garden City, NY: Doubleday.

Sanders, Heywood T. 1980. Urban renewal and the revitalized city: A reconsideration of recent history. In Donald B. Rosenthal. *Urban Revitalization.* Urban Affairs Annual Reviews, vol.18. Beverly Hills: Sage.

Savitch, H. V. 1979. *Urban policy and the exterior city: Federal, state, and corporate impacts upon major cities.* New York: Pergamon Press.

Schlozman, Kay Lehman. 1984. What accent the heavenly chorus? Political equality and the American pressure system. *The Journal of Politics* 46 (November): 1006–32.

———, and John T. Tierney. 1986. *Organized interests and American democracy.* New York: Harper and Row.

Schoenwald, Jonathan M. 2001. *A time for choosing: the rise of modern American conservatism.* New York: Oxford University Press.

Schwartz, Alex F. 2006. *Housing policy in the United States: An introduction.* New York: Routledge.

Schwarz, John E. 1988. *America's hidden success.* New York: W. W. Norton.

Scudder, Samuel. 1972. HUD seeks to reduce its ownership of inner city abandoned properties. *National Journal* 4 (February 26): 371.

Seidel, Stephen R. 1978. *Housing costs of government regulations: Confronting the regulated maze.* New Brunswick: Center for Urban Policy Research.

Semer, Milton. See: U.S. Dept of HUD, 1976.

Shenon, Philip. 2000. Samuel R. Pierce, Jr., ex-Housing Secretary, dies at 78. *New York Times* November 11. www.nytimes.com.

Sidney, Mara S. 2003 *Unfair housing: how national policy shapes community action.* Lawrence: University Press of Kansas.

Silver, Christopher. 1982. Neighborhood planning in historical perspective: New uses for an old idea. Paper presented to the 1982 meeting of the Urban Affairs Association, Philadelphia, Pa.

Skocpol, Theda. 1995. *Social policies in the United States: Future possibilities in historical perspective.* Princeton: Princeton University Press.

———. 1996. *Boomerang: Clinton's health security effort and the turn against government in U.S. politics.* New York: W. W. Norton.

Smith, Janet L. 2006. Public housing transformation: Evolving national policy. In *Where are poor people to live? Transforming public housing communities,* ed. L. Bennett, J. L. Smith, and P. A. Wright, 19–40. Armonk, NY: M. E. Sharpe.

Smith, Shanna L., and Cathy Cloud. 2010. Welcome to the neighborhood? The persistence of discrimination and segregation. In *The integration debate: competing futures for American cities,* ed. C. Hartman and G. D. Squires, 9–23. New York: Routledge.

Stack, Carol B. (1974). *All our kin: Strategies for survival in a black community.* New York: Harper and Row.

Stanfield, Rochelle L. 1977a. Civil war over cities aid: Battle no one expected. *National Journal* 9 (August 6): 1226–27.

———. 1977b. Government seeks the right formula for community development funds. *National Journal* 9 (February 12): 237–43.

———. 1977c. The Latest Community Development Flap: Targeting on the poor. *National Journal* 9 (December 3): 1877–79.

———. 1977d. Three rays of hope for the ailing large cities. *National Journal* 9 (April 16): 589–91.

———.1981. Cashing out housing: A free market approach that might also cost less. *National Journal* 13 (September 18): 1660–64.

———. 1982a. Low-cost housing aid battle may be a zero-sum game without any winners. *National Journal* 14 (May 22): 918.

———. 1983a. If vouchers work for food, why not for housing, schools, health, and jobs? *National Journal* 15 (April 23): 840–44.

———. 1983b. Housing focus—ramshackle planning. *National Journal* 15 (October 15): 2122.

———. 1983c. Pierce, HUD's "nice guy" secretary—it's almost as if he isn't there, *National Journal* 15 (August 6): 1642–46.

———. 1993a. The ward healers. *National Journal* 25 (June 5): 1344.

———. 1993b. Tall order. *National Journal* 25 (July 24): 1862–66.

Steiner, Gilbert Y. 1971. *The state of welfare.* Washington, DC: The Brookings Institution.

Stegman, Michael A., ed. 1970. *Housing and economics: The American dream.* Cambridge: The MIT Press.

———. 1979. *Housing investment in the inner city: The dynamics of decline.* Cambridge: The MIT Press.

Sternlieb, George, R. W. Burchell, and J. W. Hughes. 1975. The future of housing and urban development. *Journal of Economics and Business* 27 (Winter): 99–111.

Sternlieb, George, et al. 1980. *American's housing: Prospects and problems.* New Brunswick: Rutgers University Center for Urban Policy Research.

Stiglitz, Joseph. E. 1986. *Economics of the public sector.* New York: W. W. Norton.

———. 2002. *Globalization and its discontents.* New York: W. W. Norton.

Stone, Deborah. 1997. *Policy paradox: The art of political decision-making.* New York: W. W. Norton.

Stone, M. E. 2006. Housing affordability: One third of a nation shelter poor. In R. G. Bratt, M. E. Stone, and C. Hartman, *A right to housing: Foundation for a new social agenda,* 38–60. Philadelphia: Temple University Press.

Straszheim, Mahlon R. 1979. The Section 8 rental assistance program: Costs and policy options. *Policy Studies Journal* 8(2): 307–23.

Struyk, Raymond J. 1977. The need for local flexibility in U.S. housing policy. *Policy Analysis* 3 (Fall): 471–83.

———. 1979. *Saving the Housing Assistance Plan.* An Urban Institute Paper on Housing. Washington, DC: The Urban Institute.

———. 1980. *A new system for public housing: Salvaging a national resource.* Washington, DC: The Urban Institute.

———, and Marc Bendick Jr. 1981. *Housing vouchers for the poor: Lessons from a national experiment.* Washington, DC: The Urban Institute.

———, Sue A. Marshall. and Larry J. Ozanne. 1978. *Housing policies for the urban poor: A case for local diversity in federal programs.* Washington, DC: The Urban Institute.

Sumka, Howard J. 1979. Neighborhood revitalization and displacement: A review of the evidence. *American Planning Association Journal* 45 (October): 480-B7.

Suttles, Gerald D. 1968. *The social order of the slum: ethnicity and territory in the inner city.* Chicago: University of Chicago Press.

Szabo, Joan C. 1975. Urban Report/Community Development Program Shows Signs of Progress. *National Journal* 7 (November 29): 1634–40.

Szulc, Tad. 1978. *The energy crisis.* Lexington, MA: D. C. Heath.

Thurow, Lester C. 1981. *The zero-sum society: Distribution and the possibilities for economic change.* New York: Penguin.

Tobin, Gary A. 1979. *The changing structure of the city: What happened to the urban crisis?* Urban Affairs Annual Reviews, vol. 16. Beverly Hills: Sage.

Tomasky, Michael. 2010. Can Obama rise again? *New York Review of Books* December 9. www.nybooks.com/articles/archives.

Turner, Marjory. 1994. The Move to Opportunity Program. Presentation at the Urban Affairs Annual Meeting, New Orleans, La. (March).

U.S. Advisory Commission on Intergovernmental Relations (ACIR). *1977. Community development: The workings of a federal-local block grant.* Washington, DC: GPO.

———. 1978. *Categorical grants: Their role and design.* Washington, DC: GPO.

U.S. Bureau of the Census. 1971a. *Characteristics of low-income population,1970.* Current Population Reports, series P-60, no. 81. Washington, DC: GPO.

———. 1971b. *Income in 1970 of families and persons.* Current Population Reports, series P-60, no. 80. Washington, DC: GPO.

———. 1981b. *Geographical mobility: March 1975 to March 1980.* Current Population Reports, series P-20, no. 368. Washington, DC: GPO.

———. 1981d. *Statistical abstract.* Washington, DC: GPO.

———. 1982. *Characteristics of the population below the poverty level:1980.* Current Population Reports, series P-60, no. 133. Washington, DC: GPO.

———. 1984. *Money income of households, families, and persons in the United States:* 1982. Current Population Reports, series P-60,no. 142. Washington, DC: GPO.

———. 1990. *Measuring the effect of benefits and taxes on income and poverty:* 1989. Current Population Reports, series P-60, no. 169-RD. Washington, DC: GPO.

———. 1991a. *Money income of households, families, and persons in the United States: 1990.* Current Population Reports, series P-60, no. 174. Washington, DC: GPO.

———. 1991b. *Who can afford to buy a house?* Current Housing Reports, series H121/91-1. Washington, DC: GPO.

———. 1992. *Housing in America: 1989/90.* Series H123/91-1. Washington, DC: GPO.

U.S. Census. 2010. *Income, poverty, and health insurance coverage in the United States: 2009.* Current Population Reports P60-238. Washington, DC: GPO (also available on line at census.gov).

U.S. Bureau of the Census and Department of Housing and Urban Development, Office of Policy Development and Research. 1977.*Annual housing survey 1975: U.S. and Regions.* Part B: Indicators of Housing and Neighborhood Quality; Part C: Financial Characteristics of the Housing Inventory. Current Housing Reports, series H150, 75B, and 75C. Washington, DC: GPO.

———. 1982. *Annual housing survey 1980: U.S. and Regions*. Part C: Financial Characteristics of the Housing Inventory. Current Housing Reports, series H-150-80. Washington, DC: GPO.

———. 1991. *American housing survey for the U.S. in 1989*. Part C: Financial Characteristics of the Housing Inventory. Current Housing Reports, series H-150-89. Washington, DC: GPO.

U.S. Bureau of Labor Statistics. CPI Detailed Reports (monthly), 1970 through 1990. Washington, DC: GPO.

U.S. Commission on Civil Rights. 1971. *Home ownership for lower income families: A report on the racial and ethnic impact of the Section 235 program*. Washington, DC: GPO.

———. 1975. *Equal opportunity in suburbia*. Washington, DC: GPO.

U.S. Congress. Budget Office. 1977. *Real estate tax shelter subsidies and direct subsidy alternatives*. Washington, DC: GPO.

———. 1982. *Federal housing assistance: Alternative approaches*. Washington, DC: GPO.

———. 1983. *Federal subsidies for public housing: Issues and options*. Washington, DC: GPO.

———. 1989. *Current housing problems and possible federal responses*. Washington, DC: GPO.

U.S. Congress. Joint Economic Committee. 1972. *The economics of federal subsidy programs. Part 5: Housing Subsidies*. Joint Committee Print. 92nd Congress, 2nd session. Washington, DC: GPO.

———. 1981. *Housing and the economy: Hearings*. 96th Congress, 1st session. Washington, DC: GPO.

———. Subcommittee on Priorities and Economy in *Government. 1973. Housing policy: Report*. Joint Committee Print. 93rd Congress, 1st session. Washington, DC.: GPO.

U.S. Congress. House Committee on Appropriations. 1972. Subcommittee on *HUD-space-science-veterans appropriations, 1973: Hearings*. Part 3, at 1294. 92nd Congress, 2nd session. Washington, DC: GPO.

———. Committee on Appropriations. Subcommittee on HUD-Independent Agencies. 1977. *Department of HUD-independent agencies appropriations, 1978: Hearings*. Part 8: Subsidized Housing. 95th Congress, 1st session. Washington, DC: GPO.

U.S. Congress. House. Committee on Banking and Currency. 1970. *Investigation and hearing of abuses in federal low and moderate income housing programs*. Staff Report and Recommendations. Washington, DC: GPO.

———. 1971a. *Emergency Home Finance Act of 1970 and Housing and Urban Development Act of 1970*. Committee Print. 91st Congress, 2nd session. Washington, DC: GPO.

———. 1971b. *Interim report on HUD investigation of low and moderate income housing programs: Hearing*. 92nd Congress, 1st session. Washington, DC: GPO.

———. Subcommittee on Housing. 1972. *Real-estate settlement costs, FHA mortgage foreclosures, housing abandonment, and site selection politics: Hearings on H.R.13337.* Parts 1 and 2. 92nd Congress, 2nd session. Washington, DC: GPO.

————. 1974a. *The administration's housing and community development proposals.* Committee Print. 93rd Congress, 2nd session. Washington, DC: GPO.

U.S. Congress. House. Committee on *Government* Operations. 1971.*Overview hearing on operations of the department of Housing and Urban Development.* 92nd Congress, 1st session. Washington, DC: GPO.

————. 1972a. *Defaults on FHA-insured mortgages: Hearings.* Parts 2 and 3. 92nd Congress, 2nd session. Washington, DC: GPO.

————. 1972b. *Defaults on FHA-insured mortgages (Detroit): Hearings.* 2nd Congress. 2nd session. Washington, DC: GPO.

————.1974. *Management of HUD-held multi-family mortgages: Hearings.* 93rd Congress. 2nd session. Washington, DC: GPO.

————.1978. *Section 8 leased housing assistance program. Hearings.* 95th Congress, 1st and 2nd sessions. Washington, DC: GPO.

U.S. Congress. House. Committee on Government Operations. Subcommittee on Employment and Housing. 1989. *Abuses, favoritism, and mismanagement in HUD programs.* Hearings. Part 1. 101st Congress. 1st session. Washington, DC: GPO.

U.S. Congress. Senate. Committee on Appropriations. 1971. *Senate hearings: Department of HUD, space, science, veterans, and certain other independent agencies appropriations.* Appendix I, Mortgage Bankers' Association of America Report. at 777. 92nd Congress. 1st session. Washington, DC: GPO.

U.S. Congress. Senate. Committee on Banking and Currency. 1967. *Hearings on Housing legislation of 1967, Parts 1 and 2.* 90th Congress, 2nd Session, Washington, DC: GPO.

U.S. Congress. Senate. Committee on Banking. Housing and Urban Affairs. Subcommittee on Housing and Urban Affairs. 1971. *1971 Housing and Urban Development legislation: Hearings.* Parts 1 and 2. 92nd Congress, 1st session. Washington, DC: GPO.

————.1973. *Oversight on housing and urban development programs: Hearings.* Part 1. 93rd Congress. 1st session. Washington, DC: GPO.

————.1974. *Critique of "Housing in the Seventies."* Prepared by the Congressional Research Service, Library of Congress. Committee Print. 93rd Congress, 2nd session. Washington, DC: GPO.

————.1976. *Community development block grant program: Hearings on oversight on the administration of the Housing and Community Development Act of 1974.* 94th Congress, 2nd session. Washington, DC: GPO.

————.1978. *Distressed HUD-subsidized multi-family housing projects: Hearings.* 95th Congress. 1st session. Washington, DC: GPO.

U.S. Congress. Senate. Committee on the Judiciary. Subcommittee on the

Separation of Powers. 1971. *Executive impoundment of appropriated funds: Hearings.* 92nd Congress. 1st session. Washington, DC: GPO.

U.S. Department of Health and Human Services. 2010. Substance Abuse and Mental Health Data Archive. Inter-university Consortium on Political and Social Research. www.icpsr.umich.edu.

U.S. Department of Housing and Urban Development (HUD). 1970. *The Model Cities program: A comparative analysis of the planning process in eleven cities* (Office of Community Planning and Development). Washington, DC: GPO.

———.1972. *Report on audit of Section 236 multifamily housing program* (Office of Audit). Washington, DC: GPO.

———. 1973a. *The model cities program: Ten model cities—a comparative analysis of second round planning years* (Office of Community Planning and Development). Washington, DC: GPO.

———. 1973b. *The model cities program: A comparative analysis of participating cities—process, product, performance, and prediction* (Office of Community Planning and Development). Washington, DC: GPO.

———. 1974a. *Housing in the seventies: A report on the national policy review.* Washington, DC: GPO.

———. 1974b. *Summary of the housing and community development Act of 1974.* Washington, DC: GPO.

———. 1976. *Housing in the seventies working papers: National housing policy review.* 2 vols. Washington, DC: GPO.

———. 1977. *Block grants for community development.* First Report on the Brookings Institution Monitoring Study of the CDBG Program. Washington, DC: GPO.

———. 1978a. *Decentralizing community development.* Second Report on the Brookings Institution Monitoring Study of the CDBG Program. Washington, DC: GPO.

———. 1978b. *Final report of task force on housing costs.* Washington, DC: HUD.

———. 1978c. *Lower income housing assistance program (Section 8): Interim findings of evaluation research* (Office of Policy Development and Research). Washington, DC: GPO.

———. 1978d. *Lower income housing assistance program (Section 8): Nationwide evaluation of the existing housing program.* By Margaret Drury, Olsen Lee. Michael Springer, and Lorene Yap (Office of Policy Development and Research). Washington, DC: GPO.

———. 1979a. *City needs and community development funding* (Office of Policy Development and Research). Washington, DC: GPO.

———. 1979b. *Designing rehab programs: A local government guidebook* (Office of Policy Development and Research). Washington, DC: GPO.

———. 1979c. *Occasional papers in housing and community affairs,* vol. 6 (Office of Policy Development and Research). Washington, DC: GPO.

————. 1979d. *Problems affecting low-rent public housing projects: A field study* (Office of Policy Development and Research). Washington, DC: GPO.

————. 1979e. *Statistical yearbook.* Washington, DC: GPO.

————. 1979f. *The tenth annual report on the national housing goal* (Office of Policy Development and Research). Washington, DC: GPO.

————. 1980a. *The conversion of rental housing to condominiums and cooperatives: A national study of scope, causes, and impacts* (Office of Policy Development and Research). Washington, DC: GPO.

————. 1980b. *Fifth annual Community Development Block Grant report* (Office of Policy Development and Research). Washington, DC: GPO.

————. 1980c. 1980 *National housing production report* (Office of Policy Development and Research). Washington, DC: GPO.

————. 1980d. *The president's national urban policy report, 1980.* Washington, DC: GPO.

————. 1980e. *Targeting community development.* Third Report on the Brookings Institution Monitoring Study of the Community Development Block Grant Program. Washington, DC: GPO.

————. 1981a. *Implementing community development.* A study of the community development block grant program prepared by The Brookings Institution. Washington, DC: GPO.

————. 1981b. *Participation and benefits in the urban section 8 program: New construction and existing housing* (Office of Policy Development and Research). Washington, DC: GPO.

————. 1982a. *Community development block grant report.* Washington, DC: GPO.

————. 1982b. *The costs of HUD multifamily housing programs: A comparison of the development, financing, and life cycle costs of Section 8, public housing, and other HUD programs,* 2 vols. (Office of Policy Development and Research). Washington, DC: GPO.

————. 1990. *Public housing homeownership demonstration assessment.* Washington, DC: GPO.

————. 1992. *Annual report to Congress on community planning and development, housing rehabilitation programs.* Washington, DC: GPO.

————. 1993. *Creating communities of opportunity: Priorities of U.S. Department of Housing and Urban Development.* Washington, DC: GPO.

————. 1992. *The final report of the national commission on severely distressed public housing: A report to Congress and the Secretary of Housing and Urban Development.* Washington, DC: USGPO.

————. 2000. *Case studies of the conversion of project-based assistance to tenant-based assistance; final report.* Prepared by Abt Associates, Cambridge, MA.

————. 2003. *Interim assessment of the HOPE VI program cross-site report.* Prepared by Abt Associates, Cambridge, MA.

————. 2010. Fiscal Year 2010 budget summary. www.hud.gov.

U.S. General Accounting Office (GAO). 1973. *Opportunities to improve effectiveness and reduce costs of rental assistance housing program.* Washington, DC: GPO.

———. 1978. *Section 236 rental housing: An evaluation with lessons for the future.* Report to Congress by the Comptroller General. Washington, DC: GPO.

———. 1980. *Evaluation of alternatives for financing low and moderate income rental housing.* Report to Congress by the Comptroller General. Washington, DC: GPO.

———. 1983. *Block grants for housing: A study of local experiences and attitudes.* Report to Congress by the Comptroller General. Washington, DC: GPO.

———. 1986. *Rental housing: Potential reduction in the privately owned and federally assisted inventory.* Washington, DC: GPO.

U.S. Millennial Housing Commission. 2002. *Meeting our nation's housing challenges.* Report of the Bipartisan Millennial Housing Commission Appointed by the Congress of the United States. Washington, DC: GPO.

U.S. Office of Management and the Budget. 2010. Federal Budget for Fiscal Year 2011, (Historical Table 15.1).

U.S. President's Commission on Housing. 1982. *The Report of the President's Commission on Housing.* Washington, DC: GPO.

Vale, L. J. 2000. *From the puritans to the projects: Public housing and public neighbors.* Cambridge: Harvard University Press.

Van Horn, Carl E. 1979. *Policy implementation in the federal system: National goals and local implementors.* Lexington, MA: D. C. Heath, Lexington Books.

Venkatesh, Sudhir A. 2000. *American project: The rise and fall of a modern ghetto.* Cambridge: Harvard University Press.

Vidal, Avis. 1992. *Rebuilding communities: A national study of urban community development corporations.* New York: Community Development Research Center, New School for Social Research.

The Washington Post. 1993a. Cisneros promises rapid change, February 20: F1.

———. 1993b. Cities may get bigger block grants, March 6: F1.

———. 1993c. New tools for blighted cities, April 11: C7.

———. 1993d. HUD seeks new direction in housing, April 17: El.

———. 1993e. Clinton loses focus, and time: Fearing taxes without gains, swing voters are losing faith, May 2: C1.

———. 1993f. Cisneros plan aims to improve public housing access for poor, June 17: A8.

———. 1993g. White House seeks to reassure big-city mayors, June 22: A6.

———. 1993h. HUD sale of foreclosed projects proposed to meet subsidy crisis, July 28: A8.

———. 1993i. Playing defense on housing, August 2: A16.

———. 1993j. Administration's renovation plan includes blueprint for fixing public housing, September 13: A19.

———. 1993k. HUD's priorities: Addressing bias, homelessness; Cisneros' plan for department puts new emphasis on racism, October 14: A29.

Waxman, Chaim I. 1983. *The stigma of poverty.* 2nd Ed. New York: Pergamon Press.

Weber, Max. 1992. *The protestant ethic and the spirit of capitalism.* Trans. Talcott Parsons. New York: Routledge.

Weitzer, R., and S. A. Tuch. 2006. *Race and policing in America: Conflict and reform.* New York: Cambridge University Press.

Welfeld, Irving. 1977. American housing policy: Perverse programs by prudent people. *The Public Interest* 48 (Summer): 128–44.

———, et al. 1974. *Perspectives on housing and urban renewal.* American Enterprise Institute Perspectives 2. Praeger Special Studies in U.S. Economic Social and Political Issues. New York: Praeger.

Wellborn, Clay H. 1972. Cities and suburbs/project rehab is upgrading rental housing in effort to rehabilitate neighborhoods. *National Journal* (January 9): 78–79.

Wildavsky, Aaron. 1979. *The politics of the budgetary process.* Boston: Little Brown.

Wilensky, Harold L. 1975. *The welfare state and equality: Structural and ideological roots of public expenditures.* Berkeley and Los Angeles: University of California Press.

Williams, Walter, and Betty Jane Narver. 1980. *Government by agency: Lessons from the social program grants-in-aid experience.* Quantitative Studies in Social Relations. New York: Academic Press.

Wilson, James Q., ed. 1966. *Urban renewal: The record and the controversy.* Cambridge: The MIT Press.

Wolman, Harold. 1971. *Politics of federal housing.* New York: Dodd, Mead.

Zukin, Sharon. 1982. *Loft living: Culture and capitol in urban change.* Baltimore: Johns Hopkins University Press.

INDEX

AARP, 271

AFL-CIO, 137

accelerated depreciation, 125, 150

Adams, Arlin, 244

Advisory Commission on Intergovernmental Relations, 185

Aid to Families with Dependent Children (AFDC), 269

Afghanistan, 283

Affirmative action, 31

African Americans: discrimination in employment,38; FHA discrimination against, 89, 91; housing conditions of, 65–66; poverty among , 38; public housing segregation of, 97; social isolation, 77; Urban renewal relocation, impact on, 173

Al Qaeda, 283

Appropriations Committee, U.S. House, 126

Independent Offices Subcommittee, 100

Appropriations bill, Fiscal year 1999, 269

Appropriations bill, FY 2000, HUD/VA/NASA, 270

Ashley, Representative Thomas (D, Ohio), 191, 193, 205

automobile industry, American, 291

back to the city movement. *See* gentrification

Baker, James A. III, 233

Ban the Bomb movement, 26

bank regulation, 55, 292

Banking and Currency Committee, U.S. House, 94, 100

Banking and Currency Committee, U.S. Senate, 94, 100

banking reform legislation, 302

Better Communities Act, 1973 proposal, 190

Black Jack, Missouri, discrimination case, 133

blight, 46, 47

Bond, Senator Christopher (R, Mo.), 267

Brooke Amendment, 102, 131

Brooke, Senator Edward (R, Massachusetts), 131, 137

Budget Act of 1974, 223

budget reconciliation bill-1981, 223

budget rescissions, 1980s, 225

budget resolution, 1981, 223

Burnham, Daniel, 47

Bush administration, 284, 293

Bush, President George W., 28–84, 293; election of 2000, 283; housing proposal, 270

Bush, President George H. W., 241–242, 253

Bush v. Gore, 283

Butler, Stuart, 262

CDBG. *See* Community Development Block Grants

capitalist ideology, 37

Carter, President James Earl (Jimmy), 152, 202, 241

Carter, First Lady Rosalyn, 241

central business districts, 170

centrist Democrats , 254

Chicago Housing Authority, 132; Model Cities program, 134; south side of, 97

Cisneros, Henry, 257
Civil Rights Act of 1968, 250
civil rights movement, 23, 24, 29, 30, 144
Clinton, Hillary. First Lady-role in health
   care proposal, 266; Senator—290
Clinton, President William J. (Bill), 54,
   253, 255–270; election in 1992, 253;
   economic stimulus package,260;
   impeachment , 270; re-election in
   1996, 269
Coalition for Creative Non-Violence,
   237
coalition ideologies, defined, 7
Cohen, Wilbur, Secretary of Health,
   Education and Welfare, 188
Committee on the Clear and Present
   Danger, 30
community action agencies, 179
community –based health care, 237
community development policy, 45–55,
   197
Community Development Block Grants:
   creation of, 182 -194; dual formula,
   202; formula entitlements, 190–191;
   geographical targeting, 205–206, 233;
   hold harmless provision (CDBG),
   190, 199; housing impact, 207–219;
   implementation of, 196–207; nonentitlement cities, funding of, 233
community development corporations
   (CDCs), 279–280
community development revenue
   sharing, 189
community housing development
   organizations (CHODOs), 246
Community Reinvestment Act (CRA),
   217, 259, 288, 303
Comprehensive Housing Affordability
   Strategy (CHAS), 207, 250
Congressional elections: 1994, 267; 2010,
   292
conservative Ideology: anti-government
   beliefs, 54,295; development of,
   28–34; poverty, attitudes towards,
   38–41
conservatives, political strategies, 33,
   141, 292
Consolidated Plan, 207
consumer culture, 25

consumer education, 303
continuum of care (for homeless), 260,
   276
Contract with America, 266, 269
Cooperation Agreement (urban
   renewal), 96
counterculture, 26
Cranston, Senator Alan (D, California),
   239, 245
Cranston-Gonzalez National Affordable
   Housing Act of 1990, 245
Crime rates, 72
Cuomo, Andrew, 260

Daley, Mayor Richard Sr., 133
D'Amato, Senator Alfonse (R, New
   York), 245
Dean, Deborah, 243, 244
de-concentrating the poor, 143, 259
defense expenditures, 34, 52
defensible space, 104
deficits, federal, 53- 57
deinstitutionalization of the mentally
   ill, 236
Demery, Thomas, 244
democratic capitalism, 15–19
Democratic Leadership Council, 254
Democratic Party, 22, 23, 26
Dolbeare, Cushing, 229, 230
Dole, Senate Minority Leader Robert
   (R, Kansas), 261, 269
Donovan, Shaun, HUD Secretary, 293
Drug enforcement, 300
Dukakis, Governor Michael (D, Massa-
   chusetts), 241, 242

Eisenhower, President Dwight D., 29, 91,
   100, 169
Electoral College system, 183
Emergency food and shelter grants,
   237
Emergency food programs, 237
Eminent domain, 167, 168
Employer Wage Credit, 263
Empowerment Zone program, 261–264
 enterprise zones, 233, 262
Enterprise Communities, 263
Enterprise Foundation, 278
evangelical Christianity, 31, 32

environmental justice movement, 68
executive compensation, 290
executive impoundment of funds, 136
Experimental Housing Allowance
    Program (EHAP), 145–146, 153, 158,
    160, 228

Fair Housing, 110–111, 250–251, 259,
    299–300
Fair Housing Act of 1968, vii, 110, 170
Fair Housing Amendments of 1988, 251
Fair Market Rent (FMR), 148, 226
family relationships, impact of housing
    on, 73
Family Self-Sufficiency program, 249
Fannie Mae. *See* Federal National Mort-
    gage Association
Federal Housing Administration (FHA),
    23, 55, 88–90, 116–119, 150, 208
Federal Deposit Insurance Corporation,
    55
Federal Home Loan Bank Act, 90
Federal Home Loan Bank Board, 90
Federal Housing Trust Fund, 294
Federal-local-nonprofit-for-profit
    partnerships, 299
Federal National Mortgage Association
    (FNMA, or "Fannie Mae"), 55, 90,
    106, 289
Federal Reserve, 52, 55, 286
federal stimulus package (2009), 291
federal subsidies to state and local
    governments, 302
feminism, 25, 32
FHA. *See* Federal Housing Administra-
    tion
Filtering, 214, 296
Financial institution bailout (2008),
    290
Finch, Robert, Secretary of Health,
    Education and Welfare, 113
Finger, Harold, 145
Fino, Congressman Paul (R, New York),
    108
floods, impact on housing, 63, 68–69
Ford, President Gerald, 148, 202
Fox News Network, 292
Frank, Rep. Barney (D, Mass.), 244
Friedman, Milton, 51

Gautreaux case, 132, 133, 259
General revenue sharing, 187
gentrification, 212–214, 218
Gingrich, Newt, Speaker, House of
    Representatives, 266
Ginnie Mae. *See* Government National
    Mortgage Association
Glass-Steagall Act of 1933, 55
globalization, 25, 34
Goldwater, Senator Barry (R, Arizona),
    30, 33
Gonzalez, Representative Henry (D,
    Texas), 226, 238
Gore, Vice President Albert, 283
Government National Mortgage Associa-
    tion (Ginnie Mae), 93, 150
Gramm, Senator Phil (R, Texas), 271
"Grate "American Sleep-Out, 237
Great Depression, the, ix, 23, 48, 50, 51,
    55, 88, 167
Great Society, 33, 113, 195
Greenspan, Alan, Chair Federal Reserve
    Board, 287

Habitat for Humanity International, 241,
    248
Harris, Patricia Roberts, Secretary,
    Department of Housing and Urban
    Development, 205
health care reform, 54, 265, 292
Home, psychological attachment to, 74
Home Mortgage Disclosure Act
    (HMDA), 217, 303
Home Owners Loan Corporation
    (HOLC), 89
home ownership, 93: program to
    promote among low income families,
    286
HOME Program, 246, 280, 282, 285
home sales, 2010, 289
homeless coordinating boards, local, 276
homelessness, 235–238, 259, 260,
    276–277
HOPE I program, 247–248, 258
HOPE II program, 248, 258
HOPE III program, 248, 258
HOPE VI program, 269, 271–276, 282,
    285, 293, 300
households, female headed, 74

Housing Act of 1937, 98, 101, 150
Housing Act of 1949, 100, 111, 168, 298
Housing Act of 1954, 169
Housing Act of 1968, 92, 111, 115, 153
Housing Act of 1970, 145
Housing Act of 1987, 238
Housing Act of 1990. *See* National Affordable Housing Act of 1990
housing affordability, 66
housing allowance, 110, 139–145
housing and "belonging" needs, 73
Housing and Community Development Act of 1974, 148, 193
housing and physical determinism, 79
housing and physiological needs, 62
housing and safety needs ,69
housing and self-actualization, 77
housing and self-esteem ,75
Housing and Urban Development Act of 1972, 136
Housing and Urban Development, Department of (HUD), 109, 127, 137, 192, 243, 257–258: Appropriations,226, 268; bill to abolish, 267; Inspector General, 243; Office of Fair Housing and Equal Opportunity, 250
Housing Assistance Plan (HAP), 149, 103, 207–208
housing conditions, 65
housing costs , 66
Housing Development Action Grant (HODAG), 230
housing finance overhaul bill, 289
"housing first" programs, 276
Housing in the Seventies, 139–141, 228
housing integration, 124
Housing Payments Program, 227
housing reform measures, 1994, 267–269
housing rehabilitation, 207–219
housing vouchers, 161, 227, 285
human capital, 295
human needs, 60, 61
Humphrey, Vice President Hubert H., 112
Hundley, Walter, 188
Hurricane Katrina, 68

Ideology, 3–4, 9–11, 293
incumbent upgrading, 213

Industrial Development Bonds (IDBs), 231, 301
integration of social services (into housing programs), 248
Iraq, American invasion of, 284

Jackson, Rev. Jesse, 254
James v. Valtierra, 133
job training, 237
Johnson, President Lyndon B., 101, 108, 175
Judeo-Christian beliefs, 17, 41

Kaiser Committee, 145
Katz, Leonard, 122
Keating, Charles, 245
Kemp, Jack, Secretary, Department of Housing and Urban Development, 242–243, 257, 262
Kennedy, President John F., 29, 92, 100, 105, 169
Keynes, John Maynard, 51

labor movement, 25
Lackawanna , Pennsylvania, court case involving, 133
Latinos, housing conditions of, 65 -66
"Law and order," political slogan, 31
Law Enforcement Assistance Agency (LEAA), 189
Lawrence, David, Mayor, Philadelphia, 169
Lazio, Representative Rick (R, New York), 267
lead-based paint , 63
Lee, Richard, Mayor, New Haven, 169
Leveraging, 216
Lewinsky, Monica, 270
Liberal ideology, ix, 20–21, 25, 28, 34–35, 38, 48, 142–143
libertarian beliefs, 34
Limbaugh, Rush, 292
Local and nonprofit initiatives, 240
Low Income Housing Tax Credit (LIHTC), 231, 279, 280,281, 282, 297, 301
Local Initiative Support Corporation (LISC), 278
Lynn, James, Secretary, Department of

Housing and Urban Development, 135, 137
McCarthy era, 30
Macroeconomic policy, 36, 50–55
Madison, James, 49
Martin, George, President, National Association of Home Builders, 146
Martinez, Mel, Secretary, Department of Housing and Urban Development, 286
Maslow, Abraham, 61
McKinney Act. *See* Stewart B. McKinney Homeless Assistance Act
Meese, Edwin III, Attorney General, 233
Mills, Wilbur, Representative (D, Arkansas), 187
Mitchell, John, Attorney General, 113
Mixed income neighborhoods, 272
Model Cities Program, 184, 263
moratorium on housing program activity. *See* Nixon Moratorium
Moody's Investment Services, 288, 303
Morris, Dick, Presidential Advisor, 267
Mortgage Bankers Association, 91, 123, 137
Mortgages: Collapse of market, 286; foreclosures, 57, 120, 127, 289; "housing bubble," 287; housing credit, availability of, 54; mortgage-backed securities, 57, 90, 87, 303; non-bank mortgage originators, 288; secondary market, 56, 303; sub-prime loans, 57, 287–289
Moskow, Michael H., 137
Move to Opportunity program (MTO), 259, 272
Moynihan, Daniel Patrick, Senator (D, New York), 113, 187
Municipal reform movement, 46

National Affordable Housing Act of 1990, 239, 245–250, 256, 282
National Association of Counties, 185
National Association of Home Builders (NAHB), 94, 135, 137, 147
National Association of Housing and Redevelopment Officials (NAHRO), 99, 100, 108

National Association of Real Estate Boards (NAREB), 94, 95, 166, 167, 220
National Commission on Severely Distressed Public Housing, 271
National Conference of State Legislators, 185
National Education Association, 137
National Governors Association, 185
National Housing Conference, 100
National League of Cities, 137
National Low Income Housing Coalition, 271
Native American Housing Block Grants, 285
neighborhoods, 70, 75, 177–180, 184
neo-conservatives, 30, 153, 284
neo-liberal, 23, 296
New Deal, 22, 23, 29, 33, 40, 45, 55, 144
New Deal coalition, 112, 254
New Haven, CT., 169
"New Federalism," 136, 185, 234
New Left, 30
Nixon Moratorium, 112, 135–136, 147
Nixon, President Richard M., vii, 33, 112–114, 135, 143, 147, 185, 196

Obama, President Barack, 57, 290–293
Office of Economic Opportunity (OEO), 184
Oil Embargo (1973), 52
Olmstead, Frederic Law, 47
Omnibus Budget Reconciliation Act of 1993, 262

Patriarchal view of the family, 32
Patriot Act, 283
Peabody, Malcolm, 145
Pennsylvania v. Lynn, 138
Pentagon, 283
Percy, Senator Charles (R, Illinois), 94, 137
Permanent Supportive Housing program, 277
Perot, Ross, 253
Philips Curve, 52
"picket fence federalism," 183
pioneers (urban), 212

Pierce, Samuel, Secretary, Department of Housing and Urban Development, 224, 229, 232, 242, 251

Pittsburg, PA., 169

pluralist model, 1

political interest (definition), 4–5

Predatory lenders, 287, 302

President's Commission on Housing, 227

Project Area Committee (PAC), 180

policy areas (definition), 35

poverty: definition, 36; justifications for, 37

power, 1

prisoner's dilemma, neighborhood revitalization as a, 210

property rights, 30, 78, 211

Progressive Era, 29, 55

Proxmire, Senator William (D, Wisconsin), 137

Public housing: anti-drug funding, 250; capital and operating subsidies, 285; community service as a condition for the receipt of public housing assistance, 267; early history, 95–105; relationship to Urban Renewal, 168, 174; rent computation, 131–132; role in future housing policy, 297, 299; role in late 1970s, 161–163; role in Nixon Moratorium, 137

Public Works Administration, Housing Division, 96, 166

Quality Housing and Work Responsibility Act of 1998, 271

race: as ethnic identity, 17; discrimination on the basis of, 97, 177; integration, 108; white privilege, 31, 299.

Reagan Democrats, 27

Reagan, President Ronald, vii, 27, 52, 223, 226, 236, 251

redlining, 93, 217, 259

Reich, Robert, Secretary, Department of Labor, 254

"Reinventing Government" report, 258

Relocation, urban renewal, 172–177

Rent Supplement program, 107–109

repayment crisis, assisted housing programs, 238–240

Republican Party, 29, 30

revenue sharing, concept of, 185–186

Richmond Redevelopment and Housing Authority, 177

Richmond, Virginia, 171

Rights language, 24

Robert Taylor Homes, Chicago, 97

Romney, George, Secretary, Department of Housing and Urban Development, 113, 115, 123, 135

Roosevelt, President Franklin D., 22, 29

Savings and loan associations: creation of, 90- 91; federal bailout, 56; federal regulation and support of, 55–56

Schemata (of attitudes), 8

secondary mortgage market. See Mortgages

Section 8 Housing Program: certificates and vouchers, 246; creation of, 146–151; contracts, 285; costs, 154; Existing Housing; 148, 151, 158–161, 228, 230; Moderate Rehabilitation, 148, 151, 242, 298, New Construction, 148, 149, 151, 153, 156, 157, 229, 298; rental assistance computation , 226; Substantial Rehabilitation, 148, 151, 154

Section 23 Leased Housing Program, 110, 146, 272

Section 115 Rehabilitation Grant program, 174, 214, 215, 216

Section 220, FHA Urban renewal housing financing, 174

Section 221(d)(3) Below Market Interest Rate program, 92, 106–107,238

Section 223(e), FHA Standards alteration, 92

Section 312 Rehabilitation Loan program, 174, 214, 216

Section 235 Homeownership program, 93, 116–123, 137

Section 236 Rental Housing program, 109, 123–131, 149, 155, 238

sexuality and reproduction, attitudes towards,32

Shannon v. HUD , 133